Take
Up
the
Bodies

Herbert
Blau

TAKE
UP
THE
BODIES

Theater

at the

Vanishing

UNIVERSITY
OF ILLINOIS
PRESS
Urbana
Chicago
London

Frontispiece: The prophet Calchas, from *Seeds of Atreus,* like
an early warning signal in the inner ear . . . (p. 171)

Photographs of *Seeds of Atreus, Elsinore,*
and *The Donner Party, Its Crossing* by Chris Thomas
Photographs of *Crooked Eclipses* by Walter Williams

Library of Congress Cataloging in Publication Data

Blau, Herbert.
Take up the bodies.

1. Theater.   2. Drama.   I. Title.
PN2039.B59   792' .01' 5   81-19774
ISBN 0-252-00945-2   AACR2

TO RUBY COHN

" . . . in the end, the shadows, the murmurs,
all the trouble, to end up with."

Contents

To *seem* is the false case of *be*. It is the passive of the verb to *see*. To *do* is the more active mode of to *be*. To *let* is the permissive of *do*. To *make* is the formative of to *do;* it is a doing that leaves a concrete result. To *say* is a kind of making, leaving but a trace in the air. *Come* and *go* are opposites of motion.

Ezra Pound, Foreword to
*The Chinese Written Character
as a Medium for Poetry,*
by Ernest Fenollosa

. . . How could you have responded if you were not there?
. . . Will you never have done . . . revolving it all? *(Pause.)* It? *(Pause.)* It all. *(Pause.)* In your poor mind. *(Pause.)* It all. *(Pause.)* It all.

Samuel Beckett, *Footfalls*

Preface

This book is the remembering of a theory:

I came to the theater, I sometimes think, with a disposition foreign to it. I don't really know, though I've been stubborn about staying there. Others are born to it but have little to say through the form and know little about it, like people who live in a place all their lives without being aware of what's around the corner. By nature, I am alternately gregarious and solitary, even secret. In my heart, I rather believe I'm solitary even when gregarious, though I don't hold back when I'm in the open, where I'm a pretty good broken-field runner with a tendency to give myself away. Those who know me best say I do it even with those who can't be trusted or when there's hardly a prayer of a return. Over the last thirty years I've put a lot of myself into the theater, which is a form that can't be trusted, and one of the secondary purposes of this book is to take the measure of that experience. The focus will be, however, on the work done mainly in the seventies, which concentrated on that aspect of the experience which is not capable of being measured because it always seems to be going out of sight.

The book is primarily a meditation, through that experience of theater, on the dynamics of disappearance, which also became the subject of the work.

There was a period after I left Lincoln Center (1967) when—as it comes to all—nothing much, but especially politics, seemed to make sense. A friend bawled me out for being "smart-ass," in a letter, about the California political situation and the New Left. She didn't see it going anywhere either, but asked what else? I'd always been partial to the what else?, but among my current anxieties was political apathy. At

Lincoln Center I had been accused of being too political with *Danton's Death*, the first play we did there, though the one certainty for me in that disaster was Danton's abhorrence of those pressing him with their politics when "there was a mistake in our creation" and "life isn't worth the trouble it takes to keep it going." Back in San Francisco, I had written a play, done there in the early sixties, in which a central character was revolted by politics on similar grounds, while "every son of a bitch is calling!" After *Danton's Death*, every son of a bitch stopped calling. I'd rather not have said that, for obvious reasons, but words lead to words and fact's fact, and that kind of fact is certainly no news in the theater, where there's probably no point in being if you can't let what happens happen and keep it going as it passes you by. That's still, for performance, basic advice to the actor.

Nevertheless, I wasn't long at Lincoln Center before I felt rather like Captain Ahab on the third day of the hunt—log, chart, and compass gone—throwing his hot heart against the whale and ending up wrapped around it, caught in his own line, sounding. Or maybe it was a hubris less heroic, even foolish, like the Yippies trying to levitate the Pentagon. There's nothing like failure to trip the images out of people. Another friend, wanting to console me, wrote to say that *Danton's Death* was my Bay of Pigs. I wrote back to remind him that Kennedy was assassinated soon after. Yet, I can't deny it, the theater has done for me what I always claimed for it as the public art of crisis: it gave my desire for political being a locus. Out of solitude—and not so sanguine feelings about creation—it was the tithe my conscience paid for the want of a public life in an age which generally thwarts it.

Who was hunting whom? At the end of that beautiful book *Out of Africa*, when she had lost her farm and her lover had been killed in a plane crash, Karen Blixen found herself looking for a *sign*. One has to prepare the looking, the right climate of mind around the eye. Then she saw the encounter between the Cock and the Chameleon. The Chameleon, turning error to bravery, flashed its tongue. The Cock was amazed for a second, but only a second, then dropped its beak like a hammer and pulled out the Chameleon's tongue. Blixen was stunned but then killed the Chameleon, which lives by eating insects, to spare it a slow dying. She concluded from the event, which was her sign, that duress was meant to be, however harsh and sudden, fate guaranteeing nothing. Defeat and victory, both abrupt. It seemed superbly part of the devastating nature of things. Soon after, the lovely hills of Ngong levelled and disappeared in the stretch of distance. I couldn't tell about the rest, but for a while after Lincoln Center, it felt as if they'd pulled out my tongue.

I saw no sign, but was preparing, with some confusion, the right climate of mind. I wasn't ready to do theater again, so stayed away from it, watching, however, out of the corner of my eye. While theater was moving into the streets, it occurred to me to offer my services to some political action group. But after years of running the show I was used to being in charge, and it would have been hard for me to serve, participatorily, in the lower echelons. Field work and stamp licking were out, and I didn't think I could break immediately into the civil rights leadership. So I wrote letters and read much and dreamed up equivocations, with some remorse of conscience, as the Vietnam War dragged on. The war on certain days seemed less senseless than other natural disasters in the deranged ecological cycle. To wit—March 1967—the RAF was bombing a tanker which spilled out near the coast of Cornwall, jeopardizing more than a hundred miles of beach, oyster breeding and bird refuges, as well as the coast of France, where the oil was drifting. It was one of those catastrophes of floating technology almost more disturbing than the experimental technology of a napalmed village, because there seemed to be no one to blame. Of course there were soon rumors that the government had hesitated to order the bombing because of insurance loss. There were pictures of soiled beaches and asphyxiated birds, guillemots, gannets, and ospreys, which were being bathed one by one to remove the oil slick, those which survived. It was going to take months of convalescence to restore lubricity for flight. I thought, looking at a picture of the burning oil, is there an albatross or an actor signalling through the flames?

However I recoil from it, there is always a reflex back to the theater. And in 1968 I returned to California to start a training program that led me in a circle around the country to KRAKEN and the work that group has done. The kraken is a Nordic sea monster whose habitat is fathoms deep. I was reminded of it in a letter by Melville who, replying to a query by Hawthorne as to what would follow *Moby-Dick,* said he was after bigger fish. Then he sounded into the self, his own object. So, in all that motion and public crisis too, I carried around the motives of solitude. There was always the sounding. The kraken dies when it surfaces. What has never abated is that ingrown addiction to the self that might be better served in poetry if I were driven to write poetry as I have been drive to do theater.

Rilke speaks of a vast loneliness of another order when a friend writes him about being solitary. The magnitude of the loneliness is the condition of poetry. I suppose there has also been a tendency from the beginning to impart something of such a loneliness—I won't claim the magnitude, only the shadow—to the act of theater, maybe to void it. The disease of politics comes and goes. The ideals of consciousness are a sorer temptation. I'm not sure what place there really is in the theater for solipsism, if not a primary narcissism, that only knows what *it* means because there can be no meaning outside for itself. If I had the courage of my convictions, I'd never think of myself. But since I do, extrapolating back and forth through the burning oil—*is it here or there?*—I've tried to create a theater form that deals with the perceptual dilemma outright. Some who read this book will remember the kind of theater I've done before, which is some light-years away from the work I will refer to now. We are genetically coded, they say, and there are traces, which I'll identify if there's a point.

That other kind of theater may have had better motives. I increasingly believe that if one has the choice, and one does, it's better to think in terms of purpose, mission, action, task, service to others than in terms of identity, alienation, otherness, division, being-in-itself-for-itself *ad nauseam*, not values but default of value. It is a matter of preferring the illusion of objective cause to the self-destruct mechanisms of a vain introversion. I say this, however, knowingly against the grain. One of the values of the work I have been doing is that, by introversion, it teases you out of thought to such a conclusion. The subjectivity is irredeemable. The equivocation turns up in our technique, not as a contradiction but as the methodology itself. The stress, as in all acting, is on identifying the objective content of an impulse. But we insist that the acting occur on several levels at once and inseparably: act, scene, agency, mirror and motive, and analytical proposition of itself. We have been trying to develop the ability to act spontaneously in ways that have always been held to be antithetical to each other, without (false?) separation of one mode of expression from another, and with rigor of form. Even if what appears is opaque—and it appears to appear so sometimes—we insist upon reaching after what it means as if striking through a mask of unmeaning.

A work becomes inarguable when it creates the terms by which it is perceived, when it becomes its own system of value, when there is nothing *behind* what it is saying, when it certifies and substantiates itself as the sole species of its own genre.

Whether we've accomplished anything like that or not is, obviously, not for this book to say. To write about what one has done in the theater can be nothing but afterimage and afterthought. Something about the nature of what we've done makes it harder to separate what there was from what I've since thought about it. That was not quite true of the theater work of which I've written in the past. I realize that the theater as theater must say its piece on the stage, in the enacting, or not at all, and that's an iron law, although in recent years the stage has shifted conceptually, like, in, and through the other arts, and even off the stage, as what is now called "writing" has shifted hermeneutically

Take Up the Bodies

off the page, being rewritten in the act of reading and projected into history, which is itself being rewritten by consciousness as a work-in-progress-never-to-be-finished till the last syllable of . . .

Here, then, I am concerned with what the works meant to me and what, theoretically, they may suggest about the nature of theater, whether they meant that or not at the time they were performed. I must of course think they did mean this or that when we performed them, although even then we realized they were being absorbed as after-thought through every performance into the realm of reflection, on and off the stage. That is really what they were about, or so we thought. It may be, as Horatio warns Hamlet when he is speculating over Yorick's skull, " 'Twere to consider too curiously to consider so." No doubt, but begging your indulgence, think on't. If there's any justification for thinking so, it may be the verifiable fact that there is never very much in the American theater about which, in performance or after, you can bother thinking about at all. Years ago I wrote about that, and for a while it appeared that things had changed. But I am still surprised at how in our theater even very good minds tend to put their intelligence aside, as if Jarry's debraining machine had taken over. Artaud says that in the theater metaphysics comes in through the skin. It comes in thus, I assume, for every generation, except for every generation a different metaphysics. Ours is likely to be skin deep.

To some the concerns of this book, as of our work, may seem naked-ly, if not niggardly, intellectual. But the things I take to be important do come out of some passion for distinction, for making distinctions that may actually be too striating or strained for theater, turning the subject over and over, so many facets as to be demoralizing. Even some who are very interested in what we do are unnerved by that; so am I. Take one abstract issue that comes up again and again, in various guises, that inevitably determines what we believe about acting and how it should be done: that is, whether or not we admit a "human nature." Brecht, for one, refuses. I don't, though I'm not sure about it; sometimes I do, sometimes I don't. But I don't mean to toss it off like that, I damn well care whether it exists or not. And the work sometimes nearly tears itself apart thinking about it.

As we can see from the choices that Brecht makes, there are practical implications in believing one way or another. For us, each theater piece is an increment in an endless act of perception. It's like, in physics, the property of "strangeness" turning through further investigations into the "charmed quark." Until scientists recently found "naked charm," they weren't sure they were telling the truth. Even now it only means that subatomic theory appears to be heading in the right direction. Because we think there's such a thing as naked charm (in the theater we might call it "presence," although we haven't the slightest idea what we're talking about) doesn't mean there is. Even in the sciences, verification is not inarguably empirical anymore, as they pass over the limits of thought toward the unthinkable. The mathematical proposition may be our highest form of faith. Despite all analogies, let us not fool ourselves, we have no present equivalent in the theater. Speaking of metaphysics, I mean that stuff is really way out. What seems to be coming through the pores is numbers. We are back with Pythagoras. (Artaud may have had an intuition of this in his rhapsody on the geometric robes and animated hieroglyphs of Balinese theater, and the "mathematical meticulousness" of its musical figures, "an exact quantity of specific gestures, . . . a sort of primary Physics from which Spirit has never disengaged itself.") But the existence of human nature doesn't seem to figure in the equations.

Or does it? Even the mathematicians don't know. And whether it exists or not, it occurs to us it might, and we still have to think about it, since the irreducible substance of any art is human, if only as a trace, though in ours it can disappear in front of your eyes. Whatever it is that we're looking at that is not what it is *because* we're looking, yet that in the person which seems fixed or determined, which "bolts up accident and shackles change"—what do we call that? If not nature, what? The point where conditioning or social relations take over from birth—the node of history—is so difficult to ascertain the distinction may hardly be worth it, surely not in so coarse a form as the theater. Yet my nature (the word is out before thought) insists that it is worth trying to make the distinction or to guess at it with the special heuristic means that the theater gives us. At the same time theater passes in and out of history, and we're not sure exactly how. The elusiveness of that passing is the matrix of the opening chapter, as history has been the horizon of the solipsism in our work. Occasionally, distinction with its winnowing fan is so active it gets the better of us *as* we're working, and we begin to feel like the Chinese mystic Chuang Fu, who took a dim (hence enlightened) view of these matters, as well as numbers: "To wear out one's soul trying to understand the oneness of things and not know their identity, this I call '3 in the Morning.' What do I mean by that? Well, when a monkey-keeper was passing out the chestnuts, he said '3 in the morning and 4 in the evening.' That made all the monkeys angry. So he said, 'All right, then, 4 in the morning and 3 in the evening.' The monkeys were all pleased."

Because, says a compulsive western voice, it *does* make a difference, now that history is statistical and on the computer. Sometimes, as in *Danton's Death*, we come upon a variation of the question about human nature which, if it doesn't drive us to despair, puts us on the

Take Up the Bodies

defensive: "What is it in us that lies, whores, thieves, and kills?" As it does, as we do, as we see in the statistics—though they don't resolve the question. As for the monkeys, over the years they appear to have wanted me to say just the reverse of what I am now saying—that these distinctions don't make any difference at all, *in* the theater. So they'd just as well not think about them, in or out. This book is clearly not for them. As for Chuang Fu, with all due respect I must say we differ profoundly, but he does force me to examine my assumptions, and our work has sweated over the distinction *he* makes about identity. Though I am indebted to him for the Tai Chi Ch'uan, which has influenced my thought and my practice, I think I know more about the theater than he does, though he probably couldn't care less. He does have the advantage of a culture with a tradition of long patience. I'm afraid I've never been very much of a monkey keeper.

That was apparent in an earlier book, in which *the impossible* was the theme, up to the regions of the unthinkable. There were those who thought the book unthinkable on quite other grounds. What some took offense about—my opening indictment of the vacuity and hypocrisies of the American theater during the fifties and early sixties—was simply undeniable. I am not concerned with anything like that in this book, whether the situation has changed or not. I almost couldn't care less. The theater is one world, however, and I will bring a few things up to date, including a view of the nearly uncrossable boundaries between parts of that world. I thought what I was saying was rather common knowledge then, manifest, and I would be doing a service by summing it all up before passing on to the subtler, more maddening aspects of what makes the theater impossible, and thereby alluring. Here I will come to that directly. I will say more in the first chapter about the ground to be covered in this book, but the impossible is still the theme—what else? since *that* we can be reasonably sure is unchanging, whether thinkable or not.

The first chapter is almost entirely theoretical. It looks at the powers of theater in and out of perspective, as if viewed in the perceptual space of my current work, which is more subliminally than overtly there. After that, I will backtrack through the experience of Lincoln Center, which was the nutritive *nux vomica*, the rancid preface to the theory, which is absorbed as the chapter proceeds into theory. Wittgenstein describes the unthinkable as what, at the borders of expressivity, one must pass over in silence. He doesn't quite mean what you can't think about you shut up about, but since that appeared to make sense when I was there, I will say now what I can talk about here, mainly personal and sociological reflections. That part of the book is a specimen of (unaccomplished) history; the rest is in the making, reflecting on the reflections. In some of Brecht's plays there are projected "arguments" before the scenes that expose the underbelly of history, putting things in ironic balance, thus: TILLY WINS A BATTLE AT LUTZEN: MOTHER COURAGE LOSES FOUR SHIRTS. I give my view, but the reader can also decide what was really in the balance at Lincoln Center, what won, what lost, and perhaps frame a suitable argument for the events. I could probably have written about them sooner, but I have never spoken of the theater except out of a body of work, which took some time to accumulate in the years between. One always wants to dispose of bad memory as quickly as possible, but the chapter is somewhat longer than I thought it would be. I hope it isn't much ado about nothing. If so, no matter, move on, the theory will hold up without it. If the chapter succeeds, however, in showing how the experience, wasted in itself, helped gradually to focus an idea of theater reflecting on itself, it will have done what I wished.

The subsequent chapters will explain the strategy of *reflexion* in our work, as if spinning in a vortex out of the nucleating imagery. There will be provision for what the astronauts call "orbital decay"—hence, "calculated re-entry" into the atmosphere of the work and the world around it. I won't take up each piece in chronological order, or as a "whole," but rather as increscent cross-reflection on the earlier theory. Each project is a variation on the main theme, a further reflexion on the nature of theater, as well as a kind of satellite tracking station for signals coming into the theater from the gods know where. I will refer to certain plays and other key works as if they were codes and, later, guides to craft. The plays I allude to are, almost without exception, among those I have directed over the years. I will also want to say something about other modes of performance impinging upon the theater from the other arts, in a period when the lines of demarcation were rapidly being erased—or so we thought—in the arts and in society, and between them. Sometimes, I will come at theater issues from the other visual arts, partly because of an overlap in performance theory, partly because there isn't a sufficient body of work in the theater at the same theoretical level. In that respect, the theater still tends to be retarded.

The book is not organized topically or chronologically but rather by an association of ideas that move laterally with and through each other as they advance upon the mirror image in the work. The work throws back reflections in theory. I am no longer sure, as I explain within, whether what I have to say about the theater (or in the theater) occurs in this form because of the idiosyncrasies of my thought or because that's how my thought has been affected by my sense of the theater. There is a tendency in the thought to be allusive and elliptical, by indirections finding directions out. I like to believe I can move in a straight line if I want to, but I don't trust it, even in prose. Nevertheless, there is a whole series of recurring topics which are of importance to the contemporary theater and the reshaping of the idea of performance: issues of space/time, structure, participation, masking, roles/persons/character, self and other, doubling, confession and intimacy in acting, process, group process, myth and ritual, shamanism, convention, environments, representation and illusion, action/activism/atavism, text and pretext, alienation, solipsism, depth and surface. If we seem at times to be circulating through the same terrain, that's because these issues circulate through each other and because the work is always being looked at askance. If we come at it from another direction, we may for a while seem to be outside the mirror frame. But there is, as with the work, an insistence on coming back, retracing a path, looking again; sometimes a specific look or direct gaze, more often than not as if in a cycling of images through monocular and binocular vision, squinting, one eye, then the other, now both.

If I appear at times to be contradicting myself, I like to think that's inherent in a dialectical process, but it may also be because I *am* contradicting myself, or very nearly so, since we will often be moving close to the edge of thought where truth shifts in the act of perception, you lose your balance, and thought slips. I will not offer Whitman's defense about containing multitudes. There are a lot of ideas—sometimes quick flashes *in* the trace of thought—but I do care about the liability of contradiction. I want to see and say as closely as I can and will make every effort at saying it as I see it, exactly. The flashes will be rehearsed, returning as mutations as on a rotating prism—and I ask the reader, where the conceptual going is rough, for the mutual allowance of second thought. In what I think, as I think, it will be hard to separate theory and personal history, the theater and the world in which it occurs, abstract levels of thought from concrete instances. In this matter, there is no priority. As with language itself, our subject—the (dis)appearance of theater—is not really a substance that can be named. It is nowhere present at once, and yet makes itself felt in the repercussions of thought as the whole language makes itself felt in every act of speech.

That's why it's hard to divide the three central chapters, which constitute a gyring movement around the axes of Theory, History, and Origins—with my own experience now on the surface, now below; and ideas of the self (entity? construct?) verging on Myth. Or the axes may be seen as three lines of perspective narrowing, through the work, in the same direction. The final chapter, which assesses the overall state of performance in the theater and the other arts, reflects on the future of illusion where the lines of perspective meet, like the three roads in the oedipal distance, or the intersection of ramparts and cellarage in the closet of *Elsinore*, the shifting habitation of a ghost. If that work seems synoptic of what we did, there is a sense, too, in which Elsinore is the mythic name for the common origin—the historical condition out of which images, the work, and the book came. Parsed, it becomes theory as well.

The Impossible Theater was constructed around the events and imagery of the Cold War as they were reflected in the plays we did during that period—not yet over, merely extended through the debate on détente, the Carter interregnum, and the inaugural of Ronald Reagan. This book is also intended as a reflection on social history—with Watergate and Vietnam in the mirror, providing the metaphors. As is the way with mirrors, once you're looking in, it may not be entirely clear whether the images are going in or coming out, or whether, so far as it is inherent in the work, the atmosphere of the period is background or foreground or, given the period, merely appearance. Sometimes, looking at the work through the period and the period through the work, the eye may grow all pupil, entirely dark. Which is, in theory as in theater, one of the main things I want to talk about.

There is also the view that what you don't talk about you can't know about, as in the Freudian "talking cure," or as a poem is words about things that wouldn't exist without the words. William Carlos Williams is often quoted by people who don't like ideas as believing that "there are no ideas but in things"; but what he really said is, "*Say it*, no ideas but in things. . . . " The extra emphasis is mine, and I will say what I can about what may be better passed over in silence—which is what, by paradoxical rite of memory, should be in the center of the stage. The great ambivalences of theater are constructed around things that are, if we knew more (or if we knew less), maybe better not talked about at all, though we insist on doing so until, language failing, we no longer know what to say. Nowadays, various disciplines are concerned with language as it determines the logic and limits of thought, and what's on the other side of it. While the use of language in the theater, or its absence, has been a major problem over the last generation, and I will discuss it, the stress will be on the theater as a language desperately struggling beyond its limits to what, possibly, may be on the other side.

What is remarkable about this other side is that it always appears to look like theater; that is, it can only be *represented*. Which is disturbing to theorists who, like Jerzy Grotowski or Jacques Derrida, are attracted to Artaud and see the consummation of theater in the refusal of theater, the abolition of representation, the search for the pure unmimetic act outside of what Nietzsche called the prison-house of language. When we think it over, we realize that what they are talking about is the separation of life from death, which is the stickiness of mimesis, the thing that can *only* be represented. Those familiar with such thought will recognize the circularity (not unlike my own), the tautological bind in the attempt to liberate scenic or theatrical language from verbal language. It's like the words which cue the tramps to *do* the tree in *Waiting for Godot*, an instance of seemingly nonmimetic play. I will say more about the circularity and the problem of representation, but the book assumes some familiarity with the major tendencies in the theater since Beckett.

Those tendencies, like Beckett himself, were resisted at first even within the Actor's Workshop of San Francisco, where some of them started. It took a lot of exhortation to bring the actors around. The remarkable thing about my influence at the Workshop was the innocence of the exhortations brought on by the novelty of my information. I mean it was all news to me. Some of it was hard to come by in America in the early fifties, and everything I was discovering went enthusiastically into the work. I wanted to share it as quick as I knew it. It was an advantage and a disadvantage. The resistance could be fierce. One of the things we've had to deal with since is that the ideas became news, very rapidly. The theater is reasonably informed now, though it may remain retarded. What is not done now is not because people don't know about it or can't know about it. There is a glut of information. But I remember the days when, say, Eric Bentley's anthologies were like a breath of fresh air in a mausoleum. Today not only a repertoire is available but a body of theory, and even the utterest squares talk about Artaud as if they were veterans of some gangrenous discharge of a bubo in the Plague. A decade ago people were going "beyond Freud"; no doubt they are already going beyond Artaud. I am prepared to believe they may be going beyond reality too. With anything of great theoretical dimension, we are fortunate if we can only return.

In the book as in the work, I am very conscious—as Wittgenstein says in the preface to his *Tractatus*—"of having fallen a long way short" not only of the impossible but "of what is possible." Perhaps my own powers are too slight for the task. As he says, "May others come and do it better." Since the work itself has not received the attention I might want for it, let me submit its theory to the generosity of time. (The event disappears, sadly, but that's what it's supposed to do.) I do this in a collaborative spirit, customary in other forms of research.

Here it is for the taking. I can only report that "the *truth* of the thoughts that are here set forth seems to me unassailable and definitive." I say *seems.* That will be the key word in this book, as in the theater. There are probably fewer ways to the truth than we think, but because of what we think, and how poorly, we need to leave the options open. One must not only choose, but also reserve the right of last refusal. The next step is inevitably at the threshold of remorse:

In everything that we do, the residue of what remains to be done. Gradually we come to what can no longer be; or what remains to be done finds itself in the service of an undoing—the necessary abuse of illusion, that dark crown. We see ourselves coming to an end, the borrowing outward of the last taking in, yielding up the disparities. We see at last that the selves toward which we aspired can never be, and if we're lucky we're the better for it. We are born several and die one, as Socrates discloses to Phaedrus in Valéry's *Eupalinos.* The others remain as Ideas. "They came, asking to be, and they were refused." The horror, I suppose, is the *being refused, not* becoming one, the several from which to choose not waiting around or, as we say these days, splitting. This book is not a memoir; time enough, maybe, for that. The autobiographical aspects, more or less allusively there, are meant as facet-planes of such Ideas, a sort of aide-memoire of motives. Rough estimate: when I was young, though there was reason to think better of myself (and many thought I did), I didn't think well enough; older, I think I should think much better, for reasons that escape me, though the dues are never paid and one may always be inadequate to the Ideas asking to be.

We are always working in the theater as if we were giving up the ghost.

Minor confessions: First, I will often be speaking of our work in the plural or the collective *we,* when what was being done, or my recall of it, may actually represent my own attitude toward it or my own intentions. Not that the group wasn't aware of the attitude or didn't share the intentions, only that an important aspect of the work was, as I say later, in the friction between us; not dissension (sometimes that), but variant ways of seeing things, the crossing biases of a final design, out of a process which elicits competing wills. Second, our work has been suspended. I am not at all sure that KRAKEN will ever continue as a group, not because its ideas are exhausted (far from that), but because we may be in a period when the group ethos can no longer support itself or be supported. While new groups proliferate, many of the older groups are breaking up or disappearing. The touring circuits are sparser, the money less available, and there seems to be a limiting longevity, anyhow, in such collective work. If there is no future for ours at the moment, I will nevertheless speak of what we did as an ongoing process, and what I have to say of our past is sufficient unto the theory which I am recuperating in this book. Given the theory, the work is in a sense still being performed in these reflections upon it. I realize when I say it that if the work should not be resumed, there will be nothing left of it but that illusion.

While I think there is a future for illusion, as I shall indicate in the last chapter, let me put aside the wrong kind with some watchwords left over from the radicalized sixties: If you're not part of the solution you're part of the problem. I'm sure I am. I do not, like Wittgenstein, "believe myself to have found, on all essential points, the final solution of the problems." I do believe I am speaking of the right problems. Perhaps someone else will come along to solve them. I doubt it. I think they are important problems because they are insoluble. I might say in advance what Wittgenstein says of his "final solution" (an unfortunate term), that the value of this work consists in its showing "how little is achieved when these problems are solved," no less when they're not.

If some of the ideas seem in any way derivative, that's a matter of indifference to me. If I was not born to the theater, I am somewhat more confident that I was born to the ideas. Whatever the work has been, I am convinced that the methodology is exceptional. It depends on an idea of the act of acting which has promise because it has to my knowledge no parallel, though there may be surface resemblances, and some indebtedness, to other modes of theater with which we have become familiar in the last decade. This is not a how-to-do-it book; I'm not sure I know how. That depends on what we're doing. That's why I will be chary of exercises, which are invented for occasions. We have logged hundreds of exercises, but in the end they are all one, and they come down to a way of thinking. Actors are now doing things they didn't do in the fifties, keeping in shape and developing skills; that's fine. But we have also gone through a period of exercises and systems as if each one might be the miracle, like water diets and marriage workshops. Each system is a skeleton key opening a door to perception, perhaps, but when we go back to look, the ground shifts and the key merely twists in the lock. The final door is, as Yeats suggests, a dreaming of the bones, to which no key exists at all. Each work we do is an exercise in craft which ends up jimmying the lock.

If I refer to a particular exercise, then, that's because it clarifies a concept or *is* a concept. The actors in the group KRAKEN are vivid with their bodies. They can literally act standing on their heads. But the validity of what is acted doesn't so much depend on its physicality—there's now plenty of that around, a mixed blessing—but rather on the virility of mind in the method. To shift from mind to matter: in pro football, after all the running guards and tight ends became great physical specimens with extraordinary agility who could do the forty in next to nothing, there was not much to choose between them when they lined up. After that, as Vince Lombardi observed, "It's all mental." And there we are, being intellectual again. For that there is no playbook.

One more thing: if it be said that this book is not finally about the theater, what can I say? except, finally, that is true. Not even theater is finally about theater, though it seems to be.

Milwaukee - New York
1981

Acknowledgments

A long career in the theater has its personal costs, not the least of which is the brevity with which some of those you care for go in and out of your life. The next illusion waiting, the memory of intimacy can be short. Sometimes the illusion is intimacy, and a faulty memory yours. It's a deceiving sort of profession, and I have no illusions about that. Nor about the depth of intimacy achieved when the work is at its best. For me, the work I did with KRAKEN—allowing for the best and the worst—is the most valuable I have done in the theater, and a large part of it was, literally, about the remarkable people I've worked with, young, younger then, who took a good deal on faith and struggled with me through, against, and to the ideas which, as a continuing legacy of the work, are the substance of this book.

Some of those in KRAKEN (or the Oberlin Group before) were with it a relatively short time, but the work was so demanding over any span of time that I want to name them all, all those thinking bodies, more than momentary in the mind: Julie Augenstein, Linda Bowden, Malcolm Dalglish, Bruce Daniel, Brent Dickey, Nicole Dreiske, Jim Eigo, Peter Ferry, Linda Gregerson, Karen Henry, Tom Henry, Bill Irwin, Denise Koch, Chris Leggette, Marilyn Millberger, David Newman, Michael O'Connor, Sharon Ott, Ellen Parks, Jack Phippin, Margaret Roiphe, Tyran Russell, Wes Sanders, David Suehsdorf, Julie Taymor, Chris Thomas, Chip Ukena, Jim Waller, Walter Williams. A couple or more have since changed their names, but I have named them here as I knew them then.

As an editor, years ago, Robert W. Corrigan gave me the chance to think out in writing what I was doing in another theater. He later gave me the laboratory where, in mid-life artistic crisis, I started to retrain myself as I trained the nucleus of actors for the group. He has followed the fortunes of KRAKEN and, in reading the original manuscript of this book, made a key editorial suggestion.

While the book was gestating, I had the good fortune to be asked by the late Michel Benamou to spend some weeks, on two occasions, at the Center for Twentieth Century Studies in Milwaukee. It was there (before moving there) that I wrote one of the two essays which were adumbrations of this book, and whose ghosts are scattered fitfully over the last chapters. That essay was included in a volume published for the Center by Coda Press, on *Performance in Postmodern Culture;* the other was commissioned by and published in the *Drama Review,* for its issue on theatrical theory. Other more or less dismembered portions of the book have been published in *Performing Arts Journal, Theatre Journal, Dreamworks,* and *Boundary 2.* Some early reflections of mine on the Tai Chi Ch'uan, expanded and altered here, were included by James Schevill in his *Breakout! In Search of New Theatrical Environments* (Swallow Press). I want to thank the editors and publishers for the previews of material which is differently focussed here.

I also want to thank the John Simon Guggenheim Foundation for making the writing of a book, for the second time, more possible than it would otherwise have been. And a final word of gratitude to my editor, Cynthia Mitchell, whose clear-eyed patience saw the manuscript into print.

H.B.

Take Up the Bodies

Take
Up
the
Bodies

Conspiracy Theory

1

When you spend most of your waking life in the dark, in the theater, thinking about it (as I have done), the platitudes about illusion improve with age. And the redundancy you come to amounts to this: If life is the dream, what is the theater? Since there are stranger things in heaven and earth, what *moves* us there? Think about it: even the familiar, outside, may move us more. The slightest infraction of daily life, the barest slight, will affect us in depth more instantly than most scenes in a play. A small disappointment may ruin a week, and surely the death of a dog, a horse, a rat may shake us more than the death of King Lear. Indeed, it is now a staple of acting technique to use the memory of the death of a dog to support the emotion an actor might need as, say, Kent or Edgar at the death of Lear. The squashing of an insect may prepare you for the murder of Duncan. With imagination enough, it may prepare you as well for suffering the moral consequences. Or, with the paranoid scruple of a Kafka, there's a methaphysic in the insect, which has its emotions too.

Then what moves us to the theater and why go there to be moved, when the routine, accidents, and psychopathology of everyday life can provide us with the emotions we are experiencing, and even more intensely? It's not the emotion, emotion is cheap. What we are really experiencing is something other—instinct scrupling, an afterimage, the integrity and shape of emotion, a sign, the consequent order of emotion, the cost, an afterthought. Theater is theory, or a shadow of it. (The two words—*theatron, theorōs*—come from the same root, the Greek word *theasthai*, meaning to watch, contemplate, look at; from *thea*, a viewing.) In the act of seeing, there is already theory. Aristotle, much abused for ideas still inexhaustibly relevant, situates theater between history and philosophy. Where exactly that is shifts from period to period with the histrionic sensibility, as history—in a linguistic space which scatters time—becomes philosophy, which is more and more obsessed with the *trace* of history, its disappearance.

Use your experience, the actor is told, even as it is being invalidated. In the human sciences—psychoanalysis, linguistics, anthropology, genetics—research is busily "decentering" or dissolving man, that "simple fold in our knowledge" (Foucault), through a network of impersonal systems, into which the very concept of individual experience may disappear like a single ribosome in the endoplasmic reticulum or a wrinkle in the curvature of space. To say the human situation is unstable is to define the human. We are rooted in a place, we are rooted in the absence of a place. After passing through the End of Ideology, we now speak of reaching the end of history, as if all motion were but flashes and specks, a paradox of gravity, being sucked through the proscenium and out the Black Hole. Nevertheless, we are still overselling the significance of *our* experience. All science aside, our experience is severely limited, by frailty, screening, lapsed memory, fright. The scattering of history confounds our sense of origins. What we are is more than what we know, and most of what there is to be known we've left behind, as in a dream. "I speak to those who understand," says the Watchman in the *Oresteia*, rooted stonily in a place, an absence, waking over the whole known world to the virtual beginning of time. "But if they fail, I have forgotten everything." If there is theory, there is also conspiracy. The lure of the theater has obviously something to do with the fact that *others* are gathered there, as if there is safety in numbers, and the repressed might be acknowledged. There is no guarantee, no more than in psychoanalysis. It is not group therapy. We wouldn't need the theater if experience served us better. What the Watchman wants us to understand is a mystery.

At least, that's what the history books tell us. As time goes on, the Chorus speaks, the Plot moves, and it's not at all clear that we know enough of it to remember. The ideal work would seem to be one in which, as Kafka says of Goethe's diaries in his diary, "The clarity of all the events makes it mysterious." But the next day he says of what he has recorded, "How do I excuse the remark about Goethe (which is almost as untrue as the feeling it describes, for the true feeling was driven away by my sister)?" How shall we ever again know the true feeling? At this distance we're not even sure it was there when Orestes, disguising his feelings, met his sister over the tomb. We lack the ritual forms with the clear events; when we have the clear events we distrust the forms.

In recent years we have played avidly with ritual in the theater, out of some eschatalogical, or ethnological, nostalgia. On behalf of liberation, we have celebrated the return of the repressed. There has been much stimulating talk about the actor as shaman or hungan, with added credentials from the Gestalt Institute. In practice, it has about as much substance as UFOs, those close encounters of the loose mind, paratheatrical. Theater, like foreign policy, has its own Doctrine of Credibility. After a period of deconstructing the ego into a metamorphosing self, we are no longer quite sure that the repressed ever returns, except as engrailed shards of guilt in the oedipal clubfoot. If there is anything like an initiatory rite left over in the form, it consists of a half-summoned remembrance between a sleep and a forgetting. The knowing that is to be known is already known but not understood until the reënactment. We see feelingly, if the event does. The *déja vu* is important. But there is something to be understood. That takes a lot of thought. We're not even sure we want to remember. Some people are honest about it, like Dr. Johnson about the conclusion of *King Lear;* he preferred to forget it.

Study the mist on Cordelia's lips: "Do you see this? . . . Look there!—look there!" Think fast. Who is being addressed? Those in the play, those watching. If by then you're not in the play, you're not watching. We are all vexed, not only Lear's ghost. How do we know what he sees, if anything? You should only live so long, said my grandmother, who never heard of the play, as if she'd written its final lines. She never heard of Marx either, who said that history occurs twice, once as tragedy, then as farce. But what do we do in America, where we are living longer, but history is only what happened once?

When and if we turn back the pages of history, we usually stop at the place that confirms where we are or where we'd like to be, what we have to prove. Not only will history prove the opposite if we look further, but it's perfectly logical that it should. History is not an exact dialectic (Marx never said it was), but it contains all the possibilities that have been imagined, usually in impure states and with the contradictions side by side. We are always looking for the nuclear event, the remotest particle of memory, *that* happening, a *dromenon*, whether to root a doctrine or to authenticate the Plot. When we're not playing things back, we're leaping ahead of ourselves. The more secular we become the more our lives are being lived in the memory of an afterlife—which is why we have so much trouble living the moment. That is the chief problem of acting, in life, in theater. It is a real problem, maybe genetically imprinted. In the theater, even though we know the French use the word *répétition* for rehearsal, we're still indecisive about what a rehearsal should be—*what do we repeat?* The technical problem reflects the ontological problem, and that always turns out to be metaphysical.

Side by side in history with the idea of progress is a natural instinct for thinking of advance as an act of recovery. Our most telling compulsion is a loss. Whether a lapsed Paradise or a Big Bang set it all in motion, there is still a fallacy of origins in the idea that what came first shall come last. That the last shall be first may be the only approximation of the heavenly dispensation we shall ever know, which is one thing we may conclude from *King Lear*. Which brings us to where we should be historically, up-to-date. We are where we are, for the moment. That doesn't, however, keep memory from desiring back. The fallacy of origins persists like the utopian dream, which couldn't exist, so perhaps no fallacy, if it didn't somehow reach back to the shadow of what it's dreaming. I mean desire *is* regressive. It wants the future in the instant. It even wants to have had it. If there's no past which doesn't include this present, there is no imaginable future which is nothing but future. Certainly it's confusing; why shouldn't it be? It's also what moves us in the theater.

I said *if* life is the dream as if it were, pushing the conditional toward the actual. I suppose we always have to ask whether it is or it isn't. Or whether there is only the one dream. I must admit to a bias in that direction (aesthetic?) from having spent, no doubt, too much of my life in the dark pondering the future of an illusion. In our time, however, the conditional has been pushed toward the actual by current events. History collaborates with illusion. One of the better summaries of the period we have not quite lived through, with the revelations about Central Intelligence, calls it in fact *The Time of Illusion*. Life as conspiracy theory, Cointelpro. Yes, it has been that way before—which firms up the theory, life and the theater dissolving into, would you believe it?, the "lift of a driving dream," improvised by President Nixon out of a theme by Martin Luther King on a yellow legal-sized pad. Of all the unsettling exposures about the CIA, the most absurd is the most alarming, perhaps because it suggests what is becoming more acceptable in less clandestine quarters. I am referring to the decade-long experiment with controlled behavior, practiced on unwitting subjects, "in normal life settings," using drugs, electric shock, radiation, ultrasonics, and psychosurgery. The programs known as ARTICHOKE, MKULTR, and MKDELTA are like the cabalistic coding of dehumanizing process, the scrambling of truth itself.

The issue of credibility is written into history, the illusion of continuity. What we normally call history, the assessable life we live in common and of which our records appear to speak, is always threat-

4   *Take Up the Bodies*

ened with oversimplification or extinction. We overdocument it or erase it. In the era of information systems, we don't know where we are, as if all knowledge (as it is) is the agency of illusion, part of the conspiracy, since we don't appear to know what we know either. Thus, the life we actually live is threatened at the extremes, as if there were still at the periphery a barbarian invader. The *via media* under tension becomes a virtually excluded middle, and all we appear to have left is the pathology of the margin, a *via negativa*, which is the path by which reason yields to the unreasoning for the sake of making sense of a dead end.

But there is an adventurism at the extremity which turns to nothingness and leaves us aghast. It's like Edmund asking the gods to stand up for bastards. And they seem to comply, as if cancelling time. The geography of the psyche is in disarray. The margin widens to a frozen sea, an evacuated and splitting center, where the best lack all conviction, never mind the worst. The suction is surreal, the spume of history. "O, I am in a mist," says another figure out of the conspiratorial world that gave us *King Lear*. There are moments of condensation where we are literally up against a wall—Bartleby preferring not to, Beckett's Hamm listening to the hollow, Hamlet beetling over the cliff, Caldéron's Julia outside the convent and the ladder gone: "Isn't this the wall it stood against?" Play Strindberg, and the walls are collapsing all around. *Who is going to stand up for the continuity of history?* A liveable life in the middle seems like a bad dream. We are bereft of mediations when things reach their most radical pitch. The worst returns to laughter or, as Beckett revises the Bedlam, the laugh laughing at the laugh, as when we were up against the wall (bleep) during the sixties. But all the time there is the desire for some negotiable balancing act amid the unnegotiable demands. It's as if, every coordinate buckled around us, the act of living becomes a sort of navigation over a fault or a continuous process of centering and decentering with consciousness as a warped gyroscope, history seasick, unspeakable, language hanging on by the nails.

The plays we remember in a cluster of images speak through time's scatter with the rasp of history. "I have caught/ An everlasting cold." (Deep Throat.) "I have lost my voice/ Most irrecoverably. . . ." Thus Flamineo in *The White Devil*, with his fierce intelligence and no illusions. He knew almost too much to begin with as if he were born twice, an uncanny student of the human sciences. Yet not enough. The linguistic space was almost all there was, making everything theater, including history. It is a condition that, in the latter part of the twentieth century, has been borne again, not only power but the absence of power staging its own reality, nothing but illusion. The condition is shared by disenfranchised artists and intellectuals who alternate between escalating and deflating their fantasies, like Flamineo, who already sensed that history might be happening without us.

We have had a generation of high theatricality in public life, subsided now, but none of it—despite the banalities and the pieties and the churchgoing waspishness of the President's men—was up to the Ur-drama of the Nixon psyche. (Nor the banal and pious actor we have recently elected President.) The Man-with-His-Finger-on-the-Button (not the missing eighteen minutes, but for the final countdown) saw himself at the center of an abstract, technocratic, global performance, where "credibility" was essential despite any opposition or censure—as if the roles of Creon and Antigone were reversed and he were upholding, solitary and misunderstood at the last assizes, some higher Law than that of the State. Because he was a two-time loser who looked even seedier botching the Main Chance, we are liable to underestimate not only the achievements, as they say, but the theatrical dimensions of the Nixon period, which outdid any reforms we thought were occurring then in the theater. To balance the staging at the Great Wall of China, broadcast by satellite to the world, there was the equally remarkable scenario for undercover operations which almost rivalled in sheer moral grime the most awesome confections of a drama by Webster, or Genet, who gave us the image of the plumbers in the Brothel before they turned up in the White House. It is chastening to remember that in our time there were on the payroll at the White House: spies, saboteurs, con men, extortionists, forgers, imposters, informers, burglars, muggers, bagmen, pimps, and possibly murderers—not to mention mere criminal public officials and hypocritical statesmen. And think of that bizarre scene in the last act that might have been stage-managed by Flamineo: a ritual drama in which two foul and godless men of power, responsible for wanton slaughter, kneel in prayer—the Quaker President and the Jewish diplomat. Is there anything more grotesque and deracinated in the crazed poignancy of rulers and prelates in the Jacobean theater?

Credibility wobbles in the illusions of power. We are almost at a loss for words. Fast becoming a ghost at the vexed end, Flamineo still knows (the superb language failing toward the catchall lingo we know) where the action is. Play the moment. Make the scene. There may soon be no one to embody it. Certainly nobody you can trust. Analogies fail. The Plot is thickening and falling apart into untellable tales. The play ends, a "nightpiece," the stage littered with dead.

If you sit in the dark, thinking, the mind goes back and forth in time and in and out of the play, as through a topological maneuver. There is a lot of spinoff. You realize that the theater causes you to think as if thought itself were transmuted to its nature. Nothing but illusion, and all too actual, as if there were no thought but theater, subdued to what it works in like the dyer's hand, as Shakespeare says in a sonnet. The play doesn't end when the play ends, or it's merely play. This attitude toward the theater would seem to condescend to the Spirit of Play, but as Huizinga says in his classic book on the subject, it is precisely the indeterminacy of play that resembles the illimitability of thought. Shakespeare's fluency in the matter is sufficient testament. The longing lover of another sonnet, wanting to be instantly with the loved one, wishes the dull substance of the flesh were thought. Unless it is, the theater is dull. "Ah, thought kills me that I am not thought." There is an entire theory of the theater in that passion.

Does the theater begin with the actor in the center of the stage? or with "the empty space"? to use Peter Brook's term. Brook didn't quite intend it, but the emptiness of that space, on second thought, resembles consciousness itself. We speak of the play of thought and the thought of play. In any case, as Huizinga says, "Play only becomes possible, thinkable and understandable when an influx of *mind* breaks down the absolute determinism of the cosmos." For me, most theater events, not thoughtful enough, are still too rational and predictable. Even in their spontaneities there is impoverished play. On the zero ground of that space, a lack of spinoff. True, the theater event must be tactile, corporeal, carnal even: the actor materializes in the flesh. But any way you look at it, the theater is a play of mind. An abstraction, blooded, spilling over the empty space.

And the mind moves in and out of the space, keeping its eye on those dead bodies, back to the determinism of the cosmos as it is written in the inflammations of history. The trouble with history is that it gets us all wrong. We are born to its double bind. Whatever it is that's determined, *we* are what makes the momentum, the madness, for the momentum is blooded too. We are suicidal and genocidal. We are randomly destructive. We violate our space by the mere living of it. We are the victimizing eyes unblessed by the victims we may become. The damage we've done to the world is appalling, immeasurable. We are the ruins of time. Is all that determined? Could we have changed it? Absurd question; there is no other course, as we see in the theater. This is a place to be ashamed. *We are what happened.* Who can imagine some turning point in the affairs of men when we might have chosen otherwise? History may occur once or more than once, but it is not exactly replayable; not even plays are. Do we really think the world would be in a more satisfactory, less politically corrupt, environmentally hygienic condition if Golgotha had never occurred or Aristotle never lived or no gun went off in Sarajevo? or if nobody discovered that $E = mc^2$? We know for a fact that America is lethal at heart, compulsively violent, its self-evident liberties predicated on the self-righteous extermination of 3,000,000 nonwhite indigenous people. But were the indentured servants and apostolic renegades who came over here supposed to stay in Europe and be persecuted and "disadvantaged," to use that clumsy euphemism? Or were those adventurers at the margin (financed by royalty and privilege), whose cruelty uncovered the Theater of Cruelty that Artaud so admired, and we admire because Artaud did, supposed to stay home and wait for the Plague while the Aztec priest, knife raised, went on with the sacrifice, politics as usual? And if time, God, politics, and the pressure of history brought them here in some ruthless manifest destiny, who after all was responsible for that? We all know now that the murderous exploitation of the Indians and the chattel slavery of the blacks were atrocities. There were those who knew it then, that we are living on bloody ground. But are the dark-skinned races who have found their roots or the women summoning up mother-rite going to be any the more hallowed for lovingkindness when it is arranged for them to practice their depredations on history? Sometimes, as the mind looks out of the theater at certain interpretations of history, the simplifications are stupendous. We can say—as I've read recently in a left/liberal journal—that General Amin was trained by the British to be the grotesque brute he is, but the British also trained Ghandi to liberate the other Indians from them. But what happened to the *satyagraha* between the spinning wheel and the emergency measures? Ghandi said he would stand in peace and pray if he saw a threatening plane overhead, but who told India to make a Bomb? And what is it that prevented ex-Prime Minister Desai—a non-violent man who deplores a gift of silk because silkworms died to make it—from acceding to President Carter on a nuclear holdback? The invisible worm that flies in the night? Come now, who will cast the first stone? And what would the theater be without it?

Theater is one of the great forms of human continuity, about the value of which it is, to say the least, decidedly quizzical. Better never to have been born, the ancient drama used to say. That, I think, is moving.

We want continuity and we deny continuity. We feel we must close off history in order for it to continue. It is like a power drain. The system is overtaxed. Too much of ourselves, we say, is attached to the past, as if it could be unattached. We develop methods for denying memory, and we have certainly lost the art of it which was known in the classical world. History is stubborn, however. The history we are doomed to relive if we don't remember it is the only history we can

Take Up the Bodies

remember. Like it or not, we *are* remembered, memory disallowing its own denial. The history that is not played again as farce is, of course, played straight by the actors. It's only history that thinks it's funny. True, all this is merely theoretical; it needs fleshing out in the theater. The past always needs blood donors. The theater is a means of transfusion.

In this book, as these thoughts suggest, I will not be speaking of theater merely in formal terms or as an art that encompasses social and political realities, which it surely does, and I will talk about them to the extent of my competence, which is theatrical. I am speaking of theater not only as an instrument of thought, but *as thought*, an activity becoming what it thinks of, something to which one becomes so habituated that, in responding to experience or letting it happen (as it will), in *being* experienced, one responds instinctively through the distressed logic of theater summoning up its remembrance of things past. I mean in theatrical terms, which can only be reflected here. We are aware of theatrical *behavior* outside the theater. What we characterize as theatrical seems to be measured by some generally accepted behavioral norm, though it should be clear in a relativistic age that no behavior is theatrical and/or dramatic except so far as we have an image of theater in the mind. What concerns us here, however, is not that image but *the* image—what, *in theater*, is the inconstancy of its constant, like an atomic nucleus, and which, either split or fused, may release into behavior forms of energy about which we may have very mixed feelings. There is, for instance, the deepening illusion that what is moving in the theater may be converted instrumentally to other purposes. That is a tendency worth thinking about twice.

Since World War II, even before, theater has been fulfilling a new analytical function in respect to historical process. We are all becoming familiar with it; it is entering the mainstream of theatrical study. The theater has provided the social sciences with a conceptual apparatus for interpreting the reality from which, paradoxically, it draws its substance as a form. The old metaphor of the world as a stage has entered the rhetoric of social analysis to assess what it is being derived from and what, in turn, it must be assessed by. About an hour before I wrote this, I read a passage in a book review by Robert Heilbroner on the managerial revolution and consumer culture: "Yet we all know that this business world is a facade, that something else is going on behind its life-consuming presence. That something else consists of the silent, order-bestowing, and disorder-creating processes of capitalism. Business is the theater in which the drama of capitalism is acted out, a drama in which the players, unbeknownst to themselves, write the very script that dominates their actions. That stunning puzzle is the central challenge of economics." Heilbroner's use of the metaphor is not systematic, as in Victor Turner or Erving Goffman, but it is sophisticated. The theater he describes is somewhat more avant-garde; it starts without a text. But the really stunning puzzle is that the metaphor has become so ubiquitous and attenuated that it is evaporating into the processes it is describing. We used to speak of the "production ethic" in industry. Now we see it as a theater production with "desiring machines" which have fantasies and a "schizo-unconscious" which corresponds to "desiring production," where the machines play their parts like persons in the reconstituted plot of capital and labor, and also write their own scripts, which dominate *our* actions. The whole thing is packaged with subsidiary rights for television and, with the new tribal reach of electronic circuitry, is performed through the global village, when it's not playing at the festival in Persepolis—converted by the Ayatollah to something between guerrilla theater and a Mystery. As fast as McLuhan could publicize the concept of World-Play, Madison Avenue and the networks produced it, and it was endorsed by various knowledgeable people in the theater, like Dewar's Scotch. Obviously, the terms of the sentence above are reversible: "Theater is the business in which the drama of capitalism is acted out, etc."—not a word change necessary for the rest.

Theater is everywhere, more decentralized than any of us dreamed in the old days, and that may be unfortunate, as Plato warned. But there it is, like the silkworm's yellow labors, leaving a stain on the fabric of apprehension. It may even be more insidious than that. In the same issue (of the *New York Review of Books*) as Heilbroner's article, Susan Sontag, writing on the imagery of disease, quotes the psychologist Georg Groddeck, who describes sickness as "a symbol, a representation of something going on within, a drama staged by the IT. . . ." In this case, as Sontag shows, the dramatization may be clinically dangerous, obscuring the etiology of the disease. The patient may be left confused, guilty, internalizing the burden of sickness instead of seeking out a plausible treatment.

In cancer, the diseased cells are felt not only to be deadly but illicit, like being occupied by a nonself—as if Dostoyevsky's Svidrigailov had shown up in the blood. The idea of some mysterious indictment grows. A judgment is pronounced. The very naming of the disease is punitive. Yet, if the self-condemnation of the patient must be corrected by a proper diagnosis, there is still the other distinction to be made: How *much* of the morality play is true? Despite the mystifications of cancer—by members in good standing of the AMA, as well as Reich's orgones or Mailer's American Dream—we are also aware that we can't

Take Up the Bodies

entirely dismiss the psychosomatic source, with its egregious trace of the IT. If we do dismiss it or minimize it, then we are faced not only with distinguishing the validity from the folklore of psychoanalysis (the two not entirely separable) but also with the old enigma—raised by such works as *The Magic Mountain,* where the disease objectifies a psychic state—about the real substance of artistic "truth." In this, as in Ivan Illich's critique of the medical establishment with its iatrogenic disorders, there is the problem of ascertaining the watershed moment where truth is washed into illusion. Caution: what applies to the cure applies to the critique.

For whatever reasons, we do conjure up and stage our diseases. Or they are staged for us. The hazard is a falsifying melodrama. When that is kept in mind, along with the cheapening theatricality of pseudotherapeutic self-enamorment—people playing roles conscious of playing roles encouraging others to play roles in a supermarket identity game of becoming what you're not and probably never will be—there can be only one true objective of theater, and that is to make *less* theater; which is to say, to reappropriate it from widespread adulteration in the social body.

Perhaps I can clarify this impossible project by keeping in focus another sort of disease, the idea of punishment which, as Freud thought, is generically related to play. "I can't be punished anymore," says Clov in *Endgame,* that mordant record of compulsive play. Would it were so, either in the psyche or the body politic. Michel Foucault, in a provocative book, *Discipline and Punish,* studied the paradox of penal reform. He showed how, as the laws of punishment became less severe along with the reduction of the ritual spectacle of torture, the power to punish was nevertheless distributed more widely. First, there was the spread of jurisdiction to a medley of minor magistracies other than the sovereign; then there developed the various structures of amelioration for crime, including reformatories and prisons; whereupon the number of acts held to be crimes increased, filling the prisons and requiring more punishment—though less brutal perhaps and intended to rehabilitate—until the idea of punishment became a subliminal motive, a social bond, without, however, the tragic sense that is still remembered in Beckett.

The proposition is paralleled by the distribution of pseudo-theater into the productive and behavioral mechanisms of everyday life, thinning out our sense of theater until we feel we've been given free tickets to the wrong play, a kind of insipid rewrite of the demystified family drama in which the son ignores the father, or patronizes him, at the place where three roads meet. To penetrate the disguise of history is one thing, to make a charade of it is another—and the displacement of guilt into weirder forms of self-punishment has still to be assessed, as we can see any afternoon on the soap operas (which are in their seriality, replaceable roles, and other indeterminacies a model of postmodern narrative). The consequent loss of critical intelligence, the widespreading diminishment of being, makes one almost wish for the return of the repression. That may seem contradictory to the idea of theater I have been developing, but when I say it appears to me there is nothing but theater, I am still *in* the theater, darkling, thinking it may not be so. That may be another delusion, like the desire to reappropriate theater from the social body, where it's probably too far gone. But there is a critical difference: I am speaking of an activity of mind.

The dissipation of theater into the theatricalization of everyday life, a pale shadow of what it shadows, is accompanied by the merger of art and nonart contexts. The metaphor of life (not quite the same as life) brought into the arts has confounded the arts and criticism of the arts, while life goes on being what it is, confounding. There is the business side of this merger—that "life-consuming presence," connected with the "art world" and the gallery structure—but here there is even more sophistication at work. It would be as obtuse to dismiss the art/life experiments as to let them happen to you uncritically or, as they say, experientially. Like the idea of participatory theater, they have amplified our conception of performance—as Max Neuhaus's acoustical field under the subway grating amplified Times Square. Such post-Happening "situational events"—derived from Duchamp and Cage—are usually constructed around a perceptual conundrum. In the subway event, eye, ear, and social reality (the creepy degeneration of Times Square) were played off each other as a series of minimal variations on the state of the art (the accelerated history of Postmodernism). That is not quite what I will mean when I speak of a perceptual space in the theater, though I have learned much from these experiments.

What I have in mind is more conservative, to use the word generically. It depends on who's below the subway grating and what's happening in the underground. I am speaking both literally and metaphorically. Ideas of depth and surface are not unlike the medical mysteries. They have been among the most controversial notions of modern art since the rearguard action against perspective pushed reality up front. It's as if Cézanne were behind the canvas like Sisyphus shoving the rocks toward the picture plane. From there on, it is all surface. What you see is what it is, ruling out illusory depth. Wanting to see it on the surface, no coverup, is the aesthetic counterpart of political demystification. The same attitude occurs in the psychology of behavior when

Take Up the Bodies

we prefer people who are "up front" and "all there," although in the theater that is something of a problem as it is not in the strictly graphic arts. We have all seen the actor who is, as far as we can tell, all there and up front too, though he may not be very much. Or there may be more to him than appears, but he has no idea as to why he's there.

The formalist ethos of the sixties and seventies was defined for painting by Frank Stella: "What you see is what you see"—a critical variant of the proposition above, which is always and invariably true. The problem is the parameters and paradoxes of seeing as related to *presence*. The thing there is what *is* there. But some of what you see is what you want to see. That is also there. Some of what you see is what you can't help seeing, despite what's there (in one sense), since it's all there (in another). Thus, there is a patina of perception on the painting that is almost more troublesome than successive layers of unwanted varnish on an Old Master. Restoration is always tricky. It may be trickier in the mind than in the hand. In order to exclude subjective laminations from the painting, the artist may be quite willing to accept, like Stella, formalistic and technical laminations—what is there making its points with art history. As the innovations proliferate, one thing displacing another, presence is a function of what is no longer present, and the immediate present (what we see?) is subsumed in the continuity of the art world (with its inseparable laminations of criticism and publicity: what we see is what we read), a privileged history if not a washout. As things turn into words, we have not only the trace of history but the basis of Conceptual Art.

Robert Lowell, in his *Notebooks*, speaks of "the mortmain of ephemera"—but his is an old-fashioned psychological voice pondering the heavy burden of things in the undertow of time through the heavier burden of language, from which history (in the unconscious) never seems to recede. At its most complex and pertinent, the commitment to surface in art comes out of an impatience with the refuge of the Freudian unconscious, compounded of language. We may, like Cleopatra, have immortal longings in us, but if they're going to show up in art, they're going to be hanging out there, exposed, like the lights in the Brechtian theater.

What we've learned from exposure of the mechanisms is that the problem of any form is the form itself. The medium by which we think is the problem of which we think. The problem with the theater, as I see it, is that there is always somebody there thinking, or a piece of him. About that, Grotowski's posture was inarguable: whether the theater is "poor" or not, it always returns to the actor, who complicates the surface as paint doesn't. The technology of the visual arts, which increases energy by directing it to a flat plane, is undermined in theater, which is forever seized upon by receding space. The actor may think in two dimensions and may even have a one-dimensional mind, but the corporeality of the body is, to begin with, a merciless skeptic, insisting on perspective, and therefore the illusion of depth. It refuses to be "reduced" to less than what it is. The actor, moreover, brings along the recessive freight of the unconscious, like it or not. Since the actor is his own most irreducible problem, there is always the danger not only of subjectivity but of solipsism.

It may be that the theater arises as a resistance to that temptation. What becomes theater is the experience we have no way of transcending without theater. From the standpoint of some recent performance theory, the use of the word *transcendence*, like the insistence on going below the surface, is a serious problem if not a capital offense. That bias is phenomenological, and I will have more to say about it. The philosophical attitude is one to which I'm drawn. Still, as much as one wants to trust the surface, the depths are unaccountably there, especially in the theater, even if illusory; especially in the theater because illusory. The limiting state of mind can be very painful, as in Beckett: "Let me try and explain. From things about to disappear I turn away in time. To watch them out of sight, no I can't do it." Beckett was drawn to the theater because—as he told me years ago when he was struggling through *Comment c'est*, submerged there in the sack—it appeared to be a surface, a containable space. He has since discovered, especially as he began to direct actors, that it's a space where, whatever there is to see on the surface, there is no alternative to watching it out of sight. One suspects he always knew it, though he usually deals with that dire prospect by not attending the actual performance.

Theater is a space of thought specifically vulnerable in performance because of the stubborn vulnerability of the actor. That negative capability is its power. The seeming antitheater of Beckett's plays reminded us of that when they first appeared, wanly, with next to nothing but actors on the scene. We forget how distressingly strange they were, those figures which (who?) leaked memory like Pozzo's watch, or behaved like the hush and babble of a tape loop in the bleak landscape of escaping thought. As theater was going to seed, it was being redefined in the spinoff, if I may mix a figure. The compulsive playfulness of this most cerebral of playwrights took us back and forth through the history of thought, Krapp's *spool* winding down to Freud's grandson on the bed, throwing out and recovering his spool, from which we came to understand, as the plays do (Beckett studied Freud), the origin of theater in the pain of separation from the mother's breast (the *Fort/da* of *Beyond the Pleasure Principle*). Then there were

Krapp's masturbatory bananas, like Socrates' wax in the *Theaetetus,* "thick, copious, smooth and worked to a proper consistency," on which time and perception "imprint" themselves so that we might remember. In Plato, the archaic space of theater comes out of the cessions of thought, historically, as an effort of recollection in the body politic; in the weakening of myth, a "memory place." As we might expect from Plato, the imprints were to be accurate in respect to perception, so we might make "true judgments," as Athena says in the *Oresteia* at the founding of the Areopagus. But how to make true judgments now, given the fractured polity and the spinoff, the lost traveller's guide to western consciousness in Lucky's speech, "quaquaquaqua," or the grandiose counterclockwise journey of Hamm through his disjunct Cartesian space to near-absolute "Zero" (those two windows at the back of the space like the eyes of the mind); or, as we see in Krapp, the hapless imprint upon imprint circling in a near collapse of memory through that lone actor's apparition of a self? Says Gogo, trying to remember what happened a moment ago, "I'm not a historian."

If my own thought has been circular here and elsewhere, it is partly because I do remember the formative influence of these plays which we did back in San Francisco "a million years ago" in the fifties, when audiences were still dismayed by them, and which remain—the allusive play of mind over the selvedge of extinction—inexhaustible. The allusiveness is contagious. Or it may be congenital. Whatever the case, the purpose is to suggest in my own thought process a self-reflexive idea of theater which worries its solipsism as it draws upon it, as it also does in worrying about the theatricalization of everyday life. The two are related, the one always liable to dissolve into the other, so there seems nothing but a performance of the self observing itself, like the Bodyworks which came as intestinal feedback out of the conceptual landscapes of Minimal Art. Or the reverse but mirroring process which came out of a Poor Theater: the new doxology of Grotowski, where the confessional seizures of the actor, once so formed, are passing out of the space of thought back into the landscape through torchlight processions and secret rites, as if the tape had snapped and, miracle of miracles, restored Myth.

It was Grotowski who, over the last generation, made us especially sensitive to the vulnerability of the actor as the source of his power. But as it turns out, the power of Grotowski is not in his vulnerability, if we can judge from the effect of his appearances here. In the end the influence of Grotowski on American theater may be less interesting, relative to the thought of theater, than the influence of America on Grotowski. The recent paratheatrical fancies in the forest seem like

Esalen transplanted and made demonic after a reading of Edgar Allen Poe. No wonder the European Marxists reject Grotowski. What appears to be happening is an admixture of Woodstock and Altamont, those two celebrated rock festivals of the polymorphous perverse sixties that were the living dead end of the Pleasure Principle's short-termed triumph over the Reality Principle. Historically, the turned-on communitarian ethos was sung to rest at Altamont by the Hell's Angels. As for the earlier and hermetic Grotowski, no question about it, he was an exemplary figure at the theoretical level, and for giving deep authenticity to the idea of acting as a spiritual discipline. The achievement was the reflection of high intelligence in the form of theater. That's what I saw in *Apocalypsis cum Figuris,* although there were always dangers in that work's postromantic beatification of the Simpleton.

Given our penchant for high fashion, one might expect that experimental theater types will have been turned on by the new Grotowski even by long-distance report. The news now travels quickly from Wroclaw. According to *Vogue,* they're going to be doing savage things in exotic places while the Moral Majority flourishes here. Grotowski's ordainment of the "holy actor" was always a funny notion in this country. The "inner being without defenses" turns out to be the same old restless servitude that D. H. Lawrence identified in the American character, the ceaseless agitation of an emptiness. Like Rennie Davis and the Maharaji. Or the new solo performances of self-parody. These are sometimes very skillful or imaginative, as with Stuart Sherman or Winston Tong, but also frenetic and forlorn. For a while, and maybe still, there were a lot of born-again theater groups doing the older Grotowski-like things. The exercises were rampant. The Cat prowled. Few, however, had the stamina for that monkish work. Nor was there much theory behind what was being done, any body of ideas in the tiger leaps and the primal screams. The invert sado-masochistic renegade Catholic elitism—like Artaud's "culture-in-action"—was never exactly mana for the masses. They both demanded, as Artaud put it, "A *presence of mind. . . .*"

What was always impressive about Grotowski, all method aside, is that he has a first-rate mind, or did before the communitarian mindblowing and mystified encounter sessions of *Holiday.* While that seems as woefully misguided as some aspects of the Human Potential Movement or the poststructuralist schizoanalysis that dreams of "carnivalization," he's certainly entitled to his worst ideas. There's no telling what may come of them. There is the liability of ideas, however, that second-rate ones diminish the intelligence if persisted in too long, and that can be irreparable. Look at the very intelligent people who made up the Living Theater, what they paraded as ideas, those Sears Roebuck catalogues of antiestablishmentarianism and instant apotheosis. "Continue," said Kierkegaard, "I'll know you where you sweat." There's been a lot of sweating in the exercises, and now in the forest, but Kierkegaard's remark is the challenge of a fierce intellect reproving itself. In the theater, whether psychophysical or pataphysical, one wants the intelligence undeterred and seizing upon itself—as Grotowski himself taught when, after years of lonely work, he seized the theater's attention. In those less formidable, paratheatricality looks like a further delusion of theater in the depletions of everyday life.

In theater we look for a rupture of the plane of being, through performance, to the plane of knowing. Perhaps it would be better to say an *eruption* from one plane to the other, an upheaval of the ground of being, as from a slip of tectonic plates below the earth—like when the Ghost appears in *Hamlet* and the ground goes under. Even before it appears, background and foreground shift, depth and surface: "Who's there? Nay, answer me. Stand and unfold yourself." An interchange in the dark with a distinction that can almost not be perceived, a shift between the watcher and the watched. Two voices in an absence, I quote it as one to keep track. From these opening lines on, the play is a theory of acting. "Is this not something more than fantasy?" Or an acoustical field? a Bodywork? or—even though it is all of these—a perceptual conundrum?

Of course the eruption is what *should* happen, though it mostly doesn't, even when the play is *Hamlet*. I am speaking ideally, of what we would make happen if we could, in our fondest imaginings. Whatever we do in the theater we are always doing on shifting ground. We have to establish ourselves all over, each time. Take the space in which we play:

Let us say, an audience comes into a room. No matter what room, and even if they've been there before, it must be a room they haven't seen. I don't mean transformed by paint and canvas, disguised, though there may be paint and canvas, and the disguises will appear soon enough. I don't mean either what has been called "Environmental Theater," with the scaffolding up and exposed and the audience moving around (it's convivial, but I've seen that room), though naturally there's an environment and the audience can move or not. It must be totalled. I mean totalled by thought. It is no more than a room and a space within the room, but a space charged with the activity of thought, breathing, as if it had never until this moment been thought before. Nothing but thought can do it, whatever else is there. The space is illumined with it, the light above or wherever it comes from or no-light, the actual light, being an act of mind, like the no-birds which sing in Keats' poem. We realize then that the space was never empty. (As Bachelard says of an empty drawer, an empty space "is *unimaginable*. It can only be *thought of.*") A similar act is required, then, of the audience. I know that's hard. We are really not adept at pursuing a thought, for all we accuse ourselves these days of mental hangups. The hangup, I'm afraid, is a refusal at the point where the mind pays for its daring and we are suddenly emptied of thought, in the declivity of a space from which we recoil, forgetting—which is why (where) ghosts come back to remind us, there is something else in the space, what else? I mean—"What, has this thing appeared again tonight?"—all those dead bodies, what *are* we supposed to think. . . ?

And thus we are back—in this linguistic space where thought is scattered like history—to what was immediately before us and what we left behind, the sort of thing plays usually leave over, what is forgotten, what usually gets lost in the two-hour traffic of the stage because we get caught up in the emotion of the scenes, the psychology of character, the personality of the actor, or, in the nonmatrixed diffusion of time, what's left over of the Plot, or because we're too familiar with it (even in fragments), we've seen it before but in the wrong way and history seems to have passed it by (and we shouldn't be doing texted plays anyhow), and because nothing in the performance is as particular, say, as Hamlet is when he quarters the thought of his mother about being too particular, since she'd rather forget it, and maybe we should. Brecht tried to get at it nevertheless with the idea of Alienation, to shake up the selective inattention, making the familiar strange so we could see it again—what he called a *gestus*, a sign—historicizing it, a technique which used to be strange but is now somewhat more familiar, though not always particular; and even so it may have to be stranger to get through time's scatter to the warp of history or to the troubles in *Hamlet* which annoyed Brecht and are too familiar, or to the end of *The White Devil*, which is not.

Look at it. The play is devastating in its final exposure. And the last words urge us—lamely? cynically? can we truly judge?—to make "use" of the punishment. But what use? The use of a play, like a set of axioms in a mathematical system, is directly proportional to the questions it raises which are unanswerable within its own framework. Again: "Is this not something more than fantasy?" Maybe it's not. In the theater, all other questions intersect in that possibility. In KRAKEN, we've tried to convert the dilemma into a technique of performance. We call it *ghosting*. I will discuss it further in another chapter, but it has to do with the uses of illusion in the process of thought. "For both art and life depend," says Nietzsche in "A Critical Backward Glance" at *The Birth of Tragedy*, "wholly on the laws of optics, on perspective and illusion; both, to be blunt, depend on the necessity of error." In the empty space, unanswerable questions. The questioning begins even before we know what we're doing, in preparing a subject, or finding one, in *apprehension*. (As I implied about *Hamlet*, a great text out of the repertoire is neither a necessary subject nor a guarantee that the questions will be there.) In thinking thus, we will always return to the question with which we started: What moves us in the theater, whatever the technique? What, in fact, moves the technique?

The play of mind becomes a habit of mind. As we turn things over and over, the theater becomes—in the doubling consciousness of the play-within-the-play—what we think about it. The result may be a methodological tautology, erasing error with more error. That's what I meant about the redundancy you (I) come to in the dark, leading to the reflections upon illusion. In reflecting on the reflections, the work itself may lead to a kind of impacted structure, moving by association and elision (as in a dream), reifying particulars to the point of exhaustion (as in dream interpretation), frustrating in its refusal of conceptual relief, not letting go of the outside shadow of a last possible meaning, like members of the Bantu tribe who will in their speechmaking pursue a comparison when the things being compared have next to nothing in common, but yet not nothing, and they appear to be satisfied with that. I'm not. Yet it appears to me that that's where the action is, *in this last space of thought*, the thing which—in an age of unavoidable introspection—is most specifically theatrical: *the refusal of conceptual relief*, the desire to get as close to the thought of theater as theater would be if, in a conspiracy of illusion and history, it were reflecting upon itself. Even as I say it, I know quite well that this is thought and not theater, although in the theater we try to make it more than thought. If we could do it as we desire it, it would be as highly charged in the body as *the first thought* that separated itself from life or mere being or whatever-was-there-before in order to become *the difference-from-life which appears to us as theater*. Whatever it is, suffice to say that my intellectual habits have been very much determined by theater, and these speculations may in significant ways, even right now, mirror that source.

A play is a world. The world must first be thought before we can understand the indeterminacy of play. The play is radical only in releasing itself to the exhaustion of meaning. That doesn't mean the meaning is exhausted, only as much as we can make of it. What get in the way, often prematurely, are the intellectual habits of an age which is either reaching irritably after reason and explanation or—through a long tradition of anti-intellectualism—refusing to give meaning a chance. I am not speaking of the congenital know-nothingness of everyday American life. The tradition I am referring to is more formidable. Possibly never before in the history of thought has so much cerebration gone into the subversion of the powers of mind. Now that somewhat more intelligence has come into the theater, the problem is doubled over, since it gives more justification to its thoughtlessness. Certainly the hardest thing to do in acting is, still, *to take thought*, and to do so in relation to the objective problems raised *in the acting and by it, as it occurs.*

The work of Richard Foreman, with its emphasis on "THINKING what is present," is a case in point. It's an important case because Foreman is clearly one of the more intelligent people now working in the theater, and, like Robert Wilson, with unusual graphic abilities. Nevertheless, while he avowedly wants to put the theater back into the mind or the mind back into the theater, his tracing of thought-revealing images is still occurring at a level where no specific idea, *as idea*, has to be thought through. Indeed, he scoffs at the thought: "Listen-speak-click of release that's no-mind. Ah!" Which is not quite the emptying that occurs when the Ghost comes or Godot doesn't—the dreadful cost of thought reflecting on a world that numbs it, because it is virtually impermeable to thought and, what's maybe worse, intolerable to think about. What we see in the Ontological-Hysteric Theater may be rationalized (Foreman has the virtue of being theoretical) as filling a space (mentally), but it does not include the "old paradigm" of determinate thought, the rationalizing process itself, within its expressive means. For that process is ego-bound, a residue of the old humanism—the presumption of trying to make sense through theater of what won't release us in the world, and what we'd maybe do better to forget if we could, because we're only human.

In Foreman, the composition—a word he rejects, preferring *shape*—is strict. He shows you what to look at, and where. The play of thought is a saturation of attention around the surface of objects and occurrences. You can't quite call what happens action. There is an order of dissociation and discontinuity. The framing is designed "to read off the 'said' from the face of thought." But he is working largely with linguistic and perceptual games. What's said is more like Gertrude Stein (by whom he was influenced) than Samuel Beckett. There is a critical difference in their respective discontinuities: in Stein, a denudation of passion, and of passion linked to memory; in Beckett, memory there only as something forgotten, but there as the insistence of what wants to be remembered through all efforts to discredit it, even one's

Take Up the Bodies

own. That accounts in Beckett for a richer ambivalence of perception. It's hard to establish identities, but you unavoidably project them on what's there. The thing to be identified is, however, provisional, elusive, chimeric (maybe), recurrent, and haunting.

The old humanistic terms won't dissolve. In Stein, in Foreman, they are dissolved, it seems to me, rather too easily or arbitrarily. The persisting humanism in Beckett is not a mere tokenism of balancing forces—some from the old world, some from the new—it is a single world moving and being moved in an almost classical structure of incoherence through interminable division. *Nothing* disappears. In Foreman, however, the prescription is: "Don't sustain *anything.*" Neither the old appurtenances of drama nor the thinking process. As a result, there is nothing like the felt cost of the "discard" in the cataleptic shape of a Beckett play, as when Hamm throws away his props. What Foreman calls the "ordeal" bears not the slightest resemblance to the far-gone ritual source that has left its initiatory scars upon the drama. It is rather the trial of the jigsaw puzzle, a very intricate one, and often witty, but neither for the actor nor the spectator, an *undergoing.*

As for the THINKING that is present, it is not really the actors that do it. The actors do not think at all *in* the process of acting. They are rather functions of prior thought. That's not because Foreman provides them with a text but because of the particular kind of text. They are not even so thoughtful as orthodox characters, but rather images of thought unthinking in the act of performance, programmed, like cybernetic bits in the register of a computer, or what Foreman calls "a more verifiable neurological bi-part system in which . . . the perceived may be read in (on) the past (the memory state upon which past perceptions left their imprint.)" The resemblance here is not to Socrates' wax but to systems theory in the recent conceptual forms of the visual arts, or to other information systems. Indeed, Foreman is at the controls of his performances as if he were at the console at NASA during a launching. It is a thought process in which the actor—picking up signals and embodying an atomized stream of thought—inevitably suffers from sensory deprivation.

But it is at least a conception of theater. It occurs at a threshold where the world-as-played has something radical about it, aware of the problematics of play and the operations by which it constructs that world. It is not a political radicalism, though Foreman admires Brecht and has directed *The Threepenny Opera*. It is, however, the formalism which attracts him, the *A-Effekt* at an extreme—as the actors have suggested in commenting on him as a director. Yet the accomplishment is there. In whatever binary form the theory can be argued. The holistic vision of Robert Wilson raises another sort of critical problem. While

Foreman is prolix about his intentions, Wilson almost refuses to talk about his. The published version of *Einstein at the Beach* has an introduction, by someone else, which does explain Wilson's effort to recover the perceptual faculties at the proprioceptive level, on the ambiguous borderline between normality and psychosis. But the "playscript" itself is entirely non-verbal, like a sequence of strip-photos by Muybridge. Wilson's achievement is of such an order that he can choose to talk or not, but he has successfully prevented others from discussing (no less assessing) his work by other than mere antiseptic description.

The observation is correct that Wilson wants to eliminate all mediation of his images. That attitude toward meaning and language is what keeps criticism in awe and off limits. His works seem oneiric, but unlike dream they are supposed to ward off analysis. The mythos grows around them that they are not interpretable, which is very different from being inarguable. What is arguable, however, is a theoretical aspect of Wilson's theater, and the delinquency in making the argument is in turn an aspect of the anti-intellectualism which has become second nature among certain intellectuals, particularly where performance is concerned, which is supposed to speak for itself. But it does and it doesn't, and we ought to say where. Whether Wilson has developed a new theater form or not, he is moving in the company of exotic ancestors, like the unappeasable ghosts which wander the countryside in the archaic Japanese drama. He is attempting to fulfill on stage the Symbolist mission—one of the more heroic ventures of the last century—of liberating the "landscape," as Yeats put it, "from the bonds of motives and their actions, causes and their effects, and from all bonds but the bonds of your love," which may have to be aroused, however, by soporific means playing over the active (aggressive) or recalcitrant (rational) forces of your personality, making you passive, docile, and therefore receptive. It is not the free-floating alertness of the analytical session, the mental readiness for play, that Freud brought to dreams. It is rather the Eastern form of negative capability, a mode of spiritualized hypnosis, which is also pretty much the theory of art that Bergson erected around his concept of the *élan vital*. While Freud, Einstein, and Stalin turn up in Wilson's titles, the work is also a-historical. As Yeats wrote in *Cutting of an Agate*, "if the real world is not altogether rejected, it is but touched here and there, and into the places we have left empty we summon rhythm, balance, pattern, images that remind us of vast passions, the vagueness of past times, all the chimeras that haunt the edge of trance. . . ," or that perne in a gyre like the Sufi whirlers. It is a distinct tradition in which, as Bergson says, "the survival of past images . . . must constantly mingle with our perception of the present, and may even take its place," completing "our present experience, enriching it with experience already acquired [and also brought to the stage by people who would not normally be there: aphasics, Wilson's grandmother, etc.]; and, as the latter is ever increasing [ideally, the pieces would last not 164 hours but *ad infinitum*] it must end by covering up and submerging the former." The almost petrifying adoration of a gesture can be mesmerising and even healing in a hurried time. The boredom we have come to understand (we had the abridged version in Beckett), but there is still the vagueness (which we didn't).

While Yeats tried to do it by foreshortening and compression, Wilson does it not by a breach but a proliferous expansion, like gold to airy thinness beat. Recently he has been exhibiting furniture from his *Gesamkunstwerk*—as if he were trying to demystify backwards to the original mystery of the ritual artifacts which were in the theater aestheticized. Mallarmé described the unitary emotion of the symbolist ethic as "evoking, in an intended shadow, the unvoiced object," to be achieved by "stroke incantatory!" It is the echolocation of a theory of art that tried to pass like the winding of a serpent synesthetically beyond the powers of language toward the divine, restoring to "reality and justice," as Yeats would have it, all that the articulations of language have denied and rent asunder.

Wilson often approaches this desideratum splendidly, but what he does is hardly as arcane anymore as it has been made out to be, and not at all undiscussable. The refusal to talk about it, however, begs the question of his subordination, even mockery, of language; and it is at this level that Foreman and Wilson, with their quite binary temperaments, meet—in the idea of a "landscape play" whose presiding genius is Gertrude Stein. It is no accident, given the ontological bias, that the language of Foreman's plays is dry, iterative, aseptic, unfigurative, and unmemorable. It is also logical that Wilson did his last major composition at the Metropolitan Opera, since he has been trying to do without language, or with poor language, what in the symbolist and postsymbolist traditions, language tried to do for itself, that is, to achieve the condition of music; even when—as in Yeats or Lorca, or in Eliot—it also tried to do it in the theater as well. Foreman and Wilson are both poets of the theater, but a theater which we should recognize—for all the prolificness of Foreman and the extravagance of Wilson—has been seriously lessened, and made anemic, by the now-tiresome side of the quarrel with words. The "kneeplays" of Wilson are part of the kneejerk reaction. Of how to reduce the importance of words or do without them, we have now seen and heard plenty. Of what to do with them neither Wilson nor Foreman tells us very much.

Until the day when we are really released from the bonds of motives and their actions, and the icy silence of eternity subsumes us all, it will remain a problem.

In the rest of what has been called Experimental or Alternative Theater—that somewhat random outgrowth of what, in the fervid sixties, was named the Third Theater—there are few things that can be discussed in this context. The Third Theater, to the extent that it existed, reflected the politicizing of everyday life. Ultimately—with performance in the streets and on the media—the dramatistic strategies of the Left succeeded in playing into the hands of the enemy by increasing the quotient of mystification. The forces of repression actually prospered, all staginess played out. And it might have been worse if we hadn't lucked out with Watergate. When all the fervor waned with the ending of the Vietnam War, we were left with another conundrum to which I'll keep returning, the old one about the relationship of art and politics.

In the indeterminacy of play, radical art and radical politics may or may not meet, but there is an implicit political component. Dada and surrealism—the progenitors of some of the more interesting "non-matrixed" experiments in performance, including the theater of protest—grasped this, with misconceptions. "I don't know how radical you are," said Lenin to a young Rumanian dadaist, "or how radical I am. I am certainly not radical enough; that is, one must always be as radical as reality itself."

At the end of *The White Devil*, the bodies are an objective problem, as radical (it seems) as reality itself. What *use* are we to make of them? They lie there with the immanence of a blooded abstraction from which, if we don't follow up the question, the reality will begin to drain. I don't know how radical we are, but our work usually starts with such problems. They are obviously insoluble. We return to them again and again, as in a compulsion dream—and as we are doing here. (*The White Devil* is not a play we've actually worked on in KRAKEN, though at Cal Arts I did a very shaky project with it, as in a mist, in the early days of thinking through a method.) The problem is absorbed into the acting process. The act of theater is a series of mutations on similar themes. In following up the question, I want to point to some of these themes as they've shown up in the works we have made, and as they conspire with the theory of theater derived from them.

The pivotal mechanism is the idea of punishment. We know that punishment was somehow taken to heart by the theater from the very beginnings, whether in tragedy or comedy, racked on the Wheel of Fortune or struck by a lemon pie in a revolving door. If there is an Eter-

Take Up the Bodies

nal Return, it moves through punishment (the ordeal) like a compulsion dream. If there is the one dream, that may in fact be IT: if not the existential disease of history, the solipsistic reduction to self. The nightmare from which Marx tried to awaken us is the one about which we remind ourselves that if we should awaken there would undoubtedly be no theater. For which relief much thanks, but there we are. In the great ages of theater, punishment was up front, and bewildering. In our own period, it may be alternately up front or subliminal, strategically distributed or a function of new modalities of power, mass slaughter or minor cruelties, insidiously lenient, but still bewildering. As for the use of punishment, that still remains to be seen.

If, as Vico remarked, jurisprudence with its rites of punishment was an "entire poetics," so theater—particularly dramaturgy with its rites of punishment—is an entire jurisprudence. There is still (as old actors used to tell me) nothing more dramatic than a trial, although trials can reflect thought—the effect of Athena's presence at the Areopagus—or a set of procedures, more or less brainless, having nothing to do with justice. The same is true of theater. There is a sense in which every performance is a trial, offering up evidence.

There is always the issue of credibility. What was true of the dramatic process in the seventeenth century is true of the juridical process as we have come to know it in our century—and not only the staged trials, the purges, Eichmann, the prosecution of the Gang of Four. There is something endemic to the process which, in the long paranoia of the oedipal tradition, cutting the drama to the brain, has changed the behavior of theater. What is justice? And so with the entire law. Crimes have been committed. What is the use of punishment? And if punishment is desirable, who would in justice mandate it? And if the punishment has been performed, what then? Suppose, as Heidigger said, the dreadful thing has already happened. Kafka's *The Trial* is an altogether different story. Or is it? Who can really be trusted to enforce the law when (as recently in this country) the covert operations designed for security under the law were directed by an intelligence chief known (appropriately?) as "Mother." And the law itself, what is it? At best, as in *Hamlet*, it is felt as an absence in the structure, with more or less diminishing presence and powers. Every look is the law. At worst, as in Kafka, there seems no point in looking. Where there are no grounds for guilt, it is simply unspeakable—and we feel guilty for feeling guilty, as if we're only being looked *at*.

When we speak of the law we are speaking of power, but where it comes from we're not sure. Neither the young Giovanni, at the end of *The White Devil*, nor the experienced Fortinbras, at the end of Hamlet, is divinely appointed. What power they assume is thoroughly problematical. Giovanni doesn't even know, until one of the (criminal) avengers undisguises himself (not as a criminal), that the massacre has been committed by his authority. The authority is about as dependable as any tyranny after a coup, racked in turn on the "torturing wheel." What applies to the guilty applies to the law. Both are benighted, and "lean on crutches, made of slender reeds." Fortinbras at least seeks a prior justification, more evocative, claiming "some rights of memory in this kingdom." He knows that the theater is a memory place. He is temperate because he knows how tenuous that is, how dependent on what you're *seeing*—and whom would he charge with capital crimes in any case? Not all of the guilty are corpses, but death never restores innocence, which was anyhow buried, if it ever existed.

What we are left with is the feeling that there might have been, once, a punishable offense, but we no longer know its nature. That's the mystery which tears open the structure of *Elsinore*. It is the issue returned to the space by the Ghost. We are baffled by the deeds that have been performed, and we're not sure, always, whether they're crimes or not. (Theory of law is now constructed, as if it were theater, on the virtue of this defect. "The principles of justice," writes John Rawls in a very influential book, "are chosen behind a veil of ignorance." According to Rawls, the choice is deliberate and desirable.) Still, theater is made possible by some glimmer of common law. It is the social contract that needs rethinking. We must now ask about any act that looks punishable, what does it entail? To what level of reality does it belong? Are the deeds merely delusional? Every work we have done has been concerned with that. Brecht would have insisted that the deeds are real, or better be—and maybe the process delusional—or otherwise they would be unalterable, and that would be the crime.

But the dead bodies—which once, in the exemplary stagings of punishment or the rites of war, told a tale—give no witness. No more than they did in the cannibalism of the Donner Party (migrants from the Midwest who were snowbound in the Sierras in 1846), which was the "subject" of a work we did. Divested of all indemnifying value, made imbecile by death, they incriminate a whole system. To appraise the atrocities of the Donner Party, there is no system. Dante might have known how to place them in his Inferno, but we improvise our judgments through a history that litters the landscape like pollution. It is a cloaca of unnameable deeds. We can only be grateful that some of the history isn't recorded. As for the horrors of *The White Devil*, there is no solace *in* the play. So, as Giovanni commands, "Remove the bodies. . . ." Nothing doing. Outside, in the world, it seems worse. Which is, I suppose, what Beckett had in mind when Didi runs off stage

Take Up the Bodies

and comes back in a hurry. These things stay with you, if they're moving. There is no question of credibility then.

The mind, ghosting itself to the last breath, is never contented. It refuses, even in Brecht, the arbitrariness of signs, the postulate of a semiotic distance in a revolutionary art. The rules of evidence obtain. I used to argue these issues at the Berliner Ensemble in the late fifties, right there up against the Wall, the most brutal signifier on the landscape, though it had to be overlooked on the stage. Now that the Wall is somewhat more—but by no means entirely—a museum piece, the political side of these existential issues is even more blurred. What is clear now is that Brecht too, absorbed into time, is becoming familiar and needs to be historicized. When we are moved in Brecht, it's not that his politics is subverted or cancelled by theater (as those who don't like his politics want to believe) but that *the theater distances the distance,* a sort of reverse perspective bringing *us* close in. We studied that paradox in a long project called *The Enemy* which became *Seeds of Atreus* and persisted through *The Burrow,* which became *Elsinore* (the traces going back, probably, to a version of *Endgame* done at the Actor's Workshop in 1959). It's the process initiated by the Watchman at the birth of western drama, when he brings the theater into remembrance out of infinity, "the grand processionals of all the stars of night" igniting like beacons across the deepest space of thought to illuminate the mystery.

Reverse the adage: If you're not part of the problem you're not part of the solution, whatever that is. Theater is the memory place where conspiracy theory is privileged. The rites of memory are passed from generation to generation, although what there is to be remembered is passing out of mind. "Look again, look again, search everywhere," chant the Furies, those gray and aged children, remembered and remembering, with their fierce intelligence, hunting the prey. There we are, looking, in the dark.

The theater is in the looking. It can do no more. The looking is performed in theory, as if life were maybe a conjecture but not a dream. The last scene of *King Lear* offers another paradigm: the dead (or dying) body in the center of the stage, another looking and dying over it, that gray and aged child, intelligence humbled, no longer fierce; the others watching and being watched, as if the looking were a kind of dying. "Is this the promised end?" The eyes glaze over the body, remembering. Up too close, we can't see. Too far back, we can't feel. That's the problem with Empathy, that's the problem with Alienation. That's the problem. Distance, which gives perspective, blurs; intimacy, if it doesn't breed contempt, blinds. All theory fails at the limit of theater, as it does at the end of *Hamlet*, that most ratiocinative play of all: "Take up the bodies." The mind boggles, yielding nothing. There's a crucial difference between that "Take up" and "Remove"—the barest shift in the linguistic space, having to do with the responsibility of a political order. There's no punishment to make use of, no amnesty even; there's a story to be told, Horatio's burden, an untellable tale. That, too, was the pretext for *Elsinore*, though it had been on my mind almost as far back as I could remember in the theater.

During part of the last decade, language failing or being failed, we tried to do the telling with the bodies. The story is too complicated for that. What was summoned up was either too obvious, already there on the surface; or, as the bodies tired, subject to amnesia—as with the erasure of consciousness over the atrocities in Vietnam, the punitive instincts at home, the secrecy, deception, and felonies that, in young and old, went right through the marrow of the body politic. Even the desire for amnesty—however justified by the willfulness of history and the criminality of our government—is the providential side of the desire for forgetfulness. But if there's a point to the theater it's to not let ourselves forget: *What did it all mean?* The Ghost, reified, wants to be remembered, with almost no boundary on thought. "Go on, I'll follow thee," cries Hamlet; then: "Whither wilt thou lead me? Speak, I'll go no further." But does he really mean that? Will he go if he likes what he hears? After *Hamlet,* there is only the dramaturgy of limit. It is one of those works, perhaps the supreme one, which by forming our capacity to perceive also gets in the way. It has the contours of an empty space. The history of the theater is a calculus of changing focus on a subject which is increasingly mist. The thing which moves us is on the edge of a disappearance. Whether in or out of perspective, we are always at the vanishing point.

Or so it appears to me. The vanishing point is, so far as I can see, the wobbling pivot of the work I have been doing in the theater for nearly a decade, with an obsessiveness, if not ferocity, that is still trying to become intelligent. It has the quality of a compulsion dream. We are always returning to the Ghost. The principal issue is perception. We insist that the Ghost will speak. Other types of theater have their own illusions.

Take Up the Bodies

The Power Structure

2

Though we probably make too much of it, experience can't be out-guessed. What we wished for, whether it comes late or soon, is not what we wished for whether it comes or not, because we are not what we were when we wished. If we could be that, what-we-were, restoring the fugitive ego of former days, its reappearance would cancel, if it came, what it came to reassess. Playing it over, that reasonable fac-simile of what is reasonably possible in the theater, is very unsatisfac-tory in life. All the water under the bridge, how to trace it? Yet the water under the bridge is more or less the same water.

Let's put a wide-angle lens on the illusions before we pass again, theoretically, out of sight. I mean let's keep them open to history. I want to do that, at the risk of a narrowing rather than a widening, in a somewhat more personal vein. I have already said, in something like vanity, that where I was in the theater is a very long distance from where I have come to be. But Destiny is strict; for each of us, one history. I trust it will not be without a sociological perspective. Thus, from the top down:

Boards of Directors are probably the most unjustly maligned people in the theater world. That's not because they aren't what they say they are, rather because they never claimed to be anything else. We keep ex-pecting them to behave by values that are not theirs. We knew when we started they were not theirs, and more often than not they show more integrity in stating what they stand for than we do. In the desire to get them to turn over the resources, we will shamelessly promise anything. The values we want them to live up to are values many of us never possessed.

Be that as it may, I recall an interview at the top of the First National City Bank on Park Avenue, when I had to think of the values I did possess. There across the table were three representatives of the Power Structure—affable, confused, steely, not necessarily in that order, nor this order: Hoguet, Rosenman, Burke: The Banker, The Judge, and The-Man-Who-Bought-the-Yankees-for-CBS. They reminded me of the Allegorical Figures out of Genet's *The Balcony*. "COULD YOU RING ME COLLECT IN NEW YORK AT PLAZA 1-2345 REGARDING THE LINCOLN CENTER REPERTORY THEATER." The telegram had been signed by Michael Burke, CBS Development then, formerly a hero with the OSS, afterwards president of the Yankees, then head of Madison Square Garden—these latter jobs really impressive, all the teams and places I ever wanted to play when I was growing up, before the Absurd, in Brooklyn. When the wire came I was in a technical rehearsal of *Uncle Vanya* in San Francisco, just before the turn of the New Year, going into 1965. As I confronted them over the table, I kept thinking of Vanya in that wild scene of the play, shooting at everything in the world that made the world frustrating, and missing. Over the next several years, however, I came to respect each of them, not because they saw the world as I did, far from it, but because they were candid about who and what they were. I realize that candor, while not automatic, comes a little easier with power, and is hardly a guarantee of virtue. But they were also as responsive as they could sensibly be to what we were, which, as time soon proved, guaranteed nothing either. So far as I could define it that day, I tried to be candid too, not shooting but pulling no punches.

Judge Rosenman was easy to respect. He was after all a hero out of my earliest political awareness, one of the Roosevelt brain trusters. We talked readily about politics. He still had a brain. He also knew immediately where I stood. I remember one morning at the Links Club on the East Side, he and I had turned up early for a breakfast meeting, waiting for the others. "Do you know where you are?" he asked. I said no. "This is the fascist power center of America." He was amused. He had evidently learned how to live with it, thinking he could put it to use. I am sure he was hoping we could. As for Hoguet, he was a hulk of a generous man who had called up a lot of loans; in the overall balance, an "optimist"—I suppose it comes with the territory—who worried about my being a "pessimist." He was fond of me but we carried on a running argument in which he would make such polar contrasts of his world and my world. "I never pretended to be a philosopher," he would say, but the distinction was pure Cartesian: his world "objective," my world "subjective." He had been given the job of Board president (following George Woods, the former head of the World Bank, the current one being MacNamara when he dropped out of the Viet-

Take Up the Bodies

nam War) at the time Robert Whitehead and Elia Kazan were still in charge of the Repertory Theater. Immediately, the shit hit the fan. Hoguet admitted having done some foolish things in that debacle, having been sucked into it, he said, by the press. He could be garrulous and naive, though the press has made suckers of people with more smarts. He also learned; not fast, but he prided himself on being able to learn, and with good reason. When he retired from the bank, he talked of wanting to run for political office in Colorado, where he went to ski, like Jerry Ford, whose mixture of honesty and clumsiness he shared. If he ran (he didn't) and I lived there, I might have voted for him, though I never crossed Republican before. His wife, a shrewd and intelligent woman, was an active patron of the Philharmonic, but he'd never had much to do with artists. Among the things he had learned was that people from my world were "weak, evasive, cowardly, and illiberal." He could be eloquent about this. "They talk democracy, then run away so there can be no dialogue." What could I say? I knew he wasn't making it up. Credibility wasn't his problem.

Hoguet worried that I might be *too* subjective, "too partisan." One time, making a point about good faith, he said he could give away $10,000,000 over the telephone with a mere okay. What was there to say except the obvious: I wasn't about not to have a dialogue with a man who could dial away ten million. He was never quite persuaded. He enjoyed these sparrings but was more comfortable with my partner, Jules Irving, who might have stayed at the Beaumont if the ten million were available, since that's the sort of subsidy the place needs. Actually, our Board wasn't too great at raising money. (When Jules, an administrative genius, stayed on after I left, he managed to keep that opulent place going by spit and glue and scrounging, with economics learned at the Actor's Workshop.) Hoguet considered me "avant-garde," and if not indifferent to money, having to pretend to be, which was worse. He liked discussing the fantasies of the avant-garde artist, though he preferred the word "alienated." He was especially fascinated when I pointed out that some artists, of varying avant-garde qualifications, wanted to get in touch with the sources of power. That was the period for it. I mentioned Norman Mailer, who would have liked to be in Kennedy's cabinet or Jackie's bed, or failing that, to sit down to a bottle of Wild Turkey with LBJ and, between the dirty jokes, jawbone him into shaping up the country.

I had to admit sharing a little of this fantasy. "The fact is," I said, "I want to change you." When people had asked why I came to New York after my exhortations to decentralize, out in San Francisco and in *The Impossible Theater*, I said, and believed it, that "it is the biggest public platform in the country." I said we would still be in principle 3000 miles off-Broadway. Soapbox, soap bubble. The book was subtitled *A Manifesto*. He was troubled by that, its subversive edge. He had read there that I was in the theater to save the world. He really believed I meant it. I did. I still do. I always said it was impossible. He was not much for paradox. But he wasn't the only one. Some in the theater who claim to be avant-garde (I never did) have the same trouble.

What people forget about boards is that they want gratification too. Since they know more about the operations of interest, it doesn't have to be instant, but it can't be forever. They're willing to accept almost anything so long as it's well written about in the newspapers. They are not as censorious or vigilant as they're made out to be. They're not all that anxious to control policy either. Even though, after the conflict with Whitehead and Kazan, the Board maintained the right (which nobody wanted published) to overrule us by unanimous vote, they never exercised it. They didn't need to, we're not dopes; if they had occasion to oppose us unanimously there'd be almost no point in having a Board, which may make sense, but in some other world than Hoguet's or mine—and not in a social institution of that scale. I'm not even sure it would be the utopian dream. If they're told by fashion that it's good, they'll fall all over themselves supporting it and, at the propitious moment when we came, they probably could have raised money if we'd done well. We did all kinds of strange things in San Francisco that our Board there approved, against the natural tastes of some of the members, because even when we were assailed in San Francisco we were being approved of, somehow, in New York. Boards have also changed with the times. Where art's the commodity, they'd rather be told it's good by the liberal intellectuals than it's bad by the conservatives they'd trust on the stock market. And in Burke's case, you were dealing with somebody who was also out there with the swingers. Beyond that, they wanted "the right things" to happen, though they didn't entirely know what the right things are, which is why they presumably hired us. Given my critique of the American theater at the time, which they read avidly, the substance of our relationship when we contracted to them was this: Here are the marbles. Shoot or shut up. When we did shoot and others didn't shut up, that was another story. I don't blame them. Given what they were hearing, I might have acted before they did. And when they did, it was at first with a soft touch. Boards have their own distinctions, especially this one.

There was a lunch with John D. Rockefeller III. "No *one* has power," says one of the Allegorical Figures in *The Balcony* (emphasis mine), and John D. III wasn't actually on the Board; he didn't need to be. He was, after all, the *eminence grise* as well as the patron bankroll of Lincoln Center—I mean the whole place, not only the Beaumont—and

Take Up the Bodies

when it needed bailing out he was the exchequer of last appeal. Lincoln Center is, said Hoguet with admiration, a monument to his philanthropy. Jules Irving and I went over to see him at Rockefeller Center, his father's monument. As we came off the elevator, there was a control console, tended by an austere white-templed Negro, at the clitoral nub of an impeccable nautilus of corridors sounding deep into the lairs of the brother clan. Somewhere in the hushed radial design—like the vanishing point of *The Balcony* (or another "house of certainty," Jeremy Bentham's Panopticon), where "we can no longer be actuated by human feelings" and "all scenarios are reducible to a major theme"—there is, we were later told (why not? we were at "the gates of legend"), the completely furnished room in which the Father died, just as it was, like a Castle Keep.

John D. III (who died recently in an automobile accident) looked a simple man. He was shy, but very adroit. He tapped one's knee or hand and slipped in a suggestion. "We want it to be permanent, don't we?" How can one argue? Jules was offended. I wasn't. We already knew we were on the line and that we'd be over and out if permanence didn't show up quick, in the reviews. The Word penetrated even this deeply. (As it happened, I was out.) What was maybe offensive was that Hoguet and Burke, who were the steering committee of the Board, felt it would be good for us to receive this gentle pressure. What did they want? They weren't sure. Other directors? other plays? a change of tone? John D. III never mentioned it. I was a little perturbed with Hoguet after all our dialogue. The funny thing is we were already thinking of compromise, having been severely compromised by the rabidity of the assault after *Danton's Death*. Rockefeller—gaunt, sharp-nosed, bleached—was careful of his diet, not watching weight but, though giving away money *was* his business (politics was for Nelson, taking in money for David, etc.), out of otherworldly sentiments. He was devoted to Oriental art and thought and spent considerable time in the Far East. (Just before his death, he left his art collection to San Francisco, not as reparations for taking us away, but because New York has sufficient culture already.) He talked of the machinations of foundations with an understated sense of his own powers and expertise. After describing one particularly artful operation of money-giving, he tapped me on the hand, quick as a bird, "Quite a business, isn't it?"

These things, too, are moving, like the "order-bestowing" process behind "the life-consuming presence" of the capitalist reality itself. The experience at Lincoln Center confirmed again that Scott Fitzgerald was, so far as making class distinctions go, a far better man than Hemingway. The very rich *are* different from us *because* they have more money. This was also apparent at the Board meetings, where only certain kinds of money could be admitted and, despite Rosenman—who passed because of his legendary status—not much Jewish money, though they opened that up afterwards when money grew tight. There was no problem with Jewish artists if they didn't make any problems. William Schuman, the composer—who pretty much gave it up for a while to become overall administrator of Lincoln Center—advised Jules and me at the Lotos Club that we could get anything from the powers-that-be "so long as you are a gentleman." This ethic was confirmed at the other clubs, the Links, the Century, the University, and at the home of John D. Rockefeller III, on Beekman Place where, however, one summer night during a party the airconditioning went out and I made a joke—a pretty good joke, I thought, only a little premature, maybe, it was only the sixties—about a permanent energy crisis, and it was as if the universe were threatened and the "disordercreating" presence were mine.

John D. III looked at me with the blank whited perplexity of a civicminded man of Calvinist origins which had gone through the mutations of social progress into a firm belief in the powers of positive thinking. Power failure as an existential condition was simply outside his conceptual framework. He'd never seen a play by Beckett and would have thought him demented if he did, though he would have indicated that more politely. Anything may be ameliorated with money. With all those millions to cool us, we sweated and said nothing more. At such dinners, where you go by private elevator and the men still withdraw for cigars while the ladies powder, there were discretions and velleities that screened hostility and threat (and other realities), if they existed, as lead does radiation. It was new to me, very Jamesian, what I had read about and never experienced, and while I don't want to make too much of it, what I learned there was probably the major accomplishment at Lincoln Center.

Meanwhile, back at the First National City Bank, there was less reserve about what Burke described, albeit nicely, as my "intellectual ego and conceit" and Hoguet attributed, alternately, to my "idealism" and my dark cast of mind, my "pessimism." That first became more than our friendly dialectic after a controversy over the program note I had written for *Danton's Death*, but they'd surely have put up with the purest arrogance if *Danton's Death* had been successful—though in the environs of Lincoln Center nobody much liked the word *Death* in the title. Critical as they were, they were still solicitous about how we were taking things in New York. I summed it up in a phrase of Dante's about Florence, the City of Permutations, chancy. They were both proven gamblers, but within more reasonable limits. The fact is things were

Take Up the Bodies

getting out of hand, despite our mutual desire to make it permanent, and they were talking to me alone because they felt I was the center of resistance to a necessary change of policy. Always less stylish than the others, Hoguet was blunter when I indicated we were thinking of Genet's *The Screens* for our second season: "Not a play where they fart in someone's face!" My subjectivity, he thought, was becoming too "negative."

I really do think it was the indecency, not the politics, that offended Hoguet, though on second tl.ought he wouldn't have liked that either. *The Screens* was a savage assault on the ideology of colonialism, and we were just becoming aware of a political obscenity attached to a moral decency. The Vietnam War was coming out of the closet. Sometimes, when I'd sit at a Board meeting, our own compromise was a little harder to look at because of the degree to which, I felt, Vietnam was a WASP tyranny. The notion of the Elect has never been banished from the boardrooms, no more than from the Pentagon. True, the aboriginal mission of the Puritans, warranting a genocide, went through a transcendental and Unitarian softening. The Calvinist militancy was assuaged by wealth, the Outer Sign of an Inner Grace. As I sat there making excuses for our being there, I'd think of the second wave of immigrants, escaping genocide, the pogroms which were part of the family folklore. The ethnics brought the crudities of American culture like a fart in the face, but I felt rather smug in the view (despite, later, our Jewish secretary of state) that *we* weren't responsible for the habits of mind that made for Vietnam (my grandmother would say, with her sense of history, that's what happens when you hang out with the *goyim*). Still, here in front of me were the men who were perpetuating an insane war which was not yet, on the public agenda, as indefensible as it came to be.

At Lincoln Center, however, they had been charged with a lot of other sins from its inception, including the rapacity of urban renewal. The arts came late in America, and in clearing away all those blighted buildings they were making up for lost time. The motives of our patrons were nevertheless distrusted at every turn. Nobody could believe they would give us a free hand. But, as I've suggested, they were as ready to embrace whatever we did as to hang Abstract Expressionist paintings in corporate buildings—if it were only more highly approved of. That was demonstrated (not by the same Board, but all WASPs look alike) with the presence of Joe Papp. In a fine entrepreneurial way, he has always been aggressively anti-Establishment. We know from the principle of preemptive tolerance how much of that can be absorbed by the Establishment. About what should happen at the Beaumont, however, the liberal critics are as baffled as any board and usually twice as pious, as we could see palpably when Papp withdrew and left a vacuum. Nobody had any ideas without dollar signs, unless it were to tear the place down, which, from the beginning, has been a cheap shot at the impregnable, another long American tradition. Sad mortality o'ersways its power, but the marble will survive us all.

For some time after I left the Repertory Theater, not only the newsmen looking for a story but others looking for a laugh were trying to induce me into some denigrating statement about the Board or the Beaumont. The usual gambit was to give me a chance to get off the hook. I obviously had quarrels with both (Jules Irving would eventually have more), but I either refused to say anything or gave answers to this effect: what's there is there, justice is strife, and most of what is wrong with the stage is in the head (about which, more in a while). I can imagine some once and future time when nostalgia over the place will arouse ire against those who threaten it by urban redevelopment, like when people got mad about tearing down the old Met; provided, that is, we survive the neutron bomb designed to preserve the building. A board or the building has always been fair game, and there's enough wrong with both of them to make for the indulgence of easy satire at their expense. I am, nevertheless, sure that in the ecology of putdowns the building will have the last laugh. In the history of putdowns, what happened to us at Lincoln Center was clearly not the least. It's not the best of memories, but I ought to follow it through. For the experience did reflect—from a rare if slippery coign of vantage—the social and psychic history of a period which was changing our ideas of performance; and it did cause me to rethink, out of obvious personal necessity, what I was doing, or could continue to do, in the theater.

When we were appointed to head the Repertory Theater in January 1965, there was still a lingering surreptitiousness about the Vietnam War. Lyndon Johnson had, after all, defeated Barry Goldwater in a landslide because the latter was presumably going to bomb the Vietnamese back to the Stone Age, as Curtis LeMay had recommended. It wasn't any great compassion for what was happening to the Vietnamese that accounted for the vote. We didn't even know the gooks yet, and there seemed to be plenty of jungle. But nuclear dread went a long way with the public, détente was not in the picture, and the Chinese were getting very big. Johnson capitalized on the anxiety with a television spot featuring a little girl, who had probably grown up doing air raid drills under her desk; she had a flower in her hand (little did he know yet about the ferocity of Flower Children) while the mushroom went off. Officially, the war was still in the annals of the unnameable, like that previous "bandit" skirmish in Korea, a "shooting peace." Since World War II, we didn't have any wars; they didn't exist. By the time we opened the Beaumont in late October 1965, the policy of deception had been established while our overseas involvement secretly grew. According to Assistant Secretary of Defense John McNaughton, whose specialty was the formulation of policy for Vietnam, 70 percent of the reason for being there was *"to avoid humiliation."* Like Hoguet over the telephone. America had given its word. In the global theater of operations, the Doctrine of Credibility had prevailed. At home, we were deep into the reality of illusion, the specialty of theater, that very compromising form. "What is our waking," says Robespierre in *Danton's Death,* "but a clear dream?" I didn't yet know, however, what humiliation is.

When we gathered for the first rehearsal at the end of the summer, the entire company massed in a circle on the not-yet-completed Beaumont stage, I was very conscious of a gift of grandeur founded on a Balance of Terror. It was not quite a Reign, but the balance was tilting, and the Imperial Presidency about to come. The decision for escalation was somewhere in the dark councils of the technocracy, the computer, and the questionable personality of Lyndon Johnson—the complete political animal with good human instincts, half consensus, half cunning. The Great Society was on the scene, the scenario in the Pentagon Papers. There we were on the stage. I pointed out that we were living off the fringe benefits of a permanent war economy. Blood money, I said, was paying our salaries. I was no doubt indulging my own discomfiture, not all that widely shared in the company. Vietnam was still open to reasonable question, as even I felt compelled to add, since I knew nothing of the politics of half the actors, and most of those we brought were nonpolitical. Just the day before, the *Herald-Tribune* (still publishing then) had denounced the "peaceniks" in an editorial. The coinage had not yet gone out of circulation, as it did when the country turned around. As I spoke I wondered who was taking notes about what, and for whom. We were, after all, making history. Everybody was watching. But, as everybody realized after Watergate, that was true anyhow.

We were all paying our tribute to invisible power, in the surface play of an invisible exchange. We were realizing, as the theater always knew, that the secret of power *is* the invisibility. The images we see in the dominance of the media, where everything is seen to be exposed, are in the service of the imageless. What we now call spectacle is the fallout of surveillance. I had begun to feel, through the immanence of paranoia, that this was true of the theater itself, which is unsuspectingly in the service of what it reveals, a kind of double jeopardy, imitating power and bereft of it. It served the theater right for setting it all in motion, the compulsion to surveillance, way back with Oedipus. The worst of that Complex was perhaps not the incest but the passion for investigation. Now, there are eyes everywhere. We are always being looked into. We do it to ourselves. But the bureaucracy does it better, more comprehensively, with its vast apparatus of investigation—records, files, traces, verifications—to which, out of necessity or default, we alarmingly consent. Danton saw what was happening in the Terror as social process, when he relinquished his desire for power to the power which is ultimately faceless, "the long slow procedural murder" with its formal stink.

But what about the faces of power we knew? Had Hoguet been present he would have had further evidence of my negativity and argued the issues; Rosenman was seeing, I think, what I saw but he was aging in the service; Burke would have listened and taken it all in. Nelson Rockefeller would have plunged right into the charges and straightened me out. Soft of heart and hand, John D. III would have managed to avoid an argument. He'd have even thrown good money after bad to do that. He'd have willingly bought off my contract if that's how I felt. He was even better than his word. There was a side of power that had a human face, and I am not being facetious when I say you could take that into heart and home. And if theater was everywhere, it was also there.

When we took over the directorship, there was still bad feeling around town about the severance of Whitehead and Kazan. Moreover, Whitehead had threatened a suit over what he considered the breaking of his contract. John D. III wanted him paid in full rather than have any more negative publicity, though Whitehead's threat wasn't taken seriously by the businessmen of the Board who, apparently, weren't breaking a contract for the first time. John D. III was also a sympathetic man. Whitehead's wife was dying of cancer. Kazan's wife had died during the previous catastrophic season, also of cancer. After the catastrophe of our own season was underway—one night after a rehearsal of *The Condemned of Altona*—there was a weird argument with my wife (we are now divorced; other times, other seasons), which started with a relaxed hallucinatory violence and went with amazing speed off some deep end. Later, when she lay sobbing, all spent, she spoke quietly of a terrible pain in her head which seemed to me like a concentrate of myself, there, spinning. IT was saying humiliating things about itself, to me, none of which I could reject; I was prepared to believe anything, it had all happened so fast. "As one trapped in a nightmare that has caught/his sleeping mind, wishes within the dream/that it were all a dream, as if it were not—such I became:" thus

Dante, with his pellucid accuracy. "But," I wrote in a notebook, "fact, it is *not* a dream."

We lived then in the Apthorp on upper Broadway. My lair, sequestered and quiet, was triangulated by the apartments of George Balanchine and Joseph Heller, over a graceful carriage trade courtyard, from whence we passed out of the gates of legend into the Catch-22 of Needle Park. The area was the center of drug traffic in New York. All the walking indigence of the universe appeared to be on the streets, stoned, sepulchral, lobotomized, freaked-out, hysterical, and not unlethal, while the pensioned old ladies dozed in the sun on the dividing islands. Down Broadway, like a scummy pleasure dome from Bavaria, was the Ansonia Hotel, built by Stanford White in an elephantiasis of rococo, where Bellow set *Seize the Day*. Every day, back and forth, I walked the thirteen blocks to the theater. There was a red-bearded Jew in a neatly collaged trench coat, army surplus, the stitching done by wire, some of it barbed, who paraded down the street with a knapsack and a springy step, humming, and when he came up behind me one time like a trilling wire in the blood, whispered into my ear, red beard on my shoulder, "Six million!" There was another man who staked out a corner below the Ansonia and made speeches as powerful as any Danton might have delivered from the Mountain, his entire body torqued to eloquence, as if seized by a wind turbine, a sublime fury, thunderous, except though his mouth was moving not a word came out of it. He denounced the injustice of eternity in a commensurate silence.

Then there was the Sphinx: a squat four-square dark-skinned androgyne in a honeycomb black hat and fatigue jacket who stood arms akimbo against a Johnny pump and smiled conspiratorially at me, only at me, whenever I passed. She knew me through and through, I was sure of it. I once drove a rented car west of Broadway, got trapped at an unexpected one-way near 11th, and in exasperation made a sharp turn into a mid-block alley I thought was free, and dead-ended. There she was, right in front of the car, several blocks from the usual, sitting back on a hydrant. She waved. I pulled away and went back to walking. There it was all around me, ambulant calamity, hand out. No wonder the period was nonverbal. All I could say was, I'm sorry.

Which is all I could say for the whole experience. Personal knowledge is not necessarily what has been lived through, but what has been truly imagined. Much of what has been lived through has not been imagined at all; some of it is irreducible to the imagination, or seems so, and for most of us some large portion of experience is unexperienced, mere dead weight of being. People do not invariably learn from experience either, as in some things practice does not make perfect. It may only debilitate or obscure. I have had a lot of practice thinking through Lincoln Center, and while history may betray twice over, in both the making and the reflection, what appears to have been so was—though I'd be happier not to believe it—no more than so, as in a Chekov play. We came, we did not conquer, we were inept. Some of those who made excuses for us said, "The knives were out for you." Certainly. We may have been fools but we were not innocent. The knives are always out. But here, no conspiracy theory.

Whether we were inept by nature or circumstance is still a puzzle. I am not using the word as our harshest critics did; they've seen far less talent that they've commended. I mean it historically, *at that moment.* The dimensions of the problem were enormous, or we made it so by trying to do everything at once: change the repertoire, shape up a divided company, avoid the use of stars, alter the economic structure of the theater, renovate the unions, develop a newer audience, protect the actors from sudden firings, open a new theater and test out the stage, use the machinery, introduce a new and radical music, bring in the blacks, take on the Vietnam War, anticipate the self-defeating excesses of protest, educate the Board, reconcile the Underground and the Establishment—and stay, in spirit, 3000 miles off-Broadway. It was a measure of our confidence that only in retrospect does it seem so boldly what it surely was: overreaching, if not utterly naive. We were too unknown, too ambitious, too callow perhaps, too resistant to "star quality," which the place may have needed then; and we failed as the moment failed, from overextension, not unlike (but not the same as) the Movement, which may also have been a failure of imagination. If there was an animus against us, too, that was to be expected. Conspiracy was enseamed in the nature of things.

Everybody talked in those days, before we came, about "the right to fail"—but failure has no rights, and Jouvet was righter in saying that the theater's obligation is to be successful. Especially on that scale, in that setting. The fact is that we failed at Lincoln Center because we weren't good enough—I mean good enough to do what we proposed to do. (Not what Irving managed to do when he stayed on or could have done if he wished to continue what he did just after I left: bring in an all-star cast in a production, *The Little Foxes,* directed by Mike Nichols, that would have been praised if it were third-rate, as it was, and Irving was never fooled—since it was always possible to do what is being done now—make the Beaumont a booking house.) What we had proposed was a virtual reformation of the American theater at almost every level, aesthetically and politically. It was worth the dare, but we

Take Up the Bodies

were simply not that powerful, aside from all excuses we might invoke having to do with the space, the machines, the critics, the knives, the Board, the sympathizers with Whitehead and Kazan, the impatience of New York, etc. etc. It is no more comforting to know that nobody else has been able to do what we proposed, though only Joe Papp has had a shot at it, and I respect him for what he did accomplish, which was nowhere like what we were after in that one focussed place—the creation of a national theater, with a company, whose apex for the moment would be Lincoln Center but which would still be conceived of within a pattern of decentralization, as well as the new latency of experiment in the theater. We obviously never got off the ground.

Here was a case where the particular loss was a general loss, because it was a watershed moment for the theater—and there was every reason to believe we were prepared for it. There was hardly any way in New York, with its want of continuity, to acquire anything like the range of experience we had brought from San Francisco through all those plays over fourteen years, and not in any mere routine, but unusual plays often unusually conceived and performed (as attested to in New York by some who later seemed to forget what they saw). For one thing, if we had pulled it off, it is fairly certain that those with adventurous inclinations in regional theaters—for which the Workshop had been (and still is) an exemplary model—would have had less trouble with their boards, as some of them did (say, André Gregory in Philadelphia or John Hancock in Pittsburgh). Others would have inclined to be more adventurous. As it was, our shift to New York was like some embarrassing culmination or levelling off of the promise of regional theater, which we had struggled to validate through the years. It was a long time developing but the model was, at least for the moment, shattered. And to some, it merely verified what was becoming apparent: the regional theaters—with their boards, their building programs, their foundation grants, and their continuing financial problems—were only part of the Establishment, and not worth troubling about. The winds of change were blowing in another direction—Bob Dylan calling that tune.

At the first sign of our failure, the axis of attention shifted in that direction, way down Broadway, along with the radicalized activism of the sixties and the emergence of a youth-oriented counterculture, to which Lincoln Center seemed irrelevant anyway, if not the Enemy. So we were left holding the golden bag. Those we were counting on for long-term support turned precipitously from us, raising the banner of a Third Theater and, in the heat of politicized enthusiasm, praising a whole series of theater events that in other, less exacerbated times would have felt puny, skittish, insulting to their intelligence. (I think of

Macbird!, which I'd read and rejected as a gross trifle. And, serves me right, an irony with every sour grape: I remember Stacy Keach coming to see me during its rehearsals and asking whether he should drop out of the cast. He hated it, thought it tawdry. We weren't using him at the time, almost didn't dare, for he was—though he didn't join us till New York—one of "those actors from San Francisco" who had been condescended to, playing Horner in *The Country Wife.* What about *Macbird!?* I advised him to see it through. It made his career.) About the time that Hubert Humphrey was proclaiming the Politics of Joy, we were being chastized for being glum. By then, I suppose we were. The critic who chastized us had seen us perform in San Francisco and liked the goodhumored energy of the company there. The problem then—as in reflecting on it now—was how to pay tribute to the exuberance, and exemplariness, of the New Politics without buying into the banalities. It was the Aquarian Age. Joy was in, along with the Apocalypse. Sides of a coin. Love's Body was in, all sides. Hair camp honey and ashes sperm and rock—the materials of a New Theater, flashing off- to on-Broadway. Ubu was one of the culture heroes, his joy, not Hubert the Hump's, every torsion of the torso back to the old turd: crucifixions and consummations, O Calcutta! the Big Bang. Speaking of preëmptive tolerance. It's hard to assess the politics, which succeeded in displacing Johnson and winding down the war by helping to elect Nixon over Humphrey. But the puerility of it had people jumping out of their shoes, which were at one exemplary performance piled at the door as a parable on property.

In keeping with the times, even our best critics were in the mood for affective simplicities with the right political opinions, until the acceleration of protest toward violence and totalitarianism—the "trashing" was already there, on stage—caused them to pull back and recant. These were the years when, through the amorphous politics, every sort of delinquency and inadequacy of performance could be transfigured by discourse (from which, at Lincoln Center, we were exempt). Perhaps the finest performance of the Living Theater was that infamous episode at the Theater of Ideas, where it assaulted a sterling audience of the intellectual power structure who had been asking for it all along. As one of them has no doubt written, somewhat along these lines, the beggary of criticism is the beatification of mindlessness. We have not yet recovered from that, as you can see if you attend any gathering of the New Theater, such as the festival in Baltimore, or now, with or without the opinions, many events in Greenwich Village or Soho.

Or even (before the new committee structure) on the stage at Lincoln Center. The one I happened to see was *The Cherry Orchard* in a version by Andrei Serban, a similarly mindless event by a director of eclectic but impressive gifts. There were even, on the disjunct slope of the orchard in the background, insinuations of the right political opinions. I won't dwell on the affective simplicities, but just one resonance from the period we are discussing: when Irene Worth—acting out Madame Ranevsky reminded of the death of her son Grisha—did a vocal routine like a bellyache out of *Orghast*, making sense neither of the character nor the moment, nor yet an "immemorial incantation on the air," as if reminded not of Grisha but Artaud, there may have been (I say this with an animus I don't much like, in this remembered context of do or die) another failure of overextension at the Beaumont; and one felt the sharp clinical eye of the doctor, who detested Stanislavski's excesses, rolling in the grave at the emotional sloppiness. I have admired that fine actress' willingness to give herself over to experiment, but in this case, literally, I don't think she knew what she was doing. As for Serban, what he did can be traced to the apparent virtues of his better work and the sixtyish archaicism of a theory he shares with Peter Brook, whom he assisted on *Orghast*—the bottoming out of sound in the percussive sound and fury of dead languages and new vibes. So far as *The Cherry Orchard* goes, this production wasn't defective because the director tampered with this classic (the new shibboleth of some critics), but because this classic, in this conception (my guess is that, outside of the now jaded discovery that Chekov is funny, there wasn't one), wouldn't serve that end.

Between the conception and the act lies the shadow. The largest ambitions require the most persuasive performance. And whatever it was, *Danton's Death*—which was the beginning and pretty much the end—wasn't that. We were by no means mindless, but the palpable fact was we fared worse than Senator McCarthy at Chicago. Unsuccessful wasn't the word for it. We were savaged pure and simple. When I left there was nothing to be said against that, what?, judgment?—even to claim that more time would have permitted the realer abilities to emerge. That might not have been so, after what happened happened. There were those who were only too ready to conclude that the place had changed us before anything happened, but that was their problem. We tend to see things in our own image. I have already spoken of compromise, but that was at quite a different level, having to do with the inherent contradictions which sharpened after the bad news came, or when we were reeling and holding on for dear life. What I did say in my letter of resignation about the "climate" having been impaired was a euphemism (as was the resignation) but also an understatement.

Yet: what *did* happen? The question is still being asked to this day by those who had known our previous work. I don't want to, obviously can't, retrospectively justify any production. I've written extensively before about how productions were conceived, but that would be ludicrous in this case. One or two things, however—not acknowledged in any criticism that I'm aware of—might be said objectively, and even usefully:

In recent speculation about the building, there has been talk about demolishing and renovating the stage. That was always premature. For in the history of the Beaumont, there had been to my knowledge no production which, like *Danton's Death*, went head-on at the still-unexplored possibilities of the total space (Foreman's *Threepenny Opera*, from all accounts, coming closest). I mean the whole bastard stage with its botched contours and true dimensions: the long-receding distance to the back wall, the vast see-through wings, the vomitoria with passages below and (usable) airspace above, the vaulting loft so large that Irving (later) had to prevent them from dividing it into a movie house, and the side ramps with electronic close-in panels—a technological disaster to begin with, used now only as expensive tormentors for the perplexed frontage; that is, the cross-purpose pro-scenium and pimple thrust. (The latest news is that four or five million will be spent to rectify the space and end the schizoid fantasy, though that still exists more severely at other levels.) Everybody realizes now that the place is so huge that the hundreds of lights in the remote ceiling are like a galaxy of dying stars, and that if you don't take precautions to give the actors amplitude and voice they will look (as we had to learn to our dismay) not only smaller but younger, and acoustically forlorn. Despite all this and my own equivocal feelings, it is still (though renovation will end such vain conjecture) possibly and by ac-cident an exciting space—not the first in theater history to pose a challenge in its faults.

I am not claiming that what was attempted in *Danton's Death* proved it, and clearly—though we kept our peace about the faults—what we tried to do was impeded or overwhelmed by the clum-siness of the machinery, if not our own. (Once the machinery was in we couldn't get it out, even when we discovered it couldn't operate ac-cording to specifications; I have no similar explanation for us.) If some things were carried too far, some were not carried far enough; for in-stance, the differential momentum of the moving crowds, whether describing a neoclassical geometry in a promenade or volatilized from the wings in a rush of Terror. (The wings, by the way, still need to be explored—given the ovoid sightlines—with mirror images or dialectically with negative space, using the fact that the audience on each side of the thrust sees a different wing and those in the center see a triangular segment of both.) Sometimes the crowds were splayed out in swift strokes, like paint on the canvas of an Action field; but the unmastered difficulty of the space, particularly the disproportion of the thrust (later built over and extended), may have caused me to hedge the intended randomness of the image and left things looking roughly, I suppose, neither consciously improvised nor designed.

There were other things people didn't like, but plain old well-blocked crowds might have spared us a lot of grief. It was a shame, given all the large productions we had done before, with a lot of complicated movement in good order. I still like the other idea and thought, whatever its faults, it was visibly there. But the staging—like Morton Subotnick's electronic score, impelled by a similar impulse and compared to which most composition for the theater is the merest Muzak—was much abused at the time. That we attempted such things at all may have been part of the overreaching. That we didn't take it any further—I mean a thorough exploration of the huge space—was probably due, after the guillotine fell, to our being too intimidated to try. I did start to think again about those dimensions in preparing *Galileo,* but that was done by another director after I left.

Recognition of what was attempted in the staging wouldn't have necessarily saved the day, but this much I know: *Danton's Death* was well enough conceived to stimulate and even inspire a lot of actors who didn't come from San Francisco and were as skeptical about us as anybody else. Several of them were reasonably well known and some of them are now "stars"; but they were abused then by association with us as they had never been before or since. There is something revealing in that. Since they had, contrary to report, practically *all* the major roles in *Danton's Death,* it would seem they were mistaken for the San Francisco actors who were wildly attacked, though they were mostly (we had planned this) doing walk-ons. All of which may only signify that the fault was wholly mine, as director. That may very well be. I'd be an imbecile if I didn't acknowledge mistakes—and you usually know the turkey when it smells to high heaven—but not even the most jaundiced New York actor in the cast would have predicted during the course of rehearsals what hit us when we opened.

After that, blackout. We were clobbered. It was humiliating. We never recovered. I wish I could say it knocked some sense into me. But, artistically speaking, the most appalling part of the experience is that it left me devastatingly uninstructed. There was nothing to be learned from such a failure (except more about failure), possibly because it wasn't a true pathos, which is why it wasn't quite humbling either. The calamity was too abrupt, like an earthquake or a flash flood against which there is no argument at all. If there is something to be said after the split ground settles or the waters subside, it has not so much to do with the justice or meaning of the event, but merely with how one survives it. If I am saying it now, it's because that became the atmosphere, if not the cause, of the ideas that followed after (some of them already latent), infusing my current work.

We laughed a lot to spare ourselves the aftershocks. There was a little book of Russian proverbs that somehow turned up in the office. Jules and I took turns reading from it aloud, a little lexicon of miseries, one more hilarious than another. *"Inconceivable!"* we roared, a watchword I had dreamed up in San Francisco the night we'd agreed on a contract with Hoguet and Burke at Trader Vic's, long-last proof that our fourteen-year effort to do it from the ground up, against every kind of resistance and skepticism, had been notarized by the indisputably biggest of Apples. *"Inconceivable!"*—meaning there was no way in the world we could fail, we'd seen the competition. Or had we? The force of the attack was so stunning and unrelieved once it came, so *demeaning*, that the heart must have gone out of us without our even being aware of it. There was no longer an issue of skill and experience, the denial of which by people who should have known better was outrageous. I felt I had squandered a legacy.

But why couldn't we have made some sort of comeback? I can't give the reasons, only the symptoms. We've seen stranger things in sports, with undeniably gifted athletes. Once the fastball hits the head, it's a lot harder to stand up to the plate. It has nothing to do with ordinary courage, you don't even know you're wincing. And then, suddenly —all the civil rights of failure withdrawn—time was compressed, it had to be done quick, we had no illusions about that; in truth, we never did. It just had to be done quicker. We tried not to run scared, but we certainly had nothing like the resilience and stored confidence that had sustained our work in San Francisco, good and bad, though it was also attacked, sometimes virulently, good things rejected, bad things embraced for the wrong reasons—we were always embattled. But Lincoln Center was altogether something else. To get some idea of the inconceivable scope of the beating, I might simply point out that *Danton's Death*—because of the opening of the Beaumont and the worldwide panoply of expectation about that event in New York City—was then (possibly still is) the most-reviewed single production in the history of the theater, and I suppose there's nothing more repercussive than bad opinion, especially out of the centrifuge of New York, over the networks and the wire services and the weeklies, and the deluge seemed unending and it didn't stop between shows. "Who, if I cried," I asked in my journal, quoting Rilke, "would hear me among

Take Up the Bodies

the angelic orders?" At the time I was preparing *The Condemned of Altona*. "Not even the Crabs," I added. I had fortunately trained myself years before not to read reviews if at all possible, so was technically spared some of the excruciating detail, though a look from Jules always told me the whole story; but I have recently, in an act of selfless masochism, studied them in the research for this book. Actually, they were rather divided to begin with, or at least charitable, but once a couple of the heavies were in and the critical mass established, the centrifuge whirled and the floodtide was overwhelming.

If we didn't run scared, or if we did, what can I say about those we had counted on for support and patience? Reading over the comments of the liberal intelligentsia we thought were allies, one is impressed with the ugly self-mortifications by which they tried to disembarrass themselves. It stinks even at this distance. Not the criticism, but the disemburdening. Speaking of getting off the hook: it was suddenly as if *nobody*, or very nearly, had seen us in San Francisco, though different critics and other theater notables had come at different times over the years, so it was hardly a single-shot deal. Now the charge was, by one of the defecting "kingmakers" (he actually used that term), that we had suffered there from the blight of provinciality, though as I've said our reputation in San Francisco wasn't certified until the news came back there from New York. That such provinciality exists, there is no question, but that it also exists in New York I thought was, among sophisticated people, beyond a feather of a doubt. What went wrong with us at Lincoln Center was, any way you look at it, pretty complicated—and I am content to yield judgment to the will of the gods—but in New York there is ordinarily a constituency for almost anything, some of that anything considered significant. Just look around. It seemed that when the king turned out to be a mere pretender, the disavowal had the force of terror that comes when you suddenly find yourself in a *coup d'état* lined up with the losing party.

All of this feels now rather like ancient history—and criticism is criticism, I've written my share—but it does belong somewhere in the archives of the holocaust now being indexed by the New York Public Library of the Performing Arts at Lincoln Center. If it were some subsequent Dead Sea Scroll disentombed, I'd want it registered therein that there are certain mouths in which the idea that honesty is the best policy makes you vomit. Which is, by the way, what Jules did one night when we were consoling ourselves over at Vorst's (across from the theater, no longer there). He was not, shall we say, a drinker, but had something like four martinis, whereupon he threw up right over the table, across Broadway, below the plaza, in the dressing rooms on his knees, up twenty-nine stories of the Lincoln Towers where, at home, his son was having a party and Jules wouldn't go in, so down to the theater again, in the corridors, also unending—it was like the opening of Celine's *Death on the Installment Plan,* where they are crossing the English Channel and, in surge upon surge vomiting into the wind, swallow it. We swallowed it. In memory of that virtuoso performance, Jules remarked one calmer dismal afternoon, "The trouble with us, Blau, is that we *didn't* have a nervous breakdown."

It was, nevertheless, a considerable fall, and the problem was how, through a growing pathology of failure, to make something out of the nothing that seemed to be left. By increments, later, out of the subtext of my licked wounds, the semblance of a method appeared in all the madness. But there we were heading toward a zero at the bone:

One night I was speeding down 9th Avenue to La Mama to take in a piece of the new action. There was a drizzle and the visibility was poor. The cabbie, a veteran grumbler, was not concentrating. I saw it before he did, too late to call out, a yellow shirt in the haze. The driver swerved, the shirt leaped, the thud sounded like both shoes had dropped. He lay in the rain. The police were casual when they came and talked of a gunman at the Port Authority. Eventually they took my name. Though we had been made kings, I noticed they weren't impressed. The truth is I felt guilty. The cabbie, his wits brazenly about him, picked up a whiskey bottle which was nearby, unbroken, and put it by the head of the injured man. One of the cops brushed it aside. The cabbie put it there again. The cop became angry. "You don't mean you got a right to hit him because he was drunk?" The man had been crossing against a light, but both their reflexes were slow. I told the police it was a draw. The victim was Porto Rican. He wore a watch and two large rings. I tried to talk to him but he was dazed. There was blood on his head from the fall, but nothing was rushed. The police were not insensitive, but they simply knew that somebody had to be him. I tried not to be insensitive, but that made *me* feel a little better. It's easy to be paranoid in New York.

When I thought it over, there'd been signs all over the place, if not so ominous as the Sphinx. Like: when we first brought the company together, we set up a series of classes and scenes to integrate the actors from San Francisco with the New York actors who had worked with Kazan. I participated in the mime class given by Carlo Mazzone-Clemente. Carlo knew I'd been a paratrooper and asked me to demonstrate a technique with him. He wanted me up on his shoulder, and then he would give a command. Up I went. Carlo braced. Command! He wanted me to stand there on one foot, quick. I lifted. But Carlo's accent is far from gone and what he'd shouted was that *he* was going to stand on one foot. So he lifted as I lifted, opposite feet, and I toppled, breaking a bone in my heel.

The paradox of this (fortunate?) fall was that it gave me more reason to think of the grounds of training. What in the world was I doing up there? More to the point, what were the actors doing up there? This had nothing to do with Carlo's teaching, that knowledgeable and effusive man. But with all the disciplines available to the art of acting, which do you choose to study, and why, and for what purpose, and in what forms?—even with mime, *which* of the many varieties? and then that question to which you inevitably return, what does any other discipline have to do with acting? and what do you mean by that, I mean, the idea of acting itself? Which, in the radical inquiry about to come, was to receive a lot of attention, along with the idea of theater itself.

These were, however, further adumbrations of questions I'd been asking before when, in San Francisco (moonlighting in my own theater), I had started to experiment in a studio with actors and other artists. What nobody in the company knew, except my wife and Jules, was that I had almost resigned from the Workshop so that I could do that more intensively—when Lincoln Center, ambition, power-lust, the whole ballgame, you name it, interrupted; though my intention was, if we had succeeded, to set up a studio there. What, however, when we integrated the San Francisco and New York actors—whose approaches to acting varied considerably, and not because they came from different ends of the continent—would we be integrating them for? At the moment it was for *Danton's Death*, and Jules insisted I cut out the acrobatics and spare myself for that. Still, the problem of training was there, theoretically and otherwise.

In the worst days at Lincoln Center, when Jules and I hardly knew anymore what to do, for some members of the company—and some concerned outsiders—training was the secret weapon. Workshops were sprouting all over town. That's what we needed. I remember riding in a cab from Harlem down to the Village with Susan Sontag and Joseph Chaikin, and that's what he was telling me to do also. I appreciated the advice, but it seemed laughingly irrelevant then, out there on the firing line, with time speeding by as it was. Some people who were putting the screws to us for not doing it immediately were still talking as if we were being given four or five years. At a company meeting before our second season—knowing also what was going on behind the scenes, with the Board—I said that training struck me right then as if a boxer were on the ropes, nearly out, only his instinct to trust, and somebody put a rubber ball in his glove and said squeeze. Or, if you'll forgive an old paratrooper, like telling them when they were besieged at Bastogne that they ought to go out to the rifle range and do some practicing with their M-1's. If you are old enough to remember, the word at Bastogne was, "Nuts." Time was short; we'd have to make do with what we were.

Besides, when I did get down to the Village, what I saw indicated that there was not that much yet going on in those workshops, whatever became of it, that could survive that stage at the Beaumont. Not then, not in that atmosphere, and probably not yet. About this issue, too, the simplicities abounded.

One afternoon I arrived somewhat late at a conference organized for the *Drama Review* by Richard Schechner. As I entered, a panelist was declaring that the exercises he was seeing in a studio were the best theater in New York. We are also still suffering from that delusion, as Harold Clurman had pointed out just before he died. Whatever the nature of the improvisations, or Transformations, Lincoln Center was another scene. Jules Irving remained there for five years after my departure, but if when I left he had used some of the workshop actors who were being urged upon us as if they were the saviors of the American theater, he'd have been murdered in the instant and they would never have survived to win Obies. As for what some of the observers thought about what they saw in the workshops, anybody who has had any experience with them knows that if you invite in a literary type (a good practice), he'll paw the ground in adoration of things which are quite commonplace, unless he sticks around and gets used to them. I don't mean because they are exceptional and happen all the time, just commonplace. Extraordinary things happen rarely anywhere. But people were in the mood, too, for affective athleticism, routines, psychophysical revelations, encounters, trips, interactions, process, Yoga, sound/movement, games. I am not denying the value of any of these things, merely putting them in perspective relative to Lincoln Center. We saw the hapless residue of such experiments in *The Cherry Orchard*. When they were most valuable, they *were* going in another direction.

To the extent that my own thoughts were moving in that direction, I resolved that if I came out of Lincoln Center with my senses intact, I'd never do theater again in such a way as to make a company vulnerable like ours was there. I can hardly imagine a situation where they would be, not like that, but what I meant was: whatever we did would be, beyond any cavil against it, so determined by its own nature that it would throw judgment off balance. And so far as we could achieve it, only *those* actors could really do what was being done, like it or not, because they had conceived it. As to what we would do to prepare ourselves, and what we would study among the plenitude of available disciplines, the intensity of the imperative would be the deciding factor. On any ground (or shoulder) that would have to be commonly shared, imperative into method. In San Francisco, we had developed a group ethos that was emerging in the new workshops, but their emphasis on collective methodology made definite sense. That was an on-again off-again proposition at the Actor's Workshop, where we were always too actively producing to see it through.

As for the actors then at the Beaumont, I've already indicated there were some very good ones in the company, some of those we inherited and some of those we brought. If I had any resentment over what happened at Lincoln Center—and I'd be a prig if I didn't—one strong part of it had to do with the effect on some of those we brought. I am still convinced that at least a few of them were among the more capable actors in the country, and some were especially promising. But if the promise didn't really show up, what in the world did anybody expect after the unprecedented intensity of that assault? Even when it did show up, as with Tom Rosqui in *The Condemned of Altona*, it was disparaged. Whatever its limitations, there was hardly a better performance in New York at the time. And he did it under terrible circumstances. If there was no conspiracy before, by then even our friends were laying for us, asking for proof. I've said that the theater always has something of a trial about it, and that includes the existential anxiety of performance, but even the self-evident didn't seem to hold up. And we were losing credibility to ourselves.

It wasn't a question of: if the heat is too hot for you get out of the kitchen. We were not weak people. There was much courage and stamina. But the tension swelled up in those corridors under the stage. It was as if we were shell-shocked and burrowed in. There were days when it seemed all sanity went, all friendship, for some of us built up over years of collaborative work—sad testimony to the theater's frail affinities, the profession more unstable than the form. As things became more oppressive, reactions were way in excess of provocations. There seemed to be no way of averting them or letting them take their course, as they will in a single production once the play is on or the run is over and the actors disperse. Here, the semblance of continuity worked against us. It was no ordinary dissension or ups and downs of morale such as we had at the Workshop. Something needed shaking up. If Jules and I did the dispersing, what would happen to the idea of a company? Yet the actors were oppressing each other, wearing each other down, and us. When we were rehearsing *Danton's Death*, the other large production rehearsing in New York was *The Devils*. Word gets around, there were reports of firings every day. We knew we'd made our own errors in casting and might have done our own firing.

But we were (mistakenly, in retrospect) taking the longer view. The actor's security seemed essential to the shaping of a company. We debated the firing and refused. (*The Devils*, by the way, was an awful production, and the famous actor who played the leading role was inadequate, to say the least. But it was treated a good deal more politely than *Danton's Death*.)

The experience was especially demeaning for the actors. Even those instinctively loyal became conspirators, day by dreary day. Away from the theater, there was no great relief. They were not exactly being celebrated in the small theater community of New York. The most inconsequential actors were doing better, and of course the large army of unemployed joined in running them down. It was hateful, it was absurd, we never felt so helpless. It had its funny moments, and we welcomed the darkest of humor, but it was very short-lived.

In *The Condemned of Altona*—Sartre's reflection on a sequestered ex-Nazi who conducts his own trial as the conscience of the twentieth century—the explosion of the planet is on the agenda. But it seemed to have already taken place in the theater. The atrocities remembered in the play seemed to incite little atrocities around the dressing rooms and in rehearsals, charge after charge and little relieved, and then—among the actors who had been around New York for years—a resurgence of the old cynicism. There was a fight with one of the actresses. I told her, after we'd made up, that she was injuring herself with a mask of toughness. She said she needed the toughness because it *was* a jungle, she needed it before Lincoln Center, and now all the more because everything that was hopeful about *us* had been shattered. She had admired what we'd done in San Francisco and what I'd written before we came. That's what brought her to us. She had a very good reputation in New York and was making it as well as one makes it. The right word about *Altona*, and she might have chanced into a large success. But she was glad I was there because it would get to me, I'd know better what it was like, it would change me too; she knew. She was not projecting. She knew her own motives, she'd been in analysis for years. I said maybe so, but what she was doing to herself was unbecoming, the worst of her, never mind me. She couldn't see it, despite the analysis. She was in hiding, I said. We are all images, she said. The bait of mirrors.

I stood there wondering about my own repertoire, feeling the growths over my face like a cuticle. No worse there is none, these laughable propositions of the unseen. Where did I come off defining her? If looks were stark naked none of us would be seen by ourselves except reversed, a series of replicas, overlaid. Suppose she came out of hiding? What? Where would that leave me? I was determined not to be changed. Yet if I looked in a mirror at that moment I'd have to refuse whoever it was I saw. In the dressing room, there were mirrors all around me, rimmed with light. I walked out, blank of error in the eye. She went shopping that afternoon with the designer and came back, thrilled, with the materials for her costume. She was positively girlish. The enthusiasm surprised me, did me good, both of us. It didn't last. The mirrors turned up, however, in my later work.

For one of the inverse advantages of our plight was the self-reflexive state of things. You could do nothing else sometimes but look in the mirror and ask why you were there, the most elemental question in the theater. And as you dwelt upon the admirable ignobility of the actors, those culpable and equivocal persons—the liable body of all theory—you couldn't help but wonder at the audacity (or perversity) which causes one to think, somehow, that it's possible to be more truly oneself by choosing to be someone else. Then you wondered, is there any choice? You could suffer through that at the theoretical level, shuffling through the cards of identity. The situation improved the theory, if the theory didn't improve the situation. There was an adamantine clarity to the issue, but when the actors returned to the dressing rooms to put the makeup on, they had to look at the overlays as I didn't—including the makeup they hadn't rubbed off—and it didn't relieve the ache.

It was hard to think of asking favors, but we were desperate to reduce the pressure. I even fantasied a meeting of the critics I knew—those who reviewed the second night—in which I would put the case: shouldn't they have done for us what, say, Kenneth Tynan and a couple of others did for Joan Littlewood in England, who was carried along for a while on her good intentions, even if hell is thus paved? Her theater was backed up even when it was pretty bad (admittedly, it was also out of the way, in the East End, not in Piccadilly) on political grounds. It was a distasteful idea and I never did it. I probably wouldn't have done it even if it made better sense, but we were fetching for rectifications. Now and then—sure, because people thought I wanted to hear it—the idea was confirmed before I said anything. Someone would insist they all had a stake in our enterprise to which—whatever the particular faults—the really concerned critics were not being "politically responsible" in the long run. I obviously didn't mind hearing it, but such things were straws in the hailstorm. We could forget the long run. I didn't know what to think. What I did know was that we were going disgraced into our second season. We were baffled, muffled, short of hysteria but not quite in control.

Control seemed out of reach. The bankruptcy of New York was also on the agenda, just surfacing, and I felt somewhat like Mayor Lindsay, on whom Mike Quill, the union chief, walked out. Quill then went into the hospital with a heart attack. In another cab, the driver said it was the answer to millions of prayers, but Lindsay—who fancied himself an actor—wasn't getting good reviews either. An older, once-black-listed actor, raging from the left wing of the thirties, said, "Those bastards, do they think strikes are fun?" Yet, while the trains might stop and the garbage pile up on the street, no actors were walking out—where would they go? Even their union couldn't protect *them.* Some we wanted, however, were keeping their distance. Nothing was going right. As I was planning *Galileo,* the energy crisis, averted in John D. III's living room, came. Power failure, another blackout. All of New York in the dark. Naturally, I took it as a personal vindication, on all counts. I walked the streets in good spirits with Robin Wagner, who had designed *Waiting for Godot* for us in San Francisco, the production that made a reputation for the Theater of the Absurd at San Quentin. As we sketched out ideas for *Galileo,* in the radiantly benighted city, it felt like the imminence of a new world. *Eppur si muove!* And yet it does move! For one night in New York everything seemed benign. At the Apthorp, the neighbors came out with candles to light me up the stairs. I felt like a king. Duncan, going to bed.

Rumor had it that we were going to be replaced. Agents were no longer sucking up to us, and those who had courted us when we came, selling the stars, were not calling. We were either unable to get some of the new plays we wanted or to pick others with any confidence. We had no constituency we could count on. If we picked certain plays, the Board would now resist; or the critics would say in advance we couldn't do them. Day after day, my journal was a record of frustration, loss of urgency, a bewildered ingathering, deterioration of sunken morale—and it seemed that nothing short of luck could recover for us the authority we needed for even the remnant of an idea of theater that meant anything. As it was, everything we did, shoring up our defenses, made me feel cheap, threatened, contradictory. Outwardly we kept our cool, and our people. Even our enemies admired us for that. There was always a temptation to speak out. I remember being very moved by a note from a young English instructor in Bridgeport (yet) who had seen *Danton's Death* and asked, "Why are you mute?"

For the actors, there were the daily humiliations. Because of the attacks, we couldn't easily use those already in the company in major roles. Going into the second season, the idea of a company was in disarray. When we were casting *Danton's Death,* we had resisted the

Take Up the Bodies

biggest of stars to play the role, but by the time of *Caucasian Chalk Circle*, at the end of the season, we were adding people to the company who either could not subscribe to what we'd have liked a company to be or would have said anything to get a part. Our own actors, looking askance, losing confidence, waited for the next blow. There was a history of dedication, but that history was for all moral and practical purposes cancelled; for some, the instincts annulled. Robert Symonds, a rather temperate man, has since remarked that in all the years he had been in New York and after we came, he could not recall the word "amateur" used about any professional actors—however scurrilous a review might be—until it was used about ours. It can make good actors flinch, and look bad. We know the opposite is true, that mediocre actors, praised, will inevitably get better and, if they're praised enough, can believe it enough to become stars. There is plenty of evidence. I can name names. Anybody who has been in the theater can name names.

Paranoia? It's not only what has been said but what will be seen once it's said. Even though some audiences manage to overcome what they've heard—and they did—I've never had any great faith in the independence of audiences; they mostly see what they've read, and in New York when the word is bad the seeing isn't so good because there are a lot of words. This is true for the most intelligent people. I've known academics who are capable of writing astute criticism of the most refractory books, and would not hesitate to take other critics apart for reading wrong, who have come up to me and asked whether I'm going to see such-and-such a play because it got a terrific review in the morning paper, and then will go and suspend all disbelief. The Donner Party took their disastrous cutoff because a guidebook of the time said they should go that way, although they were advised, in person, by one of the greatest mountaineers, who had just been there, that the route was dangerous. They believed what was down on paper.

None of this justifies what we did or, over the indifference of the years, makes it better; and the behavioral patterns of the New Theater, despite appearances, are not that radically altered. If I dwell upon the hurt, it's because I was never so conscious until that experience of the self-mortifying basis of the idea of acting, the always potential expense of spirit in a waste of shame. In any case, I felt often about the actors as I did about the Pietá when it was taken out of the Vatican and brought to the World's Fair in New York, put under blue light by Jo Mielziner (who designed the Beaumont stage), and fifty million people passed by. It was abraded by the eyes and never the same. The director, fortunately, can go and hide.

Where are these actors now? Like most of the good actors in America, they are in Hollywood, doing the sort of thing that would guarantee their professionalism if they returned to New York, although it can't help but reduce their capacities. The irony is not lost on me (nor on them), in view of what I'd written in the past about other actors. Do they have alternatives? Not really. Groups and workshops are mostly for younger people—and after their experience at the Actor's Workshop in San Francisco, most regional theater seems rather tired. It is sad to see them now—even those who are "doing very well"—in soaps and other idiocies on the tube, bits and pieces in the movies or, better than that, playing second fiddle to actors who once even admired and envied them, and to whom they were clearly superior. Of all the things that happened, that's one of the hardest to swallow.

It all caused me to think, too, of the petty vanity of the director, not the overweening choice that brought us to New York, but the more fundamental one, structured into the theater as we mostly know it: the desire to rectify the actor, "to get a performance out of him," or even to make of a role a turning point of a life. I blush back to the times when I must have scared the life out of them by the intensity of the conception, in the overreaching, trying by the ardor of my own Idea to cause the actors to do things they could never conceivably do (nor I, for that reason), their wanting to do it out of their love for me, or the attraction of the Idea, the two confused, and the way that could turn to hatred when it didn't happen; and sometimes—for this happened too—mutual desire striking flame *in* the Idea and (why it happened and why it didn't a mystery, for I have seen things ill-conceived take fire too) taking us all beyond ourselves as, for a while, we thought it might do at Lincoln Center. That may in the end have been the tragic fault of *Danton's Death*, not the paucity of its conception—for say what they would they could never convince me of that—nor a mere failure of execution, but some unaccountable blindness in the pitch of desire that, for all the reach of its conception, let the prize, the astringent grandeur of the play, escape us, escape me, and nearly ruin some of the lives.

What I am talking about lies past all mistakes because mistakes, too, are absorbed in the theater all the time, and forgiven, the worst casting, the most embarrassing detail. I know, they have been absorbed in some of the sorriest things I've done that were subsequently applauded, and in the applause the actors, who disliked in rehearsal every moment of what they were doing, then began to perform as if the mistakes never existed and the outcome was never in doubt, and the travail forgotten, as I suppose it should be. In that context. But in reflecting on this over the years, I have wanted to develop a way of working, an acting method, in which there would be no delusions about getting a performance out of an actor, for the actor would, in the very nature of the

Take Up the Bodies

conception, decipher his own; and (ideally) by the time what was being done were to be performed, the mistakes, the vanity, the blindness, even the criticism—under the ceaseless self-correcting scrutiny of the process—would be withered away, and what is there would be, in the structure, all that could be there, *for that is what it is.* In a sense, criticism would be irrelevant (we always say it is, but we don't believe it) or frustrated, not because we don't want it (we do) or because there aren't things to be talked about (there ought to be more), but all of the talking would be a useless glancing unless it inhered in that. In the perception of most performance, the seeing of a play, there is invariably an anterior performance, real or imagined (the more so if the play is known), by which the thing in front of the eyes is being perceived. It sets the standard. It may even cast other actors *as* it is being performed. That may be involuntary, but it happens. What I was after is a mode of performance whose standard, *you* know, is only its own. It resists the saying how it ought to be done, for it may even be hard to guess how it's been achieved. Whatever other standards are being invoked, there is no way of recasting what is there.

That is a far cry from where I started at the Actor's Workshop, way back at the turn of the fifties, when standards all over the country were still being taken from Broadway, and we even used to copy our sets out of the old *Theatre Arts* because, give and take a little imaginative revision, that's what designers were taught to do in the schools. We borrowed both plays and performances. There weren't many ideas to pick up, but nobody told us you were supposed to have them. All through the history of the Workshop—but rabidly in the early days, when it was considered mere intellectualizing—the actors were divided about the ideological course I had gradually defined, and the experimental choices. They were prepared, however, to jettison last doubts when we went to Lincoln Center; after all, it had been my adamance that got us there. The policy had paid off, including the ethic of a company. For all that, they suddenly found themselves more dependent than ever. Rejected and abused, the actors were wondering whether everything they'd been taught had gone wrong, and all our resolute "commitment" finally exposed as a lie.

In New York, there was almost nothing supportable left to say. If we were talking at all, we weren't talking about ideas, we were talking about jobs (a word we'd hardly ever used). In San Francisco, Irving and I had managed to keep a large number of disparate people together for twice seven years through every adversity, and when salaries were less than lean, or non-existent. While other actors circulated at the fringe, there was always a strong nucleus. We prided ourselves on the continuity. Now, though morale would appear to stabilize itself, even the nucleus was an illusion. There was no alternative: we had to think of firing people we had worked with for years; and eventually, after I left, Jules got rid of nearly all, not without much torment—nor with the conviction that, as all the criticism implied, there were much better actors abundantly around. When I was in Los Angeles, at Cal Arts, he called me once to meet him in Las Vegas. Jules loved to gamble, but with method. There was hardly even a hunch now to guide him. He was debating a final clean break, which hadn't entirely been made. Even contemplating it was painful. What did I think? He made the harder decisions, and a couple he couldn't quite make. I don't think that shadow ever disappeared from the Beaumont stage while he was there.

We went to the crap table and some guy went wild with a series of runs, calling on us for luck! At dinner we reminisced about our last time in Nevada, just after the appointment to Lincoln Center had been publically announced.

That, too, was a controversial event. We had gone on a retreat to Lake Tahoe, to get away from the newspapers and sort out our ideas. San Francisco, which was always listless about supporting us when we were there, was shocked at the news that we were about to go. There was civic turmoil, television debates, letters to the editor, opportunistic politicos; and an actor who had just showed up at the theater a couple of weeks before threatened to do us in. We went around with a bodyguard, one of our stage managers who had studied the martial arts. Later, when William Ball's American Conservatory Theater went into the vacancy, it profited from all the outcry by running up a subscription before its first season that we hadn't achieved in fourteen years. If there was remorse in the city, there was also dismay among those we left behind, who had also accepted the ethic of a company and for whom the Workshop had become a virtual way of life. They were bereft. They were also thrilled at the confirmation of what we'd done, and encouraging. We were very grateful. Others were outraged by our going, or at least played it for all it was worth. (I just read an article in a new San Francisco theater magazine, and they are still playing it—and why, as if the living cliché were scored, does the animosity last longest with those who had sacrificed least? Others had better reason:)

R. G. Davis, who had founded the San Francisco Mime Troupe within the Workshop, was particularly incensed, went public, and stayed after us. When I was rehearsing *The Condemned of Altona* in New York, Jules told me—as if our local miseries weren't enough—that Ronnie had made a "nearly libellous" attack on me in *Studies on the Left*. Actually, by the time we accepted the invitation to Lincoln

Take Up the Bodies

Center, Ronnie was no longer very active at the Workshop, had just about withdrawn. He had come there with a passion for Brecht after a Fulbright abroad, and served as an assistant director for several years, along with Lee Breuer (now director of the Mabou Mines), André Gregory (Manhattan Project), and Ken Dewey (who died in a plane crash during one of the Action Events for which he became known). The vitality and experimental inclinations of these young people had been very helpful to me in the perennial conflict with our older guard about what the Workshop should be all about. Ronnie worked with me on *Endgame* and *Galileo,* and we were very fond of each other, though we also argued about the Workshop's purposes relative to the personalities in the company and, specifically, about the absence of a definition of Style. (I have written about that elsewhere.) It was also just about the time when "the decision-making process" was on the radical agenda, and Jules and I "made no bones," as he would say, about who was finally running our company. Ronnie was frustrated by that, but we shared—more than any others at the Workshop—a desire to make it into a "Popular Theater" on the European model, such as Vilar and Planchon had established in France, Littlewood was trying to do in England, or like the Berliner Ensemble was supposed to be. It would be a place where students, workers, and intellectuals would converse, the bourgeois sweat would be wiped off the seats, and Marx and surrealism would embrace.

Even at the source, there were problems with the conception: The Ensemble was a proletarian theater in a walled-off totalitarian city, made famous by the bourgeois intelligentsia on the other side; Littlewood was hardly known around the corner from Stratford East, the workers' quarter where she'd set up, and had to make it on the West End; Vilar's money came from DeGaulle. And in San Francisco, our audience was unregenerately middle class (as was most of the company), and those who did care about the workers disliked our existential plays. The repertoire, to which I tried to give a dialectical structure (or see it as such), was always throwing the audience off balance. It wasn't until the New Left came into the picture, and the sit-ins began with passive resistance, that *Waiting for Godot,* say, seemed to make political sense. The Old Left preferred *The Crucible,* and Sean O'Casey. Still, from the time I returned from Europe in 1959, I was dedicated to the notion of Popular Theater, and I took it as a mission to Lincoln Center, as Vilar had moved it into the Palais de Chaillot. As one looks around the country today, there is nothing that even vaguely resembles the idea, certainly not the levelling off into regional theater. I'm not at all sure anymore that it is really possible in this country, where we are too decentralized in thought and conviction, the scale of difference defeating the theatrical scale which the idea requires. Without imposing my choice on possibility, we seem limited now to local initiatives, scaled down. Even in France the notion was considerably shaken up in the May Revolution of 1968, when for a moment Marx and surrealism did embrace, tearing up the seats and nearly bringing down the house, only to discover just how sticky that bourgeois sweat really is.

The dream vanished (it had already really gone), Ronnie went (I was told) berserk on television, denouncing our betrayal; as I gather, particularly mine. In the article in *Studies on the Left*, I was a bigger fink than Kazan, who had testified during the McCarthy period for the House Un-American Activities Committee, which had finally shown up in San Francisco and kicked off an era of protest when the police hosed down a demonstration on the steps of City Hall. It was an era in which Ronnie became a charismatic figure, and his subsequent career is a chastening afterimage. He was always outspoken, which I liked. I never thought much, however, of his political savvy, which struck me as Clifford Odets left-wing. As we were about to go to New York, the Mime Troupe was playing the parks in San Francisco, becoming a model for street theater and El Teatro Campesino. It flourished, travelled abroad; and Ronnie went through a more systematic political education. He was forced out of the troupe later on when—in a thrust toward participatory democracy—he also became an authority figure and was rejected by the feminists, who say he invented them. He then ran a Brechtian institute in Berkeley and apparently came to feel, as he analyzed the political scene of the later seventies, that the Workshop, of which he sometimes despaired, was the model worth emulating. To the extent that these years do resemble the fifties, he may be right. Epic West has since closed down, and Ronnie went east, at last, to make it there in the conventional sense. He recently produced a piece by Dario Fo, but with no illusions about its political impact, rather as something he could justify to himself while making a living, though I gather he didn't stay east very long.

At Tahoe, in 1965, the windroot was churning other ground. There was a company back in New York still performing—at the temporary quarters of the Repertory Theater in a huge quonset off Washington Square—in Arthur Miller's *Incident at Vichy*. We hadn't yet seen the actors, but we were technically in charge. Miller says in the play (a character says it for him) that he doesn't want our guilt, he wants our responsibility. (In *After the Fall*, performed by the company earlier, he had made his peace with Kazan's guilt.) We had done *The Crucible* and *Death of a Salesman* (and I paid attention), but he never had my guilt, which was, in principle and temperament, more labyrinthine. And we were priming to be responsible on our own hook. Yet, "Caution:" I

Take Up the Bodies

wrote in my journal, "I must think very carefully now about what I'm saying because nobody will *not* believe me anymore." (Thus, the topside of the Wheel of Fortune.) The emergence of the Workshop seemed like a triumph of the historical sense—which had been energized in the underground by the Absurd—and we were trying to consolidate and extend that achievement at the advent of the Great Society. It was important to distrust my own rhetoric, no less that. But there was also the impetus of a new political consciousness, and it seemed like a time to put it all together, "the deepest possible subjective life and the widest possible public statement." I wrote after that: *"THE WAY DOWN IS THE WAY UP."* I forgot to add that the reverse is also true. Nevertheless, we wanted to be able to say to the actors—specifically those who were still hung up on the Method, which still dominated the acting in New York and infected our own people—"ACT. SPEAK OUT. PERFORM."

If there is the history of a period in that enjoinder, there were competing strains in my thought. While I was warding off the more self-indulgent versions of "the Private Moment," as in Strasberg, I wanted the intimacy of "the Embrace," as in Buber, the intercourse of I and Thou. Was the one possible without the other? When Kazan had spoken earlier—as he gathered his company and defined his objectives—about a new actor transcending psychology, what he seemed to forget, I noted then, was that the American actor "had never understood Freud to begin with, no less Jung. Both were primarily men of reason and intelligence, even if one explored the anarchic id and the other fell in love with the spooks. What we have to purge is the compulsive egocentricity of the actor-in-love-with-truth. No more Narcissus upon Narcissus. This actor reaches out to be certain *he* is there. The obsession with the Method was an aspect of perturbation about Identity. One must hearken to the cellarage not *retreat* there. What we must encourage is not 'playing off' or 'making eye contact'—these are mechanistic ideas (like Donne's eyebeams twisted on one double string)—but *embracing* the Other. *I* look to him because I *know* he is there. *I* will take care of itself by forgetting itself in the Other—not immolation *in,* but bringing *out.*" Bringing it back alive, I said. "Look there, look there! What we are looking for is the shape of the mist on Cordelia's lips." You couldn't hope to see it on the stage at Lincoln Center. It was some years later before I took another look at that, studying the degree to which the nuances of acting theory are but traces of the historical moment, indices of presence depending on how much identity you think you have. That very problem has become a kind of subject matter in our work. Once you get close in to the issue, as we shall see, the italics (above) will shift with the ego.

We were at a friend's lodge on the North Shore, just over the line from Reno. It was winter, we were the only ones there, except for the caretakers. We laid all the congratulatory telegrams on the sideboard and Jules, quick to order, started to outline his charts while I thought about *Danton's Death* (we knew immediately we were going to do it), and how I might reduce the large cast of characters to a manageable number of actors, because even at Lincoln Center there would be budgets (as our general manager Alan Mandell used to say, "No difference from the Workshop, only more zeroes.") If I were to do it today, it would be with half a dozen or so actors, and maybe the better for that, it having occurred to me even then that it should be done as if it were *Endgame*. ("The deaths of Danton and his friends," I was to write in the controversial program note, "in the burnt-out Olympus of their Utopian dream, evoke the waning of the dying gods." With a little more caustic to the melancholy. . . .) But we didn't do it like that. It wasn't that we lacked the audacity, we might have done it another time. We were, rather, feeling expansive and wanted to take on the challenge, the stage and its machinery—it would have seemed an evasion if we didn't, or so we thought. And this was a period when, at the Workshop, I had been doing very large productions taken very far in physical conception (they could neither build them as meticulously nor afford them in New York, what with the unions and the scene shops), on the principle of "risking the baroque." Actually, I have never lived down that presumptuous fantasy, the desire to do it all at once, the hubris which probably did us in at Lincoln Center. The reductive scope of my present work is still overweening. The narrowing down to a needle's eye is another expansive ambition, an imperialism of austere means. The conceptual elements at play are the equivalent of electronic turntables with their annular rings. "Nothing turns," however, "unless it means," I wrote. Little did I know that it might not turn at all.

Occasionally I think back to the scope of that bare space, and the space surrounding my first thought of it. The snow was everywhere, silent, deep. We were not far from the site where the Donner Party, not able to make its crossing, built makeshift cabins that were later—when they were forced to eat human flesh to survive—twenty feet under the snow. At night we drove over the state border to Reno, to gamble, as Jules did years later, and died.

The day before Hoguet and I agreed that I should "resign" from the Repertory Theater, President Johnson had delivered his State of the Union message to Congress. He asked for a 6 percent increase of taxes for the Vietnam War. A coalition of Republicans and Southern Demo-

Take Up the Bodies

crats (not yet New South) had taken over the House. Before that, as the second season proceeded, we had race riots in Chicago and danger alerts elsewhere. Senate peace doves were warning Hanoi not to execute some captured flyers and thereby escalate the war. The Common Market—a Cold War creation—was turning into a prosperous European community which would eventually be matched by Eurocommunism, and even France was going along. My wife and I were having dinner in Stockbridge with William Gibson and Arthur Penn and their wives the night Stokely Carmichael announced that whites were no longer welcome in SNCC, and Black Power took over that scene, leading to the short and bellicose ascension of H. Rap Brown.

So, suddenly, we were honkies. There were some who were prepared to believe that before the escalation of black demands. Soon after we came to New York, there was a meeting at Actors Equity initiated, as I recall, by Joe Papp, who has always been admirably ahead of everybody in bringing minorities onto the stage. (I should add that when we felt like an abused minority, Joe sent us a letter of encouragement saying, on the basis of his own experience, that the negatives would pass.) Most of those connected with institutional theater in the city were there. Without any severe pressure, but pressure enough, we were being asked to agree to preferential treatment for blacks. James Earl Jones and Leroi Jones (not yet Imamu Baraka) were also there, along with Frederick O'Neal, the Negro (the word was still in use) president of Equity. We had not yet announced the cast for *Danton's Death*, which everybody was awaiting and the newspapers were trying to ferret out. Actually, James Earl Jones—well-known then but not as he is now—had already been hired, with two other blacks in the very few key roles, and others to come in the many doubled smaller parts.

As the meeting wore on and everybody was raising his hand and swearing affirmative action, I began to feel infringed upon, and when it came my turn to give witness to our good intentions, I refused to say anything about our casting. I said instead that we intended to reserve to ourselves the artistic if not civil right to make choices on conceptual grounds. (I didn't say the usual about competence or talent.) I also said that we'd not achieve equity for blacks in the theater, no more than in the mainstream of American life, without plays that are written for mixed casts and plays that are, at deeper perceptual levels, miscegenated. I mentioned Beckett and Genet, who were then still very marginal and still resisted. I said one could think of their plays as miscegenated, as some of Shakespeare's are, not all, by mythic content, and deracinating time; and the Greeks, not only by further archaic distance, but adulterated grounding in the fertile crescent of the Middle

East. I also suggested that Brechtian alienation permitted integration through a historicizing distance. (But Brecht was also still resisted and never really made it in America, at least then.)

I realized there were some plays not quite at the distance of the older classics which might seize upon a time lapse and pass (as I thought we might with *Danton's Death* which also, it seems, disperses history into mind). But some plays, I said, are also more stubbornly situated where they were, the environmental or material reality harder to subvert, as in Chekov, or undesirable to subvert because history has already been sufficiently abused by the easier liberal misreadings. While I could imagine, say, a black in the role of Undershaft in *Major Barbara*, off-hand I didn't think it was a very illuminating idea, and it would take an unusual conception of the play to convince me otherwise. (Not because I wasn't in favor of revisionist productions, I was, and had done them and was always looking forward to such concepts, but I didn't normally see them. The issue of black casting was not, indeed, separate from the whole problem of revisionist performance, and had to be thought out with the same theoretical stringency—but more of that in another chapter.) More often than not integrated casting, like updated classics, felt arbitrary and shallow. Whereupon Fred O'Neal remarked in an avuncular way that he had once played the judge in a drama by Elmer Rice and after five minutes—so he assured me—the audience forgot he was black.

I said that was too bad, if true, but I didn't believe it. Obviously I might have done better not to reply at all, but those were the days of hubris. I explained as tactfully as I could why I thought he was deluded. I have been in such audiences, I said. What probably happened was that either they were condescending or he was very gullible. As a liberal myself, I'd been trained to color blindness in economic and social matters, but that's a necessary fiction and I know when I'm seeing black. When I see black on stage, my liberalism and my art may be at odds. Long before we were told by blacks to see black because they are proud of it, I trained myself to see what is *materially* there (including the force of a fiction), and I assume that if black is there, or some variant, it is *meant* to be there, to *be seen*. If it's not meant, it shouldn't be there. We are imperceptive enough, I felt, without the theater helping us to deceive ourselves in the wrong way.

Leroi Jones, who had listened to all the testimony in silence, then said—not because he liked what I was saying or wanted a theater the way I was seeing it—"The man is the only one here talking honest." Black separatism was about to emerge, wanting its own theater, calling a spade a spade. Jimmy Jones said nothing. I didn't know if he disagreed with what I said, or was honoring my refusal to divulge the cast, or was being circumspect for his own reasons. Gladys Vaughn, who was also there and had directed Jimmy at the New York Shakespeare Festival, told my wife (they were old friends) that he thought I should not have said what I did. He considered what I did a serious mistake, as Gladys did. Politically, they were surely right, for whatever report came out of that off-the-record conference, it was not to our advantage. Jules bit his tongue as I spoke, but made no move to reverse any bad impression by promising anything more or announcing the cast, which I was half-hoping he would do.

The ceremonial appearance of the Muslims at the CORE conference in the summer of 1966 betokened the scornful end of Integration. And despite my discriminations *about* casting, the abandonment of the integrationist ethic was, in my opinion, the sorriest mistake of the civil rights movement. As for *The Fire Next Time*—the escalation of the rhetoric of Black Power—if the Constitution is not really color blind, violence is. There is a self-cancelling limit to the pound on demand which we have seen in the subsequent backlash. The blacks who were more than polemically out for blood seemed to forget that "the pigs" had more guns and would certainly use them. If they didn't forget— and sometimes they didn't, they were proving a point—their testing out proved disastrously correct. The leaders of the Black Power movement were virtually wiped out or exhausted, by legal action, harassment, assassination, exile, imprisonment. What was really outrageous, given this predictable and inevitable outcome, were the blinded or asskissing whites who were encouraging "black rage" at the time. No social movement can make any claim for itself, not in this country, if it is even rhetorically based on the division of black and white. That anybody could approve violence anymore—after the frightful experience of the twentieth century—was simply astonishing. *Danton's Death* (whatever one thought of the production) was a prophetic gloss on the issue: violence abrogates identity as it claims it, and the abrogation may outdo the claim.

In the long view, and on my worst days, it didn't seem to make any difference. I had forgotten Faulkner's prophecy (how he was derided for what seems almost self-evident): the Jim Bonds were by slow accretions going to take over the western hemisphere, the idiot's howl embracing it all. There was also the long-term prospect that, in the world at large, black would have its deadly evolutionary turn. There was, in both senses of the word, enough bastard white to assure it. Meanwhile, to round out the state of the world around my resignation, the Chicago police were having a busy time of it, as they would a year later at the Convention. Now, however, they were looking not for enraged blacks or trashing radicals but for the killer of eight student nurses, the worst massacre since that St. Valentine's Day which Brecht used in *The Resistible Ascension of Arturo Ui*, in which by gradual degrees the tyranny takes over, and there are bodies all over the place.

Aline MacMahon was with us then, playing Tribulation Wholesome in *The Alchemist* on the Beaumont stage. A superbly gracious lady who had, when I was still a student at Stanford, been exceptionally kind to me, Aline was rattled a bit by the plays I was disposed to. She was rather in favor of plays of reassurance, while no less realistic about things as they happened to be than the most worldly of us. She is far more worldly, and very wise. Aline's husband was Clarence Stein, one of the pioneer city planners, and a man who knew the New York skyline and Central Park, which we both loved, like the palm of his hand. Clarence was growing old. "This age, this dying," Aline said, "I don't know who made it up—but he deserves a kick in the pants." Aline began her long career in both theater and film as a showgirl in (if I remember what she told me) the Green Street Follies. "Things don't really change," she said, "only our relations to things." But something had gone out of the world, she had to admit. Clarence and their dear friend Lewis Mumford had been confident of things. Clarence, after all, had conceived the great waterways of the St. Lawrence, the greenbelt, and the Appalachian Trail—compared to which risking the baroque seemed like tinker toys. Look, they said, that city wasn't there, now it is! Presto! Lidice reversed. Only the time is confused.

So, in the sixties, the Marxist Herbert Marcuse did a revisionist romance on Freud in *Eros and Civilization*. It was one of the ideological gospels of the Movement which had no ideology. Marcuse would have had us reach back to subhistory for the archaic-mythic residues which, mated with technology's power to banish scarcity (about which we're no longer sure), would give us a nonrepressive civilization. Not Prometheus, builder of cities, but Narcissus and Orpheus, who came back from the dead. They gave us an imaginative precedent (no sociological model) for arresting them. Marcuse actually wrote the book in the fifties, reflecting the affluent stasis of the Age of Ike dreaming on Utopia lost. Afterwards, in one self-reassuring preface after another, he tried to dispel the obdurate Freudian pessimism, that bleak clinical vision of our civilization and its discontents which, like the analytical process itself, the theater also rememorates. By a kind of Ali shuffle around the Reality Principle, Marcuse shows how the Revolution will be achieved. We will break the bondage of history by taking up each historical cause, in one incarnation after another: the Third World, the students, the hippies, the blacks, and (in 1974's edition) women. "The reason to be a revolutionary in our time," said Danny Cohn-Bendit, whose relationship to Marcuse was a double take on pedagogy and authority, "is that it's a better way to live." Or so it seemed, until his friends were shot up or exiled, and Cohn-Bendit changed his mind about the way he was living, and the celebration of revolution turned to terrorism.

That hadn't happened yet. As I left Lincoln Center, the war resistance was accelerating, and the incidence of fanaticism was rising. It was hard not to admire some of the young people, however savage or vainglorious, who were about to go underground. They were living our sublimations. Nothing important, I reminded myself, is done without fanaticism. But I no longer knew what I was fanatic about. Meanwhile, the idea of Death—better kept out of the play's title and under the table—was beginning to get some columns on the Leisure and Living pages. People were getting older, the national mean getting middle-aged and senior citizens becoming an important political con-stituency, even as the youth culture was prevailing. One felt it at the personal level, the aging, but what with the war, the pollution, the gar-bage strike, the power failure, reports of overpopulation, triage, car-cinogens, and still no solution for nuclear weapons, we were rather surprised to find, nearing the final quarter of the century, that we might be undertaking our own end. We were not quite providing for it, however, since—though we were busy in the prospect—we did not really believe we would succeed. The high achievement of oblivion would not be reported on the report card. But the paranoia grew. Relieved one time to be out of New York giving a talk in Western On-tario, I saw Buddy Hackett on a late-night show. He was describing his early days on the saloon circuit in New Jersey, when he was young and scared enough to have to drink till four in the morning whenever the local bookmaker wanted him to. He wouldn't mention the man's name, he said, because the local bookmaker isn't local anymore. "Wherever we are," he lowered his voice and raised his heels, peering around, "we can step on his toes."

The next morning, at breakfast with Martin Esslin—who, when Beckett was still a doubtful figure, made our production of *Godot* at San Quentin the keynote of *The Theater of the Absurd*—we heard that Beckett had won the Nobel Prize. We wired him over the Canadian bacon, but he was hiding out in Tunisia. In China, about the same time, Mao's wife put out an ideological manual for artists. In Thailand, we had set up a secret air base. The Vietnam War was spreading out. The largest and most powerful air force in history was bombing Indo-China with the most advanced aerial technology—"smart bombs" guided by TV cameras or laser beams. I went to look at my old neighborhood in Ocean Hill-Brownsville—the local bookmaker gone, all black and Porto Rican now—looking like it were blitzed. Even in the old days, that was a place where you got an eye for an eye. I kept thinking about those bombs, somebody's going to get even with us for that! One afternoon, over drinks with George and Mary Emma Elliott (who didn't stop calling in New York), the novelist Verlin Cassill told of starting an article on the Warren Report, but in the middle of it, having discovered a series of contradictions, he broke out in a cold sweat. Maybe they had planted the contradictions to trap him! So he filed the article away. He was suffering a stiff neck from sleeping too much in a draft. Herman Kahn took LSD, and Martin Luther King was booed in Watts. I wrote my friend Mark Harris, half seriously, to ask him to tell me what to do with the rest of my life.

It was strange, after twenty years in the theater, to be suddenly and totally adrift. Now that I'd been forced to it, I didn't quite know what to think over, not yet, except what I'd better forget, since I couldn't undo it. But that would inevitably be thought in the long mixed annuity of the unconscious, just as what I am remembering now, for all that it has been thought, is the mirage of a larger history that, with other things that had been forgotten, would be the undoing-that-had-to-be-done in the subsequent work.

I had still been working on Brecht's *Galileo* when the end came. We had finally yielded to the pressure for stars, and Rod Steiger had agreed to play the title role. But when he was advised (by agents? friends? our enemies? we were making a list) of what a wreck we were at Lincoln Center (this is my reading of it), he withdrew, presumably on psychiatric grounds, producing testimony from a doctor that he was emotionally unable to go ahead. We had become friendly in Rome, where he'd agreed to do it. When he called in New York, after a long inexplicable silence, I knew he wouldn't. It was very awkward when he came to explain, almost like you're turning an actor down for a job. He was then at the top of his career, with an Academy Award, conquering worlds in the movies. He had always wanted to play the role and might have been splendid. We had announced publically that he would do it, subscriptions were up, and the withdrawal sent our stock with the Board plunging.

When I came home from the First National City Bank, I took my books on the Renaissance, on Brecht, and my notes for the production, and placed them neatly on the shelves. Jules and I had talked, and I persuaded him to forget any misgivings he had about staying. By then, there was no reason not to. We had known each other since we were students at NYU, before going to Stanford in 1947. It was a relief not to be doing *Galileo*. (After all, I had done it before, turning Brecht's methods back upon him, one of the productions in San Francisco which, praised in New York, brought us there.) With Steiger out, it seemed doomed. I wrote in my journal: "One doom cancels another."

Actually, the last play I directed at Lincoln Center was called *In Three Zones,* by Wilford Leach. It was going to open the Forum, but I refused to put it on, though we were urged to by many who saw it in the previews. All disasters seemed to be coming to a head just then, and we had a series of them on that production. Whatever it was, it wasn't what I wanted. I had had it. Everything had soured, maybe I couldn't see straight. Will Leach later became artistic director of La Mama and now works with Joe Papp. Ellen Stewart couldn't have found anybody more unflappable for her unmethodical place. He was disappointed at my calling off the play and would have preferred to go ahead, but he didn't complain. Will is tall, soft-fleshed, round-faced, unconfessional, sly. He likes things that just happen, pattern over logic, and not too serious. He looks at you with slew eyes when something interesting is afoot. He used to visit an astrologer, who told him that we'd not picked a propitious day to open. It was the Day of the Dead. "Astrology is not predictive but descriptive," writes Roland Barthes, "(it describes very realistically certain social conditions)."

Lake Tahoe at one end, Lake Placid at the other. An immense zero between. I went there with my son Jonathan to relax it off, and to pay Jonathan an old promise. I read of my resignation at breakfast, amidst reports of disorder in Red China and the first thirteen-alarm fire in New York history. The company was shocked, Jules cried. The obituary was on the front page of the *Times.* Everybody said I "came off well." (Shortly after, Robert Brustein, one of the critics I'd thought of assembling when I was fantasizing some relief, wrote about my departure that "it is a melancholy decision for which we all bear some measure of responsibility"—and reproached himself and others who "became impatient for results.") Jonathan, who would be eleven the following month, said as we drove into the winter country that "people can't imagine endlessness." That same night our bird Petey died. We skied and skated and did the bobrun and watched Joe Namath make history over the Colts in the Super Bowl. Appraisal of Johnson at the New Year was that his downgrading was only temporary. Adam Clayton Powell was another casualty that week, having been denied his committee chairmanship. He claimed it was a racist move, which it undoubtedly was, but there is also a Nemesis for living it up. Two dissidents down. There seemed to me something unjust and unrepresented, but due process does what it must.

Knowing the difference between the process and your own bad choice is quite another matter. The most shameful thing I ever did in the theater was to withdraw from the program for *Danton's Death* the long note from which the following excerpts are taken:

"The French Revolution was a series of small nuclear explosions climaxed by the Reign of Terror. It came at the end of the eighteenth century when Enlightenment looked over the abyss to anarchy and, in our own time, absolute unreason. The Terror was designed by the Committee of Public Safety as an instrument of order. 'Terror, but not chaos.' The bloodletting seemed required by History. Terror, according to Robespierre, Castro, Verwoerd, Mao Tse-Tung and President Johnson, is the moral whip of Virtue.

"This is not to equalize all aberrations of Power, but to recognize— as Buechner did at twenty-one—that nobody has a premium on tyranny. By fault or default, from whatever good motives, we are all executioners. 'What is it in us that whores, lies, steals and kills?' The question may be hard tack for a new season. But we may as well begin where our world leaves us; with the Balance of Terror. We would hold our peace if we had it. . . .

"The heroes of the Revolution were responsible for murder, rape, arson, cannibalism, atrocity of every kind, and the horror is they were no more (or less) sadists than the men responsible today for releasing napalm over the jungles. . . .

"The Terror is the mind's revenge on itself. . . . The guillotine, introduced as a humane method of capital punishment, quick and surgical, is the absurd chop-logic of the bureaucratic mind, like the tumblers [sic] of the computer that decides how many people are expendable in the next holocaust. People submitted to it as we submit to our own most impossible conceptions. . . .

"The Revolution may have been a time when, for their little day, the poor were the terror of the earth. But the guillotine was the debraining machine of the bourgeois world. The executioner, like Eichmann, was a respectable man, an obedient part of the mechanism. Revolution comes from oppression, but the price indices rose then as they do now with Viet Nam. Buechner creates a scene where prosperity promenades while murder is laughing in the streets.

". . . 'What is it in me that denies me?' [Danton] cries. . . . While Robespierre is tormented by Duty, Danton suffers from a disease which knows no name; in another time it might have been called the Sloth, that disorder of the soul which turns back upon itself death-breeding doubt, the boredom of the hyperactive mind which sees unnaturally through life while possessing death. . . ."

That pretty much covers the territory over which stormed philistines and intellectuals alike, whether or not they'd read the note. It also covers some themes which are germane to this book. The newspapers

Take Up the Bodies

reprinted very little of it, the two opening paragraphs above and the line about sadists and the jungles. What I've left out refers mainly to the romantic temper of the men who conceived the Revolution, the mythic imagery in front of which the bloodlust was played out, the fearful symmetry of creation and destruction, the sexual contrast between Robespierre and Danton as objectified in the guillotine, and the grandeur of Buechner's pessimistic vision.

The note had been used in the first previews, along with a plain historical summary of the Revolution. But after a great deal of complaint, which seemed to distress the actors and others associated with the production, I agreed to withdraw it, leaving only the historical material. I did not withdraw it because of audience hostility, nor because of pressure from the Board or the newspapers, but because of the effect upon the actors, who were already nervous about the opening, many of whom had never been in an embattled theater before, most of whom had no politics whatever and found even the inclusion of a note strange. That much the San Francisco people were used to, though they always had mixed feelings about it; and this one made them nervous too. Even so, I resisted until I was persuaded that too much was at stake in this first production to imperil it with a note; when principle started to look like vanity, I gave in. I don't believe I would ever do anything like that again. I don't suppose I'll have the opportunity.

After all, how many productions about to open in America ever have editorials attacking the director in advance? Two days before the opening, for instance, the now-defunct *Journal-American* wrote that I had "already come in for deserved rebuke for a very bad performance." The editorial found particularly offensive the idea that President Johnson, along with Mao and Castro, "supports a policy of terror as 'the moral whip of virtue.' [Blau's] article went on by implication to impugn the motives of President Johnson's policy in Viet Nam." The word *sadist* was found objectionable. After pointing out that various theatergoers were shocked by what I'd said, the editorial reprimanded me for "the nasty show of pseudo-intellectualism" that I'd put on. The *Times* gave the story a fair amount of play, but there were similar implications about the offensiveness of my attack on President Johnson.

If we defused the peril with the conservatives, and we didn't, we had a mixed and confusing reaction among the liberals and radicals, in letters and phone calls and in the lobby. Some, like Sontag and Chaikin in that same cab ride, did the expected: they simply reproached me for having taken it out. They were right. I explained, but there was really no argument convincing to me, so I could hardly convince them.

Others, however, were more imperious on the subject than the *Journal-American*—not so much critical for my having withdrawn the statement but for having made it in the first place. The odd part was that they came down on me for what they appraised as the naiveté of my politics, and proceeded to lecture me on the true meanings of the play. The actuality was that they believed what came out in the papers or in the gossip around it or, if they saw the note, came inexplicably to the same conclusion: that I had attacked President Johnson by lumping him with the others. And when *Danton's Death* was then performed, they attacked it (with other objections) for tendentiousness, as if I were reducing Buechner's vision to a simpleminded politics. They felt this was not only damaging to the work, but even to my best intentions, of which they were still trying to approve, and some took it all the way back to the politicizing they found in *The Impossible Theater: A Manifesto*. Of all the reactions to the performance, that seemed—though triggered by the controversy—the most identifiably predetermined, and misguided. Political *consciousness* there undoubtedly was, but I don't see how anybody can read past the first page of that book, then or today, and not recognize the subordination of the political impulse to the *impossible* itself, although I wish I had some answers to the politics. That's what the book was about, that's what all my work had been about, and still is, that's what *Danton's Death* was about, and this book is a variation on the theme.

About the place of politics in the art of theater, I shall say more in the theoretical matrix of the next chapter, as an aspect of the idea of origins and the displacement of history into process. But the issue was especially confused and confusing, for all of us, in the period when the program note was written. Maybe not. Maybe it is more confusing now that we are left with the disenchantments. However that may be, I want to discuss what I did say, as it reflects on agitations within the theater brought on by the politics outside, and maybe on some current discontents.

What I was saying in the note is surely apparent in the quotations above: there is something in the very nature of power which incriminates, and constitutes its tragedy. What the statesmen I mentioned had in common, however different they were, is that they felt compelled to have people murdered in policy or principle. Nothing new; one of those self-evident truths that men of power not only relive again and again, but that we need to think over again and again, the more so as our principles shift with political sympathies, forgiving an atrocity here that we denounce there. As Bernard Knox, the classical scholar, wrote in a very recent article, commenting on Euripides' one-line

Take Up the Bodies

reference to Calchas' oracle in *Iphigeneia at Aulis*, "It's as if Euripides were saying: 'There is no need to explain it. This is the way of the world: if you are a man in the seats of power, sooner or later you will face a choice just like this one.' " As in the world everyday—mere witnesses to the illusions of power—we have to adjust our principles between Munich and Entebbe. But elsewhere Euripides does try to explain it—and even to dissuade power, against hope, from fulfilling its nature—and the other great dramatists have tried to explain it, or if they can't explain it they re-represent it, and it remains a mystery.

My sentiments about Vietnam were clear enough, but if anything the statement was intended not as a political but a moral reflection; and while I might very well have attacked him on another occasion, I was not particularly trying to denounce Johnson, as some even sneered, by placing him with the others—for one thing, I happened to admire Castro, and still do (though I have to adjust my principles). I had only a short while before written about *Danton's Death* in *New York* (the old *Sunday Herald Tribune Magazine*), which had asked me to do a foreword to our season: "It speaks across the years to a century in which we've been killing people all over the world. It is a revolutionary play with reservations about the Revolution. It knows how at the very limit of exaltation the heads start kissing in the basket, and vision drowns in blood. The clairvoyance of the drama is awesome and impartial; it takes no sides. Castro might ponder it, and those in this country who impeded Castro when he came down from the Mountain, prophet and visionary, like Danton. The play is not simply talking about the brutes who killed beyond reason, but the idealists who kill in principle. I think, therefore I am. The murderous permutation becomes *I believe, therefore I kill.*"

The note itself says that "the true Revolution has never happened," and indeed I was hoping that some of the idealists in our country —never mind Johnson—would also ponder the drama, because already in 1965, when the Movement was just generating its eventual frenzied response to the escalation of the war, I was worried that the revolutionary impulse would be crippled by its own excess. As I suggested in my comments on Black Power, that is one of the main reasons I chose the play. You could already see it coming. The armies of the night and the race riots had not yet reached that point, nor the activity of the Panthers or, later, aberrations like the SLA; nor had we yet seen the Days of Rage of the SDS types who would, finding themselves up against the wall, go underground with the Weatherman. But it wouldn't be long before we'd be seeing various liberal and radical types in the sanctuaries of higher thought (it's hard to say it without sounding like William Buckley) justifying and even encouraging a spate of actions from simple lawlessness to outright violence. The scenario is now familiar, and which of us wasn't divided? I have already mentioned the Living Theater when they were freaking out the Theater of Ideas. The subject that night was "Theater and Therapy." That was, however, near the end of the line, like a coda to the craziness of an era. The whole thing was brutally funny. Some of the intellectuals left dancing equivocally in their tracks had started with an earlier innocence.

I remember getting an appeal, in 1963, from *The Drama Review* to make a statement about the Living Theater when it was closed by the IRS for not paying its taxes, and then gave a forbidden performance behind the padlock, rapturously reported by *TDR*. I wrote back that the closing of the Living Theater, however regrettable, seemed an open-and-shut legal case. While we wanted to be vigilant about what was called the narrowing of free expression, the theater was perilous and manic enough without our all getting nervous over their delinquency. "When we first heard of the secret performance after the Internal Revenue Service had barred the doors," I said, "we were not inspired to Genetic ecstasies for it all sounded like a comic opera of sentimental anarchy, an inexplicably dumb show—not civil disobedience but the most adolescent kind of law-breaking." An article in the *New Republic*, which had spurred *TDR* to hurry up a forum, saw a portent for the future in this clandestine event, as if the participants were primitive Christians. "A theater of the catacombs, that?" I added. "The Church would have died underground of dry rot if it had been founded on such rubbish." As part of the therapy that evening five years later, Paul Goodman said just about the same.

Back in 1963, we felt a definite kinship with the Living Theater, but the air was not being cleared by dubious allegations from our side. There were in fact institutions, like the Pacifica Foundation then, which *were* suffering unjustifiable harrassment by the IRS, but nobody was doing the cause of justice any good by confusing the two cases, as was done by some who felt later betrayed. We were moving into those years where the cases would have to be taken one by one, if you were to preserve any moral sanity. There would soon be plenty of reason for double alarm, as the campuses were occupied and banks firebombed, wires tapped and draft files bloodied, students maced and computers exploded. In that atmosphere we would all be hard-pressed to make the right distinctions. One didn't want to blow one's mind too early in the game. The melodrama of the IRS is only a sample of the ways in which people with normally good minds were, through the improvisational excitements of the period, lured into a lapsed intelligence. That's the larger issue that concerns me here, rather than the fact that, in 1965, a few of them were slapping my wrist for being simplistic about President Johnson and *Danton's Death.*

When I said parenthetically before that I had rejected the play *Macbird!,* one reason was that it abused President Johnson, and others, with parody to the point of slander. Despite the ending of the war, what has happened in the country since that confused man was driven from office indicates that the complexities of power are beyond the indignities and radical pieties that were heaped upon him. Before writing about it here, I hadn't looked at the program note in years. It seems to me that what was at stake there is no different now from what it was then, although both Mao and Johnson are dead, Castro is doing his killing in Africa, Carter's human rights were suspended for an occasional junta or the Shah (and now a lost election), and you'd need to change Verwoerd to Botha. And I wouldn't quite know what to do about it if I were in power anymore than any one of them.

"What wouldst thou do with the world, Apemantus," says Timon of Athens, "if it lay in thy power?"

That's another one of those questions we keep asking ourselves in the work of KRAKEN. It is also probably the critical question in the politics of the Left which, having no power, is no longer sure that it has any feasible programs either. For members of my generation raised on modernist despair and liberal values (a maybe untenable combination), the problem has been complicated for a long time. That was reflected in what I did say in that ill-fated note, as well as in the condescension to the politics I supposedly brought to Lincoln Center. The turmoil of the sixties exposed a serious contradiction still not resolved, though the first term has been tempered by the disillusion: on the one hand, the temptation to go along—if only to break one's own paralysis—with the expedient politicizing of behavior we saw in the Movement; on the other, a resistance to political solutions, which came from the disenchantments of the forties, revulsion against the sellout of social progress to World War II, the revelations about Stalinism, and the "moral realism" of the end-of-the-ideological fifties.

The thing is that for some, politics was already over in the sixties. And all the radicalism was the recidivism of a last fling. As with life, so with theater. Even while they were sponsoring *Macbird!* or *Birdbath* or *Viet Rock* or *America Hurrah,* they were instinctively acclaiming such an apolitical work as Pinter's *The Homecoming,* which begs not only the political question but almost all questions that it raises with far more sophistication. (For certain radicals that seemed to make no difference; and for all the distance in quality between *The Homecoming* and the other plays, it makes sense that the *New York Free Press*, then publishing, named it one of the "canons" of the New Theater.) It was also apparent to those who did ask questions that Peter Brook's very accomplished staging of *Marat/Sade* aestheticized the political content of the play, perhaps improving it, perhaps not, but being very much attuned, for all its inventive dissonance, to the bone-wearier politics of the dissident times.

Whatever we were attuned to in *Danton's Death,* it was certainly not the politics that was imposed upon it. In the play, the bone-weariness of Danton contains all the contradictions. The performance came just before the time when, as I've said, many intellectuals—even those who could read the meanings only too well—were going to be very equivocal about violence, whether in Chicago, the Pentagon, Watts, or worse. "As we read today," I wrote then (in the *New York* article), "about the wars of national liberation or the civil rights movement, the play is an augury of tomorrow and tomorrow and tomorrow." True, if the rhetoric had only been matched by a production inarguably convincing and better received, we might have had—in that unprecedented forum, with everybody paying attention—some real indication of the impact of art on politics. But then, what kind of politics is that? to be caught up thus in the ultimate equivocation, an image of history as self-mortifying momentum? Well, there is a saving margin in the mind for which I wish we'd made the case, despite all controversy, as you'd want to do for grace. Almost all the great poets of the nineteenth century tried their hands at a Shakespearean imitation, but Buechner alone had the trueblooded catastrophic instinct for the strong toils. "The outside danger revealed by [the] great story is that any revolution, whatever its just cause, may become through annihilation of reason a tale told by an idiot signifying nothing. The true Revolution is never over. Nobody owns it, neither the Negroes nor the Asians. At a certain moment in time, he who shouts [like Lucille at the end of the play] 'Long live the King!' may be more revolutionary than he who shouts 'Long live the Republic!' " Or even than the actor signalling through the flames—with the incendiary approval that the time extorted from us—burn, baby, burn.

That reflects, I think, what my politics tends to be and what characterizes the work I do when it is at its best, the incessant turning things over, tomorrow and tomorrow and tomorrow, as if there were no last word—though I undeniably want to have it. *That* tendentiousness suffuses the work I am doing now. It suffuses it with all the more intensity (I'd guess) because of the experience of Lincoln Center. I said there was nothing to learn from the shock wave when it came except how to endure it. I still don't know whether I've learned anything from it that I might not have known if I'd never been there. Aside from the plain defeat, what stays with me—the strongest retrospective presence, perhaps melodramatized in the remembrance—is the image in the mirrors under the stage: in the abashed body of desire, the critical liability of the impossible. That still depends on a better self-conception than I thought was left me then. The liability of the criticism was that in the end I might have come—scourged and without the shadow of an achievement—to something less existentially instructive than Danton's disease, the Sloth. But if it felt like that, that's the glamorizing trouble with retrospection. Inconceivable! It should have happened, but does it matter? The knives were out, there were other causes for the failure, but the bottom line is this: "What is it in me that denies me?" All justification—and all politics—becomes meaningless at that level, and we return to the compulsion from which we came, the mortal danger of solipsism, where all acting starts, or ends.

I do not like it, but that's the way it is. The Revolution can be damned when it comes to that.

Origin of the Species

3

"Sir, thou hast nothing to draw with, and the well is deep: from whence then hast thou that living water?" (John 4:11):

(. . . in the kraken's wake:) *What we want to show is not only the structure we have come to but the conceiving process in the structure, what led to it and what leads back to its sources, in the world, in us, in the friction between us, the work, each other, the rage, the work, each playing upon the other, receding, the world, our gravity; a memory trace in a spoor of association,* the thinking through. *There is always the haunted and critical moment when what we're after is almost not-there, the moment of Appropriation, the stepping back:* Act? how? why? where? what for? for whom? and to what End? *Why am I doing this in the first place? and can we? and since there is always the likelihood that nobody is listening or, if listening, cares what it means, what difference does it make? It may be that we are all listening to different voices, this candle, that flame; not for love or money the same light:*

The self's voice (wherever it speaks from) goes in and out of hearing. The genesis of a work is not where it seems. *Did I make it happen? or did it just happen?* The actor wonders. Where things come from—the roots and shadings of ideas—is, if you think about it, subject to the thinking, temporal and interminable. It's hard to know at which end of time, now or before, things occur in the act of reflection. To trace the source of a body of work is to be involved in an infinite regression, as when the dreamer scans (or interprets) the body of a dream.

Act? how? why? where? what for? for whom? and to what End?

Nevertheless, I will try to suggest, *in the way I think about it*, not only where the work came from but how, in the slipstream and nerve ends of thought, it acquired a method, gathering up motive and memory.

After my departure from Lincoln Center, the research was not linear, either conceptually or geographically. Since the place where it evolved had something to do with what it became, the thought of the work will take us to Oberlin, where the group was in residence and the first piece was completed, and back (temporally) to Los Angeles where, at the new California Institute of the Arts, the questions above were explicitly raised in the training process as I thought that out. What happened at Cal Arts is part of the social history in another turbulent institutional setting, but I will deal with that briefly. In discussing the conceptual strategies of the work, I will allude to one project or another, not necessarily in chronological order nor to review it as a whole, but rather as reflective facets of the theory which, perceived in the process, is being remembered in this book. I will try to define what seems distinctive in what we were doing, but as a pretext for further theory. Later in this chapter I will dwell upon two long projects that never actually came to performance but gave us—through an obsession with the indeterminacy of origins—the basis and texture of method. I might say they gave us something like *a methodical indeterminacy*, in which elements of the process go in and out of focus with the question of origins.

In this last quarter of the twentieth century, we are obviously not the only ones thinking about the principle of indeterminacy in the arts, or science. In any generation there is an infrastructure of ideas which governs the possibilities of thought; it's as if there is a conceptual ceiling on the problems that can *be* thought. Our work resists the ceiling but reflects the problems, and I will discuss them further as we approach the work. They are both ontological and political. We are always capable of being deluded as to where we are and how we got there, what we think we believe and what, in both personal and social reifications of thought, that actually represents. Ideas bend to the curvature of time. You believe, so to speak, where you *are* in history, while time curves back upon itself. If that brings the future to the insant, it also burdens us with the past. We're never quite sure how much of what seems to be entering consciousness—in the displacements of history as in the distortions of dream—was already there. Nor are we sure, as Freud points out in discussing memory, where it was when it's not in consciousness. Both Marx and Freud speak of time as a kind of alchemy. In the alembic of history, we *dematerialize* the sources of value, as in the sublimations of the unconscious. As a result, we are always puzzling about beginnings, the determination of thought by

Take Up the Bodies

history and, conversely, the impact of volition upon origins. In our work, we are very much concerned with this puzzle, the self's voice wavering in the distinction.

When I first came into the theater, however, the voices I really heard seemed formed, emphatic and, when not classical, mostly Russian. With Chekov, Stanislavski, Meyerhold, certainly Tolstoy (who finally abhorred the theater), no small-mindedness. Everything begins at the level of soul: a reform of being, ethics, purpose. "Don't come into the theater with mud on your feet." One doesn't act, one makes a life in art. To the best of one's ability. Between the desire for such a life and the actuality of it, there is an archipelago of questions extending all the way back to the ancient world: "Are you alive? Where are you living? What is your life?" says the Stranger, holding something back, giving Orestes' message to his sister over the tomb. This life. Something holds it back. Whatever that may be, part of the problem which keeps you from being part of the solution is the conviction (out of the credo of Modernism) that art is always about art, the double bind, the thing that takes life from the thing that gives life as it is. That's not quite what the Russians had in mind. Look at yourselves, how you live, it's awful, says Madame Ranevsky, not realizing that change would burst into the orchard like the beggar from the Lower Depths. Came the Revolution, they were in the same bind, my Russian masters, life-as-it-is coming into the theater with mud on its feet. Meyerhold tried to live with it even more dutifully than Stanislavski—letting art serve life, historically—then denounced it as lifeless. Meyerhold disappeared.

He seemed remarkably authentic because seized by history. *The rage, the work* . . . there was another bloody seizure in particular: the death of Trotsky. It was not staged as it was intended, but it was better theater—the drama of socialism cut to the brain. Imagine: skull smashed, face gored, with the mutilated pregnancy of tragic power —the lonely-man-in-exile struggling against the attack, throwing books, inkpot, dictaphone, bloodstruck emblems of intellect in the body, and then the body itself, almost wrenching the murder from the murderer with the ice axe. It was as if the savagery of thought that made the Revolution was every bit as lethal as the weapon. And of course it was, though it didn't save him. Even before his death, Trotsky was as stained with blood as Danton. Yet it was the size of it one admired, the theatricality of the Idea, like the feverish metaphysics of Dostoyevsky. I wanted the fervor of such conviction in a work.

Yet: "Art remains alien to the revolutionary praxis," says Marcuse. And so it may be for those who have not suffered a vicious politics, like Solzhenitsyn in the Gulag or Kim Chi-Ha in Korea or Reza

. . . bloodstruck emblems of intellect in the body, and then the body itself . . .

Baraheni in his accounts of torture in Iran: "Azudi has shattered the mouths of twenty poets today. . . ." The critical distinctions between art and politics are swallowed by such a line. We certainly have no way of judging it—no more than we did the plays that came over from Eastern Europe in the fifties, seemingly Absurd (more simplistic than Beckett or Ionesco) but closer to realistic. No matter what the subject matter or the motive, we say, it must still be art, as if we know what makes it so under any conditions. As our work developed, we were to turn specifically to this dilemma, and quite uncomfortably, in a project on terrorism called *The Cell*, to which I'll refer in a later chapter.

Draw upon life as art will, there is a formal impassivity at its selving core, a distancing, a desire to not-be-there, which history sometimes *doesn't* allow. The irony is that at the secret level of one's art, where fear gives birth to possibility, there may be an ambivalence about be-ing exempt from victimization—as if not to have suffered that way is to be unprivileged, embarrassed by history, disadvantaged. I said in the first chapter that our work pivots on the idea of punishment, which was engrafted in the theater from the beginning. Terrorism and torture are extremities of that motive which tears the mind in the body out of thought. In some sense we are always thinking about it, the dread and humiliation, even when we censor it out. The alternative to history is indifference, or the appearance of it. People are suffering, the Buddha smiles. The Cultural Revolution smashes Buddhas. When John Cage, following Buddha, says there's just enough suffering in the world, you want to smash John Cage. Making a life in art is not always a case of live and let live. So long as the impulse to activism wants a theater, that will be true, even if activism is apolitical and moving out of history, as with the reconstructed Grotowski. In either case, there is the turning to the life we live outside of art to which art attaches itself with a vengeance, as if art by itself is not living. But what is?

Which returns us to the questions over the tomb. All theory of theater converges there. That's where the real acting takes place. "Are you alive? Where are you living? What is your life?" When we speak of what Stanislavski called Presence in acting, we must also speak of its Absence, the dimensionality of time through the actor, the fact that he who is performing can die there in front of your eyes; is in fact doing so. Of all the performing arts, the theater stinks most of mortality. Buber said of Hasidism that it is "the only mysticism in which *time* is hallowed," somewhere "on the borderland of faith where the soul draws breath between word and word." It is a superb definition of what theater should be. The secret of any craft is mastery of time. Odor of time. Ordure. Which led Artaud to the Plague and the Theater of Cruelty, and a hellish assault upon the faithless words. But when "hell itself breathes out contagion to this world," Hamlet cautions himself to be cruel and not unnatural, maintaining the finest of lines between life and hell itself, words words words with no breath at all. Some of our work—which was especially attentive to language in the nonverbal period when we started—deliberately stalks this fine line, the words coming as if shot from the heart of perception in a near breathless rush.

The Zen archers say, "One shot—one life." You don't release the arrow, the arrow releases you. We require an idea of acting in which everything in the act is *breath-taking,* as if you are being breathed from out the rigor of the structure as from a tautened bow. The bow is history, which is made of language, and which we struggle to overcome. It would be absurd to claim the serenity of the Zen master in this. That is a world elsewhere. We are living within the dilemmas I have been defining, in this meditation on the origins of the work. We are too willful and egocentered—probably unregenerately so—and we can only pretend that we are not racing with time. Since an early work, *Seeds of Atreus,* a theatrical meditation on the beginnings of time, the delicacy of the struggle has been to work out some liveable unison between panic and grace. "All holds," as the Furies say, but only when "the cord has been stretched to the breaking point." Even then we have our doubts. There is a sort of brain fever in the process. What comes comes from a certain precipitousness of spirit which trembles on the letting be. That, so far as we can hold it, *is* the structure. As if in one long breath. One works for the irreducible, a history in the living eye. The question is always, what history?

Stop-time. That dying animal which enacts its own future wants to abolish time. It releases itself to its absence in something like a *déja vu.* The displacement is unnerving. You are not where you were. It is like the recollection of a previous existence. The neuromental aspects of theater are elusive. Unpredictable in the actor, incalculable in the viewer. *In the friction between us, each playing upon the other, receding.* The actor who thinks he is all there is suffering a delusion. With mortality as a base, Presence is fragile, subject to change (and chance), yet persisting through that. Breath blood nerves brains, the metabolism of perception. Beckett suggests what is at stake in the marvellous threnody between Didi and Gogo. There and then, they are not what they were, they are what they hear. They make a noise like leaves they whisper they rustle like ashes like leaves listening to themselves breathing a heartbeat away listening to the others listening

lds," as the Furies say, but only when "the cord has been stretched to the breaking point."

like ashes like leaves, perception in a time warp turning us inside out, this enormity of being, breather and breath. The grids of perception cross; mind and body, the watcher and the watched, theater and life. In the theater, if we think about it, we breathe each other, giving and taking life. So, life; we can widen the theater.

One of our most elemental exercises has to do with training this form of consciousness, in the work, each other. Thus, *now,* doing nothing but breathing (and *taking* time, take *time*): You are living in your breathing. Stop. Think. You are dying in your breathing. Stop. Think. You are living in your breathing. You are dying in your breathing. You are living in your dying, dying in your living. (Take time, breathing.) Stop. *Show.* The doing without showing is mere experience. The showing is critical, what makes it theater. What makes it show (by *nothing* but breathing) is the radiance of inner conviction, the growing consciousness that it *must* be seen, what would make the word come even if there were no breath. The first dimension is the mantic heart.

For the theater has a passion for compulsive utterance. It completes itself in what might be better unspoken. Theater is a mystery for good reason. We see what should probably not be seen, that from which, really, we should turn away. What makes it so? Thinking makes it so. The intensity of the passion is a function of that. One wonders what keeps us there, on the edge of a breath, looking, the desire to be looked at? the nature of the compulsion, the watchers and the watched. "The players cannot keep counsel," says Hamlet, "they'll tell all." Hamlet warns them not to "o'erstep the modesty of nature," though it's certainly clear that he can't follow his own advice. If the great performance is a full confession, it is also a critical act, exegetical, as we can see from the commentary on the play-within-the-play:

OPHELIA: Will 'a tell us what this show meant?
HAMLET: Ay, or any show that you'll show him. Be not you ashamed to show, he'll not be ashamed to tell you what it means.

That doesn't mean he knows what it means. The plot having fallen apart, and the character dispersed into thought, the play-within-the-play has become, reflexively, the nuclear image of all theater. The essential act is the watching. Not only the mirroring, but being-as-mirrored, with the nucleus splitting. However that may be, the idea of theater developing in our work is derived from this model. It is a matter of following through the implications, and insinuations, of our most self-conscious drama—from *Hamlet* through Pirandello and Genet—which has virtually been predicting its own disintegration. The kind of theater we have been thinking about, with the subject always receding, moves inevitably (if confoundingly) on as fine a line as this, having to do with *the substance of seeing:* Light proceeds from the eye like ideas from the mind. Reflected. Both are compounded of, what? aether? the most weightless of material things. When we think about it, the light fades and the mind sinks. Stop. Think. The weight of the world *out there,* its sinking gravity—that's what frightens and disheartens, time running out in all directions. We look for meaning, and all the evidence in the universe is merely circumstantial, and circumscribed by the others, also looking. So we close ourselves out before the terrific uncontainability of things, precisely because they *are* all there, or seem to be, too much, always less than we know, more than we are, not quite equal to what we see for all the showing, heaving up a profound emptiness. Is that the condition of seeing? The mirror, like nature, blanks. Lights, lights!

I am describing the epistemological basis of a process which we're trying to show in the theater, along with the psychic consequences, restoring it to meaning through the most disheartening aspect of it. For the theater is not so much concerned with an empty space (in Brook's sense), but with an empty solitude, striving to explain itself away. There is a social grounding to the apparent solipsism of these ruminations in our collective work. In recent years, as the body politic grieves for want of consoling purpose, we have been searching for the last exemplary models of community. We forget, however, the ambivalence which may always have been the strongest motive in the gathering for performance. We are lonely and do not want to be alone; not being alone, we are lonely. There is the inconsolable body in its divisions, refusing ultimately to be consoled. Isn't that what the theater reflects, when most deeply gathered into itself? It is the motive that lies behind the most expansive forms of theater we have ever known (though we have never really known them). Look at the plays, see what they show. Aeschylus, for example, when we remember beginnings, who preserves the model of the great Panathenaic Festival as a mote in the Watchman's eye: at one end of his career the embattled City ("pity the host") in the figure of the defeated enemy; at the other Prometheus nailed to the rock: "This is the world's limit we have come to; this is the Scythian country, an untrodden desolation." Sometimes the poetic justice in what history chooses to remember confirms our worst fears about a place in history. Aeschylus was in Sicily when he wrote *Prometheus Bound.* We shall never know what he was doing there, far from the Athens he loved, nor why his last tragedy was written in what may have been exile, nor why and how he died; no more than we shall know why Shakespeare gave up the theater and withdrew to Stratford, the clue of the coat-of-arms being somewhat less memorable than Prospero's broken staff.

The world, the work . . . if what we choose to do in the theater also reflects what we remember of theater, that model of the world, there are some things in the theater that we can only *remember,* making an issue of it in the work. The forms represented at the City Dionysia or at the Globe are no longer available to us; we have seen no evidence of it in my lifetime. Whatever the gathering was, it no longer is. Even the remnants in other cultures—as if to spite our theater's new ethnological curiosity—are now suffering from the disintegrative encroachments of a postindustrial world. Everywhere, the aboriginal dance of the bones is coming out of the bush. If the old forms of theater are preserved, in the halfhearted protection of national treasures, it will very likely be as museum pieces, for tourists. As the jets come and go in the "underdeveloped" countries, what's happening in Bali seems to be the equivalent of what's happening in Britain, and what we periodically despair of at the Comedié Francaise, that museum, where loneliness has always been in the center of the stage—though all society sweeps around and applauds it, with snuffbox, cashbox, or broken heart. As we think, in the foyer there, looking at Molière's chair, of the paradox of the gathering—what it is that we come to witness or celebrate—we may also remember, as I do here, that Molière himself died (betrayed?) "strangled," according to one account, "by the copious outpouring of blood from his mouth" after being seized onstage (was it in that chair?) by a convulsion, which he covered with "forced laughter." That he was, like Hamm? (about whom we can't be sure), playing the Imaginary Invalid seems almost too good a story. "Don't be scared," he is said to have said to Baron, the great actor whom he'd nurtured like a son (though Baron may also have been one of his wife's lovers), "you've seen me spew out much more than that." Though he died in the arms of two nuns, they were strangers—and he may have been buried in an unconsecrated grave.

> Empty? I saw it was empty. I was full.
> I saw the same.
> I saw the unseen good old man falling.
>
> . . . .
> I saw the smooth body in the blossoms of sin.
> Then saw you not his face?
>
> . . . .
> I saw a woman eating that man.
> I saw the earth without form and void.
> I saw something to be told for the telling of which we all wait.

Old human life, new human life, fancied human life, avid, I saw.
I saw footsteps in the garden.
I saw we are explainable and not explained.
I saw we will leave the emptiness an emptiness.
I saw we will go on craving.

These are portions of a long tape going in and out of hearing, back and forth in time, in and out of the source and through the stored memory of *Elsinore*, a work we derived from *Hamlet*, whose memory system is not confined to that text. So far as I can remember, we never thought of Molière while we were doing that work, but in retrospect he seems subliminally there, like the thought of theater, which is seeing what we saw. *Elsinore* is a self-reflexive work which circumnavigates an empty space. The actors, hearing their own voices, gather again and again and finally in the bewildered circle of a collective identity that is betrayed, forgotten, and fallen apart—with a sharpening of the craving for the fullness of that space. It can never be explained, but we must explain it.

Much of what we do (taking life from the thing that gives life as it is) is a means of learning to live with the necessity of the aloneness, sufficient unto it. Even the forms by which we show are composed of the *insufficiency*. Let me explain, by maybe complicating the subject. I mean by subject the solitary self whose nature is insufficient, like the solitude which listens to itself. Here we move with a kind of deliberate slippage of thought into the precise but indefinable intimations of *otherness* that we experience in, say, Shakespeare's sonnets, where "insufficiency our hearts doth sway." We also composed, some time after *Elsinore*, "a theatrical essay" on the sonnets called *Crooked Eclipses*, the title suggesting the disjunct realities with which we were dealing, the strategy of their exposure through performance, and the problem of perception at the indeterminate center of the work. It is perhaps the major problem of contemporary thought: not only what we're seeing but how we see it, and how—according to the principle of indeterminacy—*the seeing changes what it is*. Of nothing can that be more rigorously said than of whatever it is we call the self. If its voice goes in and out of hearing, that's because the self was—as we've seen in the line of thought from Nietzsche to Derrida—a linguistic problem to begin with; the moment, drawing breath between word and word, we try to identify it, and something disappears.

What we are left with is a *specific* grammatical vagueness which, nevertheless, transcribes a disconcerting break in the apparent continuity of being. Shakespeare gives us, in perhaps his worst pun, "when first your eye I eyed," a parodistic version of what is called the "shifter" in linguistics, the sign which acquires a slippery signified only because it is "empty" (the referent not quite there), so that we're obliged in naming the first person with that pronoun, or any person with any pronoun for that matter, to hedge the identification: not that, *this*; not this, *that*, though this and that are also shifters. The pronominal *I*, however, that designation of a self, is the shiftiest one of all. Our language preserves, in its errancies, that state of being, no matter how well we master its syntax. The intrinsic emptiness of the shifter tells us what we are. ("Not merely is the first person singular detestable:" writes Lévi-Strauss in *Tristes Tropiques*, "there is no room for it between 'ourselves' and 'nothing.' ") Every gesture of the body, its mere presence, caught up as it is in this shiftiness of language (even when the words are unspoken), is an insinuation on the features of time that is already out of mind.

If the theater models the world and the world is a shadow of theater, it is language which models them both. The self, we hear, is a construct of language, not an entity but an *appearance*. In our work, we turn the subject over and over. It is the mirroring of language, world and theater in the refractions of the performing self, a subject slipping away (but getting a lot of attention from the "human sciences"), that we tried to encipher in the (dis)articulations of *Crooked Eclipses*. I shall say more about our acting methods later, and specific qualities of performance, but in *Crooked Eclipses* the actors do not relate to each other as in a conventional play, or even an unconventional play where, in the dispersal of character, the emphasis is still on the priority of acting egos in their relationships to each other. The work subverts the normal dialogical character of interpretation. The actor does not concentrate on the other person but rather *looks* with the other person at the *subject matter*—which is, in its reflexive dimension, the insufficiency of the autonomous subject, the vanishing enterprise of the self as a contingency of language.

The crooked eclipses are seen by nothing but flashlight. In one, at the start, a solitary actor—"contracted to [his] own bright eye"—is caught up in a solitude of mirrors in the plenitude of an empty space. He is virtually gasped into focus by the other actors, there between word and breath, but otherwise invisible. Light moves over the emptiness as if thought (we see the actor, we hear the words):

> Ah, yet doth beauty, like a dial hand,
> Steal from his figure, and no pace perceived;
> So your sweet hue, which methinks still doth stand,
> Hath motion, and mine eye may be deceived. . . .

We are practiced in the eye's deception. The actor is eclipsed in the reflection, then reappears, something stolen in the figure. In the play of

Take Up the Bodies

mirrors (held in the dark by the other actors, who are also mirrors), the image is given back to the shadows behind the light, from which the image is a projection. The actors lighting with the flashlights are always "expressing" through the light the emotions of the actor(s) performing. There is a very precise continuity of emotion out of light into darkness and back, no reference plot, no character, but a common vision of the stealing motion, as if there were one emotion which, traced to any one actor, appears to be discontinuous, even unmotivated. As the structure develops, the actor is displaced by others, with their own reflective antecedents of repressed or exposed thought. What we are after is the conceiving process in the structure, what I called earlier the spoor of association, the moment of Appropriation when what is figured in the words is apprehended in the space. It is a process of *presencings* and mediations in order to grasp the elusive subject, a collaborative act of understanding.

Theoretically—since each is an image of the other, projected into space—the light could come up on anybody at any time; they are all to be at the same pitch of *enactable thought*. The center of energy is the darkness between. The play within the play, featured in darkness, is articulated by the flashes of light. The presence of the solitary actor is a predicate at the slipping edge of consciousness, as substantial as a finger on the button. (The flashlights are the actuating mechanism of the performance not only externally, in the play of light, but also internally, up the arm which holds one into body and mind. If you hold one and compel thus the play of an imagined scene, to which you're privy but excluded, you'll have some sense of how, involuntarily and voyeuristically, the hand squeezes the tube and emotion accrues in the observer, like an inexpressible desire *to* perform:) Not that, *this;* not this, *that.* Like the metonymic moments of a self. At the margins of thought, an emperiled existence, doubled back—concentrated like empathy at the manipulable thumb. *Watch.* When the light shifts, and an actor who held a flashlight is revealed, the emotional intensity is ("no pace perceived") at another level of being than was apparent in *that* actor when last seen, by an almost geometric leap. If you don't watch, or refuse thought—expecting other continuities (narrative, a role, a psychological fix)—you won't even know how it got there. Such, as we say, is life. We can hardly believe it. The intricacy of the syntax is such—as with the emptiness of the shifter or the substance of the quatrain above—you may have to look a second time.

Still (that crucial word), the eye may be deceived. The nature of the performance is an occultation. The *unmotivatedness* is a precise symptom of the elusive subject. The term is used by Jacques Derrida, the

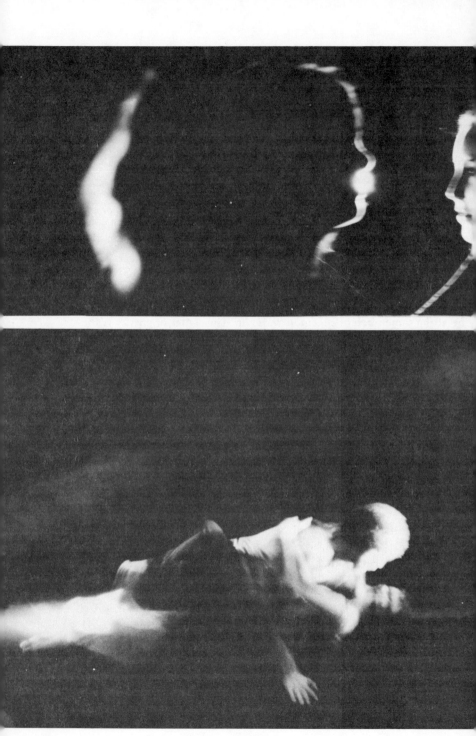

. . . a common vision of the stealing motion, as if there were one emotion . . .

philosopher of "deconstruction." This is a theory of literature which, in refusing any concept of embodied meaning to the presence of words, denies the autonomy of any single textual source. Although as theory it has the liability of its virtue, which is theatricality itself, deconstruction helps to explain, if not entirely justify, the revisionist practice of much recent theater. (In the first chapter, I spoke of the performative obsessions of the last generation. When the theatricalism of the sixties subsided in political life, one of the subtler things that happened to it, another form of going underground, was that it was—in the human sciences, philosophy, and literature—recycled or [re]sublimated *as theory*. What I am describing in our work we discovered through the work, but it might also be described by such theory. As I shall explain, however, we struggled against a tendency which, in deconstructionist practice, is supposed to be playful but now seems doctrinaire—and that is a gratuitous subversion of meaning.) In his critique of western metaphysics, Derrida speaks of a world of signs ordered hierarchically by an Oedipal Father. It is a coded world. Any movement of thought is merely another cipher of "the instituted trace," the semblance of an origin which is institutionalized by language. In a parricidal effort to abolish the idea of origin from thought, Derrida warns that this trace has (like love in the sonnets) "no 'natural attachment' to the signified within reality" (no identity, no objective reference or enclosure of meaning, no name). The absence of origin, or phallocentric source, puts *"in question the idea of naturalness* rather than that of attachment. . . ." In the language of deconstruction, truth is *undecidable*, for there is nothing to refer it to, only more language. The attachment is to the structuration of thought.

The same might be said of naturalness in acting. It has no decisive referent either. Not "life," not "experience," certainly not "Nature"—and, after Hamlet and Pirandello, neither the Author nor an authoritative "text"; and only the merest fiction of "character." What we take to be natural, then, is a matter of *mediations*. Which is the method of *Crooked Eclipses*. The performance is a spectrum of shifting behaviors whose attachment is to the structure. The structure is an act of collective perception, also shifting. The watcher lit, what we see in reality is (what actors are normally taught to avoid) an "unsupported" emotion—embodied sign of the insupportable in experience—whose path moves not through the (false) continuity of a "role" but from actor to actor (there are no roles, only actors) in *a constellation of prospective meanings*. All of what is seen is but mere trace, trace of an entity *becoming*, in love (and not really that either, since these are actors acting), gratuitous or ungrounded. The theatrical "thing" seen is a moving field of interdependent presences, not a series of psychologized behaviors in a frame of drama. In the disjunct light, behavior is ruptured, reflexively looped, *abstracted* (in a double sense); not-there, or too much so; stealing from the figure or, no sooner seen, still, stolen away.

I will return to *Crooked Eclipses* in another context. The sonnets were obviously not written to be staged, but it was the desire to embody meaning in the presence of words that caused us to try. I have always read them, moreover, as a virtual manual of theater craft, an ontology of theater. They suggest, in poem after poem, that the deepest seizure of theater is an evacuation of meaning. Or, as theater is a time-serving form ("the waste blanks" of time), an imprint of meaning upon emptiness. In the beginning, where there might have been a Word, there is now, as in *Hamlet*, only suspicion. "The air bites shrewdly," but it's made of words. As the words keep the play from being exactly the thing, the merest *seeming* appears to be the genesis. Seeming is seminal. Psychosexual. In theater as in love, the subject is disappearance. That makes, in performance, for a sort of doubled jeopardy. Performance, to begin with, is always under suspicion. The lover knows by heart that it's a matter of credibility. Or paranoia, where the delirium of appearance covers up for stage fright. "What, has this thing appeared again tonight?" If it doesn't, the play is obviously in trouble. And if it does, can we really believe it? If we ask too many questions the subject is likely to disappear, like the dream of love, into the questions, so that the questioner is left with the dreaming. And the fear that it might be theater. Thus, as in *Elsinore*, there is the interpretative problem known as the hermeneutical circle:

We judge the credibility of appearance by referring it back to life. As a standard of the credible that seems, as I've suggested, another delirium, taking its cues from the theater—with all the indeterminacies of illusion and resistances to illusion, including the illusions in the resistance. In the figural play of thought, theater is second nature. The very thing which appears to *in*validate the form also appears to give witness to something "beyond" it or "behind" it . . . but what *is* it? As the voice used to say about the Shadow, only the Shadow knows—but we're not so sure about the Ghost. "Is this not something more than fantasy?" As soon as you think about the theater, you return to the question. Between the conception and the event falls the Shadow, which is the matter of origins, suspended in appearance. For the Ghost is the thing which is only a trace, *the origin of the memory from which it appears,* a shadow's shadow. All we have (as with everything in the theater) is the evidence before us, the *ap-parency,* neither a father nor a ghost but an armored pathos, visor up—face of a sign sign of a face, the

Take Up the Bodies

image of a ghost claiming to be the Father, which is why we have trouble believing it or knowing where it came from, or how, by what forbidding power, *that* thing, which compels its disappearance.

The Ghost is the thing which is not-a-thing, like the trace in the unconscious which, as Freud conceives it, cannot return *as such,* but only as a *prospect,* precipitous, scarred, scary, and circuitous—yet something desired, *preferential,* as if chosen by memory from what it wishes to forget. The paradoxes are dazzling and haunt our memory, as the power behind the Ghost possessed our work and will haunt the rest of this book. The Ghost is the stimulus of an enigma arising from the infrastructure of theater which seems to limit the revelation of its illusory power. "I could a tale unfold. . . ." But the tale is still unfolding through the dubious play of words or, still, historically, in the illusions of silence (an *abandonment* of words). It is an impossible prospect. What we hear in the unfolding is the echo of a will to power conscious of its own powerlessness—forbidden as it is "to tell the secrets of [its] prison house. . . ." (Is it merely a coincidence that Nietzsche later spoke of "the prison house of language"?) A believable ghost is a hopeless thing. Yet it is a model of theater within the theater, even when it doesn't seem to appear, or equivocally, as in the Closet—seen and not-seen.

The ontological problem is not only knowing who we are but where we are in the topography of illusion. We are drawn by its appearance (the illusion which won't *stay)* into the circuitousness of thought where there seems no meaning except appearance. It is as if some trickster in the universe were leaving a trail of riddles to indicate it is not a trick at all, our being here. Yet how can we be sure? All the data of existence—like the libidinal codes of the unconscious (the stuff of dreams)—is no more than a series of clues which can only be ghosted. This process of ghosting became our process. The circuitry of thought is mirrored in the muscles. The very body of thought is a deciphering. A performance, scored, is like reading the scars, or graffiti, on the body of a ghost. The work *looks* like that, an act of *speculation,* seeming the way it sees.

Sometimes, watching the actors warm up, in the ablutions of an exercise, you have an intuition of meaning. An actress is doing a backarch. You watch it in the mirrors around the room, remembering that the women curve to the ground with no effort at all, reaching out to it even with a single hand. In contrast, the men are rigid in the spine going back. (A phrase of the Ghost grieves for the loss: "All my smooth body.") It's harder for them to make the bridge. No sooner thought (though widely becoming thought), it is a banality of meaning. The making of a work is a wrestling with banality through the data, shifting hand-over-hand, wide-eyed, through the dreamwork of thought, summoning up the clues.

In everything we do, an insistence upon meaning. The structural *reflex* is to delay it, however, *draw it out*, look again, defer it, as in dream interpretation, measuring appearances in a perpetual scanning of images (like the dial hand of the sonnets over the waste blanks), exhausting all signs—say, the data of rehearsal—to *in*significance, until the prospect-of-meaning bursts through to its own exclusion. We are not content with mere sketchwork on a disappearing subject, the mere ontological status of the work, its *thisness* or *thatness*. The truth is we want the pronominal I to stand still, stop shifting, complete the goddam circle. This is not an objective, it is a passion. What's the matter? *Matter,* as they say in *Elsinore* (punning off the Mother's cue in the Closet)—from which, entropically, the meaning runs out. It's as if, having taken all meaning for our object, we are conceiving a structure which attempts to crush the fluency of meaning into a single identity with the force of a blooded abstraction. The work is dense, there's no denying. It solidifies itself against interpretation, but allows no respite to the act of interpretation. In short, it wants to *know*. That is the passion which becomes an objective—or what Stanislavski called a Superobjective—fusing subject and object. That's what moves us. That is the play-within-the-play-within, the Mousetrap. It cries out as if deceived by its own closed sysem: *I want it and I don't want it!* The being-of-meaning, that banality, is not enough. There is something insidious in the process. As Ithamore says in *The Jew of Malta*, "The meaning is in the meaning"—a basic intuition of advancing semiology, although of course Ithamore can't be trusted, a man who goes around poisoning wells.

It may seem from what I've said that what we're trapped by is, despite its elusiveness, one of the now staple themes of modern thought: the relativity of knowledge as an effect of consciousness. But in this appearance of a habit of mind is a crucial distinction in our work. We all know that meaning is relative. Relative to *what?* It's that simple question which structures our investigations, gallingly, with the abrasive energy of self-distrust, against the imminence—the most detestable illusion—of the self-evident. Of which there seems so much that (it sometimes feels) the only way to think about it is to think about it all at once. Which accounts for the impacted motion of a helical structure of thought. The damnable thing in the space of theater is having to move thought through time, which always leaves us with a "questionable shape. . . ." That's the vise of speculation. The attention

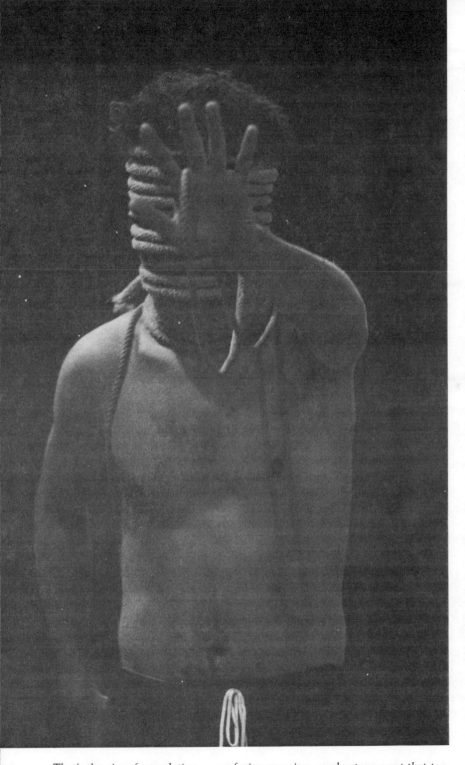

That's the vise of speculation . . . refusing meaning—*and yet we want that too.*

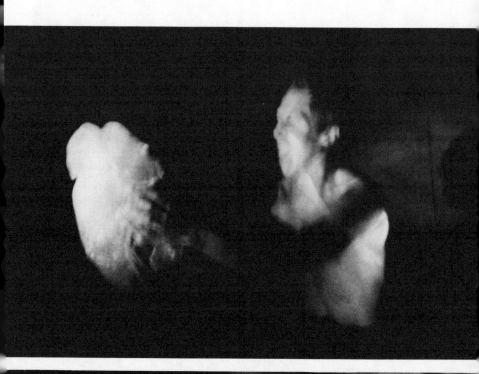

Maybe in the end we do get what we want, the opacity, some collision with the irreducibl

of perception is extremely concentrated, but there is that structural in-determinacy (in things? in theater? in perception?) which makes the very act of perceiving alter the nature of the thing perceived, refusing meaning—*and yet we want that too.* That doesn't mean we get what we want. The experience we are dealing with is not relativity of percep-tion, but the evidence of *opacity.*

"How do I know the universe is like this?" says the Tao. "By looking."

We look, and look again. There are two ways of progressing in art (by that I do not necessarily mean improving): one takes place within the dominant tendency of art history, a style, for instance, passed on; or a problem, as when space is refined by one artist and then another within the formal terms of a painting, with respect to the frame perhaps, or its absence. The problem may go through generations of successive investigation, with the space as a given, drawn and quartered. Or, as in the early gray paintings of Jasper Johns, the en-caustic scumbled surface may take the space away, denying its possibility. The painter's act is radical, but it occurs very consciously within the long dialogue of art history. Space is no longer credible within the frame, and thus the painterly annulment of the pictorial site. It might as well be turned to the wall, like the picture (? we never see) in Beckett's *Endgame,* which is also—frame, gray wall, play—a shifter. But in some painters, space is not only a problem to be solved, another notch in a conceptual task, but something to be *seen* in the actual world. Possessed by a real frog, Monet painted an imaginary garden with only the frame distinguishing it from the world. The medium became his way of quieting the ripples in the lily pond. Or—as we'd al-so feel it in Proust describing the same landscape—the demoralizing commotions of time. Technique seems rather to take back from the real world what it perceives there. We perceive the opacity.

If there is anything special in that, it is the absoluteness, the intensity of will, with which we try to penetrate it. All right: what's there is there. What we see in the mirror is the mirror. Maybe in the end we do get what we want, the opacity, some collision with the irreducible, the thing that takes life from the thing that gives life as it is—that history in the living eye which blurs in the trace of myth. Seeing is blind. Yeats: "Empty eyeballs knew/That knowledge increases unreality. . . ." As I think back over the most physically audacious images in our work, it is the desire behind the empty eyeballs which seems to dominate the scene, taking the breath away (literally) between word and word: as when Agamemnon in *Seeds of Atreus* walks in "the red act" over the royal carpet which blackens and rises like the Furies to entangle him; or the actors square dance like dazzled oxen into the canyon walls of *The*

Donner Party, Its Crossing; or the Hamletic figure in the long silent struggle of *Elsinore* throws himself in a rage against a figure of the Ghost and bounces off, stunned by the impermeable, the subject of desire; the figures rising and falling:

I saw: Will in the beginning.
I saw the soldiers shoot.
A cruel blow: I saw it lash out, bite, recoil.

As they fight, pursuing each other like the shadows of origins, the mind races *backward* through the remembered narrative of the source play, a reflexion of the text reflected—in which origins seem like Original Sin through ages of rising and falling form:

I saw them take up the bodies.
I saw them fight and one said, Well! I was born to fight.
I saw the King drink to Hamlet, a jewel I saw bleeding.
I saw them bleeding on all sides.
I saw hands and arms in the air.
I saw the King is a thing.
Is she dead? is she sleeping? I saw the Queen with her
    lion-red body, her wings of glass.
Where is this sight I saw?
I saw him comply with his dug before he sucked it.
The cup at her lips I saw, a hit, a palpable hit!
I saw each one by itself, one accusing, one defending, one
    separating these two.
I saw them wrapped in each other's arms.
I saw a man confused with the armor he wore. A ghostly hand
    pulls it off, the other holds it tight.
I saw a young man trying to know old flesh.
I saw nothing neither way.

Thus the tape starts. It continues through the fight and elsewhere in the performance as a kind of conceptual music, testing and displacing eye and ear, soliciting and "correcting" interpretations by the viewers (actors and audience), coming out the "front end" of Shakespeare's play with the relative speed of thought. There is an accelerating momentum of the reversed story into the sources behind the source, the Ur-*Hamlet,* the myth of the myth, as far (back?) as we can remember—where the mind blanks.

Sometimes the myth leads you back to the opaque social body. It seems even more intimidating, as in a figure of *Seeds of Atreus:* No physical activity, virtually pure concept, the actor (male) in a long blue gray sheath of a costume, on cothurni, a gun gray phallus, un-armed. The actor looks feminine. The figure is Athena. What we hear is her hard "advice into the future," the impeccable and abstract power of the

Sometimes the myth leads you back to the opaque social body.
Is any terror just? . . . We concluded with a vigil.

proposition, "not to cast fear utterly from your city." We are asked to accept those "just terrors" without which there can be no justice, no law and order, no governance. As we were finishing *Seeds of Atreus*, in early 1973, a truce had just been declared in Vietnam, but the war was hardly over, nor the disorderliness of the period. What did she mean by a *just* terror? We were confronting the use of punishment, the classical problem, the Freudian problem. Our rehearsals were taken over by arguments as to whether we could leave it at that. Is any terror just? Danton's problem. Is the social order, then, necessarily repressive, even cruel, reflecting some essential denial in the human order? And that other denial, in an emerging feminist context, what were we to make of it? I mean Apollo's defense: the male chauvinist mystery of the immaculate conception of Athena out of her father's skull, another enigma of origins, "born unnurtured in the dark of the womb"—and thereby denying mother-right.

When we were completing *Seeds of Atreus*, the illusions of liberation had far from subsided. To eliminate guilt and expel fear from the body politic was a therapeutic mission. 69 varieties of Dionysian ecstasy had been proclaimed through the land in innumerable versions of *The Bacchae*. It was a classical scholar revising Freud (Norman O. Brown) who had valorized Love's Body in those polymorphous perverse days. We had to deal with our own wishful thinking, but there was Pallas Athena's decree, implacable through time. So far as I could see into the future, her advice stood. We could no more argue away that cold intelligence than we could dismiss the power behind the specter of the Ghost, for which the Ghost seemed an oedipal decoy. As we looked back down the originary trace, what was the prospect? Was it possible in *Seeds of Atreus* to justify to ourselves anything like the celebration at the end of the source play, when the transfigured Furies are led with rejoicing to their hallowed precinct, where they would "sit in shining chairs beside the hearth"? Negotiation with the Furies seemed an absolute necessity; the celebration seemed—to me at least—shocking, insupportable, unreal. Some of the actors, however, younger than I, conditioned by the risen hopes of the period, argued vociferously for the celebration, regardless.

We concluded with a vigil. It was powerful. Nobody denied it, but not everybody among us was convinced. It wasn't really a conclusion, but it seemed (to me) inevitable, returning to the beginning, stonily, becoming the Watchman, *before* the end of the war in Troy. Actually, a truce had just been declared in Vietnam. But we knew it wasn't quite over. And if it was over, where were we? We had gone through a myth of the myth as far as thought could take us, but there was also history, imperturbable, and we were still looking for signs.

If we didn't suspect life for what it is—"Seeming, seeming" (*Measure for Measure*)—the theater wouldn't be what it is, the form that plays with our realities because we are fundamentally suspicious about their existence and meaning. We can play too much. And one of our problems with history at the moment is that we may be doing just that: in the absence of meaning a surfeit of play. In this matter we go at risk, the very perplexities beguiling. Thus, Nietzsche: "You have abolished the world: what world is left?" Nietzsche denies that it is the world of appearances—the true world gone, we have abolished the ground on which appearance stands. The snake in the garden is still the ground-root. He (it) is not what he seemed. (Or seems?) Beyond good and evil, he is simply there. Which is reason enough to keep a wary eye. What seems perfectly natural can be suspected on precisely those grounds. We don't trust it. (Nor those who, like Sri Ramakrishna, would have us embrace the snake.) Somebody once said paranoids have real enemies too. Who can be trusted? Real enemies have paranoia too.

It was on some such grounds of wary thought that, a few years ago, in reassessing method, we turned to Kafka's last story, *The Burrow*. It is a masterpiece of paranoia, maybe over the edge. We had been working at ground zero, we went below. Like the creature of the Burrow—not a character but a consciousness—we were possessed with technique. The story is a manual of craft. We constructed a series of exercises from it and around it, a provisional summing up. They remain in the repertoire of our method (about which we say all exercises are *one*), like a seminal madness.

The Burrow is the model of a work-in-progress. It is a perceptual space. It resembles Plato's Cave. Or the cellarage below the ramparts. It is as if we are back at the theater's inescapable substance, the interplay of reality and illusion, seeing and sounding, the beleaguered center of seeming, in-terminable. The creature of the Burrow is an artist, a master builder, subtle to a fault. In the deepest recesses of the Castle Keep, the creature is also vulnerable to a fault. The Burrow is a defense mechanism to outdo all defense mechanisms. Below the protective moss, in the maze (what is the moss? the creature has a beard, but is it male? the Burrow suggests a womb, is it pubic hair?), we study the sequestered shape of panic, its self-punishing creative force, the defenses pinioned on a murderous rage, the microstructure of institutional hatred and violence, what the theater as an institution seemed founded to appease.

In all the cunning corridors, below history, one feels the intelligence of the demonic. Give memory a chance, and it will try to forget. It is the power of theater—the incumbency of its technique—that it turns the mania into the memorable. ("Well said, old mole! Canst work in the earth so fast?") It insists on remembering, with a legacy of particularity. We come to the vastness of the Burrow through the circumference of the needle's eye. Inside, a quiet and harrowing mixture of consciousness and monstrosity. There is no-one there, only trails. The creature of the Burrow is like the actor who draws upon that part of the self which defines itself by an absence, torn by an awful dependency on an outside which is incessantly disavowed—in that very solipsism slipping away, hiding, disappearing into an absence, its lair, an unfinished illusion of a self.

"The world is all that is the case," says Wittgenstein, in the first proposition of the *Tractatus.* In the Burrow, nothing but case history. Nothing outside the case can be imagined, nor can the thing be imagined without its space. (According to the creature, "the place of disturbance" is located by "experimental excavations"—as with the archeology of Freud.) So, an exercise, putting the case:

The actor is there *(each one)* before the space. The space is there, but it must be carved out. The Burrow is not-there until it is constructed. Silence. The actor moves (or is moved?) into the space. The first step is a territorial imperative. One holds one's breath, breathes, a trying out. Think: not any step, but *that* step, the first trace upon emptiness, the exactitude, the subliminal terror of it, like the first drip or stroke of paint on a huge canvas—the lease of destiny. Now, the space is established—until the other moves *(each one).* The step might have been retracted like the first word x'd out on an empty page, but while the page can be torn up, nobody the wiser, the actor is out there, seen, the others there—the very pulse of thought is an observance, the flick of an eye; nor can the step really be retracted if you think. From any point of view, the structure extends, infinitely, breathing and being breathed, *in thought,* undeniably *there.* The structure is very simple, elemental, minimalist—but it is a power structure. Absolute. With ambiguities of control and domination. Look! something moves. An error in the construct! from someone's point of view *(each one).* The entire being of the actor is summoned in the process of becoming to keep the structure *as-it-was.* Don't move. Reflect. *Be* still. *But more than that. . . ?* What is exercised is the conception. Immaculate. The Burrow is built upon a fault. It is doomed to failure. Which is to say, it is doomed. Which is exactly what it is meant to be.

The basic form of the exercise is an incremental extension of the earlier meditation, through breathing, on the double play of mortality. Here, the consciousness is directed outward, in all its paranoia. Being in the Burrow is *being breathed.* The experience is something like the interiorization of the idea of destiny. The reductive intensity of the exercise, most alive at the edge of paralysis, is the paradigm for the more volatile structures of which the performed work actually consists. The Burrow is—to use Chomsky's term for the reflection of the nature of mind in our grammar—the "deep structure." What happens in the space—in the surface variations of the structure—may be more or less physical and more or less verbal, but exhaustion occurs at the level of the psyche. As with the creature of the story, it is a many-minded labor with an almost prohibitive attentiveness to detail. Outside the Burrow, we couldn't manage: the concentration, the fastidiousness of the follow-through (and the ambivalence), the body taking notice, old dead connections being made, sending and receiving signals (voluntary and involuntary), the stethoscopic listening, questions questions questions, the painstaking course of a particular, a clue, a fault, stirring memory and desire. The actual doing is a calculus of desire—for a "perfect" structure—point by point approaching the limit of the impossible from the zero with which we begin, *that* consciousness, there *before* the space, a carnal makeshift—the actors' bodies as "animal matter" from which the inexpressible shape of the creature emerges, *not-one*, the mental presence so palpable, the two fusing, that the animal gets lost in the corridors, in gray matter.

The Burrow is an autonomic system. Even when, as we elaborate the basic exercise, there is a complex verbal surface over the kinetic images, it is "pure" behavior we are after; between word and word, a kind of particle physics, the most rudimentary materials of theater: void space pulse cadence noise dark light breath motion systole diastole; stored memory, a critical network, through the nerves, the multiphasic shadow of consciousness, brainwaves, assuming the proportions of a great rough beast, as it seems to do in the story. The Burrow is a bloody mental construct, like a performance, an abstraction blooded. It is full of violence, repressed and released, crafted by illusion, designed to ward off evil, a cry coming up from the ground.

What ground? The Burrow is almost geometrically composed, but it is vegetal, cellular, ovular, spored. To stand, and unfold the self: an untenable task. I spoke of the actor stepping into the space, but he may step crawl roll back into it at will, or project himself there; no down, no up, and (in concept) gravity defied. The actor is not really sure, once the premises are accepted, through what element he moves or what figure is really there, as if a withdrawn mirror had left an unsteady reflection behind, all space refusing balance, as if the ground had been withdrawn and there were no ground at all and one's whole strength of being went into the labor of holding on, the physiological equivalent of that mode of energy in a void projected in the *concept* of Hamlet or

Danton ("What is it in me that denies me?"). We think it is the primary energy in the theater, and it acts now on behalf of the structure rather than toward a superobjective—though it may be, in the absence of the old basis of drama, a new ground for action, perhaps the major action which is left to enact, with a sense of the singular consciousness *as* a structure.

The structure is the means by which we think through acting about acting. In the Burrow we dwell, explicitly, upon one of the oldest dilemmas in the art of acting: the controversy over inside/outside (variant terms for surface/depth), which comes first? There is no outside (or bottom) of the Burrow even when it appears so, in the story, only the immanence of the bottoming out. In the exercise, the psychic definition of the space becomes, then, a practical issue, since it also involves a definition of the perimeters of a life. When the rehearsal ends, what then? Or, to what extent does it ever end? which further defines what it is that we're playing back. Where is the one—inside? outside?—who creates the creature who creates the Burrow? Mind/body? The bleeding of the creature, in Kafka's story, is through the forehead (a brilliant stroke). The Burrow is created with the brain. The cerebral activity is the Burrow, its very bowels. There is, for the sake of method, nothing else. In the Burrow, as in the body of a dream, cerebral is genital. To use the jargon of recent theater: psychophysical, psychosexual. So: an erotics of theater. The Burrow *is* the technique. We call our rehearsal method *burrowing* when we don't call it *ghosting*.

As a structure of investigation, the Burrow imposes the puritanical discipline of anointed paranoia. The value comes from staying rigorously with the elements: space duration rhythm distance scale, the reflexive monitoring of the indeterminacies of time and motion, an unremitting perceptual vigilance. There is in the concept of the Burrow, as I've implied, a terrible desire for a perfect achievement—and the immanent rage at any subversion of the conception. "Not quite in the center, carefully chosen. . . . the chief cell." I am reminded of Beckett's Hamm in a fury to be right in the center, perfect, a revenant: rooted in a place, rooted in the absence of a place, and the insistence on being there. Then, one of the primary issues of any acting technique: *Centering.* What *is* the center? for the actor? for the entire performance? again, approached as a limit, a matter of perception, not a given. The point is—*where?* The core of technique, elsewhere in Kafka: "Two tasks on the threshold of life: To narrow your circle more and more, and constantly to make certain that you have not hidden yourself outside of it." He says nothing about locating a center, only the narrowing down to it, like Stanislavski's circle of attention. The entire pressure of performance is, however, toward the center, the truth hid there, exempt from seeing—the impossibility of it.

For, as metaphysics comes in through the pores (Artaud), betrayal oozes out (Freud) with every breath. The energy comes from the secretion. The mastered intimacy of craft is a vast exposure. All the defensive precautions of the creature are projected outward, but inwardly inflicted. Self-sealed, solitary, secret, the actor confronts his paradox. Suddenly, there is the rustling of another creature, there, "which is immediately reduced to silence between my jaws. . . ." I tell the actor, work on this animal. He is beside himself with the impossibility. Not one but several! There is splitting and substitution, more than several; as Clov says, "a multitude." The Other is there and the others are encroaching, the threat of otherness: You mean I am not self-contained? whole unto myself? nothing but a substance contingent on a relation? *What relation?* How many? Unsexed? As the actors say in *Elsinore* across the empty circle at the breathless end of an ensemble agon whose structure is indebted to the Burrow: "What is the matter, my lord?" "Between who?"

Doubt we can live with, but opacity drives us crazy. Doubt has expectancies. Things may clear up. But there is no peaceful coexistence in the Burrow, because we're never sure who is existing with whom. There is the abyss between subject and object which, in the play of language (and its failings), is the entire subject. In the endurance of that reality, the illusions of the Burrow are indecipherable from those of the theater. Inside/outside, surface/depth—it is all appearance. The perfect structure must be made from that.

The methodology for constructing the Burrow incorporates the most basic concerns of the actor: concentration, focus, circle of attention, public solitude, emotional recall, units and objectives, task-activity, a memory bank, otherness, doubleness, duration and endurance, the self as source, and that which compulsively expands the circle—in the equal and opposite necessity to drawing it in—fantasy projection. The energizing principle of the Burrow is the flow of an absence, negations within negations, like the illusion of reversing wheels on a strip of film. The fanaticism of the process is a perceptual delicacy, like grasping the sparrow's tail in the Tai Chi Ch'uan. The structure of the Burrow, like those meditative and kinesthetic forms, is a system of endless closed variants, sensory perceptions glossing themselves by turning back, a ceaseless rehearsal—achieving or lapsing, by its over and overing, into a state of clairvoyance.

To the degree we draw upon it as an acting method—or rather, as the method is drawn into the structure—it is with the intention of releasing into consciousness the contents of the unconscious, like the creature of the Burrow seeing "the spectres of the night in all the helplessness and blind trust of my sleep, but also to confront them in reality at the same time with the calm judgment of one who is fully awake." It is at this level that the awesome silence of the burrowing becomes sound and, as in dream interpretation, becomes language. The consciousness of the actor, ideally, is like a chambered nautilus, in which (to begin) only the rhythms of the self are heard, heartbeat and metabolism, the sound of the listener's own sense listening to the other's sense. The protective corridors are also access routes. They resemble, in strangeness, the structure of the ear, vestibular, a labyrinth. The lifeline is the language out of the murmur of silence, the word within a word, unspeakable. (Yet I shall try to speak about it in subsequent chapters.) Abstracted or liberated from building a character, these basics of acting are the elements of a theater event. The technique becomes the thing itself, without giving itself over to mere improvisational process. The form is as absolute as we can make it. We are paranoid about that. The burrowing is a strenuous discipline—a mental act performed by a carniverous animal. It is obsessed, like the actor, with the perfect leaving of a trail that offers no evidence of itself —yet leads, infallibly, nowhere else.

The structure of a performance is the moving inscription of its method. The method has its own history, which is a premonition of performance; in our own case, the staging is skeptical of its own stages. One moment interrogates another, as each work does. The idea of burrowing had actually been anticipated by the long study (nine months) we did in the early seventies on the trace of *The Enemy*. There was more than a trace of personal history in that, stemming, I suppose, from the experience at Lincoln Center. I was not conscious of it at the time, but the paranoia of New York must have drained through some quick circuitous vent into our exercises. *The Burrow* was a culmination.

When we were first psyching out *The Enemy*, the group was in residence at Oberlin, in Ohio, the landscape as flat as a *tabula rasa*. We came there after more than a year's training—averaging six to eight hours a day behind closed doors—at California Institute of the Arts, which I helped to conceive and launch, and then left in another controversy. Out there, the Enemy appeared to be the Disney Family. The institute had been, along with "the Florida project" (Disney World) and a futuristic city, one of "Walt's dreams." An elegant lady, one of the members of that Board, first told me of these dreams. We were at a party in my honor in Walt's office. I believe it was the first time it had been used since he died. The room was preserved at the Disney Studio like the (alleged) death room of the original Rockefeller in his domain.

Take Up the Bodies

While there was something more outwardly wholesome about the Disney tradition and the Family, rumor was that Walt was on ice for eventual resurrection (by some elixir, perhaps, of recombinant DNA). Chairman of the Board—before he went off to the campaign that would bring Richard Nixon to the White House—was H. R. Haldeman. A certain aspect of that campaign was something of a Disney production. It was helped along by Disney money, and some of the Disney PR—USC, Quaker, Christian Scientist—went along with Haldeman to Watergate. It was Haldeman, however, who shepherded through my appointment, after a letter came down from another Board member in San Francisco who warned them that I was "controversial." The lady, in her sixties and in perfect trim, practiced Yoga and was an occultist. She wouldn't confirm the rumor about his being iced, but she did have conversations with Walt. She was quite wealthy. Her father was the discoverer of natural gas. Her husband was a reactionary to the far right of Reagan, but she was one of the subtlest women I've ever met. You could trust her. Los Angeles is a stranger place than New York.

As an American cultural phenomenon, Cal Arts was a sociologist's dream—the daring anomaly of it, in that setting, with those sponsors, and the hip crowd of artists, intellectuals, Happeners, gurus, freaks, and guerillas that came from all over the country to occupy the weird possibility. For all that, and because of it, Cal Arts was the most promising conception for training in the arts that the country has ever known, saving Black Mountain perhaps, which was a model but on a smaller scale. In conception and during its start-up period, Cal Arts was a way-out mixed-media psychedelic Bauhaus (although it occurred to me only afterwards that among the meanings of *Bau*—the word Kafka actually used—is Burrow).

You drive to Valencia, a "new town," over the hills above the San Fernando Valley. The complex of Cal Arts is an escalated pink brick air-conditioned megalith over a freeway running through the canyons. Leo Carillo and Gene Autry had ranches in the area, where they still shoot an occasional western and you can still see an occasional rattler. Valencia was dreamed up by the real estate developers to receive the urban sprawl which *is* Los Angeles. Walt's dream of a great "community of the arts" was to be incorporated in the totalizing environment, and we had our own postmodernist fantasies of artist studios in the shopping malls. The environment is a little unsteady, since it is situated on the San Andreas Fault near Palmdale, where they built the piggyback bombers—a city with a self-image as an experimental disaster area, which the residents took as calmly as gunfighting at the OK Corral. Some who came to Cal Arts, however, were not so calm and suffered in the continental tilt from the rather widespread phobia about California breaking into the sea. There were a lot of jokes of the kind that Freud records in his essay on wit and the unconscious.

Indeed, there was an earthquake shortly after the opening in temporary quarters at the Villa Cabrini—an ex-Catholic-girls-school in an olive orchard near beautiful downtown Burbank. Where the nuns once prayed, the nude swimmers "co-counseled," faculty and students together. It is easy to stress the eccentricities, and there was a good deal of plain junk. The attractive thing about the eccentricities is that they were often amusing and inventive. Moreover, a good deal of thought had gone into the sometimes carnival-like atmosphere of Cal Arts, including what artists think about, how and where, and what if anything they should study other than art. The dominant theory was the obvious one that most schools ignore, that knowledge comes into the arts in unpredictable ways from unfathomable sources, and you had to allow maximally for that. Some of what was taught at Cal Arts was unfathomable. It would have sent most conventional academics up the wall, but it was the best situation for learning I have ever known. If you had the stamina, the learning could be nonstop. While some things were not "taught" at all, counting on living as learning, some of the more disciplined study was in very exotic subjects. There were Marxist-Leninist seminars along with courses on Cannabis Myths and Folklore, and Chinese Sutra Meditation—the urgency of History in a prelapsarian state. A concert might consist of South Indian ragas and Tib drumming, along with serial music and Bach toccatas, the world's "musics" gathered as in a jam session. The idea of the Free University, a dubious fringe benefit on a straight campus, was second nature to the curriculum at Cal Arts. The emphasis was on *Critical* Studies (one of the six Schools), more or less analytical, but theoretically what needed to be thought about, because of the social and historical crisis—whose locus was then the Vietnam War. There was, naturally, a School of Film, and the entire place seemed at times like a video feedback environment.

They were designing bionics for underdeveloped countries at Cal Arts before it showed up on television in the slick million-dollar varieties. They were also ripping off thousands of dollars of equipment and throwing television sets out the windows as a form of Conceptual Art. The student body was an activist body politic that had, after all, grown up in the generation of Affluence and Abundance, where you simply broke the toy if you didn't like it and expected your unreproving parents, brainwashed into permissiveness, to provide another. The ethic was refined at Cal Arts by the leftist participatory notion of common property: what's everybody's is mine. There were all kinds of ironies and absurdities, and sobering exceptions to the far-out rule. There was straightforward humanistic thought by first-rate academics, and superb instrumentalists were performing those Bach toccatas. The tabla players and the Tib drummers were masters, and so were those who taught composition on the digital and analogue equipment in the electronic music studio. There was also innovation mixing art and politics, as if on Nam June Paik's video synthesizer, which was also developed there. Womanhouse was conceived at Cal Arts as a purgative collective fantasy within the *Fantasia*. Situated in downtown Los Angeles, across from MacArthur Park, it became a model for feminist enclaves elsewhere. The Modular Theater, which I designed with Jules Fisher, is one of the more audacious theaters in the world and can more or less do what they couldn't do at the Pentagon— achieve levitation.

When, however, the quake did occur, and an unfinished section of the freeway curving spectacularly into the hills below Valencia tumbled to the shaky ground (better than in the movie), maybe we should have realized that something was wobbly in "the Concept." At the Villa Cabrini we lost a couple of buildings in the quake, but the guerrilla artists went on excavating the orchard (which still belonged to the nuns) and the weirdos kept smoking dope or passing out Genderfuck (though the Burbank police sent over helicopters for surveillance). The painters and sculptors who were displaced by the quake went over to studios set up in a warehouse rented from Lockheed. The fact of its being empty didn't register, but Lockheed was wobbly too. Layoffs in the aircraft industry began shortly after, and several years later there was the scandal needing government subsidy for Lockheed that reached over to Prince Bernhard and the Dutch government. In 1969, ten days after Richard Nixon took his oath of office, an oil rig spilled off Santa Barbara and a controversy was developing over spoilage of the Florida Everglades by Disney World. Meanwhile, around Valencia, the bulldozers were still bevelling the landscape for intermedial split-level junkfood living, and the stuff coming over the mountains from Los Angeles was not what Sir Francis Drake saw like an overhanging fog when he first sailed along the coast. The pollution was filtering into the canyons and would eventually do in those snakes. We would be done in, however, by another kind of infiltration, though we tried to keep our eyes open.

In the atmosphere of the late sixties, Cal Arts was quickly radicalized. In that unlikely crucible of unorthodox art and activist politics underwritten by right-wing money, there suddenly appeared to be enemies all around, far Right and far Left. It was the Left that engineered the final confrontations that led to my going in their defense. The Disneys had been bewildered and often repelled by what they heard was happening. They were also amused, even proud, recognized it as extraordinary, and tried at first to keep hands off. For some of those on the Left that wasn't satisfactory. For them, Cal Arts was the last desperate effort to believe in an institutional possibility which existed for the people in it, and was governed by them (no matter who put up the money, *that* ripoff), before taking to the hills, to hard drugs, or to the underground. They developed their own Doctrine of Credibility. In order to test out the political reality of the scene, they practiced a post-Dulles brinkmanship, upping the ante on dissidence, with the Disneys as sitting ducks, and the moderates as buffers. Some of *them* you couldn't trust. Some people, perfectly reliable otherwise, should be spared by the mercies of time from anything like crisis. Ethical memory is short, will shorter. It was another impossible situation, in which it was hard to know finally if you could even trust yourself.

Yet, impossible as it was, it had given me the laboratory in which to take up the problem of training that I had left behind in San Francisco and speculated on, with cloven heel, in New York. I was so immersed in the work that it continued even through much of the controversy which, this time, was almost entirely political. Tested, the Disneys became what the Disneys are. They can be lethal. It runs in the Family, as labor organizers learned in the union-busting days of the silver screen. Because the theater work was so rich with potential, I didn't want to go and might have stayed, but the political impasse was such—and by that time, the lies, even among friends—that I went. In Oberlin, the training process which was already intense was totally concentrated. In that isolation—nothing in Oberlin but Oberlin—there was no distraction from the work.

We started again through a regimen of exercises: associative and reflective, structural, ideographic, physically charged, always verbal—and including the beginnings of a vocal sequence constructed like a performance. I wanted to ingrain the idea of performance *in* the method, rather than propose it as an outcome. But what, first, was the grain of performance? During the period between Lincoln Center and KRAKEN, my mind had been impatient with everything I already knew, and it was drawn to the ethic of *deconditioning*, as in the martial arts and the spiritual disciplines. So, when we started, we started all over again. That, too, became something of an ethic: an instinct for ground zero, as in the breathing exercise I have already described, or the construct of the Burrow. What was already known might be known deeper, but there was an internal need, recurring, for a systematic forgetting.

We worked back to the known by a kind of estrangement, taking nothing for granted: uses of the body, what the voice can do, occupying a space in an endurance of time. We explored forms of memory and degrees of behavior, from the unmediated self (and is it a fiction?) to the idea of character (which became a field of inquiry). The acting graded itself away from the center in the actor (another fiction?) through a spectrum of behavioral possibility like a palette: person self role actor persona character mask double and shadow. We did exercises on types of imagination: auditory, visual, tactile; materialization and disappearance; not only subtexts but fantasy texts and collective fantasies, systems of association. We experimented with a series of improvisational techniques, moored to character or utterly dispossessed, from the purely plastic to the ideographic—throwing the stress this way or that way, upon the continuity of the "inner life" or the contingency of "outer circumstances." Stanislavski used those terms in "building a character," but we were thinking through inflexions of the mimetic, articulating the expressive differences between representational and gratuitous play, as if they were (as they are) keys to identity.

Sometimes the body was the book, or in the beginning was the word: we were verbal and non-verbal, through stages of identity, or stagings of identity, from the undifferentiated OM to the pronominal I of the ego-powered I AM, with self-registering doubt as the wellspring of metamorphosis. We were interested in the *principle* of metamorphosis—rather than, like the Open Theater, transformations of roles—as it released residues, impregnations, and latencies from the unconscious. While I personally distrusted all quick intimacies with archaic forms of thought, we developed exercises based on the desire for lost realms of experience and possibilities of belief, lost words and, therefore, powers—reimagining the self, for instance, as Thrones, Dominations, Principalities, and Powers. We did a series of exercises on figures of origin and evolution—and among the metamorphoses were those of Fire, Air, Earth, and Water. But nothing came up more instinctively in the encouraged skepticism of the actors than the deflation of an archetypal posturing. "The world is in the bonds of action," says the *Bhagavad-Gita*, "unless the action is consecration." In an unconsecrated world, and with severely limited powers, we tried to nurture a discipline that would understand what consecration meant. So if, as we did, we came across a fragment attributed to Aeschylus in which someone cries out on seeing Dionysus: "Where have you come from, man-woman? What is your country? What is your garment?"—that would not so much send us dancing back into rituals from which we were irretrievably cut off, but rather into exercises where we would think—with all the intensity of a bad dream—through the division of the sexes as that primal division in the self which has put us at a loss for origins. We looked about in other disciplines (as everybody was doing then) for techniques of "re-integration," but it was the errors and illusions of dissociation that clung to us like the poisoned garment of the centaur. In their desperation the exercises were a means of throwing it off. But it was a killing garment, from the theater's oldest consecrated ground.

I have already pointed out the etymological union of theater and theory, and I wanted to carry that essential insight through at the level of acting method, theater being the means by which we theorize. Sometimes, however, the theory seemed purely technical, like, what is the visual equivalent of perfect pitch? But the acquisition of a technique is an act of discovery, which may at times feel like an aberration. We remember, for instance, that people with brain damage may have photographic memories. In a sense, the development of a technique may systematize the damage, turning it into theory. To repair division, the methodology im-pairs. There were other powers (or, as in *The Burrow*, powers of the Other) we wanted to restore. We know that children have a capacity for eidetic imagery that we lose as adults, possibly as a condition of socialization—for otherwise we'd be in a blur between something like a dream vision and conscious reality. How could we approach that state, not by cancelling consciousness but by increasing it? "I too have made a mouth of my eyes," writes Shakespeare. In the exercises, we wanted to cross all the synesthetic lines—also remembering, as the line implies, that even when the body is the book, seeing is saying.

In the daily conduct of our lives, we require good sense, discretion, fair play, the ability to live and let live; in theater, we seek the power to live twice, and for this we require the parapsychological capacities that are refined, say, by the disciplines of Zen, Yoga, or St. Ignatius: the mystic light, x-ray vision, clairvoyance, second nature, second skin, the mantic gift. The highest art requires *invisibility*—the capacity of volumetric presence which is felt as not-there, overcoming inertia. When we sought such powers in our adaptations of the spiritual exercises, we didn't automatically assume we had them—nor even that we could ever quite define what we were after. As for the reality which was, in the process, being intensely abstracted as performance, it remained as a reflex of consciousness, like the stain of history in the mythos of Achilles' shield or the images in the replicating convex mirrors of a Van Eyck or Petrus Christus, which give an interiorized magic to the milieu of the domestic madonnas. Spiritualize the discipline as we would, it was a real world that was being numinously remembered.

In each exercise, ideally, an executable datum: whatever the dimensions of thought, however metaphysical, the thing to be done *can* be done, by simply doing it, like watching yourself die in a mirror, or live (as with the dying and the living in the breathing). If we were interested in the mystic light, it was not to be left to mystic guesswork or a sentimental occultism, or a falsifying stimulus. For instance (to use an exercise adapted by other groups in the period), it is possible to instruct the actors—as the Yaqui seer Don Juan instructed the anthropologist-pupil Casteneda, to find a spot; that is, a place-to-be, a secure physical space for which animals have an instinct. The tendency is to want to excite the exercise prematurely, or arbitrarily. The actor looks. He is told that the spot will be threatening. Maybe it will. But why? It is unlikely that the actor will experience anything near the trauma that Casteneda reported, not without the initiatory preparations, the systematic tutelage of Don Juan, and the unbearable length of time. But now the spot has become a fiction, and the temptation for the actor is "playwriting." So far as the exercise is concerned, the fiction is a fake. What we are after is not the dramatization but the immediate experience, consciously performed and, at some internal limit of apprehension, theatricalized.

What, then, to make of the spot? Nothing. The point is that nothing is as nothing is done. It is true that an actor in perfect stillness may induce a state that is nearly psychotic, but the objective is not to have an experience but to find the spot, and the doing can be done even if the spot is not found. In that respect, it is a rudimentary lesson out of an acting primer. The substance of the experience, for our purposes, is what is constituted by the process of consciousness into the real content of the exercise-structure. The pretense of an experience one is not having remains a fraudulence (I am trying to say this without judgment) unless the absence is absorbed or the fiction of an actable threat admitted—in which case it is a usable fiction. The playing *at* being threatened is what we want to minimize unless that *is* the point or unless (because we have no prior objection to what is called "indicating") it is a means of investigation, which may be more or less conscious, still finding the spot, but passing over it to something else, which may be it. When I say, however, that there is in each exercise an executable datum—a thing to be done concretely—I should add that it is more easily controlled in the most basic exercises, where we try to perform at the barest existential level. In one way or another most acting techniques do that, although for us one of the basic issues is whether, at any attainable level, the pretense is eliminable. We are not reducing things to be "real," but to understand as far as possible the disputable appearances of reality in the art of acting, and to materialize in those appearances an act of understanding. What we study through the exercises are the meanings that accrue and the perceptual liabilities that are incurred by varying levels of pretense, consciously deployed, but very soon eluding consciousness.

It was at Oberlin—with the self-reflexive instincts of the group becoming highly formed—that such awareness became its own subject. All the exercises involved problems of perception. If seeing what was there was a problem, where it came from was another—the other side of the Nietzshean coin whose surface is rubbed bare, a currency with indecipherable origins. No matter what the source, we were interested in "the teleology of an impulse," where it was going and where it would take us. In a series of "impulse exercises," we worked on this idea: that in any gesture of any order—out of the vast repertoire of gesture seemingly possible for any person—there is an innate selective principle and a latent structural rhythm moving, wherever it came from, ineluctably to its own end. It was as if that had been inscribed in the body by the indeterminable encodings of unremembered time. So all the actor had to do, having made the gesture, was to follow the impulse without interruption—that is, rational intervention—as if it were destiny, even beyond exhaustion. We usually began this exercise with very extreme or even violent gestures that you'd hardly expect the actor to be able to sustain, either because he'd burn out quickly or be hurt. But if there was no pulling back—when, indeed, the actor might be hurt—something like a nascent rhythmic principle would be rediscovered, and it was as if he could go on, without harm and without end, with more than second wind. The very momentum of it—by some inexplicable short circuit in the psyche—would appear to lead back to the source, where the energy of the impulse would be replenished, often at the point of exhaustion. (If the gesture weren't strong to begin with, accelerating the process, then the exercise requires extreme patience, the principle remaining the same and the replenishment coming at the point of boredom.) We have always been attentive to the genesis of an impulse, the originary source, as it enters the network of perception—like the course of the particular in Stevens' poem, the cry in the air which, thinning out, becomes so densely part of the scheme of things that it disappears in the perceiving, as if that were the source.

This reflexive concern for the beginnings and ends which escape us carried over, later on, into exercises meant to develop an equally reflexive feel for *what-comes-next*—as if, with all the options, only one thing can. When we were in Baltimore, the composer Stuart Smith worked with the group on a musical piece called *Towers*. After a rehearsal of the first part, a sound texture, he stressed the teleology of the musical impulse: "What you're getting is too much information. Get more from what you offer. Cleaner." The cleanliness he was after was like an encoding in the genes in which the future could be ascertained, in the presentness of the past: "What would be the history of that third sound? the first of that third? the second?" There were no notes to read—the score was a graph, the bars and lines of a landscape—but the history was in the perceived dynamic of an interior design, and he wanted that in the performance. What was by then inherent in our method was the sense that what comes next, as if by historical necessity in the act of performance, is the formal assertion of maximal content. It is in that respect that the ideal work would be thoroughly improvised. But though we have, in recent exercises, been closing down on the outside possibility, we know it is wish fulfillment, at the extremity of method. On the contrary, the work is thoroughly scored—one of the problems always being the abundance of the information. I shall explain later how we contend with it in the process, but we have refined the method so that we have improvised our way through the abundance to the perception of possible sequences, always looking for the formal principle, that necessity—in the same way that we move through the exercises, improvisationally, as structures to be fulfilled.

One of the reasons for the almost unmanageable abundance is that the exercises are focussed in a pattern of reflective commentary, as they are being done. There is an almost ceaseless spinoff. I shall discuss that further too, but it was at Oberlin that we explored the idea of *watching* as a mode of action and a generative force in the performance. We say about our work that if one watches those who are watching, they appear to be the real centers of energy, from which those performing are only projections. There are also, by the watchers, projections upon the projections. The root of behavior is, thus, in the act of perceiving. The performance is enabled by reflection.

One of the exercises we do—among a whole series of variants on projection (and introjection)—was derived from the Japanese puppet drama, the Bunraku. Like *The Burrow*, it is an exercise in authority and domination, a power structure in which the supreme power is, or so it seems, volitionless. In the Bunraku, no strings. In the exercise, two actors pair off. They study each other, an extended act of contemplation. Neither puppet nor puppeteer is designated. The choice arises from the act of contemplation. The aim is to develop a negative capability by complete dependence. One surrenders to the other in the acceptance of an act of will. The study continues, very formal. What is known about the other—the useful and activating information—seems to increase in proportion to the propriety of form. The less random, the more possible, the greater permission. There is an *unacted* transmission of energy, as if from the animate to the inanimate. The power of the operator, or master, is a filiation of directed energy and received otherness and, as the other goes passive, an inwardly responsive accord, an adventure, master to puppet, puppet to master, each to each, as if the flow of energy were invisibly reversing and the inanimate were the engendering force. The puppeteer discerns and embraces a repertoire of possibility in the puppet, intrinsic or projected—what, perhaps, without the puppeteer the puppet could not play out alone, or the reverse. In studying the puppet, the master becomes aware of shape, heft, jointure, points of resistance, limits of balance, skin texture, coloration, breath, smell, pulse—the extent of manipulability, and the desire; in the puppet, through the self. Yet, in the spectrum of reflections—as in the Taoist mirror, which receives but holds nothing —there is, ideally, no space for narcissism, only the washing away of projections, the emptiness of symbols; the nothing that is not there and the nothing that is. One moves, the other moves, or is moved, *one*—a spontaneous function of transmitted desire. The forms observed and the puppet obeying, will-lessly, it is soon not determinable at all, as you observe, who is moving whom.

In the Bunraku itself, there are three manipulators: the master, unmasked, placid, cool; and two assistants, hooded. The master controls the torso and right arm; one of the assistants works below the puppet to stabilize it and maneuver the legs; and (the one qualification about no strings) the other assistant, with the delicate utensil of a stringed instrument, operates (but in full view) the left arm and hand. (We have also done the exercise with a complex group like this.) The doll itself, until moved, seems delicate and not quite life-size—until it is suddenly lifted by emotion to the full principality of itself; before then, the dominance of attention is disproportionate, an emblem of a paradoxical power. The manipulators are literally—with a reverence to the task of making gestures that are to be seen as *acts*, not in themselves but in the puppet—servants of the puppet they master. The puppet is expressively human, sometimes terribly passionate, full of longing, bereft, suicidal; the unmasked manipulator is an unmoved mover. The face is unreadable, an empty glass. The whole is a dance. As the doll performs more powerfully, you keep asking yourself, if not carried to forgetfulness, where does all that emotion come from? It appears in the object, but it can't be there.

It is an act of consummate ventriloquism. The master is utterly impassive, effortless in the body; all three. But then you wonder if they are really the source. It is something more than ventriloquism, surely.

There is an infolded grace in the performance which cycles the mystery of its source among the moving figures, including the doll, which is now thoroughly evocative. There are also reciters and musicians present, seated and off to the side, framed in high stiff triangulated collars; and hooded functionaries who pass back and forth within the scene, clearing things away, stooped to be unobtrusive, but not pretending to be hidden—sometimes their dark backs rising unexpectedly like the earth's body (I am sure the metaphor is unintentional) into a task. But it is all abstract, emblazoned in the doll, incited too by the ideographic writing on the lecterns in front of the reciters, and the vocalized bravuras of the narrative. A clack of wood, things move. They move in concert, yet each in its own measured and alien place: the estranged twang of the shamisen, the seemingly liturgical text, half-chanted, and the exposed manipulators, *showing* the work in art. The very efficiency is a cadence, part of the dance.

The reciters beside the shamisen also act, but not quite mimetically. A woman, for instance, is rendered monochromatically on a specific pitch; they use facial masks to convey the emotions of which they chant, or the production of the emotions compels the face into a mask. When finished, they sit back, observing. They appear to move in and out of performance states, through graded suggestions of behavior—as in our own performance technique, which is sometimes abstract, sometimes mimetic, sometimes eerily between, often analytical, with no breach between analysis and performance. As the actors pass in and out of the space, they seem to exist in an ambiguous limbo of will, hypercontrolled form and indeterminacy. By the time of performance, the indeterminacy is *in* the form, not improvisation—as it is not in the Bunraku. I don't know to what extent there is a conscious analytical component in these compositions of the Bunraku, whether at all. Around the puppet, it is quite calmly fabulous. We are pitched differently, with a different purpose. In rehearsal or performance, a cognitive desire. There is a kind of running commentary in the act of watching, as if things would disappear if they were left unsaid. This activity of reflection is like a biophysical seizure. Whatever is projected into the space, from whatever source, is screened, stimulated, and cycled through that.

A by-product, however, of the reflective activity is a patina of the fabulous over whatever is projected into the performing space. We worked at Oberlin at learning how to orchestrate the commentary. We wanted to refine the ways in which every "enactment" or "event" would be seen and bespoken. What evolved was a performed discourse. In the absence of authorizing myth and ritual, there would be a sonorous animation of value in variant narratives, as though that which had been engendered before our eyes had existed from the beginning of time, the stories told and retold, as if there were an "oral tradition" within the form. Or it might sound as if that which was being performed, even if just then discovered, had been prepared—like the interlacing music and gesture of an arcane theater—by long hermeneutical tradition. There was an actualizing power in the pretense, and we constructed exercises for the exegesis. As with the Chorus in ancient drama—but again with a different pulse—the dance of reflections became an activating stream of consciousness and another mode of action.

It took us quite a while before we could articulate the profusion. The seeds of craft in KRAKEN came out of early reflections on the nature of the Chorus in the *Oresteia*, which combined with the exegetical process to give us the structural idea for *Seeds of Atreus*. But in that work, as finally performed, the idea dominated the process and subliminated, if it didn't extrude, the germinating reflections of the actors. *The Donner Party, Its Crossing* released more of the process into the structure, but it wasn't until *Elsinore* that the personal discourse integrated the entire performance, the structure shaped by the play of the actors' thought. The thrust of this work came early on from a response to this question: If the first actor dissociated himself from the Chorus, could we structurally reverse the process or, rather, could we make the process of association and dissociation the seedbed of an evolving form? We were not seeking the universal embrace of oceanic feeling that gave us the sonorous but undifferentiated OM of that period. We were interested in a more articulated consciousness, still responsible to the mediating reality of the ego. So far as we could make out the nature of the Chorus in the *Oresteia*—particularly in the lambent and nearly inchoate lyrics at the beginning of the first play—it was the consensus of guesswork and speculation, half-truth and inspiration, mantic heart and vain prejudice. Their view of reality existed on the margins of myth like the history of Herodotus—with amazing collective intuitions beyond any single intelligence, and some of it inaccessible because lost with the ancient dance.

At the time we worked on it, we were looking for a summary voice for all the disparate inadequacies of our thought on Vietnam, including the (inevitably failing) analogy I have already made with the war in Troy. As we worked, the characters emerged out of the Chorus, self-chosen, and passed back into it, differentiating themselves out of the pressure of individual or imagistic necessity. They were mere appearances, like those messengers who seem to materialize out of the deep structure of the drama to bring news from afar. They'd say what they had to say, being there, refusing themselves—because it seemed

Take Up the Bodies

untenable—the sustained duration that character requires. The appearances would merge with each other, images adhering, washing others away, character and actor, in the diminishing reverberations of myth across history, whatever it was that wanted remembrance fragmenting, replicating, transforming—one becoming another, maybe the half-shadowed suggestion of character, an intimation, an inscape. The one seeming permanence was the Chorus. The drama was a Book of Changes. Something like a collective unconscious would begin to form, a reservoir of clues and signals which had to be interpreted. In the concert of reflection there'd be a movement toward collective understanding, momentary, which scattered in the profusion of association and imagery, failing and haunted, going back to the unconscious—divided off—only to surface again in the reflective surround. A *structural rhythm* developed from these collective fantasies of the actors as their separating images, drawn from the drama as from an elusive gospel, rehearsed each other as in a mutual dream, mutating, prompting, releasing sealed information; out of some marred fiction of recovered memory, the viscous shadow-text of myth.

Later, the Chorus forgotten, the structural rhythm remained as a technique of investigation, and as the matrix of other work. Along with the explorations of this choral idea, there was a category of exercises having to do with self-questioning propositions that mythicized the self. They were very personal explorations, at the edge of narcissism, but were again designed to administer unconscious content in a perceptual framework, as if the questions were being watched through the transparency of the persons. For instance: If you were to be punished for your sins, what form would that punishment take? *Do.* There are those who say they can forsee exactly how they will die. How will you die? *Show.* When you die, what will die with you? what forms? what images? as when the last man who saw Helen died. *Show.* Or, an exercise in regression, in which the actor plays back his entire life from that very moment, through a set of spontaneously chosen nodal experiences, including first love, betrayal, puberty, guilt, earliest memory, back through birth and prenatal states, to which—in the teleology of the impulse—memory leads, though it will lead to more and more of what has been forgotten farther and farther back each time the exercise is done. The enactment is to be carefully differentiated so that we can virtually see what age the actor is at any moment, even while the backward unfolding of the performance is as continuous as the changing figures of the Tai Chi Ch'uan. Or, on the other side of nothingness, through the preconscious, the reverse: back to where we are, but never quite there, staging identity in a similar performance. This exercise may also be done in a matrix of reflective commentary, which changes what is remembered. The particular stage is not only to be revealed but may also be responded to positively or negatively by the actor *in* the performance; which is to say, criticized, refused, replayed. So, too, the propositions above may be examined in the enactment—a refusal, for instance, to accept the reality of sin, however the punishment is rendered. As in the Tai Chi, the Other is drawn into the orbit of consciousness, and defined, by performance. The presence of doubleness is always there, in the moving body.

The systems of the body were also a major concern at Oberlin. All exercise systems which emphasize "body work" have a certain virtue and a certain arbitrariness about them, even if the body work is spiritualized or disclaimed as such and, as with Grotowski, called associations. All method feels like little but regimen until the unique problems are stated, and the associations are flowing on the right frequency. Habitual procedures with the body will keep the channels open, perhaps, and it is important—as it was during that period—to distinguish the priorities of gut and spine from the customary behavior of the customary extremities in familiar kinds of acting. But a physical aptitude is a response to *need,* and the body follows after, refining itself to the felt intensity of need. The Bedouin, for instance, tends to be lean and swift because he has vast distances to cover in the desert. Forest people are squatter, long of torso, large of hand. There is not so much space to cover, and locomotion takes a different form. I don't know why in the world we'd want, say, a fat actor, but if for some peculiar reason we did, then the discipline of the Sumo wrestler would be relevant in our training. Like the weight lifter, he has weight because there's an efficient dual gravity in that mass: supported in pride, supported in physicality.

For various reasons, one of the systems we continued studying at Oberlin was the Tai Chi Ch'uan, which was taught at Cal Arts by an astute, surprising, and metaphorically gifted man named Marshall Ho'o. Aside from its intrinsic values, the Tai Chi has become a reference for acting method, as well as a source and analogue for an idea of theater. I had studied with Marshall Ho'o before we started at Cal Arts. What drew me to the Tai Chi was the commitment to evanescense, against my grain. It has the allure of an exercise and a spiritual discipline with the character of a performance. In that respect, it differs from Yoga which, in its highest virtue, is drawn to immobility, and a burning away of the body. By contrast, the Tai Chi is a form of moving meditation. The fact that it is performed standing was a not inconsequential feature in a period when all kinds of body consciousness, including our own, brought actors down to their hands and knees, with maybe too quick a predilection for the uncontrollable mystery on the

Take Up the Bodies

bestial floor. There was something eminently civilized about the Tai Chi, chastening when you're after the monsters.

For the actor, it is helpful in dealing with the insoluble dilemma: action or motive, being or becoming, inner or outer—which comes first? the doing or the conceiving? What is the connection between the source of energy and the theatrical use you make of it? The slowly revolving hand of the Greater Heavenly Circulation repulses the monkey. The hand, withdrawing, takes nothing with it, except the emptiness, supplying the void. They say: the *yi* (consciousness) directs the *chi* (animating spirit, breathed, gathered being), but not in any strict temporal priority, rather in the intercourse of Yin and Yang. I suppose you'd have to think of lifting the hands when you first start, what else would you do? But I have seen the Tai Chi done with closed eyes by people in love with themselves dreaming. If they were actors, they would—as Stanislavski put it—love themselves in art, not the art in themselves. The Tai Chi is metaphysical boxing—the body alive, the eyes alert. What happens through practice is very much like what happens to the actor when his technique is most accomplished. Craft passes into art when, surpassing function, it becomes gratuitous. Almost before thought, done. The gestures are impossible unless you have the vision, the vision is impossible unless you do the gestures. Insufficient to begin with, they materialize each other. The form is the actualization.

What I also liked about the Tai Chi is that the forms are a repository of learning, an accretion, a body of lore and a lore of the body in its motions. Though one sees them done loosely (and there are different schools), one hesitates to violate the forms—especially when it is discovered that the forms, done accurately, solicit what is individual in the doer. The separate but inseparable figures are elusive and inexhaustible. In reality, how *does* one grasp a sparrow's tail?

The perspective of the Tai Chi made it easier to talk about problems in acting, and instead of acting upon them, let them act upon us. In a craft oriented toward production as the theater is, perhaps the chief problem is to discover how *not* to do the thing that must be done. What gets in the way of performance? Fear, distraction, vanity, anxiety, ego, narcissism, sentimentality, the obsession with results, dislocation, no mooring, lack of gravity. The Taoist *wu wei*—volitionlessness, nonaction—is against the grain for most of us. In those days, marked by instant affinities to the Far East, we could be sentimental about becoming soft, slow, passive too. More often than not, the result was torpor. Yet the cleansing action of a true craft is an attitude of reverence toward the moment, letting it happen rather than making it happen (even saying it, my mind holds itself in reserve), relinquishing oneself, getting out of the way. "Let be," says Hamlet, at the center of indifference, where the activist power of Western thought, inevitably failing, touches upon the East. For the moment, the excruciating choice between to be and not to be disappears into the abyss. Another sort of energy arises from quietude, the intrinsic strength of an interior calm, the fusion of opposites, a gathered force, like the white whale's "mighty mildness of repose in swiftness."

The Tai Chi was a clarifying glass, but the old argument about inside and outside in acting would have been jettisoned years ago if it were as simple as the forms feel even when they escape you. As we well know, it's the simple that complicates. At one level, each to his own instinct. You don't look where you don't get it. If the inside is alive for you, then you go inside—as Walter Payton likes to do when he's running; if the outside moves, then you move with it. That would seem to make elementary sense. Aside from what happens naturally, where you choose to go depends on how you're stymied. Like Yin and Yang, opposites may have a virtue and interdependent powers. As Jung points out in *The Secret of the Golden Flower*, if one is cramped in conscious mind, one may have to work with the hands until the cramp of mind is released and just lets things happen. But this new acceptance of the nonrational and intuitive has to be understood as the compensatory motion of a process. Letting it happen "would be poison for a person who has already been overwhelmed by things that just happen." There also comes a time when one is prepared to accept from without, arbitrarily even, what one could never accept before—time for a "reversal of one's being" which is both an enlargement and "a singularly appropriate expression of the total personality." Coming *when* it does keeps it from feeling like a violation of being and the most deeply-rooted instincts.

To recover time is another (illusory?) power of the forms. "Take time," the director says to the actors, meaning don't hurry, don't push, don't get anxious, don't. Sometimes, in the press of rehearsal in conventional theater, working under deadlines, the most solicitous director says take time and can't conceivably mean it, his very function denying it. "*Take* time," we used to say in the exercises, where we had time, like a litany, another proposition, "Take *time*. . . ." We did a whole series of exercises *on* time, figures of time, in time, measured, discontinuous, expanding momentarily through space, in thought, immeasurable. Reflected on, time is the medium for forgetting it. For the time being. The aleatoric slowness of the Tai Chi is important, the almost musical consciousness *of* time moving outside of it. Still, the inclination of our work (or my temperament) was always to be critical of the forgetting. We also had to remember that, while the Tai Chi is a performance, it is not theater—which, for me, is always at the moving edge of history. Yet even there, the forms are illuminating. As in the Creative hexagram of the *I Ching*, Progress is a conservation, the moving forward is a going back. The mystery is in the repetitions. (Almost all techniques of acting aim at the idea of the return, establishing a mystery and repeating it. To take a simple example: an actor turns upstage. Usually, we forget what is most effective about it: the abstractness of form as it removes itself from the human connotations associated with the front. The back is not especially expressive. The force of a turn upstage comes from the expectancy of a return. There is the residue of a ritual structure, the basis of a second presence.) The Tai Chi is a ceaseless rehearsal, a perpetual present moment sowing the seeds of a returning future. One performs it, sentient among the successions, outside of time, with timeliness. The sequence, whether for exercise or meditation, has its proper duration. There, here, now, in the incessant and impeccable changes, is an imposing stillness. "Movement," according to *The Secret of the Golden Flower*, "is another name for mastery." The mastery of movement is to be moved.

There were two other aspects of the Tai Chi which were attractive: the doxology of the circle (a structural principle in *Elsinore*; counterpoint to the square dance of *The Donner Party, Its Crossing*) and the myriad of mirroring forms. The circularity, repeated, presumably activates the dark and light forces of human nature. Mutability and mortality. They are contemplated through the metamorphoses, the changing avatars and darkling embodiments, parting the wild horse's mane to perceive—what? The Tai Chi seems to relegitimize the Romantic moment, but it is also a martial art. Those lovely gestures are lethal. The Other is the Enemy. Or may be. It is momentary in the mind, a fitful shade of thought, like the doubleness in acting which energizes thought by taking the breath away.

The vanishing is what the actor is after, what's there and not there. Shadow and breath are the declensions of the actor's art. Immaterially in the body, they constitute a definition of the actor's being. The dead in Purgatory knew that Dante was alive when his body cast a shadow on the ground, when the shadow moved. There is shadow within shadow, measuring time. There is a shadow in the eye of the beholder, who becomes all eye. Breath is the shadow of a shadow, yet the tensile strength and lifeline of being—a skeleton key. Radiance in the actor is the shadow's brightness, illumining a breath. The Tai Chi is a corporeal reflection on shadow and breath. It stresses clarity in vacancy—movements which are exact, clean, and pure, even while inseparable and indecipherable. The circle is its secret. There is a mysterious lucidity in the circle which one can only approach with the imperfect calligraphy of the body. Yet one tries, as an act of faith and self-respect. (In *Elsinore*, an immense effort of collective will was to go into the rounding by the seven actors of "the seven corners of a circle.") I was growing impatient with performance, in or out of the theater, uncleansed of irregularities and carelessness, as if artlessness were a thing of the spirit. The Tai Chi knows that the spirit is exact. Like thunder. Like gravity. Like grace.

"Grace is grace, despite of all controversy," says a wit in *Measure for Measure*, but there was controversy too in the training. It had already proceeded rather far at Cal Arts, but after a couple of months of isolation at Oberlin, we sensed the introspectiveness of the environment merging with the self-reflexiveness of the work. What we lacked was an outwardly sustaining motive, a *subject matter* for the exercises to counterbalance the density of the inner life, the allure of the elusive subject. We tried one thing and another to which we have come back since, but we couldn't settle then on the right subject, issue, theme, text, whatever. I'm not quite sure why that was so, probably some indeterminacy in me, a desire—probably too overweening—to find the thing which, after some years of silence, would say it all.

The impediment was somewhere between a principle and a neurosis. It may also have had something to do with the social psychology of group process in the period and, given the personalities of our specific case, with the buck stopping here. While others were picking up only too literally Artaud's proclamation of "No More Masterpieces," it was some anxiety about a masterpiece that kept us from carrying through any piece at all. The word *piece* was itself an index of the period. I came into the theater when they called plays *productions*—but in the politics of the sixties that word had fallen into disrepute along with the system of value from which it came. The actors were young. They had grown up during the period of the Bomb. They had no great expectations about the idea of permanence. They spanned an age from the introduction of disposable diapers to the theory of disposable art. They didn't share my anxiety about masterpieces, and that may have impeded me even more. They would have been content with something exploratory or partial, something, moreover, in which they could try themselves out. They needed the exposure. Other groups were doing things, weren't they? which were just this side of improvisation. If the actors were growing anxious, it was more about what was holding me back.

If I was growing vulnerable, and I was, it also had to do with the discrepancy of age. I was just about twice as old as some of them, and most theater ensembles in that period were peer groups, or in other ways communitarian. They accepted my authority with very little question, but it was a time when authority was severely questionable and being put to the test—and if they weren't testing it, I was doing it myself. There was a tricky dynamic to it all. The plainness with which I assumed authority didn't necessarily validate it. Sometimes it felt like a form of manipulation to which they were only too ready to respond. They were themselves divided between wanting more guidance and wanting more mutual sharing. It's doubtful that some of them would have chosen to work with each other if they were not working with me (and that continues to be so). They were learning to live in long-term ambiguity during the development of a work, but that competed with the desire, out of their own fears, for more definitive answers and directorial choice. In any event, they expected the leadership they granted me unresistingly at my insistence to justify itself in *what* I did as well as how I did it. Authority can disappear in the laborious difficulty of it all, as it disappeared in the Donner Party going over the Wahsatch. There were times they simply wanted the authority. That's what they came for and they were disappointed when it wasn't decisively there. But perhaps there was a manipulative illusion in my own mind—giving myself a reason for not experimenting further, though I was tempted, with the distribution of power. Other groups have gone through crises of leadership. When we did, it was more than anything a subjective affair—my losing confidence in where we were.

In the studio, the faith of it, the bodying doubt. There were long stretches when I'd mainly—and uncharacteristically—sit and watch, my presence a strong factor, even when silent; the watching a motive force. An actor would move, like a crab backwards. Someone was shadowboxing with her voice.They had their own motives, but were sweating through the puzzle of my will.

Being young, they also had alterable purposes—much more than mine—and they had every reason to want to get on with it. Having cut my ties to the conventional theater, as well as to the training program at Cal Arts, I was now thoroughly dependent on these actors, because they had come there with me, although the nature of the dependency— in the isolation of Oberlin—was understood the other way around. Whatever the dependency, the issue is always survival. In the theater, I have never known anything else. The decision to reduce downward, however, to a small and mobile unit made the problem of survival something other than what I was used to at the Actor's Workshop. For all its insolvencies, that was essentially a bourgeois institution in a specific place, and with a more or less settled disposition as to what the theater was and what it should be doing, and how—for all the controversy and the experimental work in our repertoire. We worried about methodology, but it never curtailed our output. When we picked a play, the rehearsal period might be shorter or longer (compared to similar theaters, longer), but we were still meeting deadlines and, good or bad, we knew the play would go on, and they went on for more than half the lifetime of most of these actors, who hadn't done a single piece yet. Anybody who has worked in the more regular types of theater knows that the last couple of weeks of any rehearsal period are something like a Watergate coverup. By then, you're trying to make do with the irredeemable, whatever you can get away with. In this new work, the psychology of completion was something else: finished when it's finished, unguessable, and—if the task were hard enough and the investigations too prolonged—more damaging. The kraken (we had not yet used or capitalized the name) was too long submerged. It was as if I'd anticipated, as the myth goes, that it would die if it surfaced.

When it did surface, in various direct and sublimated ways all of this got into the work. The actors were devout. They were loyal beyond the call of duty, shifting with my enthusiasms and speculations, and making a creative issue of the confusions. The arduousness of their work was something you could never have persuaded actors to endure in the early fifties, even the best of those who gave stability to the Workshop. This is not meant as an invidious comparison; there were other priorities then, and they could probably never have abided the interminable preparations for performance. It wasn't until the late fifties, when the regional theaters began to feel reasonably secure about survival, that training became, for a while, something of a fetish in this country—spurred on by money made available, to discuss it, by the Ford Foundation. (There was a time when the Rockefeller Foundation—because Ford had already taken the lead on operating expenses—would give money for nothing but training, while the theaters thought they still needed it to survive.) As theaters became more established, they began to worry about going back and picking up the loose ends of acting technique, especially as applied to "Style." Voice was first on the agenda. The villain in the piece was the Actors Studio, with its Method. As the critique went (and there was reason for it) little attention had been paid—in the concern for personally-rooted behavior—to what was being said and, if so, whether or not it could be heard.

In the sixties, we began to hear a lot more, some of which I'd rather not have heard. (And to be fair, now that characterization is in again, there were few enough actors who made instant reputations in the off-off-Broadway scene who could compare in that respect with the Studio actors they were dismissing.) Nevertheless, there was a more valid concentration on training in certain of the small groups. That most of the actors were young and untutored, with no investment of experience in an older system, made it possible for a more detailed and daring study

Take Up the Bodies

of neglected, and nonbehavioral, techniques, tried out with less resistance. In 1957, I had virtually to beg actors to be in *Waiting for Godot*, and I can hardly imagine what kind of opposition would have been aroused by ideas of training which were, through the sixties, indebted to the breakdown of the old coherence of behavior which is reflected in that play. Where's the action? It appeared to be in the groups, and their preoccupations with roles games transactions tasks, and undifferentiated sound/movement in the collective resonance of the ensemble.

Group process was the creature of a period which, first, had chosen instability as a life-style and, later, so far as the theater was concerned, had no better choice. The life of a group is, by the nature of the thing, in a nervously transient state. By comparison to the Workshop, a group is itinerant. In the sociology of institutions, it is held that groups do not move irreversibly deathward as individuals do. But continuity is also a function of number, that is, the size of an institution or a culture. The Workshop endured in San Francisco while people came and went, and it had a reasonable lifespan. In the novel history of theater groups, social theory wavers if it doesn't fail. The group is more like an elemental molecular organism, dissolving and coming together at best, consuming itself to extinction at worst. It may even be more vulnerable to the degree, as in our work, that the nature of what is being done is almost inseparable from who is doing it, so that the actors cannot be easily replaced. There are not, overall, many groups that have survived for very long. With rare exceptions, they start out young. They don't age in their own service. They usually disintegrate before maturity, when the task of earning something more than a marginal living also enters the behavioral structure. Some which started off impulses hearking back to the sixties can't resolve the participatory dilemma, rejecting leadership and needing it. One of Grotowski's achievements was that he was able, over the years, to draw upon the cohesive integrity of actors aging on their own behalf. The hermetic isolation was important. (So was government subsidy.) No sooner did his group come to America than it was as if the virus of dispersion entered the organism. On their return to Poland, the original unity was gone.

Part of the paratheatrical mission of Grotowski's *Holiday* was to recover a lost innocence. In America, characteristically, we lose our innocence not to maturity but to impatience. The disintegrative forces are all around us. The years are wasted, they divide us. It is remarkable when a group like the Mabou Mines adheres through all adversity to middle age. The best people rarely stay together long enough to make use of themselves to each other, to grow and learn and prosper, if only marginally. In Oberlin—that thin margin in the vast middle—I still had a terrible desire for continuity, ingrained at the Actor's Workshop in San Francisco. But this was an altogether different proposition, and one of the things that accounted for my indecisiveness was that, even against my will, I seemed to have done a lot of starting over again in recent years.

In the midst of this dilemma, President Nixon shocked everybody by stepping up the bombing in North Vietnam. On an impulse of outrage, I suddenly decided to do what I'd never done before—despite my reputation for politics in the theater—and that was to organize an event out of an immediate political motive. Some of the actors were astonished. On the basis of their training, they had every reason to believe that "my aesthetic is an aesthetic," as I said back at Cal Arts during the controversy with the Board. In some earlier political turmoil there, I remember saying to the actors, some of whom wanted to skip a rehearsal to participate in a demonstration: "I don't care if a bomb drops next door. We work, then go out after and clean up the rubble."

So, they had good reason to be taken aback when I proposed stopping rehearsal to organize a whole protest. Some were immediately responsive; some were, as usual, apolitical. One of the actors, a black, had been reading George Jackson's prison letters and raised the question as to whether the war was his business to fret over. He didn't even raise the question, just a cool eyebrow. He didn't participate. Almost all of the others did. The work was suspended while we held a mass meeting, organized the campus, mustered support from civic groups, and cooperation from the local police. The event was called *Invitation to a Burning.* As the flyer for it said, it was intended "as a preface to specific political action to stop the bombing and finally end the war. . . ." I stressed the sense of collusion and impotence that many of us were feeling. "It is no substitute for the political work that must follow and sustain itself, but it is also meant as a political act." While a delegation including the college president went on to Washington for simultaneous delivery of letters of protest, television cameras came on the campus (the networks turned out) to broadcast an event which spread over the entire town.

Oberlin is a place with a radical history. It had been the northern way station of the Underground Railway before the Civil War; it was the first college to admit women; the early feminist movement received an impetus there from the founding of the WCTU, which was radical in its puritanism when breaking the bottle was a political act; and the college was the first to introduce physical education into the curriculum—in the pure ancient sense of a sound mind in a sound body (our own psychophysical ethic). To this day you can still see white-haired elderly women in hiking shoes striding up and down the streets with great vigor. When we arrived, the new director of athletics was Jack Scott, notorious spokesman for dissident jocks, later more notorious for having ferried Patricia Hearst across the country when the FBI and everybody else were looking for her. The man brought in by Scott to be assistant director was Tommy Smith who, up on the stand to receive the gold at the Olympics, raised his fist in a Black Power salute. Scott's parties—with dropouts from the NBA and NFL, leftist academics, blacks—seemed like a way station for the new radical underground, or fellow travellers, including (occasionally) myself and the college president, who later chose to drop out of the academic world.

There were demonstrations, more or less angry, on campuses all over the country, but Oberlin seemed an ideal setting for *Invitation to a Burning.* (It was bound to get a few seconds on the few minutes of national coverage.) There was a procession which approached the four corners of Tappan Square from different parts of the town. There were giant puppets, masks, a choir in black robes with fine singers quickly radicalized from the distinguished Conservatory. The trees (spared by the elm bark beetle) were saran-wrapped. Dancers moved among them like infinitely displaced persons. The centerpiece was a huge symbolic pyre. The totems to be burned were structures of personal belongings, "things we own and maybe some things we love, no great sacrifice but nevertheless some part of ourselves." The instructions said they should be nothing haphazard, rather beautifully designed structures, "something we'd like to live with. But they will be destroyed. The act is meant to be a reflection of one community, in the heartland of America, on the devastation of others very remote, which sometimes seem not to exist." An Loc, we pointed out, was just about the same size as Oberlin. An electronic sound, composed for the event at the Conservatory, was broadcast by the campus station and picked up by radios, volume up, in windows all over the town. It was capacious, solemn, and elegantly ominous. There would have been a helicopter if it had gotten off the ground, but that was the only mechanical failure. (The other gaffe—anticipating the seventies, when dissidence turned to environmental action—was when smoke from the pyre went up into the trees and turned some of the ecologists present off the war protest for the moment.) Nevertheless, the size of the town and the history made for an almost perfect form. On the square are commemorative arches for the Oberlin missionaries who were—while evangelizing among the heathen—killed in the Boxer War. Atop the arches, torches were ignited, and below, the choir sang hymns.

The climactic moment came when a couple of hundred people (there were differences on the body count, some say more) lay down before the fire as if they were dead. Some threw belongings into the flames as they diminished, the clothes right off their backs. It was all very beautiful and very moving, except I was troubled by the symbolic dying. Not because it wasn't appropriate, but because it had been induced when, sizing up the awesomeness of the scene as the people watched the burning, I tapped one of my assistants and *told* him to lie down. When he did, reluctantly, others followed suit. A setup. Even in the communal sympathy spanning continents, art and politics conflicted. There it was again, the easy vulnerability of collective sentiment, and the manipulability of any crowd. A true emotion on a false premise—nothing but theater again—and what does one make morally of that? After the first wave of directorial omnipotence, I thought the bodies were disgusting. I couldn't wait to get back to the laboratory.

When we did, the others were troubled too—even those who had worked day and night to construct the pyre and organize the processions. They were not so much troubled by the dying at the fire—nor the feeling that the whole event was finally more aesthetic than political—but about the purpose and motives of the work and—with the participatory ideal alerted—my authoritarian decision to stop. What were we, really? The rain beat that night on the high-beamed pitched roof of the old wainscoted gym (with its long tradition of physical education, Oberlin had a plethora of gyms) where we worked virtually in secret. A track above circled our perturbed circle. Above it were abandoned offices with antique barbells, faded portraits of old teams, and bats that now and then sailed over the space like that "austral" avatar of the Host in *Finnegans Wake*, "so entirely spoorlessly . . . as to tickle the speculative to all but opine. . . ." We suddenly felt lonely in the heartland of America. Despite the national coverage, we were isolated and uncertain, far out of it, nowhere.

Political sentiments had been stirred up by the burning, but there was nothing like political unity among us. What was the basis of unity, except the fact that almost all of them had been my students? It was in the malaise over this question that the work on *The Enemy*, about a month old, acquired a particular impetus: in order to define ourselves as a group we would—like tribes, gangs, families, states—create a myth of the Other. The whole arc of the acting process was inherent in that idea. As with *The Burrow* later, *The Enemy* became our craft. While there was much that was frustrating about it (including the fact that it was never completed), the study of the Enemy soon became a productive and generative concept instead of mere work on a piece. It looked in the mirror and extrapolated the already developed habits of reflective thought; it taught the actors to watch as if watching, like

Take Up the Bodies

readiness, were all; it proliferated strategies of performance that we could barely manage then and haven't exhausted yet; it was as adhesive as the idea of origins and profuse with illusions about them, seminal and centripetal, forcing us to think out the intervolving dimensions of inside and outside. It became a rich metaphor for the anamorphic shapes of reality, even when, as in the Tai Chi Ch'uan, the existence of the Enemy was figured as an absence.

Datum: the Enemy that appears by default is not an honorable and respected enemy. The Enemy that comes out to meet faintheartedness is a minor figure, "small fry," like the others snapped up by the creature of the Burrow—not what we were after. The Enemy we wanted to know is the sinister aspect of the Other, the Familiar, the Double, the Secret Sharer, perhaps all that survives of the Beloved—what makes your hair stand on end. Our greatest temptation would be to embrace some spectre of the Enemy prematurely, aggrandizing the self in the process, while the mortal Enemy, scornful in the realm of Archetypes, was laughing at the presumption. The Enemy is the one you want "writhing in the essential blood," as Eliot wrote, "or dangling from the friendly tree." The Enemy might be fiction, chimera, product of paranoia—yet something more than our own psychic field distorted, made monstrous or feeble by the perversions of dread, an inverse reverence. If we believed in God, the Enemy might resemble that amazing idea of Isaac Luria of Safed, the *tsimtsum*, God's withdrawal into Himself, a cosmic reduction into hiddenness, a primordial space for the existence of something other than God and His pure essence. If not God in exile from God, then the self fallen away from the self, reserving a void for the idea of strangeness, and the thing which embodies it. The very conception of the Enemy might be the Enemy. Still, there is the conception.

The Enemy's mask is inscribed by history with lines drawn by our earliest childhood fears. The idea of the Enemy is what was dreamed for us before we dreamed. Our dreams retort to our denials: we are being dreamed. The Enemy is doing the dreaming.

There were a couple of actors, one especially, who from the beginning didn't "want to remember the things that cause us to believe in enemies. I want to forget," he said. "The Enemy is what I want to forget." He was asked if he could forgive instead of forgetting. "If you forgive, you haven't forgiven. The only way to forgive is to forget." At the moment, I found the idea "hideous, reprehensible" and said so, for starters throwing the six million at him, that unessential blood. Or was it? The conceit of forgiveness infused the investigation. Was the Enemy a forgiving and a forgetting? "The best person here," said another actor, "is the one who resists it most." Resists what? "Thinking about it." But once we started, we couldn't resist.

Mostly, we proceeded on a suspension of disbelief that didn't need much suspending. While we might prefer to deny the Enemy or call it by other names—like the *hysterica passio*, that mothering emotion which Lear tries to hold down—somewhere, it seemed, there is (as the Tao says about the Mother) an Enemy and the Enemy has a name. Does it have a gender? If there is suspicion about the mother, there is psychoanalytical ground. Lacan's mirror phase, for instance, where the grounding dis-appears. In this conceit, mothering is mirroring. In the spiral of misapprehension out of the womb, the mother is irremediably there, and the mother's mother mirrored, projected onto the child, image upon image mothering back in a kind of counterfeit nurturance—back through the mirrors receding through the first glint of the mirror where the self seen by the forming child is the incipiently imaged *condition* of a growing paranoia, the self seen on the Enemy's face.

But there were those who, with the emotion of the Furies, would reject that mothering source. There were also those, like Sartre, who would dismiss the father as well, who might have been the Enemy if not stripped of rank by the good fortune (for Sartre) of death: "There is no good father, that's the rule. Don't lay the blame on man but on the bond of paternity, which is rotten. To beget children, nothing better, to have them, what iniquity! Had my father lived he would have lain on me at full length and would have crushed me. . . . Amidst Aeneas and his fellows who carry their Anchises on their backs, I move from shore to shore, alone and hating those invisible begetters who bestraddle their sons all their life long. I left behind me a young man who did not have time to be my father and who could now be my son. Was it a good thing or a bad? I don't know. But I readily subscribe to the verdict of an eminent psychoanalyst: I have no superego." Unfortunately, most of us do, and if the Enemy escapes gender, it may be a matter of timing. (There is also the long metaphysical tradition that the Enemy *is* Time.) If the world is in any way a mirror of the self, the question becomes *when* does that other image also appear in the mirror?

In the post-Freudian schema, the age has kept falling towards infancy. In recent studies of pathological narcissism, however, a distinction is made between the earliest cognitive awareness of a Self and an Other, the out-there and the in-here. There is the delayed appearance of a double image. According to this theoretical view, nothing appears in the mirror until something else does too, or until the perceiver

Take Up the Bodies

realizes that something else is there that is *not* oneself. So, no plot, no trauma, no analytical history, rather a series of occurrences in a self-observing process. The Chicago Narcissists have tried to make a therapeutic praxis of this good description of postmodern drama, permitting the one self to identify itself through the other, by letting the transference take place through the therapist. In this process, the Enemy is presumably erased or, as in the solipsistic methods of contemporary art, *reduced*. The reduction takes with it, illusorily (yet denying illusion), the ineradicable fact of pain, the tragic cast of being, from which Freud never flinched, nor his major disciples or apostates, even Jung, when he departed this world into archetypes and occultism.

In his commentary on *The Tibetan Book of the Dead*, Jung speaks of the *Chónyid* state, which is a bewildering reversal of the aims and methods of the conscious mind, "a sacrifice of the ego's stability and a surrender to the extreme uncertainty of what must seem like a riot of phantasmal forms." The *Chónyid Bardo* is like a deliberately induced psychosis, involving hellish torments, beastliness, and dismemberment of the *Bardo* body, that dissociated "Experiencing of Reality" which is, they say, the substance of karmic illusion. In a meeting of East and West, the swiftly executed square dance just after the opening of *The Donner Party, Its Crossing* is a kinetic preparation for a journey to that state. The obsessional figures move in silence. The Party has been summoned to a going-away celebration by the Caller who, in a many joke, tears off his shirt in the greeting and bites his arm, declaring himself a cannibal:

> The music's started, so heed my call
> Places all, oh, places all
> You've paid your money to have some fun
> So hitch up your wagons and follow the sun
> We're takin a journey, a promenade
> But time's a-wastin, I'm afraid
> The fiddler's a-rarin, don't be blue
> We're gonna dance till the bones shine through
> Take your belongins, don't be in a rut
> Everybody ready? Now bust your gut
> Little bit o heel, little bit o toe
> Circle around and don't be slow
> Honor your partner and now decide
> To yell like an Injun at the Great Divide

The latency of dismemberment is in the apparent gaiety. The theme is varied in the moving figures. The bodies are the "belongins." The

"We're gonna dance till the bones shine through" . . . The Enemy is dancing with th

psychosis grows with the exhaustion of the crossing and the gradual breakup of the unity of the wagon train, which is also the dance. The Enemy is dancing with them.

In *Elsinore*, the condition is more advanced at the outset. After the apprehensive gathering of the actors in a circle, a single figure rises into the space. He seems to resemble Hamlet but he is speaking Claudius' words: "My offense is rank, . . ." In a quick series of repercussive shocks, the time is out of joint. There is "a riot of phantasmal forms." The lone actor's flayed body seems to be tearing itself apart, as if it were being dismembered from within. The ideograph is a virtual effort to induce the psychosis—words flying up, thoughts remaining below—in a revulsion of being against "the primal eldest curse. . . ." As the symbolic dismemberment occurs, another figure circles the circle of observers in a hallucinated run (the mortal coil, the massy wheel, the stricken deer of the source-play). The word *murder* is sounded three times, as if the deed (is the running *from* or *toward?*) were being pulled out of the vocal cords. Reality is invaded, but we're not sure by what.

Jung acknowledges the connection of the *Chönyid* state in Lamaist doctrine to the profound Freudian intuition of the ego as the seat of anxiety, where deep-rooted fears resist the bursting out of unconscious forces in their full strength. The actor's body in *Elsinore* is like a seismographic transcription of these forces. The recorded shock of self-abuse seems to have been scripted by the Enemy. The subsequent action is like the repetitive decodings of analysis, which is itself threatening, the *sounded* extension of the shock. "No one who strives for selfhood (individuation)," says Jung, "is spared this dangerous passage, for that which is feared also belongs to the wholeness of the self." *What are we afraid of?* That would appear to be the crux in a concept of the self, the essential blood of an act of theater. But while Jung is translated in the passive, the dangerous passage is not: we live in an *act* of fear which is the history of its appropriation. What has been achieved by Western thought, according to Jung, is *not* a useless split but a subtle differentiation of subject and object, the establishment of a world outside the self on which the self can project its anxiety. "Here we seek and find out difficulties, *here we seek and find our enemy,* here we seek and find what is dear and precious to us. . . ." (Emphasis added.) Unfortunately, this consummation cannot last.

Unlike some of those in the theater who were (and are) playing with Archetypes and banishing the ego, Jung recognizes that the ego was liberated from the subhuman and the suprahuman (what he calls the "psychic dominants") at enormous cost. He says it was a heroic and necessary undertaking. The crossing made, nowhere does he suggest that the bounty should be surrendered. He does see the liberation, however, as something less than final. For the Enemy may have other ideas, if I may transpose his thought back to our own. The projections of the ego shift and change, as if the Enemy were the shape of desire that doesn't want to be final at all. The object of enmity which can be punished, enjoyed, destroyed if necessary disappears into the karmic landscape, like the Donner Party in its crossing from east to west, "lashed/ plains streaming from the snouts of beasts,/ the buried steps churning new roots." When, as in the settling of America, the landscape seemed to disappear—"No meaning but a habit of distance"—the anxiety in rage turned back upon the self, the landscape built upon a fault.

That is the territory of the mind through which we come in pursuit of the Enemy, who is forever doubling back. The horizon, as in *The Donner Party, Its Crossing*, "flows under [the] eyelids like blood. . . ." What we pass on the journey is not the mere skeletons of old forms ("boneache, stump and molar,/ hanks of horse, the oxen's scuttled jaw"), but living fossils, zoomorphic, not fossilizable. The techniques of the unconscious ("What do the wishbones say?") bring us to the depths where things survive that we'd almost rather not talk about—that, we thought, had disappeared from the face of the earth. That was the sense we had in the work on the Enemy, as we did later in the Burrow, where the Enemy seemed to split asunder and reproduce, invading from all sides—the body so besieged, it seemed to be divested of any power to resist. In the Burrow, the multitude of enemies is legendary, but not even legend can describe them, for "they are creatures of the inner earth. . . ." So, fear of surprise, fear of being taken unawares, from behind (as Freud realized about paranoia, fear of being buggered). We are talking of a paranoid consciousness in which, as in the paintings of Francis Bacon, even shadows bleed. Wherever the enemies are, the Enemy is, keeping its distance. There is no reciprocal trade agreement nor non-aggression treaty. The invasion may or may not happen, but it is feared, desired, tempted.

One of our purposes—in that long temptation—would be to name the Enemy and thus give ourselves access to it rather than ward it off, to make its powers, seeming inimical, serve us more powerfully. The danger was to collapse the Enemy into the self, as if the world were scot free. Our views of the Enemy might be diverse. Some might, recurrently, insist upon the denial or the forgetting, but that too would be recorded. We would construct the spoor of the Enemy from our separate sources (and skepticism), each of us offering what little he knew, even (if possible) the negative evidence of a refusal to believe the Enemy exists (indubitably the harder task). The aim would be to

Take Up the Bodies

develop a composite view something like those drawings the police make of a suspect when all they have is bits and pieces of information from the partial witnesses of a crime. All information would be rigorously construed. Not everything would be admitted. There would be strict rules of evidence. Like the Devil (another inscrutable figure, not necessarily the same), the Enemy is precise. Whether eternal or not, its nature is coded by time. Each of us is reading different signs. (It takes millions of years to work out an instinctive relationship between a predator, say the coyote, and its prey—what goes for the jackrabbit doesn't go for the sheep, although the idea of the predatory goes for us all. The Enemy is that idea.) If we used the word *myth* in describing what we were creating, that was itself a metaphor more or less realizing itself in the quest, as an accretion of projected value over time. Like love, the Enemy is an imaginative discipline.

In the exercises for the project—many of which persist in our work as technical concepts—we accumulated a virtual doomsday book on the Enemy. All of the following describe sequences of investigation, some of which overlapped: Origins of the Enemy; Names of the Enemy; Faces of the Enemy; Avatars, Masks, Disguises; Strategies of the Enemy; Politics of the Enemy; The Allies; Where the Enemy Lives; The Passion of the Enemy; The good Enemy and the Bad; Dreams of the Enemy; Possession by the Enemy (Incubi, Succubi, Familiars); Exorcisms and Spells; Talismans, Fetishes, Symbols; Casting Out the Enemy; Revelations of the Enemy; Oracles; Gospel, Secular Confessions (The Word by Which the Enemy Lives); Blasphemies, Imprecations, Abominations; Search and Destroy Missions; Victory Over the Enemy (Imagined); Burial of the Enemy; Its Resurrection; Loving Thy Enemy. About the Enemy, the actors became, each of them, a Central Intelligence Agency. In the acting process, there was a double agentry:

Each of us knows what to the other is unknown. To possess that knowledge from another—in the context of this investigation—certain forms had to be observed, a technique, a protocol of inquiry. Gradually, there was a mythicization of the material. The actors became adept at something like conjuring, summoning up the Other. Say the magic words, and the Other appears. It can be done. Anybody who has ever loved knows the process from its unloving moments. Sometimes, with the loved one, it's not even a word, merely a vocable or a gesture, the merest flick of an eyelash—and the Enemy is there. In the group, different actor, different magic. The actors became fabulous to each other. This was encouraged by particular exercises, not only the conjuring. For instance, the Oracle. As part of any mythic quest, one consults the Oracle, again with magic words. Who is the Oracle? Choose. Each of us is an oracle if the right questions are asked. We can all be invoked in the act of perceiving past the appearance of what we are. The Oracle is a mirror. Like the mirror of myth, it appeared in many forms: there were single oracles and double oracles, masculine and feminine oracles, hermaphroditic oracles, and group oracles. Sometimes the oracles were Janus-faced and double-voiced; sometimes the voice you expected to answer would not answer and the other would, or it would answer but in the other's voice; or it would answer but in the other's mouth; or in double features with triple tongue. There were again innumerable combinations, but the Oracle was always an image-construct in an imagined place.

The forms of the Oracle were sometimes "natural," the actors sitting face to face in conversation, sometimes ideographic. They were often visually striking and spatially complex. Sometimes they were very difficult to execute physically. The vocal image could also be very intricate. It was the state of mind, however, which was the enigma, and increasing habituation to slanting and gnomic thought that became second nature in the later work. Here, too, was a perceptual test, the necessity of attending to the slightest inflection of value. The resistance of the Oracle was also an issue. But since the premise of the exercise was that we all have oracular powers, one may even give an oracle by default. As Freud says in describing "A Case of Hysteria," "He that has eyes to see and ears to hear may convince himself that no mortal can keep a secret. If his lips are silent, he chatters with his fingertips; betrayal oozes out at every pore," even as the metaphysics comes in. Even with the trustiest of oracles the watching was essential, the meticulousness of the hearing. There were always hidden signs, illicit messages, subterfuges, traps. It was, after all, the world of the Enemy through which we were moving.

For all we knew, the Oracle was the Enemy. In the exercise, the Oracle would be chosen in terms of what the actors already knew of each other. They soon became aware, the more they knew, how little that was. Still, each "nature" among us would provide a different series of answers to the same questions, another set of clues. The actors became adept at assessing each other, weighing the value of the information, its timbre, bias, and reliability. It was a structure of both intimacy and distance. Ask a direct question, the Oracle of course rarely gives a direct answer. The Oracle can be evasive. So can the questioner. Oracles speak in riddles. But in this structure, riddles do not exist. Answers depend on what you want to hear. The Oracle takes the form of the speaker's desire. You've got to take the Oracle to heart.

So the art of questioning was developed. The actors became very skilled at making an inquiry roundabout, again making things more fabulous. A habit of indirection entered the work, finding direction out. It was important, however, that the questions be exactly phrased, and that they be asked in certain ways (to be guessed at) under particular conditions. The given circumstances entirely altered the nature of the questions and the answers. The one question that can never be answered is: "What do you mean?" We cut off the exercise when that occurs, or when anything is explained. What would appear to be deliberately obscure, and it is, is another order of intelligibility, very exact.

We have records of these dialogues, reams of them. They were decoded and analyzed for recurring themes and images, and often played back in other forms. The exchanges are mostly too long and too allusively imagistic to represent fully here, but the following is a partial list of questions that were asked in the multiple exercises of the Oracle. Many are generalized here as they were not there, summing up a tendency. In an actual dialogue, for instance, the word *enemy* might never have been used, though the Enemy is the object. Many of the issues were pursued and incorporated thematically in the subsequent work. The perspective of the pronouns is masculine (as it is through the book), but obviously gender and sex were at the crucial sticking point of many of the questions:

Is the Enemy death? Is the Enemy time? Is the Enemy there? Is the Enemy there when you look? When you love someone, do you take on his Enemy? Is the Enemy what is different? indifferent? Does the Enemy chafe? Is the Enemy silence? Does the Enemy live by the book? Was the Enemy born of a woman? When the sheet is tucked in all around my flesh, will the Enemy look at me then? Does the Enemy respect me? Can love defeat the Enemy? If you look into an infinitely clear sky, do you see the Enemy? Does the Enemy unbalance the scales? If the fool persists in his folly, he becomes wise—is excess the Enemy despite the fool? Where does the Enemy hide? Does the Enemy try too hard? Does the Enemy show mercy? pity? trust? Is the Enemy honorable, or a lie? What is the age of the Enemy? Is the Enemy lonely for me? How fast does the Enemy travel? What roads does the Enemy take? Does the Enemy dance like a bear? pounce like a wolf? Does the Enemy teach? Does the Enemy shed his own skin? If I prepare a place in the presence of mine Enemy, will the Enemy lie down beside me? Can I be comforted against the Enemy? Is the Enemy a burning babe? Will the Enemy hold my hand? When I meet the Enemy face to face, will he disgust me? Does the Enemy laugh when I cry? Does the Enemy spill the beans? Can I look upon the face of the Enemy and not turn to stone? Is the Enemy a side issue? Is the Enemy blocking the drain? Does the Enemy disturb my peace? Is the Enemy a crutch? Who are my allies against the Enemy? Can the Enemy hide behind glass? What is the

Enemy's coat of arms? Will the Enemy observe the rules of battle? Is the Enemy thought? Is the Enemy thinking of me? thoughtless? Does the Enemy know his own mind? Does the Enemy shit? without trouble? Does the Enemy wish my death? Does the Enemy do me harm? Is the Enemy the one you want to kill? Does age strengthen me in this folly? Does the Enemy punish me for my sins? Is the Enemy a number? a color? Does the Enemy really know me? a bird? a fish? Does the Enemy care? Does the Enemy rest? If my Enemy ravished me, would I be whole? If he toppled me, would I stand stronger? Does the Enemy ever think of me? Does the Enemy fight at close quarters, or does he shoot at a distance? Am I impotent before the Enemy? Does he cripple my sex? Does the Enemy give me another chance? Did the Enemy need to fight me on this score? What do I tell my children about the Enemy? Why doesn't the Enemy turn it off? Will the Enemy humiliate me? Why? Can I not be sure of lying before the Enemy? Does the Enemy know I'm lying when I lie? Is the Enemy in the mirror? Is the Enemy behind the door? What does the Enemy know? Does the Enemy really know? Does the Enemy have ears? Does the Enemy have a pleasing shape? Does the Enemy know I don't care? Can I beat the Enemy at his own game? What are the terms of peace?

We didn't know, that's for sure. We couldn't quite liberate the Enemy into performance either, partly because the actors couldn't believe in any objectification. Whatever the forms of our aggressions, it was the instinct of the group, reflected in these questions, to see the Enemy in ambiguous and subjective terms—and to the degree we did that, the material proliferated beyond us, too many dimensions. This was further complicated by the linguistic situation of the category of otherness, which fractures it into cross-reflections and impacted projections, so that the otherness of the Enemy was virtually dissolved into the structure of the unconscious, with its capacity for displacement, substitution, replication, and disguise. Soon even the Oracles were confused. Which was which? Who was the Oracle, who the seeker? We succeeded in confirming the psychoanalytical thesis that the unconscious *is* the Other, but in that confirmation the idea of the Enemy escaped. Rednecks, Birchites, the Radical Left, Terrorists, and the coal miners on the day I am writing this have no qualms about objectifying the Enemy. But we were victims of another kind of class distinction, not *out there* but *in here*. If, with the group, I pointed high above and said, "You're a Vietnamese peasant, that's a plane overhead, where's the Enemy?" the eye would go up and the arc of association down, with ballistic precision, striking one's own breast like a stigmata.

There was something admirable about it, there was something revolting about it—the powerful insipidity of our solipsism. The actors kept saying *my* Enemy, *your* Enemy. I kept insisting (the director in me, *my* Enemy), *the* Enemy—an archetype, like Satan, although (notice the qualification) he is not necessarily, as I said before, the *Enemy*. My error was to have looked on the Enemy as a substance, the privileged form of negative otherness. This of course assumed the most egregious error of certain kinds of modern thought, a substantialism of the ego or the subject. The actors, who quite properly cared not for the philosophical logic of what we were doing, rejected the latter but not the former. The assumption of a privileged ego was instinctive. They might doubt their existence as a proposition—or momentarily lose the ego in the process—but not as a lived reality. Which is to say, we may be disintegrating all over the realms of thought, in the shiftiness of the linguistic subject, but we go on behaving as if we are unified in the thinking body. What was a lived reality in our contention with the Enemy was the introjecting habit. There were serious implications, socially and politically, not to mention psychologically, in the refusal to label the other *that.* By turning the Enemy inward, we give him, her, it just the free play out there the Enemy wants. The Enemy is a shifter. By acknowledging the Enemy at all he, she, it wins. But how, I also wondered, do you not acknowledge what is surely there, if only the charged absence of a negating other, the primal antagonism at the empty center of being?

"Confidence in the principles of an enemy," says Kant in *On the Nature of Peace,* "must remain even during war, otherwise peace could never be concluded." *Can* peace be concluded? In this war, even the Oracle doesn't know. The Oracle hears everything and answers what it must. There are words the Oracle may appear not to hear, or will hear and ignore, or seem deliberately to misinterpret. Yet the answers are always there. Opaque. You hear what you want to hear. As for the magic words to summon the Enemy, one has to be prepared. The proprieties observed, the words spoken, another will appear, as when Faust summons Mephistopheles. But is it the Enemy? In presence, a double unfolding, and then the phases between, like the Woman Weaving at the Loom in the Tai Chi Ch-uan, or when between a man and a woman who are in love and seem to hate the words are said and a *third* seems to materialize, the reflection splitting, like the Ghost in the Closet Scene, though *materialize* is not perhaps the right word, for one sees it and the other doesn't.

The reflection is the imperative of other reflections: We are not condemned to be free, but rather confronted by the demand of the Other. The Other, as it emerges from history with all the authority of illusion, is always the oppressor, no matter who appears to have power. This is so on the psychic and social levels. (The opening of the contents of the unconscious in the West was, for instance, an invitation for the hordes—a term used by Freud and Genet—to arise in Africa and the East, a virulent otherness, making its demand.) If we were not quite ready, in working out *The Enemy*, to concede the illusoriness of the world-as-object, the very nature of the quest encouraged the solipsistic reduction. The thinking went like this: The adversary is an excuse. It is your own grievance that has found a voice. You strike at the Other (or the Other strikes) because it seems to be an affront, holding your heart in its hand. What we call love complicates the matter by obscuring the grievance, the brute facticity of an absence that supposes a self-reflection.

Who is the Enemy? It is said, no man strikes a single living face. Lest these ideas seem to be incapacitating, with no operational efficiency at all, let us hear another voice that, taking time, understood the dimensions of the problem: "The target and the battlefield exist everywhere, yet do not exist anywhere," said General Vo Nguyen Giap, who (for a time) liberated Vietnam with that perception.

Missing Persons

4

It seems natural to think of the theater as the theater thinks of itself, as interchangeable with dream. The stagings of the unconscious are similarly duplicitous; they appear to be doing one thing but are really doing another. The theatricality of dream is what we remember, the hallucinatory events which seem to be wholly happening. We tend to forget, however, what is being dramatized, the *dream-thoughts* played out in visual and acoustic images. In dreams, says Freud, we "appear not to *think* but to *experience*. . . . Not until we wake up does the critical comment arise that we have not experienced anything but have merely been thinking in a peculiar way, or in other words dreaming."

In theater we often favor the dreaming for the wrong reasons. We put the premium on experience and thereby ignore the nature of dreams. According to Brecht's critical comment, we are still digesting our dinners and prefer not to wake up and think. Or we muse over the "baseless fabric" of Prospero's revels, forgetting that his "old brain is troubled" and the paranoia unrelieved by love and forgiveness. Even in the Epilogue, after the promise of calm seas and auspicious gales, the "ending is despair" unless "relieved by prayer"—and the old brain of Freud told us, without a hedge of romance, just how unlikely that is. *The Tempest* is an early draft of *Civilization and Its Discontents*. If our little life is rounded with a sleep, that sleep is ideational and, whatever the dream-wish, the dream-thoughts are not promising.

There are times—as I recall the work I am describing—when it has the feel of a troubled sleep. In that work, the idea of performance seems to be hallucinating. Actually, it has been thinking, in a peculiar way. The central experience, as I've said, is the activity of reflexion, as if it

145

were the embodiment of Kant's theorem that time and space are necessary forms of thought. Reflecting on it, I realize, is not quite doing it, but there is a sense, as with dream, that what you say about it is a continuance. If none of it ever really existed, if I were simply making it up as I go along, the theoretical implications would be no less true —like false memory, or even lying, in the interpretation of dreams. There may have been in what we were doing a self-fulfilling prophecy, since it was obsessed from the beginning with the dynamics of disappearance, which made (it seems) for its inevitable but (in theory) conceptually deferrable end.

As for the self it was fulfilling, the subject of the dream, that's harder to identify. We thought of it as collective, but on the selvedge of solipsism. The mental activity is physically exhaustive, tonic, always ready to fall apart—a swift momentum of interfacing fantasies, metabolizing from person to person in a dazzle of identities—until the persons disappear in thought. If you were to see *Elsinore,* for instance, it might look like that dreamwork within a dream which rejects its interpretation. *Elsinore* was derived not so much from *Hamlet* as from the remembrance of *Hamlet;* or I might say out of its anticipatory memory of us, since we can only know it (it seems) as it wants to be known, reflexively, in a devastation of signs. To the degree that our sense of history is Hamletic, it is something like the thought of Hamlet through which we see it, as if there were nothing to thought but that thought, thinking making it so. In the dispersed narrative of this reflective process there is only the trace of an origin, specular, where even the presence of the actor is speculation. As with the flashlights of *Crooked Eclipses,* reticulating the dark in a structure of dream, there is the staking out of the missing person, the indelible datum of invisible presence, the precipitous subject, the always subliminal quarry of our work.

So: what we do is about who does it. But where in the world does it take place? And who is there? When the subject becomes its scene, they may both go out of sight. We speak about the play of thought and the thought of play, which places and displaces. All thought is a detour, said Freud, from the memory of gratification. The detours are endless and repetitive, as in the Burrow, as if something in the unconscious were mordantly switching signs. The project of *The Enemy* was gratifying only in memory. The actuality was unnerving. It left us, however, with the intuition of a theater form, and a legacy of content, that appeared to be nothing but the detours, always delaying gratification, with the subject as the scene.

It is a form seemingly concerned with its own origins, as if all it can remember is itself, no matter what else (whatever subject, whatever

Take Up the Bodies

text, whatever source) appeared to be there. As theater, it is an activity of consciousness in which origins disappear, the subject is unstable, and you can't be sure of the end. The grammatical shift between scene and subject with an ambiguous (or nonexistent) object (the *who* to *where* to *who* that constitutes the doubling play) seemed to be all that was left of theater since the characters lost their author and then got lost themselves in the devolution of authority through the lapsed identity of the person to the shiftiness of the role, almost dispossessing the actor (not to mention the director) who had to find another scene. The self is such a scene (like the deposed Richard in Pomfret Castle), a site of thought deceived into presence, living just this side of completion in thought. The Enemy was not a concept, but the prospect of a concept, an *abeyance*—a structure of incompleteness waiting for a sign: in the friction between us, the seeming the silence, each playing upon the other, the silence, receding . . . Artaud speaks of the victim (actor? audience?) signalling through the flames.

The silence of another—intolerable. The only defense is the silence within. It sinks through the space of thought with the acceleration of a falling body. The silence *between* is an agony. Was the Enemy the right name? Life goes without saying. The suspension is familiar, a modern classic, cinematic—but the film is running backwards, and all you hear is the hum of the projector, reel after reel, too loud, white light on the screen; not silence, but the upswept murmur of time, an incessance, seditious and self-defeating, as if in the transaction between the self and another all the voices of history were speaking at once. No wonder. We are told, and increasingly believe it, that nature and culture are but the fallout of language. Every reflex of behavior is inescapably spelled out. Not the absence of a sign but too many signs, as if any structure we might conceive is there before we start, exhausted by the writing, like the Kabbalah xeroxed.

In the theater that writing is a special enigma, because of the instinct of *mimesis*, the murmur doubled over—text upon text, subtext, occulted, interminable. Among the performers, there is also what Freud calls an "economics of nervous force," variable rates of being in the dimensions of antimatter; that is, in the exchange mechanisms of the unconscious. What we think of as silence, the inaccessible, how do we enact it? We are never quite sure whether to sustain it or break it. In the craft of acting, there is a metaphysics of timing. How long? asks the actor, how long? And how, out of the murmur, to say it *now*? Do we really have the words? We no longer trust the texts—in any kind of writing, on the page or behind the eyelids. The body—locus of living meaning, poor in expressive means—has told us for the time being as much as it can. The body, too, is unstable and reawaits the Word.

Communication (that hopeless word) seems to occur, when the silence is finally broken, in a weightless medium at the edge of absence, like a dialogue on the moon.

Exercise: Don't speak *above* a breath, but let the words *draw* the breath, in a cycle, words inciting breath, breath becoming words, breathless.

At the wedding of two actors in the group, a young priest officiating quotes Rilke (in words we can barely hear) *on two solitudes expanding to meet each other, in an overriding grace; two figures whose shadows touch. The actors have composed the service,* choosing their words. *I am moved by the vows, as by the sanctification of a void.* Self time voice memory mask: *shadow became shadow, crossing. At the end of all sacraments, the massive ceremony which divides* (like dreams); *a unity of negation, blank, fathomless, memoryless, and unexplained; a derision of marriage that can't, in any service, be named away.*

At the apex of craving, tangled, even art goes dumb. There is the silence which is dumb and the silence which is doom. There is also the silence which excludes us, that blank at the immitigable masked core of things. When that seems to smile as if it knows, the reaching self is fury, as if it were in danger of being cancelled. Yet there is a stimulus in the perceptual system. The very denial of self may be felt as a path of energy, an electrified probe in the thalamus of the brain. One thinks of Artaud, whipping his innateness. The impulse is toward *disclosure:* exposing the scene, coming out of the Closet, opening up the disguised subject, confession as ablution, stripping bare. The liability, for all that, is a form of hiding. The confession may be a coverup. The Closet is another Mousetrap. The self is especially vulnerable as a structure of thought.

Nevertheless, whatever has been vital, and engendering, in recent theater has played upon this vulnerability. There is the desire to come out of hiding. We've seen it in the formal principle of Alienation (Brecht), with its use of masks, as in the informal dispersal of theater into the streets, where the masks are presumably taken off. Sometimes the masks are worn into the streets, but that's considered *less* of a disguise. Whatever the case, the more self-conscious the stage becomes the more it worries about being a lie. Inevitably, the limiting condition of selfing in the theater turns out to be the degree of theater in the theater. Sometimes we want more, sometimes we want less. Whatever the origins of theater, it has always struggled with the desire to be something other than what it is: duplicitous or equivocal—the intention being to return it to the real, some purer state, as before, where desire was, and didn't fail.

In the idea of a theater *beyond* theater, there is always the image of no-theater *behind* theater, like the shadow of the sacrament. The ambition—as in Eliot's model of the Mass, or Grotowski's paratheatrical paganism, or Derrida on Artaud—is to banish *representation* and derealize performance into communion or (Grotowski's more secular word) a *meeting.* To the marriage of true minds, no impediments. The desire is for an even higher order of disclosure, *revelation,* or (since for Derrida there is a theocentric seduction in that word) life itself as "the nonrepresentable origin of representation"—the giving over of the self to the not-self, naked, *unacted,* to the more-than-self (the Logos erased or resurrected), made visible.

Yet is the *act* of performance the path of a lie? mere subterfuge and concealment? Yes, and no. All forms have rules. The theater's rules (like those of dream) are the rules of self-separation, and even a consenting self-delusion. We know when we go to the theater that we will be deceived. It's only a matter of time, time-serving. "Now, mother, what's the matter?" Even out of the Closet, there is no other matter. The truth of the form still depends—despite the post-Brechtian ideology of exposing the staging devices and undoing representation—on a pretense of ignorance. We take a willful innocence into the dark. The self reveals itself according to the laws of its nature, reflexively, as the conscious subject of apparent meaning. No sooner started, the process acquires a patina of deceit. Every attempt at demystification is another illusion, adding another layer of mystery to the opaque.

I have suggested that demystification may take the form of *more* theater. But if we persist in the de-theatricalizing process, immuring mimesis, unfrocking the apparent lie, we are left dumbfounded. There is another image from Rilke: We are in front of the mirror. We have forgotten our roles. We rub desperately at our makeup to take it off and be real. A smudge of disguise remains. There is a self-mocking arch at the eyebrow, an exaggeration, a grimace at the edge of the mouth. Now we're ripping at the disguise, mask after mask—as in the famous mime—until the flesh tears. The mirror breaks, an ontological parody, neither being nor acting. Or worse yet, we are victims of plain miscasting, whether by destiny or the self or—what a horrible fix!—as if indeed "It is chance that is infinite, not god," as Artaud would have it, or Derrida; that second phase of Creation where repetition is erased and it all seems undisguised, yet somebody, somehow, in in the wrong part. Of course, from the viewpoint of the performing self, any designation of a role is the cutting off of a disclosure from the pure libidinal body—as if there is no way *not* to be miscast.

What is strategic, however, about the telltale piece of makeup, for the theater, for the self, for the self in performance, is that it may enter the syntax of theater. You can't erase it, but it brings an *unassignable* resilience to the form, as if consciousness of the factitious were challenging on its own ungroundedness the now categorical imperatives of ceaseless *difference* (no makeup at all, the forgetting of repetition, destroying imitation) that we see in Artaud, Derrida, and the immaculate deconstructions of post-Structuralist thought. In our work, the betraying piece of disguise—voluntary or involuntary—*registers* in a fracturing process of thought drawn between word and breath as an increment of perception. Between identity and otherness, there is no pure sonorous stream of imperceptible difference, but a suffusing gamut of *articulations*—not-I, not-Other—from which an intimation of a self, deriving itself, gains whatever expressive value it has, in the corrosions of mere expression. There is a subversive energy in the process which may be paradoxically used for building a character, but the problem now—at the heart of the work, in life, a substitute for the subject—is believing in a character you want to build.

In that process, the following truths may not be self-evident but seem engrailed in the dream-thought of theater:

The disguise that sticks is a map of the invisible. The realism of performance is the remnant of a mask. We are no longer sure that keeping it on is any the less true than taking it off, even if that were possible. We are always looking for fresh gestures of released being, but we are always discovering that they have already been made, contracted before memory. To know oneself is to be foreseen. We are already bespoken. The voice coming out of the mask is always an ancestral voice. We have not yet found an alternative to the recognition scene. The meeting is still over the tomb. The tomb is representation as it represents itself—sign of the murdered father in the bloody circle of that sign. Orestes plays at being the Stranger, then has to play at being Orestes. In that circuit of performance there is the simultaneous current of the "person" playing the "actor" playing the "character" (more or less conscious of acting, even when there is no character and he is presumably playing "himself"), of whose credibility we have no way of assuring ourselves anymore, since the text has been confiscated by history and the terms discharged into each other, the character fractured to roles, the actor deconstructed and the stage all over the place. There is still the undeniable unity of the corporeal body—an apparent coherence in a specious now—but otherwise (and because of it) the entire nature of acting is up for grabs, including the separation of self from self in the playing, raising the question of *who*, actually, is acting. What we can say is that somebody is.

. . . not-I, not-Other . . . . The disguise that sticks is a map of the invisible.

In this circuit of performance—with its exponentially charged consciousness of the old doubling paradox of acting—the way out appears to be the way in. Or is it the other way around? The desire to void the circuit of any re-presentation or form of disguise is the correlative of the desire to strip politics of anything in the systems of power that sustains it by masking. We are always looking for a theater where the boundaries are erased—particularly where there's a hierarchy implied—between function and person, character and actor, illusion and truth, self and other, art and life, inside and out. But these binaries are merely symptomatic misstatements of finer divisions, which need a more rigorous thinking through in the acting out. (In recent times the problem has been dealt with by the easy currency of a facile holism, collapsing the terms. It's like proving that being is becoming by lifting the wavy line and dot from the visualizing circle of Yin and Yang. The Tao, disguised, is laughing up its absent sleeve.) The divisions are stratified by experience, stubbornly, with the irredeemable makeup. And the performance, knowing that and even making an issue of it, may be the closest approach we have to the undisguised shape of a meeting.

That other nakedness, then, do we never achieve it? in love? another mask? another kind of performance? even at the altar? We warn the lover against performing as we sometimes do the actor. *Don't act*, we even say. Then, as in the reversals of the sonnets, we change our minds. *Act. Don't try to hide it, you can't.* Since the self is only a construct, it is not concealable. It is all there at face value, on the surface. The mask, which is nothing but surface, is as naked as can be. It doesn't turn around or shift aside. It is nothing but confrontation. ("Spirits have no back," says the ancient lore.) The invisible is manifest. The purest act is the grace of pretense. In the conjugations of self, there is only the pretense, makeup smudged. The offense rankles, coming and going. We do not like even the vestiges of a coverup. No matter. In the deepest suffusions of love—who will deny it?—there may be another disguise: essential.

As in the unconscious, concealment occurs in a dangerous zone of repression. We have learned from Freud, however, that the repression is strategic, a potential storing up of energy, a transfer from the unreliable economy of the social order to the uncanny economy of the psyche. "Hide fox, and all after," say the actors in *Elsinore*, splitting, and splitting the words, as they fracture the dubious circle of collective identity—recoiling at the end from the false or falsifying ground of a meeting. (The line is displaced in our text from the scene where Hamlet has just stowed Polonius's body with a "certain convocation of politic

Take Up the Bodies

worms. . . .") The actors withdraw behind the audience, concealed, leaving the space empty to thought. For the moment, a self comes out of hiding, dubiously, drawing them back. As with Hamlet, the act of concealment, played, is a libidinal drive, transgressive. It is a spur and a solicitation to the self's identity in the search for truth.

It is also a search for lost power, intensity, the fuel of force. "Not as strong as I used to be," says one of the older voices in the wordplay of the opening square dance of *The Donner Party, Its Crossing*. "Well, ya can't sneeze at experience." (Somebody sneezes.) You don't know what to make of it either. "Round as a dollar slick as a mole/It's got no tail but find that hole." The callings of the dance are a series of riddles. It's no accident that the earliest theater was addicted to riddles. The hiding is a revelation. Experience tells us that the processes of displacement in the unconscious are doubled over in the mechanisms of theater. In the theater—which conceals in order to expose—there is always an Energy Crisis. This is all the more true as the principle of authority, which formerly determined what images were to be brought back from the unconscious, was turned on its head: "Two legs up and two legs down," sings out the Caller, "baby's in the tub, papa's in the ground"—but we're not sure there is any ground, only the grounding, a circling of the square dance in the intricate figures of the journey. In the theater, as in the unconscious (after all), the journey is a form of desire. There is a similar journey of wish fulfillment after the dance over the tomb when, in the ungrounding drama which *Seeds of Atreus* remembers, the Stranger (apparently) puts off his disguise.

Wish want will dream desire—what? How to keep it alive? It may have to go into hiding, like the Caller in his riddles. The dancers shuffle in another direction, a voice says more than it knows: "You have to be shifty in a new country." As for the theater, what can be said through the form is not due to the concealing or the shifting alone, but rather to our *awareness of the language of desire* inherent in these displacements, the self hiding and not hiding. "Comin in, goin out—that man was born goin all ways," says one of the women of the Donner Party about Hastings, that enigmatic figure of the guesting self, always just over the horizon, who wrote the guidebook that took them over the perilous route, as if some brainy opportunism in experience were determined to deny the value of experience, since he'd never yet been where he sent them. "You better not be laughin at me, you bastard!" cries a figure of Donner into "the wild blue yonder," where the otherness named Hastings exists, though he is actually part of our history.

The wagons are picking up speed in the dance, the actor's bodies clattering in the image, the Party pursuing the dream and sensing disaster. The actor who is singled out as Hastings refuses even the openness of the role, wanting *to play it all* and not—with all that real estate out there—be foreclosed in the journey by an assignment of "character." The other *actors* (named in the following sequence) are trying to keep him (it) bounded, in focus, as they lurch, wishbones shaking in an apprehensive dance of bones, toward the self's atomic and metamorphic future:

> BILL: Here we go, over the Great Divide!
> DAVID: I'm gonna piss in both oceans.
> WES: Boom!
> PETER: That's the long and short of it. Can you imagine? No color. (He is looking at the Great Salt Lake.) A light at an infinite distance!
> DAVID (as Hastings): Hastings Memorial Highway! (As the Teamster): Ain't no one comin through, I told ya. (German accent): My name is Hardcoop. Died in transit. You can't sneeze at experience. (All sneeze.)   They'll abandon me, you'll see!
> PETER: Hastings is a tall short fat-skinny man. Never takes off his coat.
> BILL: Speculation, pure speculation.
> DAVID: Killed seventeen Injuns, ate my dog. *I'll be anybody I damn well wanna be!*
> LINDA (always keeping the rhythm of the dance): Designs fail, desire counts, you need the competence to carry it out.
> DAVID: Fuck off!
> WES (Donner voice): You, Hastings!
> DAVID: I wanna be Lavina Murphy!
> BILL: Speculation, poor speculation.
> PETER (to DAVID, as they cross in the dance): Hastings?
> MICHAEL: Look—headwaters of the Sweetwater!

The line comes out of Michael's silence. The sequence condenses a double process: to move from the Great Divide to the Sweetwater is to be abandoned in several roles, or to have no role at all, yielding the independence of the actor to the exigencies of the wagon train. The difficulty of the crossing is reflected in the technical rigors of the dance ("you need the competence"—and the endurance—"to carry it out").

The actor is, then, a function of the journey, but not as in some new theater events (say, the plays of Richard Foreman), a function of the *external* design, since the nature of the journey is defined through the process by *the self-determining choices* of the actors, who often *refused* to do otherwise. The same was true of the migrants in the historical crossing: one journey reflects the other. The sequence is about Hastings and about David who—through all the months of improvisations —was, more than the others, identified with Hastings, but resisted being fixed in a role, even one so open-ended, though he might momentarily want to seize it. (The historical Hastings died actually trying to become the Emperor of Brazil!) We were quite conscious in the process that the ambivalence was part of the subject. The act of being conscious was not a mere rationalizing of the ambivalence but (as with consciousness itself, "pure speculation") a subversion of its object, scattering it to the winds ("poor speculation")—as if the ambivalence were, nothing but motion.

In the westering of the self, the figure of Hastings is all we have left of a hero, the missing person. In the design of *The Donner Party, Its Crossing,* he is constituted as an avatar of the journey by all of the actors, collectively, tempted by and resisting the anarchic individuality (a form of the Enemy?)—a paradigm of group process, without the premature and gratuitous embrace. It is a way of crossing the Divide (sum of all divisions), though the Sweetwater is obviously an illusion, clearly not-there, seen in the mind's eye, a double illusion (thought-space, Edenic space), mere passing. Time and space are actually, in the Nietzschean rather than Kantian sense now, only things measured by the rhythm of the dance. "Designs fail desire counts. . . ." The headwaters remain the self.

In the psychopathology of theater, the missing person is a seminal proposition and the disguised life a generative principle. We may *think* in those terms what may never have occurred to us without them, because they insist upon *being thought*—though the speculation (*watching* thought, like theater theory) may be more or less up to its subject. To avert the inference, however, that a psychopathology of theater applies only to a psychologized theater, let me point out that there are critical dimensions of concealment even in the dramaturgy of Brecht, where the cards are supposedly laid on the table. For the action *shown* is substituted (as in the mechanisms of the unconscious) for another which is *not;* that is, the scene played is always pointing to the scene which, in the social world, *should* be played, and would be, if our politics were unobscured. Mother Courage closes her pocketbook on the action which is not-there. The turntable is a hermeneutic circle, particularly at the end of the play, where war woman wagon seem to return again through the objective distancing to the disabling structure of the unconscious, where the energy is concealed that enables. If the circuit of performance is again closed, it is not before the *illusion* of power (not-power) has been released. It is not quite what Brecht meant in theory, but the theater has its ideology too, a fractional difference, turning the table in its own way.

The property of concealment is, then, an aspect of the grammar of theater which posits the certainty there of life. To that extent (legitimately?) the margins blur. What does he *want?* we used to ask the actor to ask of the character within the Action framework of the Superobjective. Then: with what force of *will*? Nietzsche, Marx, and Freud—each of whom tried to salvage the will from the free enterprise of repressive capitalism—taught us to ask the same questions of behavior within the political economy of our psychic life or the libidinal economy of our political life. If there is an interpretation of reality, individual or social, we have to ask what the interpreter wants. They were all explicit about that: *what you want is what you'll see*. But how do we see what we want? So much of it is hidden, hidden from ourselves. Recognition of the problem has brought about a significant change in the theater: we used to ask what the character wants; we now ask what the actor wants. As if he knows. The uncertainty is not necessarily disabling. The acting may come out of the desire *to know*, the force of it depending on the will.

As there is always a tissue of language which, eluding consciousness, accounts for the expressive potential of words, so with the impetus of concealment. In art religion politics love, the power still comes from what is hidden; that *is* the mystery, though it may sound like a tautology, and is. Were it not for the concealed, moreover, we might never be able even to conceive of love. "Get the message?" says a slightly inebriated, slyly psychotic friend who riddles me long distance in the middle of the night, as if the unconscious were sending up instructions over the phone. The message is the message, only too clear, what Freud clinically observed, what my friend knows only too well, what her refrain conveys: *"Get* the message?"—the meaning in the meaning: that even the disguises of paranoia (are there any other disguises?) are transparent, a playing out of all the possible variations on the delirium of refusing to love. The word for unconcealment is *alethia*, lovely on the tongue, like a whisper waiting to be kissed.

In tracing the insubstantiality of the self through the insubstantiality of performance, we are at the place which Freud calls, as the dream-wish goes out of sight, the dream's navel. It may be the same place where, as in *Measure for Measure*, "prayers cross." The substance of love in performance is a rich heritage, inherent in all spiritual disciplines —to which, recently, we have been looking for concepts of acting, as Gordon Craig, Yeats, Stanislavski, and Michael Chekov did in the past. Whether or not the self exists as a stable ego with a continuous history may not be so crucial as whether it is momentarily believed in, sponsored, as the currency of an offering. The meeting solitudes are a consolatory whole. We love in the *idea* of love, loving ourselves loving. In that sense, love is an imaginative discipline, as it is in Shakespeare's sonnets.

In the psychosexuality of acting, one looks for the wished-for fac-simile, that exquisite reciprocity of performance when actor and other embrace in the playing, embrace the playing itself and thereby exalt it (for the moment) to more than play—but in a rare modesty of mutual pretense composing a relation, a meaning in the meeting, if only the pretense—self infolded in self, the nuclear dream. It is perhaps the best illusion we have, union in otherness, as the dream of a possible Action is written off with the self in time. It is related to what Stanislavski calls the public solitude of the actor. Shakespeare writes of it as "the perfect ceremony of love's rite"—the rightness of the writing ("in eternal lines to time") being the structure of the unattainable and an unattainable structure, where self-love possesses the eye, coupled, and is not a sin.

Nor a deceit. We tried to play through that longing in the myriad divisions of *Crooked Eclipses,* whose presiding motive, like the self, was the inverse of the Enemy. Or so we thought. If the sonnets were obviously not intended to be staged, there's a question whether some were even meant to be read by anyone but the person they were ad-dressed to. But who was that? Deeper than scholarship, inevitably a performance, the autobiographical problem is what the sonnets are about: an autobiography of the self without a subject. Or is it the other way around? Whichever the case, they have the power of confessional poems so utterly confessed they almost evacuate the subject of the self, so that we wonder who's there doing the confessing. There is very little clear incident, no narrative. But there is a hidden story, involving the Young Man and the Dark Lady, and other shadowy figures, a series of missing persons, including the Poet, the "I" of the poems. The perfor-mance was a speculative inquiry by the group into the evidence of absence, "a quest of thoughts, all tenants to the heart. . . ."

In all we do, heart beats over the problem of perception: what we see because of what we want and what we don't because of how we see it; what we'll never see perhaps because it's all seeming, "nought but shows," and we're never sure that the heart is trustworthy, beating as it does through time—the bloodstream of the missing person, the medium through which the theater moves.

The sonnets embrace the process, and the process embraces the son-nets. *Crooked Eclipses* was a summary image of the self assessing itself, hopelessly, in the act of performance. The "imperfect actor on the stage" is a paranoid embodiment of the life unlived because not wholly moved by love. It is a matter of overcoming the resistance, stage fright. Self-seeking, self-knowing, self-obsessed, in the act of reflection, self-loving, and "with his fear . . . put besides his part"—the actor acts to be acted upon, moving and being moved, unmoved. We begin in a space of contemplation, the actors in a whorl of genders, encircled by

". . . a quest of thoughts, all tenants to the heart. . . ."

. . . what we see because of what we want and what we don't because of
how we see it . . .

and encircling the audience, man and woman man and man woman and woman, still, coupled and solitary. Quietly, and then with syncopations, these words are spoken: "What is your substance, whereof are you made,/ That millions of strange shadows on you tend?" The tendance is the theme. Behavior splits in a glint of substance through the mirroring choreography of the flashlights. There are degrees of acting, permutations, a palette of acting styles, *precipitations.* The sequences enacted are views of who-and-what's there, circuitous and partial, maybe obscure, like the sonnets, which are baffling teasing obsessive, so dexterously audacious, quick, and mental about love— about love and acting—they are almost demoralizing, like love itself.

Which almost returns us to silence, but not quite. For Shakespeare, though the end of love may be silence, it is love that returns us to language, which gives love the power to triumph over time. We still associate the sensations of the body with the symptoms of ecstasy in love (or acting), but it is not, according to the sonnets, the body which transports us to the invisible, out of time. Only words can do that—which is why, in lovemaking, for all that we're told don't say it, we feel that we *must* say it, and the one who tells us don't say it wants to be told.

In the sonnets, the broken sacrament of love remembered is summoned up through an erogenous universe made out of words. The words are inexhaustible, like their subject. Even when memorized, memory can hardly contain them. The incomprehensibility of love is precisely in its comprehensiveness. It is either too much or not enough. The heart is swayed by insufficiency, either in the object of love, because nothing human can be understood to have such power, or in the self, because only too human. The loved one is the farthest expression of the self's conception of itself, a field of infinite difference, articulated, where "every word doth almost tell my name. . . ." For us, it is the naming of the acting process, the self subject to "variation or quick change"—the "name buried where my body is. . . ."

The self may also embrace itself too easily. But the little burning Babe is fierce. Lovers embrace but love is not embraceable. The loved one is inaccessible, an absence. A missing person, with a mind like steel. Love seeks love, in the sonnets, by compelling it into thought, "grounded inward" in the heart. It is an imaginative audacity "delivered from the brain" into the utmost assumption of all that which, for the duration of loving, *one* is not: "flesh stays no farther reason. . . ." The initiation in love is synesthetic, living *through* the boundaries of the senses, but in loving the eye is in the mind, and because of that the entire material universe may be introjected by the act of love, in the image of the loved one, who is seen only by the world which is known only by love which can only be thought—"But, ah, thought kills me that I am not thought. . . ."

Naturally, we are never quite sure that the loved one isn't the Enemy.

The lacuna in the sonnets is not only that between lover and loved one, but between subject and object, word and thing, actor and act. It is the appropriation of all binaries into the dream's navel of a resolution in the whorl of thought that is the wonder of the poems, the chambered nautilus of a performance, like the design of the space in which we played. Here the lyric mode achieves, with an elegance of apprehension, a state of action—the power of illusion resisting the ineradicable division. The I and the Other are not mere opposites, nor are they one and the same. That's what we tried to understand in *Crooked Eclipses,* by showing it, an impossible project, since the subject is what—as Hamlet says of himself—"passeth show. . . ." Yet the idea of love gives continuity where we fear its loss. The laws of love are the laws of continuity, even among things that are radically disjunct, deterrent, like the fear *put besides* the actor's part. In that sense, love is a structural model, the ordination of a self, as if a bridge were to materialize over an abyss which is merely thought, like a restoration of the smooth body of the Ghost.

For all their dwelling on absence, the sonnets know too that the idea of love is historical, the body irredeemably scarred. The power of love, its chills and fevers, depends on a tradition of love which was once not only sanctified but economically and socially privileged. The language of love secretes the principles of mastery and domination, bondage and servitude, out of which comes, as in Phaedra, the desire for "the passive content/ of dry silence and solitude"—unspeakable repression, self-inflicted. "At this juncture of nature and culture, so persistently examined by modern anthropology," says Lacan in his lecture on the mirror stage, "psychoanalysis alone recognizes this knot of imaginary servitude that love must always undo again, or sever." Unless I'm looking at an imaginary mirror (which may be), the sonnets were there before him, but in this matter it makes no difference what discipline, whether psychoanalysis or poetry, has priority—since they confront the same illusion. While love may have been born in dispossession, one can thank one's lucky stars that one can love at all, or think one loves, since love is a cultural invention—like language, like the theater, like the actor, like the self.

The problem is: they are inventions on which the patents are running out, fast, like the film going backwards through the projector.

Reversing the film: in discrete and successive acts of mind—against the disappearance of the person in the "millioned accidents" of history—we posit the quite incredible, undeniably powerful idea of a continuous self. The idea requires the faith we require of love. If not by meeting, then a provisional solipsism, as in *The Donner Party, Its Crossing*—the perfection of a single solitude, in a blaze of moments, "like the sudden dazzle/ of the thinnest blade." Or the narcissistic actor in the flashlight of *Crooked Eclipses:* "But thou, contracted to thine own bright eyes,/ Feed'st thy light's flame with self-substantial fuel," a speaking pronoun in a play of names on a nameless subject. At loose ends in history, in resistance to being diffused by the naming, one subtracts from oneself everything that is not oneself, that illusion. Sanity may depend upon the fiction. "Lay plans for the next shadow," says one of the Donner Party, just over the desert—where property and past have been abandoned, and the social contract, the wagon train in disarray, the road nothing but wheeltracks, the ghost of a dance; and the cannibalism about to start.

The desire for continuity in the self is a flow of consciousness, from one work to another, the spoor of shadows, shoring up the ego, reinforcing it, sustaining it, even against its own depredations—the more so the more strenuously threatened. That is one of the major functions of the work, implicit in its method, the image by which the method moves. The starting point is, as I've suggested, a reflexive state of mind spinning radically on its own axis, down to the last shadow, the subtraction we *won't* make, not if we can help it, not even in the stunned, disjunct consciousness and nearly absolute stasis of the deathstink below the snow:

> Which if, rarely, this condition, no matter with, this condition nevertheless, finding myself here ssss scanning never stopping eyes constantly, as you suppose, slowly arching, almost out of each other, I could not, my wife here, in the pitch, this small child this smaller child which are getting, they were all brought, you see, hardly, here smaller and smaller nevertheless, and colorless, apprehensively over the prospect, brought, *I will*, sniffing in its own stench for a structure in which to awake sss sss sss sewing buttons on my eyes *yes?* to silence them tapping in the dirt, of course, a finger an arm in a nutshell a foot but consequently of many parts, tapping, I said to her, the bitter end singing in its sleep, everything everything, all I knew, *damn you! and the rest yet if*, never mind, perhaps it is a stomach falling sss into the earth, and if not, because of the air it could have been elsewhere which is drawn, *nothing in the air but air*, into itself over the trees, why. . . .

The snow is a metonymy of consciousness; so are the flashlights.

Take Up the Bodies

The members of the Donner Party come to this Pass—as the evolving text eventually described them, after months of verbal and nonverbal improvisations—"rising falling moving volitionlessly toward the mountains drifting and spinning at a touch," the slightest breath of body against body turning them in performance like flurries of snow, "an interior pressure of motion" moving though they can barely move (no pretense in the actors, who are literally exhausted), the dispossessed and separating bodies "massing powerlessly," clinging and falling, uplifted, "into the massively falling power of snow" (still, even on the ground, lifting and falling like snow, in the figures of the enduring dance). They constitute the snow which buries them, like consciousness, the subjects becoming the scene.

In *Crooked Eclipses,* the flashlights are what they appear to be, instances of self-perception, guiding the eye which "seems seeing, but effectually is out. . . ." They also imply the force which "governs" the actors "to go about"—nearly immobilised in function, blinded by desire—in a repertoire of "quick objects" perceived by the eye (including fantasies of betrayal in love, the worst erotic imaginings), of which the mind has "no part. . . ." The insubstantiality of light abrades upon the sensibility of the exposed actor, who is drawn to it and quartered by it, with an opposing instinct to hide in the dark. One wants to be en-lightened but not always when one is the subject. The works are bound to each other by such images which, soliciting consciousness (immaterial as light), resist the loss of ego even when, as in the snow, it must yield itself powerlessly to the massively falling power, as one surrenders to the flow of the *chi.* The exercise in volitionlessness takes great strength of will, in the willingness to surrender—almost impossible to act. There is, then, an exploration of the dissolution of ego and *the release of consciousness into structure, becoming an image of the ultimate subtraction, the death of self, which —as it materializes—is refused.* In that respect, the works are emblematic arousals of residual will fighting off the loss of self in the striations of thought, like the yellow leaves in the sonnet which *shake against* rather than quiver in the cold of the bare ruined choirs.

"Look what thy memory cannot contain," says one of the greatest of the sonnets, holding up the mirror to the insidious devastations of time. We performed it as an orchestration of breathing—nothing in the air but air, words drawn into breath—a kind of sacramental gasp into *self*-consciousness, the solitude mirrored by mist. There is a pressure in the work corresponding to the challenge of its "origins." The effort is to define the image on the imminence of a collapse into mystery: "*Commit* to these waste blanks" (emphasis mine), the breathing space itself, even when stinking. In this theatrical image constructed from a non-theatrical source, we were very conscious of words coming off a page, the text behind the text inscribed on the air, the writing of *voice*, that testament of the self, even before words, which is both transparent and opaque, like the spoken words (above) from (below) the snow. In that immobilised image from *The Donner Party, Its Crossing*, coming out of the dark, as in the quick illuminations of *Crooked Eclipses*—who is speaking? More of a *voice* than a person, barely a self.

What is the voice? All we know is that something comes up through the nervous system which is incommunicable and disjunct, bereft of flesh once out of the body, silencing the body as it goes—all the more as it goes into language, which is the history from which it came. Even when not voiced, words inciting breath, breath becoming words in *a remembrance of breathing*, voice, giving voice, voicing. (Simple dialogue from a rehearsal:

SHE: In that Hastings exercise, you asked me what
    I want. I didn't answer exactly.
ME: What do you want?
SHE: The most shocking intimacy.
ME: With whom?
SHE: With you.

As voiced in performance, there was the intimacy and the phrase about intimacy, displaced, spoken by the same actress, shocked [whose voice is now my voice on the page, as it was when she first heard the words in the text]. The shock was a *double entendre*, induced by the journey being remembered through rehearsal, where the motives of history and the motives of the self, leaving their traces in the voice, were subsequently deciphered into a text. But how much history was already there before it was voiced, before the words even reached her lips?) Somehow, but inexpressibly, the voice seems attached to that prospect of a self which is both an addition and a subtraction, the reality which exists on thin air—the deepest substance of any vow, unvoiced.

We are totally in the dark. The actors are invisible against the wall. They hold the flashlights below their faces, the lights going on and off, now this *that* now that *this*, through successive masks of aging, an undertow, lights passing from one to the other, and back, "Like as the waves make toward the pebbled shore," a murmuring surge, voices through the rhythm of light-waves (an articulation of speech, light, facial masks), words also passing among them, "in sequent toil," syncopated and divided, impeccable, through a commonly felt meditation on Time—"Each changing place with that which goes before," a litany

         Take Up the Bodies

of words lights faces masked, as if the poem, spoken, were *un*written and the ego gone, an interiorizing of memory that is, in the minutes hastening to their end, nothing but *succession*, oceanic, a *for*getting of self, as if, too, the meditation wants to *un*remember the momentary history between sentience and succession, presence and spoiled being, the epiphany of the crooked eclipses, *before* the blemishing "parallels in beauty's brow"—and so to become, eclipsed, in all identities, all agings, *one* voice, but to accomplish it by embracing and sustaining and then eliding the differences, sustaining, as with the words, instead of summoning up remembrance, summoning *sounding* . . .

And so, too, sounding, the final lyric of *Crooked Eclipses* is meant to be a discrete image of negative capability, the term which Keats invented for Shakespeare—that self-annihilating identity which distributes its presence through one body after another, now you see it now you don't, as we might tease a thought through an eternity of speculation without closing it off, no reaching irritably after reason before its time. The lyric comes soon after a sequence in which the figure of a woman is dragging another on her back across a long shaft of (grounded) light through a (relative) infinity of space to the light's source, alluring and harsh, originary. We have a sense of laborious and ineluctable patience draining itself out against all skepticism—denatured, ungendered, the self no longer an issue—to the edge of doom. What there is, after all the feverish quest of love, is the full, and simple, weight of burdened insufficiency. It is the ideograph of a desire so brutalized into being by the rigors of love it is almost joyous—not quite pure will and never sufficient.

The final lyric is a collage, as if the sonnets were sounding themselves. The estranged and solitary actors illuminate each other selectively across a space that appears to have no ground. Not a self, but a vertiginous remembrance of the self choirs its substance in hopeless fragments of desire, as if it could be, might be, a prophetic soul dreaming on things to come, outlasting if only in fragments the resistless measures of time, "swift-footed/ roses of shadow/ Time," like an indestructible wish hallucinating, the perfect likeness of a past, which is all that prophecy ever dreams. As we approach an ending—the actors disappearing in the flashlights counting down—the word Time is like a knell, Time recurring, with (I thought) a beautiful insufficiency in the air, the consummation of an image that won't hold still, something stealing from the figure but imperceptibly there, like voice, like thought (the thought of theater vanishing into thought): the persons missing, but in (for the sustaining moment) a marriage of true minds.

The idea of the mind as a kind of theater was not alway a vertiginous concept. In Hume's *Treatise on Human Nature*, perceptions make their appearance, gliding and coalescing in a mental landscape in a quite civilized fashion, secure in the coherence of their passing. But in the theatricalizing of experience through history, Hume's is a rational holding action. The rupture of thought had already occurred. In Hamlet's wild and whirling words the gliding and mingling perceptions split and fracture in a dazzle of instants like the obscure half-life of fissionable matter, or the "genital" and "acategorical" thought admired by Michel Foucault in an antioedipal text: "This is philosophy not as thought, but as theater: a theater of mime with multiple, fugitive and instantaneous scenes in which blind gestures signal to each other." It is not exactly such thought but the thought of it, distressed by the blind gestures, for which we have been trying to find an embodiment *in* the theater as it appears to be torn apart. It is like a reversion, or *rendering*, of theater in which there is a last oedipal struggle against the blindness, the very life of us entering the mind reflecting its own content, thought feeding on thought as if it were flesh, "consumed"—as with a seminal figure of the sonnets—"with that which it was nourished by." Cannibalism—the ostensible subject of *Seeds of Atreus* and *The Donner Party, Its Crossing*—is another name for the structure.

In the derivation of *Elsinore* from *Hamlet*, the text is not only deconstructed but dismembered. *Elsinore* is—in that sense, the grotesque image coming from its source—the funeral baked meats furnishing forth the marriage table. As remembered, *Hamlet* is a play of broken sacraments and maimèd rites, proclaiming no more marriages because, in the madness of true minds, you can't trust fathers or mothers, and especially love. In the amplitude of its consciousness, that "mortal coil," there seems to be all we know of self time memory, and every mask. Sometimes it seems as if we are thinking through *Hamlet* and *Hamlet* is thinking through us. There are times when the words are like the hebona in the ear which killed off the seminal figure; yet a whole theory of theater in that distilment. The play, for the actor, is cunning about craft. It became, through the investigations of our previous work, the genotext of *Elsinore*, which serves now as something of a prototype of the theory I am remembering. That is no doubt because of *Hamlet*, a ready field of reference that is never what it seems. We came to the play not because we wanted to do "a" *Hamlet* (one of the ultimate desires of doing theater), but because it seemed to be implicated in what was already *there*, in the emergence of method from the earliest work on *The Enemy* to the immediately preceding work on *The Burrow*, which seemed coterminous with the cellarage. When you think about it as a source, it slips away, as if denying its own origins, or attributing it to us.

For the play appears to scourge all prior dispositions toward its text: subverting every trace in the mind of previous stagings, the biases and defilements of incursive thought. When Hamlet, at the desperate edge of the farthest thought, arrests the speculation and says "Let be"—it is to escape defilement in another detour. The words are, in their astonishing understatement, a relinquishing limit of introspective consciousness which, *in that moment,* jumps the barrier of text and stage. The caveat is to the interpreter as to "himself," the character-as-interpreter, the interpreter to the actor and the actor to the interpreter in the hearsay of the text. "Let be." If it be not now, it will be now. (The readiness which is all is also a matter of reading.) The assent to an absolute yet contingent present feels at the moment outside of time, yet in time, outside of thought. If it were conceptualized, it would be defiled, the (already confusing) plenitude of the present. Hamlet's only means of getting outside the rottenness of Denmark (I am interpreting) is to get outside of thought (he can't). The letting be is easier said than done, and in any case not more than a moment. The merest semblance of a man (Osric) appears next, all defile(d), another appearance to be interpreted. He summons the actor back to the play, which never lets well enough alone. In the play of thought there is an apparent diffusion of consciousness which is, however, *imprinted* upon the appearances of its performance, clarifying the seeming in the subversions.

It is this imprint of the diffusion, through appearance, *back upon* consciousness that makes the play—so far as there is in our lives any life of the mind—the closest thing we have to a collective myth. In a world of crossing solitudes, each one to oneself, that may be the only real unity we have. As for interpreting the blind gestures signalling to each other in the crossing, that remains what it always was, *a perceptual act* (or as they used to say in the schools, a matter of reading readiness): *what are you seeing and what does it mean?* the readiness of the seeing inscribing itself on what is seen, like that first telescopic eye looking upon the false moon and seeing not the glory of God but the dubiousness of man, thought scratched upon the eyeball. In the theater the very thought of that thought is a consuming redundancy of the form, the more indelible the seeming the more remaining to be seen.

The thing about *Hamlet* is that it seems to have seen it all. Which is why we see through it as we distrust it, never quite sure whether it is informing or deforming our seeing. That quickening incertitude spread through the gravitational field between *Hamlet* and *Elsinore,* which is an intense development of the idea of theater as reflexion, both the mental process and the mirroring, charged in the body by the mind's reading of the mirror's image and the mirror's image of the mind. We say: we think by means of *Hamlet*—as if it is the only language we have

. . . thought feeding on thought as if it were flesh, . . . that once-smooth body. . . .

(not only the words)—what cannot be thought with the mind but that by which the mind can think. To be sure, as I've already indicated, the play is more than a play; it is a habit of consciousness which virtually created the state of mind by which it is now perceived. Its meanings are played back upon it like a curse. They accumulate on the body of the text as upon that once-smooth body of the Ghost, like alluvial deposits, the accretions of history screening history, subject itself to the corrosions of time. *Elsinore* is the pattern thrown upon the screen by collision with the corrosions. The entire field of vision is a crooked eclipse. The density of association is such that it feels, structurally, like brain damage. Hamlet appears in the lesions. "Foh! About, my brains."

In a letter to Jacques Rivière, written in 1924, Artaud describes a nervous breakdown, a "focal collapse" brought on by "a kind of essential and fugitive erosion of thought, . . . the impulse to think at every stratifying endpoint of thought, by way of every condition, all the branches of thought and form. . . ." In what I have called the thinking through, we have tried to think thus, theatrically, without the collapse—the mind imitating itself as a kind of thing among other things projected in space in a seizure of form, erotic body of the word, possessed by images, quick objects, partial identities, ideas flashing in every direction. At the stratifying endpoint of thought the images seem inexhaustible—like those wells in Utah which (so the histories report) the Donner Party came upon in the crossing, from which they could draw water constantly, the water always coming back to its own level. (Not all of the wells were like that, however. In the next chapter I will say more about how we conducted the investigations, the liability of saturation in the method, and the risk of its watershed moments.) Organizing the superfluity of material thrown up during rehearsals is like classifying events in a cloud chamber or gathering up the shards of myth.

Lévi-Strauss calls the science of myths "anaclastic," referring to "the study of both reflected rays and broken rays" as if he were describing the signifying light of the crooked eclipses tracking the missing persons. So, too, our study of the myth of the *Oresteia* in the early seventies—the branchings of thought and form—was anaclastic. As the subject became the scene, I saw the playing space as a kind of reversal of the eye or an optical glass bending time, subjectively, and so space, expanding or diminishing it in the dimension of memory. The space was a field of memory, always eroding, as if memory like a mandala were the space of a future. The physical scene was rectilinear. The actors were distributed around the periphery in a designated space of thought, moving in and out, not as characters but as reflections of characters or,

The space was a field of memory, always eroding, as if memory like a mandala were the space of a future.

more tellingly, like remembering nodes of time, iconographic. A large floor was painted in curving bands like the geometrized ground of meditation in a Tantric shrine, those power diagrams of vibratory color which are also soundings. The soundings were suppurating, however, with ruined and acid color, hard-edged, mylared (a reflecting surface over the black bands), so the bodies were mirrored downward in flashes and fractures as they moved, as if standing on their heads, some part of the body cut off, or disappearing into the ground.

Appearances were synesthetic, amplifying space, which seemed to be arcing, short-circuited, or collapsing upon itself. The beacons which signalled the fall of Troy came vocally through the darkness like the birth of thought. A quivering gesture in the hands flared into a figure of speech rising chorally in the mind and around the fertile crescent as over the whole known world. It was thought with the speed of light whose actual cadence in the air seemed—because of the long time-inflected distances of imagined space—slowed, stately, recessive, stilled. Out of the remembered text in remembering voices came, from mountain top to mountain top, something like a geography of myth—or the flaming of thought in a warp of time between myth and history, as the obscure voiced beacons crossed through two thousand years of contracted memory to ignite "the staggered flame" of the altars and, as if burning the seminal fluid itself, the "deep-stored oil of the kings. . . ." The imploded space was a power diagram in which the reflected and broken rays of myth were, like Agamemnon in his blood-bath, drawn, scored, sounding, into an anatomizing network of ideographic thought. Stratifications of memory in striations of sound: cry of war cry of eagles cry of gods, "the high/ thin wail of these sky-guests"—like an early warning signal in the inner ear; and then, in that sounding labyrinth of grievous time, cry of sacrifice into the stilling winds, remembered, cry of the virgin daughter twined with the voice of the prophet who seems cursed by the cry caused and who (in the Aeschylean text) never appears but is everywhere (Calchas, as in the mirror of Cassandra), materializing in space as if time out of memory were also there, the voice of prophecy itself, scored, ceded to the structure, premonitory—the generic impulse of thought dreading thought, voiced, driving reflection back through a space of blind gestures and signs to the source behind the source, *first thought,* "the fledgling, the nest, and the tendance," the myth of the myth, its origins.

This entire image from the opening of *Seeds of Atreus*—which I've tried to suggest in the cadence of its occurrence—is a remembrance of the earliest chorus of the *Oresteia,* that obscure but luminous evocation of an indeterminate time which is also being remembered there. The remembrance is an inquiry which moves not along a linear axis

Stratifications of memory in striations of sound . . . , as if time out of memory were also t

but, like the remembrance from which it is drawn, in a spiral, a nebula, or a widening gyre. In *Elsinore* it does the same even more exactingly, with a desperate longing for the "perfect circle" of recovery of the disappearing myth, that poignant mental function of "the mortal coil." When we think through *Hamlet*, we're not even sure the myth was ever there. It is immaterial—as Lévi-Strauss says in defense of his interpretations of Bororo myths—whether the psychic sprawl of *Hamlet* over history occludes through the medium of our thought or whether our thought occurs through the medium of *Hamlet*. Without disrespect to a so-called "original," it is the (maybe nonexistent) Ur-text to which we direct the force of the inquiry. That is the focal act which, in Artaud, brought about the focal collapse. We are nevertheless looking, as Artaud did, as *Hamlet* itself apparently did, for the source's source.

Thus, there is a sequence in *Elsinore* (there are no "scenes") where a figure-such-as-Hamlet, not-Hamlet, inscribes the enjoinder of the Ghost upon *his* body, ferociously, as upon the tablet (of the text). It is the climax of an outburst of emotions which range *ideographically*— both actor and narrative reeling backwards, *as if in an instant of time, the whole play*—through a spectrum of behavior(s) commonly associated with Hamlet: the hesitations and remorse, the reflexive fury, the "ratiocinative meditativeness" (Coleridge), the regressive symptoms. We spoke of that sequence as "the palimpsest"; and indeed the two "texts" (the performance and its "source") were as rubbings of each other *(that* rub?), bearing some undecidable truth between them. The "reading" of *Hamlet* in our text was like those radiation studies made in the restoration of paintings, in which the x-rays penetrate the epidermis to discover not only an original, but an indeterminate series of prior forms and colors, no one of which is certainly *the* original anymore, for that has disappeared into whatever constitutes history— the intuition which, as Kant said, is time. The performance is a sequence of decipherings.

In *Elsinore*, the unresolvable textual crises of *Hamlet*, like the literally *inimitable* character itself, are appropriated by the structure of performance. In any normal production of "the play," specific choices have to be made that are necessarily reductive. The casting itself does that. How old is Hamlet? Even if the makeup is ambiguous, or the actor's demeanor, it is a definite bodily image that decides. So, too, if the actor happens to be stout, or thin, he gives an interpretative aspect to the remark that Gertrude makes (and that German critics once took literally) about his being fat and scant of breath. Or there is the old problem of protractive and accelerating time sequences in the script that can't entirely be accounted for on logical grounds. Or the feigned madness: who is aware of it and who not? and is it that? how much and when? why? and what does the actor who is playing Hamlet think? In the structure of *Elsinore,* these issues are undecidable and constitute the network of reflection. The dilemma is there *as* a dilemma, consciously sponsored as it may be thought. Time's extension, for instance, may be deliberately precipitous, as in the palimpsest sequence just mentioned, where the Hamletic figure collapses regressively (a focalizing collapse) through the backward-reeling mortal coil into an image of a curled-up infant, suggesting also the sleeping King in the garden, into whose ear is whispered, as if they were the words of love (the whisperer is a woman), "To be or not to be" (killing words, the hebona? motherly love?). In that instant, more of the text is *there,* even as the characters are indeterminate and the text is being decomposed.

The strategy of *sub*version is taken over from the structure of *Hamlet* into the nature of the work being derived from it. The process of decomposition depends on the miming not of plot or character but of the trajectory of an interior force. Hamlet may be, simultaneously or in serial, younger and older, male and female, in primy nature—rose and expectancy still—*and* fat and scant of breath. He may also be the one who knows, in a clairvoyance beyond words, that to be or not to be may not really be the question, although the one who knows is not *one.* We are aware of Hamlet's "nature" as it is revealed in the *playing* of the play, which is customarily played from Hamlet's viewpoint (certainly so if a star is in the role), even though the scope of the play has temporally widened, "his brains still beating" through our brains into a combinatory puzzle of critical self-consciousness, the proliferating library of texts laminating the text. What confronts us now in the vain desire to perform it as-it-was or as-it-was-meant-to-be is the distribution of the play—which is after all a cultural institution—into the libidinal economy of our mental life. What we call the text is a fecundating and disturbing excess. The play we are now playing is like an overdraft on time. We may in fact have as many images of the many Hamlets, imagined, played, written about, or alluded to, as history has required. "Sir, a whole history."

In the experimental theater of the sixties, there was an almost militant tendency toward the discard or renovation of texts. Our own course moved from hypotheses of gradual displacement toward the idea of the text as the initiating pretext of thought—the axial moment winding back to what is felt before thought, a base of unceasing speculation from which proceeds the appetite for thought of which Brecht's Galileo speaks when he thinks of science. I was always conscious of the distance between what was (once) there and what could be seen from where we were. It was neither a matter of updating the plays, nor doing our scholarly homework and projecting ourselves back into the past, nor some juggling act of pseudohistorical mediation. History was the impasse. It existed between us and a text from some other period (in the accelerations of recent art, other periods are reducing themselves rapidly to previous moments) like the sudarium over the face of Christ or the shroud over Hamm in Beckett's play, eyes blanked, black glasses, handkerchief over that, nearly sealed into consciousness—consciousness like a peephole in nature widening out, the interior vision playing upon the displacements of memory like the passage of the years. The text became the sign of what-that-was, passing, something other than what it appeared to be. It was there like a racial memory, fathoms deep, emptied of origins, drawing us to the forgotten. The doors of perception, however, did not necessarily open at what, in the text, appears to be the beginning. Not anymore.

Where does *Hamlet* start? Or: where to enter the *Oresteia*? Through that first dazzling reverberative nearly mind-cancelling chorus that disinters history through myth? Maybe through the network of imagery: birds beacons food axe snake seeds flesh, the tentacular net itself, that blooded abstraction? The instincts of the actor may be, naturally enough, still through the "characters." But if so, how are we to adjudicate the behavior of those abstractions in the face of history? There is a delineation of sexual power in the displacement of the man-woman Clytemnestra by the mannish intelligence of Athena, but what about the negative reverberations aroused today by *that* idea, which includes in her decision the seduction of the Furies, appropriating their primordial and maternal energy for a patriarchal state? Should we, following Brecht's advice, strike the offending lines? Should we attempt to enter the structure through the womb of the Furies? or might we come up into the text from the soil below the tomb? or the deep-stored oil of the kings? Or, "knees grinding in dust," the phantom queen remembered? Helen, and the god of war? the Trojan horse? sneak in there? We try not to close the door on any access. Once in, we may *discover* Clytemnestra, we *awaken* Electra, we touch the conscience of Orestes and bring him home. But since they are hardly what we thought they were, we make no pretense of leaving them intact. (Notice I use the plural, since no character is assigned to any actor: in the work on *Seeds of Atreus*, not until much later; in the later work, not really at all.)

Character—the most common approach to plays—was what we referred to or sought after, not what we assumed. Even if we turn to it as conjecture, the supports of character are frail. They distribute themselves into the structure of apprehension, a figure here, a hint there, a trace of behavior, the ruptured semblance of an old heroic self,

I am Orestes, how did I become Orestes?

character as a symbiosis, a speculative limit, rather than an objective status. When Orestes, then, returns to the scene of the crime, it is not only to avenge his father (who is he?) but, the centuries having passed, to reassess his myth; but not merely to give it another interpretation as, say, Sartre did in *The Flies*. Orestes is, like Hamlet, a victim of retrospectively impacted consciousness. He is accountable to the memory of destiny and to history's account of *his* destiny. The actor *is* Orestes (more so, now, than the fictional Orestes) *before* he encounters the text. He is returning to meet his own image in the pool of history. The demystifiers have also had their crack at him, he is a demystifier himself. There are, meanwhile, other actors making claims upon the role. But Orestes—the one burdened by his myth—must rehearse its meaning. The actor must say against all claims, ideological modifications, and suggestions to the contrary: *I* am Orestes, how did I become Orestes?

For Orestes is the name of an estrangement. He brings to the text a critical attitude born of twenty centuries of dissociation from the narrative which first gave his experience form. What *did* happen, however, at the trial on the Areopagus? Orestes was not there, according to Aeschylus, when the terms of the agreement with the Furies were finally drawn and the Panathenaic convention approved it. (The Furies, moreover, have gained over the years a lot of moral support and are calling for a retrial, in which they are unlikely to concede what they once conceded. Or *do* they have a choice?) Orestes comes back to Argos as Hamlet returns to Elsinore, with a similar sense of dispossession and—having acquired it from Hamlet—a similar distancing instinct, involuted and overly reflective, self-absorbed. The nature of the self-absorption needs to be understood: it is not unlike the patient prepared by Freud for psychoanalysis, "explicitly instructed to renounce all criticism of the thought-formation which he may perceive." Only, unlike the patient, Orestes already has the power—prepared retroactively by Hamlet—to let his ideas *be*, be *there*. No sooner there, however, he is instructing the ideas—not "absolutely impartial" but not stopping their flow either, as if he can even banish the censor, so that the always conflicting judgments are wholly his own.

It's not that he can't solve the dream but that he knows, almost in advance, how little is achieved when it is solved. He also knows, as if he'd read that crucial footnote in Freud's *Interpretation of Dreams*, that "every dream has at least one point at which it is unfathomable; a central point, as it were, connecting it with the unknown"—and that any solution concedes that connection. That's enough to drive him mad, if he thinks about it. So we, in our relationship to both texts. We are crossing a vexed history back to a no-longer-stable myth. (The appearance is, if we can deduce anything from the opening chorus of the *Agamemnon* and Orestes' disappearance at the end of *The Eumenides*, it was hardly even stable then.) In all that we undertake—whether with myth or history—that instability is a driving force. The subject is always an obstacle, like a dream, a self-interfering pattern which doesn't exist at all except in the self-conscious inspection of its own unfolding in the determining pattern of time. If there's anything vital to it, the energy spins out of that; that is, what is not-yet-there and maybe never was—like the activating presence of the missing person whom we also traced, as in dream, in the texts of history, as if history were the dream. Marx speaks of it as the nightmare from which we're trying to awaken, but it's a habit of history to make us forget:

This nightmare, for instance: The Donner Pass is a mountainous region of possibility in a dangerous climate if you arrive there at the wrong time. The story as reported—in contemporary documents and subsequent histories—guides our research and throws us off the trail. It is inevitable, given our habits of thought (now highly developed), that we will be thrown off the trail. "DON'T TAKE NO CUTOFFS," warns one of the young survivors, writing afterwards to a friend back east. Good advice, but how can we help it? The cutoff (fine word, *cutoff*, for this story) turns out to be a series of detours—repetitious, compulsive, circling, and self-consuming. So is the story. There is a certain violence in the act of telling. It comes from the first tellings of the survivors, inevitable gaps and distortions, all the telling and retelling, including our own, but a system of approximations, sifted and refined by collective fantasy, including not only the encroachment of our present on that past, but the fantasy of the past itself. A story that can be fully told, we're now likely to believe, can hardly be the whole story, an irrelevance. (Is there any such story?) The story insists through the detours—as with any trauma remembered out of repression—on the true language of its final sounding.

In the case of a historical subject, we can only document it so far. History is the ambiguous medium. The extremist density of history is quicksilver to the mind. It runs away with us, not to be seized in advance. You have to catch your breath. There are faint articulations out of hearing, merely to be guessed at, words out of joint like dissevered limbs, words about those words in the histories, other rubbings on the originary source. That's why we were never able to make "dramatic" decisions in the composition of *The Donner Party, Its Crossing*—I mean decisions in favor of drama at the risk of falsifying the reported events or making up events that were never reported. All we know from all reports—to illustrate the problem—is that there were two last survivors in the mountains before the final rescue party came: the out-cast German Keseberg, who had cut his heel accidentally and couldn't move; and Tamsen Donner, who had refused to go with her children earlier because her husband George, also wounded, was gangrenous and dying. Did Keseberg kill Tamsen Donner to eat her? That question echoes through all the histories. There was the circumstantial evidence of a bucket of her flesh and blood in his cabin. There was the symbolic evidence of that cloven heel, very tempting (to us). Keseberg did not deny eating her, but denied killing her to do so, on a stack of Bibles and bended knee to his dying day many years later—when it would no longer have mattered to confess it.

Or would it have mattered? In either case, there was no historical evidence to verify what actually happened. So we never tried to "resolve" it for dramatic purposes, nor other obscure elements of the story. We dwelt upon them incessantly, however, and they nurtured the manner of our telling. Since we are interested in the reality of the *historicizing process*, we did not resort, either, to a *Rashomon*-like take-your-pick of several versions. The Donner story, as we perform it, is the inquisitive texture of the story we think it is. That, too, has its distortions, suppressions, and displacements. They are so torn from context, like the report of a dream, that we can hardly recognize them—our own hidings. Still, with the double vision of second sur-vivors, we try to see what we're doing and concealing, turning that back inside the work, the charge of a baffled awareness. It is an effort to convert what little we know into everything we want to know, like releasing energy in particle physics. It has little to do, then, with dramatizing the indeterminate events of the story but rather with ex-pressing an indeterminacy elicited by the story and articulated in the telling. The story is useless—except to the degree that it evades us. In order to see what-it-is that we're telling, what we rely on is not what "really" happened—no more than Freud did with the Rat Man—but a host of resistant memories that gradually adhere to our own until, in a reversal of subject and object, we feel that we are being remembered.

The narrative is allusive, guesswork, speculatively there—like an unidentified virus. The elements can hardly be labeled like a *gestus* of Brecht. An ordinary narrative misrepresents by reducing. Here, the structural model is not narrative but language (even when we're being nonverbal), because language has the staying power of transformation independent of events. There is no immediate equivalent, as with a character, in reality. The method, as in the interpretation of dreams, is to construct from the traces that have been left behind a construct with its own traces. As I've said, the deeds of the Donner Party cannot be morally classified as they might have been by Dante; there is no ethical system in which the history can be adequately registered, even if wholly known. So we refrained—as we ran up against the impermeability of what happened—from imposing judgments upon it. Instead, there was a kind of hypnotic rememoration of merging signs, as the story started to tell us, also guessing. It's the restlessness of the guessing that narrows the margins of guess, like the declivities of the Wahsatch canyons in which the Party was trapped. You find yourself where there's no turning back. Like the oxen so critical to the journey, you can only keep moving in the traces, even if seemingly going nowhere, spinning wheels.

The exercises we did to prepare the work were backspins of those spinning wheels in the becoming of a concept, wheels within wheels, in the constant turning of the square dance: *"Circulate! . . . Spin chain the gears!"* Time's rack, wheel of fortune, another figure of the mortal coil, nature's cycles in the turning: the journey is something more than the sensations through which it accumulates, but it accumulates in the sensations. After the early exuberance of departure, there is the long slow asseveration of motion through smoky heat waves and powdered ash, soft eruptions of the sage, ceaseless plains, winds and dogging sun, swollen rivers and the bloated horses floating upside down, alkali in the air, quicksand beasts sweat, the aromatic pungency of campfire, night-motion, tics, monotony on the wagon, disease diarrhea trachoma desert-blindness heat mirage sunburn blackened skin lye-torn lips, "achin bowels" breaking wind, "dust on [the] temples like a scab," eating dust, sulphate for the skin, Epsom and Glauber's salts, laudanum for extreme pain, amputations done with a plainsaw to gird them for the cuttings later, endless physics nausea headaches from mountain fever, dysentery from dirty utensils, stink of sulphur, bad cooking on buffalo chips ("hard stool"), ill-preserved foods spoiling; and then the real test—grass diminished, stock gaunt, nerves frayed, food scarce—when water starts freezing in the pail, cold nights, the mountains ahead, and time running out into winter; the physical details convulsed into a semblance of meaning, hallucinatory, not all "used" in the performance but nevertheless there, subliminal, like the chilling refrain, "Snow is falling"; culminating in a sequence in the "cabins" below the snow where—pristine above, the stench unbearable—they gag and retch up the whole experience in a concert of anguish—one long cramping round, a libretto of the same turning—to which they have come through a desert of bleached bones. "Grind, grind. . . . Fuckin wheels!"

If *Elsinore* is a meditation on origins, the journey of the Donner Party, as we made it, is a crossing of space into time, a time warp. The motion of the wagons across the continent is like the slipping planes of a geological fault. There is something incontinent to it, this quest for a possible genesis of a vanishing presence. In America, though the land has closed down into suburban developments, the problem remains little different from that described by Henry James in *The American Scene:* "a society trying to build itself, with every elaboration, into some coherent sense of itself, and literally putting forth interrogative feelers, as it goes, into the ambient air." Both the passivities and the aggressions of American life lie, in the aggregate—even now in the late twentieth century—"waiting, a little bewilderingly, for their justification, waiting for the next clause in the sentence, waiting in short for life, for time, for interest, for character, for identity itself to come to them. . . ." The New Jersey shore houses James is describing are of the same order of incoherence as the bones on the prairie or the cannibalized bodies at Donner Pass—our history spreading over the landscape like old beer cans at a campsite in the Sierras—from which the self withdraws, on the buckboard of its own motion, mimed, isolate, whether congregating or alone, a monody, "Back and back and back. . . ." The motion of the crossing is the flow of an absence over the shifting ground, "farther now to where you came from,/ probably, than to places/ you can reach by going on." There is a further warp of time back into the narrowest spaces in the vastness of the landscape, the usurping locality of the body, without a place, "bones inside those bones," usurped.

Thus Keseberg—banished from the company for stealing a funeral robe from an Indian pyre (he was later permitted to return)—sees the wagon train moving away—"whitetops contagious as gulls/over a running grave"—and, into the ambient air, puts forth (this *imagining* of a Keseberg) interrogative feelers. He reads the "wishbones" on the prairie, the droppings and leavings of earlier crossings, crossings almost before time, as the migrants join in an impeccable straight line, moving, hand-to-hand and leaning away, a support system, the wagon train stretched in the dance to their maximum hand-held distance, pivoting on a single actor, a wheel filling the entire space, as if the years were turning in the continental tilt—about which the isolate Keseberg declares, in a prophecy of bones, that "every one of them/ will groan like old nails in a sunken/ wheel pulled out in the reversing/ shudder of feared light"; single actors letting go and turning within the tensile structure, supported, caught up in function, as if fording a river (but more abstract than that), in the utmost orchestration of the seeming unity of the doomed journey. Or, later, frantic across time, the old enfevered figure in the desert, Hardcoop, not wanting to be abandoned, running in place at high aimless speed, a geriatric refraction of Lansford Hastings chasing the dream, back and forth from present to past, trying to catch up with the wagon train that is neither here nor there, a tremendous upwelling of decrepit energy and displaced ego and age, rambling about "sex-starved kids in the backseat hitchhikin without a seatbelt pukes and suckers eatin each other . . . still growin up," in a burst of bifocal language, wanting to come of age, but "goin down the drain like I'm up beyond orbit *zzzzz!* (tonguing it in a raspberry like a racing car) if you really knew a little galaxy all the way out here in the desert by myself travellin on the salt flats past the speed of light 200 million winners"—the imploding pursuit of self and atomizing menace of America—"all in the death seat aimin the telescopic rifles at each other Injuns Mormons white wasps black and we're plumb blowin it Lance"—the apparition of Hardcoop/Hastings still running tumbling crawling after the wagons in an impacted stagger of split motion, avid and lethal, the ego becoming id—"blown all this jizzim a thousand times more powerful than the sun whoosh you hear the signals you hear you hear!? I'm being squeezed in Lance I'm gonna disappear wrappin around myself like a rubber glove pullin off put on the brakes goddam it! who do you think you are? reverse reverse (the long line of the wagon train reverses) *I'm turnin inside out!*"

What is yielded up by history in that furious performance of splitting consciousness—the body but not consciousness exhausted—is another stage of reflection on the void between origin and actuality, documentation and imagining, a spoor, a runaway spool, a demented memorial, a patterned energy like a vortex through which, breathless, the latency of meaning moves, or a tunnel of dust in the snow. "What is given, then," writes Merleau-Ponty in *The Visible and the Invisible*, "is not the naked thing, the past itself such as it was in its own time, but rather the thing ready to be seen pregnant—in principle as well as in fact—with all the visions one can have of it, the past such as it was one day *plus* an inexplicable alteration, a strange distance—bound in principle as well as fact to a recalling that spans distance but does not nullify it." He speaks of the recalling that *spans* distance, which suggests crossing *over* it, and we've had the illusion of such a spanning. I would, however, put the stress on the crossing *through*, as if the past were *in* the distance; no as if about it.

Before returning to cannibalism as a structural principle, I want to say something more about it as a content. When we first approached the Donner materials, I was wary about facile deductions about the American experience, although I'm not sure we always avoided them. As a general proposition about America, cannibalism tells a real tale, particularly if—remembering it in the loomings, surmises, soundings, and try-works of our great epic—we don't make it seem as if America

Take Up the Bodies

(now that the Japanese and Russians are doing in the whales) has an uninterrupted monopoly. Take, eat. Since the Fall, or whatever fault or breach in nature brought consuming into consciousness, the literal eating has become a metaphor of perception. I have already cited the Shakespearean line, "I, too, have made a mouth of my eyes." That arch-perceiver Hamlet is "of the chameleon's dish: I eat the air, promise-cramm'd—you cannot feed capons so." The King—whose own words fly up and thoughts remain below—doesn't like words running away from events, since you can't keep the story straight. "I have nothing with this answer, Hamlet, these words are not mine." The Queen is silent. "No, nor mine now," says Hamlet, consumed with that which he is nourished by, words words words—summing up the intricate immateriality of language and origins in the body of perception. Since *Hamlet,* consciousness consumes on every continent. It fattens in the mirroring of identity at the mother's breast. Some eat with more grace and credibility than others, as a matter of genes or faith. There are mere devourers. But we are all, looked at keenly, eating air, badly nourished.

What *was* characteristic of the Donner Party was its conspicuous lack of reflective consciousness, during and after the events—so far as existing records show, and the memoirs. What the survivors of the recent plane crash in the Andes called "the terrible mountain silence"—the endless boredom and periods of depression that made them suicidal—appears not to have produced anything similar in the Sierras. One senses it only in Keseberg, but that may be our own psychological expectancies projected upon descriptions of his outward symptoms, as well as the state of mind that presumably goes with the cloven heel. Others, like the teamsters—the mere hired hands who went along on the journey without the sustenance of the family unit—appeared to relinquish themselves to the dying, but took no action upon their lives. Suicide requires another kind of consciousness than that which went on the wagon trains. One can hardly imagine George Donner, the nominal head of the Party, or Jim Reed, the actual leader, asking with Camus—in the famous existential response to other disasters—"Why not suicide?" Once the pioneering was over, at the introverting end of land's end—an enforced stasis stirring up the migration within—suicide became a statistic in America.

We expect ghastliness to release ghosts: unspeakable, unappeasable. There seems little evidence, however, that the horrors of cannibalism at Donner Pass engendered anything but to-be-expected bad memories, conventional at the conscious level—leaving us with the mystery of the lasting scars at the level of the unconscious, which is a construct of our time which solicits what it asks for, as it may not have done for them. Of course, that was an age—even if the stock were not inoculated—of greater discretion in published report; and we are also inclined to believe today, as I have already suggested, that what you can't say you are unlikely to feel with the dimensions that the language for it brings, if only as inner speech. (Time's murmur has muted voices.) But maybe that *was* the language for it. Even the diaries were discreet as if the nature of the person couldn't bear to bring the horror down to the page. At the level of the unconscious, then—for a people who had to be immediately functional—perhaps an interactive saving grace.

Thus: normal bad memories, except for Keseberg, whom they later named "Monster of the Sierras." He seemed—something more than seeming? no projections now?—to bear the mark of Cain. He was publicly mocked, had terrible business misfortunes as if he'd been plotted against, a series of premature deaths in his family, and two surviving daughters, epileptic, one of them weighing over 250 pounds! Keseberg's later suffering—though he seemed to have the nature for understanding it in metaphysical dimensions— was socially imposed. He was ostracized, not forgotten, as if a scapegoat were required. He had the attributes for that too, from all accounts: the temperament of a stranger and a foreigner to boot (a strange concept in a new land), better educated than the others. When circumstances warranted, he was there to take the projections of fear and self-hatred. (His revenge is history, which makes him the most memorable among a lot of sketchy characters. We were tempted to start backwards into the story, with that extraordinary meeting in Keseberg's ruined brewery—out of earshot of the yelling epileptic daughters—when Tamsen Donner's daughter, a mere child in the mountains, now a senator's wife, came to ask the German whether he had murdered her mother. In that large vacant space—two witnesses present, four chairs formally arranged—he denied it again, literally on his knees. We never used the scene.) It does seem congenital in the American character to need a nucleus for blame, even when, later, we punished nature for its crimes by despoiling the landscape and, gradually, with more and more foreign incursions on the unconscious, learned to punish ourselves.

None of the available documents, however, are capable of philosophical dimension. Maybe the better for that, truer to the American experience then, more existential, purely phenomenological—the censorship only instinctive, the screening not artful. There was no mentality, except maybe Keseberg's, disposed to tortuous and self-incriminating introspection, like the kind we displayed in *The Enemy*. All this affected what we were doing, what we could do, and how we did it. The main source, and the most emblematic, is the diary of an Irishman named Breen. That major document of the ordeal is content with the barest denotation of occurrences, weather reports and, over Christmas and the subsequent horrors, Catholic pieties. Its psychological value lies, however, in what it doesn't reveal, doesn't say, doesn't care or know how to say, by some queer instinct, perhaps, protecting sanity (quite insane)—the thing not seen at all. The members of the Party were a practical, self-interested, but hardly involuted people. There might have been another story if Tamsen Donner's diary had survived. She was, with Keseberg, the most literate person among them (with her trunk of books, the histories make her the most sensitive). The longest sustained memories came, years later, from the children, although it's hard to know how much of that has been gilded by generous eyes wanting to look away from the worst.

Still, a considerable pathos comes through their memories, as we project upon them. How to deal with that? Eliza and Georgia Donner, for instance, eating human flesh cheerfully, not knowing what it was, their older sister Frances knowing, feeling guilt, but unable *not* to eat—that does come down to us. The little girls had fantasy feasts, or pretended to feed their dolls. There was the time they ate the firerug, piece by pacifying but nearly indigestible piece. Then there were the dead babies or the baby infested with lice, who had to be bound to keep from scratching itself to death; and that dreadful sequence when Keseberg, in a fit of temper, threatened (did he mean it? probably not, but we are taught in our psychoanalytical age to see all utterance as meaningful) to eat the little girls.

For all this we needed a structural idea: *where does it all take place?* we constantly asked ourselves, stumbling over the landscape. The weird budgeted emotion of Breen, for instance. I don't mean that we were concerned with characterizing him; we weren't, though his *type* was easy enough to make present, in various shapes and shadings. I mean the temperament of Breen, the placing of it, as one strain of feeling in the crossing. The strongest sign of conflict in his diary is a brief account of an argument with one of the women over the weather. "She is a case," he concludes. Otherwise, bare of feeling, too barren to be baleful, except as *you* realize what is actually happening on the other side of the entries. It is remarkable, you think, that the dogs lasted as long as they did, or the hides on the shanties. Nobody violated anybody else's property either. The telltale entry: "Mrs. Murphy says the wolves are about to dig up the dead bodies at her shanty. . . ." Then, at the first direct intimation of cannibalism, the understated: "it is distressing—" a massive inflection of feeling in the gaunt report. There is a certain inadvertent poetry: "heard some geese fly over last night saw none": a *haiku*, the memory of an absence, nobody there. That came after the only actual notation about intentions to eat the dead bodies. The psychological blankness is a reflex in Breen; the desire for psychology, confession, analysis: our reflex—the structural idea forming around the incommensurability of the two.

About the grisliness of the events, we wanted a certain elegance in the reimagining, distancing the distance. The first cuttings were done, as if in anticipatory dreams, through a transformation of a sexual act, also imagined; and by a child, thirsty, as an incidental annoyance before the long desolation of the salt flats—the incipience of dread brushed away like you brush away flies. We also looked for unexpected inflexions of eloquence, as in Keseberg's answer to the rescue party's harsh questioning about the incriminating pot of blood: "There is blood in dead bodies." We didn't use the line, but wanted to preserve the impulse, though it would come up in other unexpected places, as a cliché out of folklore would become a grotesque vision: "Push on to the Pass!" Sometimes we felt we were really doing something quite demented, which was characterized by the use of another document, Jim Reed's diary, written mainly in the wastes of snow when, after reaching San Francisco, he crossed back with the rescue parties. The following entry occurs after passing what they called Starved Camp, a snowhole of frozen bodies that had been eaten. Here the desire was apparently to set down the revulsion, although Reed also withdrew from it, and the powerful emotion he did convey came, as it does elsewhere in his diary, through repetitions of a single abstract word (with, here, the marvellous verbal): "The clouds still thicking terror terror I feel a terrible foreboding but dare not communicate my mind to any. . . ." Imagine writing that in a storm in a little book and with icy fingers; imagine that being written with anything but icy fingers. And the problem was how to enact it, or rather (since enacting it would turn Reed into Randolph Scott in a late-night movie) how to think our way (thicking) across those mountains in a theatrical language which connects that terror with the remains of the story.

The terror terror was multiplied by two (taking the rhythm from Reed in other contexts) and transposed to a bizarre sequence, in our work, where he is being tried for killing a man in a sudden outburst of desperate tempers. In the encounter, as reported, Reed's wife had been struck, and we kept that. In his testimony, arising out of a rather crazed giving of witness by other members of the Party, Reed (Peter, in the passage below) confuses the stabbing of the man with the hunting of buffalo (a major form of recreation on the prairie, as well as a source of food)—the western myth flaring into the ancient myth of the desecrated god. The two "events" were replayed in the same motion, animal and human victims fusing, in a murderous frenzy of *macho*

"There is blood in dead bodies."

". . . knew I had to kill that bull he was crazy sweatin with gold hair beatin down . . . his red protein eye beatin fearful . . ."

shame (not Reed's so much as the actor's). The action is performed within the now-manic rhythm of the square dance, the collective hysteria (another event involving the setting of a broken leg, without anesthesia, is being replayed at the same time) subsiding at its climax into the falling of the first snow—the language of which is the amputated remnants of the preceding frenzy, which gives the volitionless massing of the snow its power, as the actors still struggle to keep the wagon train moving. The contradiction of will in the body—the necessity to keep the wagons moving *through* (by means of) the passive energy of the snow—is the deep structure of the image sequence, the terror of the performer at what, though it can't be achieved, must be *done* nevertheless: the terror of the snow (as described in Reed's diary) which comes out of violence:

PETER (as Reed, riding his horse Glaucus in swift pursuit of the buffalo): Couldn't even grasp the handle much less pull a trigger, that blade, suddenly I was very ashamed, edge of steel, *bang bang* . . .
(BILL, the enraged teamster Reed had killed, is rising and falling in his dying, which occurs over and over.)
DAVID: In order to do this dispassionately you have to be mean and ugly, and none of us wants to do that.
LINDA: Daddy goes huntin, he don't care
　　　also shot an elk and a grisly bear
PETER: . . . saw that bull terror terror terror terror sixty feet ahead of me, never spurred Glaucus before, never had spurs before I came on this trip, steel in the side *bang* saw that bull chargin palm up and I knew I had to kill that bull he was crazy sweatin with gold hair beatin down [BILL, who has gold hair, now heaving on the ground like a shot buffalo trying to move] and I was on top of that bull drenched with water (grabs BILL by the hair) his red protein eye beatin fearful and I took aim in the left eye his bloodshot eyes spinnin back eyes in his skull goin through his gold side (JULIE is pulling on WES' leg, setting it) and I pulled the trigger partin flesh six times . . .
(BILL screams. WES screams. LINDA continues chanting. DAVID—as a teamster still at the trial—is assailing Reed because of his money and status:)
DAVID: Bloody showoff, the rest of us don't have the right to throw our weight around like that.
　　[He is also assailing PETER, the actor who gets to play the "scene that the others don't."]
PETER: . . . pulled the trigger six times (he is stabbing BILL in the eye) flesh partin and he was sweatin gold that red protein eye gushin over my wife . . .

(LINDA opens her mouth in a silent scream which comes in rage
   from PETER as he stabs ecstatically and she watches JULIE cutting
   WES' leg.)
LINDA: O my God my God . . .
BILL (rising): . . . snow is falling . . .
LINDA: . . . and and . . .

And the already split narrative fractures into the snow with the images,
hair eyes gold breath falling, rising and falling in the almost disembodied voices of the actors who push on, rising and falling, through the
exponential terror to the Pass.

I have included this longish passage from the text to illustrate how
even the smallest cue from the documents may have been absorbed
through the disappearing history into the process of thinking through
the subject. When we started on the Donner project, there were several
writers working with the group. While they didn't survive the long
ordeal (an occupational hazard of writers with groups), the early
discussions were valuable and some of what they contributed stayed
with us—lines, images, strains of thought. One of our first instincts
was toward a stylistic flatness, the elegant two-dimensionality of a
comic strip as it might be extrapolated into the blown-up dimensions of
a Rosenquist painting. I was very wary, however, of anything like a
Pop treatment, the danger of which was a trendy parody, though I may
have been nervous about what no one intended. Still, a couple of us
were troubled by talk of the whole story being seen from "without" as
if "through glass" or, as one of the writers put it, "a wax museum, card-
board figures or landscape cutouts being manipulated by the actors."
There was a kind of distancing in that—an irony in advance, second
nature to the time—that I didn't want.

I mean, so far as my own sensitivity was concerned, there may again
have been a generational difference at stake. As we started on the project, I remembered only too well the attitudes which had prevailed
around Café Cino and the Judson Church in New York during the
campy heyday of the New Theater (and Dance), derived from Gertrude Stein and the cheapest aspects of the Theater of the Absurd. I
disliked it intensely. For all the gaiety and highjinks, it seemed
dehumanizing. Not wanting to be solemn, it was essentially un-
serious—at that soft end of the arc of the avant-garde when the
necessary primitivism turns infantile with sophistication. In a glitzy
clumsy in-group way, it was all surface. I make an issue of this not
because such theater events are of any real importance in themselves.
They were a superficial detour around the critical issue brought on by
the diminution or disappearance of the hunting daddy who doesn't
care, the dispersed godhead falling with the snow. When the authoriz-

ing figure disappears, it does lead to procedures of repetition—as in our own work and thought—and serialism, at the permutating edge of which parody displaces mimesis. Something of this was reflected in the consequence of the snow, all the actors gathered, descending, into a heap of jumbled bodies, suffocating, legs and arms in the air, "The Cannibal Pile," where parody was given voice, vociferous, with unabating pain, and buried.

There was always something obdurately humanistic about my own sentiments which accounted for that sequence, which was also a reflection on the effort of the ego to reappropriate itself from the affliction of group process. While I certainly didn't want to psychologize the history as a drama of individuals (made up), I did, somehow, want to get *inside,* unwilling as I was to accept the dominance of an aesthetic of surface. There had to be a way in which we could be participants in the journey without it being a mere participatory exercise. Could it mean anything to us if we merely manipulated the surface content into an aesthetic structure, however elegant? Or did there have to be some imaginative *endurance* of what they endured? In short, did we have to eat flesh? and how? (without resorting either, as in some events of the time, to real surrogate meat, bloodying the stage, and chewed on). I have already indicated that we didn't want to provide a constructed drama where history left an open mystery, as in the cause of the death of Tamsen Donner. There were parallel dangers: the cannibalism might be merely used as a counter, a module of information in a structure, something to be played with like fluorescence or numbers in the progressions of a conceptual piece; or it would turn up, if we took it too seriously, as melodrama. To play with it, to merely glance off in our associations—without the residually authorizing licence of myth, as in *Seeds of Atreus*—had the liability of being merely exploitative. Eliot navigated that fine line way back on the cannibal isle of *Sweeney Agonistes,* which also couldn't avoid parody and, as a result, was necessarily unfinished if not abandoned. (I could see them at the Judson picking up no more than the impulse that went into the buck and wing of the minstrel show *"Under the bamboo tree. . . ."*) It seems apt that, for his fragments of an Aristophanic melodrama, Eliot used this epigraph, from the Oresteia: "You don't see them, you don't—But *I* see them: they are hunting me down, I must move on."

We had been through a period in which things had been catching up with us, but in the passage to the seventies we were still indecisive about guilt. On the level of individual psychology, we were being told that guilt is a useless emotion and were being advised to get rid of it. On the social level, however, we were being prodded on all sides by the strident logic of a radical will to take on—for what we did to the land,

. . . we hauled those competing motives with us, variously agitated, like the oxen breathing horseflies of doubt.

the Indians, the blacks—retroactive guilt for our history. As we moved in the traces of the Donner story, we hauled those competing motives with us, variously agitated, like the oxen breathing horseflies of doubt. As we pushed on to the impasse—trying to decipher a meaning in respect to ourselves, the past revealing itself reversed through the repetitions of our anxiety—it was the recurrence of the immediate world, slackening off from the turbulence of the sixties, that nevertheless kept turning the wheels. That turned out to cause a displacement, a detour of thought, from the cannibalism to the crossing that became our real subject—what in fact brought us in a cycle of thought (embodied in the square dance, with its tautological turnings) back to the cannibalism we had far from exhausted in the previous work.

The repetitive impulse was a kind of engenderment. ("Honeybee shimmies to warm its hive/ chicken eats a ladybug to keep alive.") It was an aspect of the search for origins and cause, what-it-is, where-it-came-from, and why it isn't better, even in California ("Old John Sutter gonna end in the gutter/ bake us some gold, John, and bread my butter"), the gist of an incompletion (". . . snowed and snowed and never emptied the sky. Blood on my breast?"), the returning seeds. It was the precarious irony of all insistent duplications, what you can't keep yourself from doing—playing and replaying against the generalizing habit of what passes for memory—a passion for particularity, antic, riddling ("Shaggy as a bear wolf at its head/ grins like a cougar eyes are red"), and sometimes fierce. We've seen it before because it insists on surfacing while concealed. ("Why seems it so particular with thee?" "Seems, madam! Nay, it is. I know not 'seems.' ") In a public form, it is the logic, even the *Logos*, of the solitary holding its own, like a compulsion dream—and only the dreamer can know the dream. It is always the possibility of another beginning.

Right out of a letter, our last line: "It ought to be a beautiful country to pay us for our trouble gettin there." But the space of imagination we'd have to cross—and the movement from one work to another—would always bring us back to where we were: rooted in a place, in the absence of a place, the work, the world, the gravity of abrasion between them, the baffled self exacerbating itself—and the history that keeps us guessing.

Even back at the surface, we'd have to make deeper soundings. In *Moby-Dick*, there is a wondrously haunting image of a dead whale, stuck full of rusty harpoons like stigmata, the yellowing carcass punctured by one of the mates to sink it, leaving a stain on the sea, the whale rolling away, anciently, like the waning of a world. In *The Donner Party, Its Crossing*, there is a sequence toward the end which came about as we gradually realized that all the whipping and whooping "Gee! Haw!" 's which kept the wagons on the move were also the measures of the innumerable steady beatings of mere groaning animals over two thousand miles of the continent so good respectable citizens might get to California on the trail of Manifest Destiny.

The oxen were important figures in the crossing. The sequence occurred when some of the human survivors were trying to make it over the mountains while some left at the cabins, starving, were poling for carcasses buried in the thawing snow. It was (I thought) one of the most elegant ideas of all, from the point of view of a dead ox, upside down, legs still above him, "Amazed/ in a rumor of beasts,/ the toppled gut chanting," twenty feet below the snow, "contours glancing," crying out for everybody's hunger. *"Sacré cul,"* says one of the teamsters, a French-Canadian halfbreed, poling, just missing, "no ox down zere, nuzz*ing.*" The word (with its echo) punctures the song of the ox, which rolls back into time with a groan, becoming one of the frozen creatures on the mountain, crawling through a storm to survive. "Snow's killin." As the halfbreed, in a nervously delicate sequence, feeds the child with his semen, giving it suck, the crawling figure fantasizes a spirit of the mountain (we have seen her before, ghosting, around the Cannibal Pile): "I see someone leanin down with a white string in her mouth." The Indians have been watching in silence, and the oxen eyes have seen it all. "Snow's old." The crawling figure is dead, about to be eaten, man and ox.

It lay there for the moment like the remains of history in the transformative music of its cannibalizing trace. What remains of the narrative—the permutated rumor of the remembrance of history—has been regressively dispersed into the navel of dream, the true language of its final soundings. The white string disappears like an umbilicus of thinking snow into the "pesky sarpent" of the ending song, the replicating figure about which a story had been told at the beginning of the journey ("such/ a big snake they hadn't ever seen"), the figure which eats its own tail, as in the nonsense syllables of the refrain, "Ri tu ri nu, ri tu di na/ Ri tu di nu, ri tu di na . . ."—which might be infinitely repeated, but can only end by dying away.

Ghostings

5

We say: the meaning is in the music. With the receding of the old dramaturgical formula for theater, musical form has become a paradigm. *We think* of music as a pure system of relations, its signs devoid of substance, referring to no entity outside of themselves. In music the play of relationships is all there is, in their strict relativity. *We know,* and learn to forget, that pitch is high or volume low depending on where it is in the order of other sounds. It is as we hear it nothing in itself. As the system changes, the values change. In this respect musical theory is economic theory. *Yet* with music as with economics, the one qualifying factor is the existence of the system in history (what the econometricians are learning belatedly), so that we recognize sound values in relationship to prior sound values, or the ghosts of other sounds. These ghosts are disturbing, these shadows of time. They make it necessary to struggle through the act of composition, in the interest of "pure music," to cancel the recognitions. But can they be cancelled? It almost seems as if the spirit of music is a ghost, or a process of ghosting.

It is what the symbolists felt about words, empty words, when they tried to bring poetry (and drama) to the condition of music. They saw the words playing upon the surface of memory like the sediment of a text, ghostly, metonymic, words not only bringing about the "elocutory disappearance" of the poet (Mallarmé), but words displacing words endlessly—like the data of prehistory or the half-forgotten substance of dreams. Like music in this sense, like dream, theater is hollow at the core, empty of value, until its signs—body act space gesture color light cadence voice word mask etc.—are retrieved by reflection within a structure of relativity. Until then, none of its signs has a reliable existence, and even then, since ungrounded in substance. Or, if substance is assumed, the initiating act of theater instantly denies it; the ground is cut away. At least that's what we've come to expect from introjection of the older drama. But the substance may also be subsumed, or subverted (if it was ever there), with a teasing serenity of self-perception. So in the almost perfect stillness at the beginning of *Crooked Eclipses,* the millions of strange shadows estrangingly tend upon the eyes of all attending. There is a kind of watchful music in the decantations of appearance. The disconcerting presence is the appearance of time.

No sound is purely made, no gesture *in absentia* from time, no image without memory, not a particle of behavior in a state of nature (as Rousseau pointed out about music). For there is always in any system the sediment of time. Which implies that whatever is coming in, something is leaking out. When we try to take its measure we call it history. As much as we are interested in pure theater—the meaning in the meaning which is music—what is important to us is the leakage, *how* it is remembered, the residue in our thinking, and what it attests to: for the self the world, "contours glancing," our essential condition in history. And there is a desire beyond that which may never be anything more than desire. It is what Nietzsche defined as the will to power—a desire to abolish "the false character of things" by reinterpreting them "into beings," as if in restitution of the missing persons. The idea of becoming is a commonplace today, much labored, but what keeps it from being disempowered is an "active determining" in the becoming which, *at the limit of letting be, refuses*—since it is conscious of the forces playing through us even then, as surreptitiously as music. It is the sounding of such forces, which threaten to destroy being, that we heard in *Elsinore*—that insidiously pacifying or passive-making sound with its ominously equivocating sibilance, a music between a choice and a forgetting, which would mean nothing outside of history.

Thus, in thinking through its formal concepts—and in the aspiration toward an affirming music—the work keeps an avid eye upon the historical world. The missing person is such a concept. There is the resemblance between Elsinore and our own warlike state, increasingly armed in its pacifications, socially and privately. It is a state in which the organization of personality seems to lie between the obsessional neurosis of the production economy, defined by Freud, and the pathological solipsism of some preoedipal stage of human experience. In the latter stage, exhumed and celebrated in the sixties and much theorized since, one even doubts whether there is anything like a productive history of which one is really a part—with the resultant inability to identify with either past or future, origins or posterity. The new post-Freudian strategies, with their emphasis upon the momentary and the immediate (what Julia Kristeva, borrowing from Diderot, calls "musication"), seem designed to adapt us to such a world. Even the most sophisticated theory appears to succumb in the process to the condition it reflects: the anomie and isolation, the rewarded impotency, and the bewildering hostility that marks even the most intimate of human relationships, until we are gasping through the exhaustion, like the actors across the seductively empty space of *Elsinore*, wondering what we even mean by *relationship*—the very word abstracting the intimacy out of existence.

As we become jaundiced through powerlessness and human lawlessness to the hope of political remedy, we may relinquish ourselves to a new conservatism, letting things take their course; or, since they are still on the scene, the human potential movements which offer in a gestalt of becoming (like certain forms of Alternative Theater) the prospect of psychic survival or personal transcendence. The "supportive" optimism is appealing, but it still isn't facing the music. As for what happens in the theater, there is a point in every work when you have to ask through the work itself: How much of what you want to believe can you justify, given the world that is being reflected upon? *Is it necessary for this act to take place?* That may seem a far cry from the music, but it is what brings the music of the will of meaning into performance.

I mean now something "beyond" or "prior to" structure *in* the structure, as if between word and breath, the knowledge that can't be discredited because it's there, you know it's there, in and out of performance—the felt actuality of it so intense it keeps returning like a compulsion dream, the scene repeated and repeated as if the replaying will dispel it (but it won't), which is how the Ghost appeared in *Elsinore*. It was as if the mechanism of dream formation were displacing and disfiguring the reliable old Ghost we remember from the "real" play, the disfigured one coming in the form of a young woman with a titanic shivering hyperventilated vengeance out of the grave (p. 167), like a demonstration of the will it took, a *remonstrance*, the *insisting* on coming back—breaking down not only "the pale and forts of reason" but the complete steel of the character armor into a metamorphic ghost of itself. The Ghost is itself ghosted in the ghosting process because we wondered much about the power behind the Ghost, and how there could be (in performance) a single corporeal ghost pretending to be insubstantial in a world ghosted by Hamlet and the ratiocinative medita-

. . . only the exactitude of the actor's dying, the *rigor mortis*, . . . thought moving so fast between the quick and the dead.

tiveness—as well as the horrors since Hamlet that were maybe not dreamt of in his philosophy.

The ghosting is not only a theatrical process but a self-questioning of the structure within the structure of which the theater is a part. What seems true in the play of appearances—as most ontological discourse has assured us in our time—is that there is no way in which the thing we want to represent can exist within representation itself, because of the disjuncture between words and things, images and meanings, nomenclature and being—all of which cause us to think that the theater *is* the world when it's more like the thought of history. It is, however, a form whose signifying power, like that of language, far exceeds what the world in its seeming opacity offers to be signified. Like Hamlet, we may have the will and means to do it—but do *what?* That remains to be seen, though its absence may invade us with appalling force, and it is *that force* we are trying to represent in the work. So, in *Seeds of Atreus*, the rising of Agamemnon from the tomb (anticipating the Ghost), with an incredible effort of rematerializing will (*why* come back?), struck dead, "till the red act drives/ the fury within the brain," beyond all possibility of rising, and rising again, but struck, the cut flesh of the confirming body arched between heel and fontanelle, inscribing its own tomb, only the exactitude of the actor's dying, the *rigor mortis*, denying between word and the last breathing what we know only too well: that there's no further life in that death, or the image of it. Or so we think. Over and over again we see things denying what they appear to say and, in the denial, almost saying it, inarguably.

In *Seeds of Atreus*, the successions of violence which break up meaning and sunder being seem to leap out of a time seal across the centuries like the beacons with the speed of light, gravely in space, the intricate cross-cut rhythms of the oncoming strife (Heraclitus: "Justice is strife") played with a terrific pulse, impeccable, the power of delicacy and the delicacy of power "throbbing with gigantic strength," all the whispers in the universe massing in the language as if crushing the air coming at the audience like axe blows. The actors had to rehearse that intensity like the astronauts preparing for zero gravity in a simulator, until they could think like that, the metabolism accommodating itself to a thought process which was at first drawing a blank, thought moving so fast between the quick and the dead. Why think like that? Because there was no way to keep up with what was being seen, no way to signify it, the swift suction of amazed consciousness, that knowledge which *can't* be seen, nor cancelled, since it seems to come all at once in a contracting space, as if there were no time. The space travelled is an interior distance across history through myth in the encircling self, the "glut of blood drunk by our fostering ground," like an annulated break in perception, the thing reflected so intense it is its own laminated consciousness, "the vengeful gore" so caked and hard it will not drain through, image pressing on idea, idea on image in a virtual congealing of time, "the deep-run ruin" packing the mind into a Black Hole—the thing imaged forcing itself up through image, "swarming infection [boiling] within," the mind's breadth but the span of an instant so that it almost feels there, *what?* "fear in the beat of the blood rain/ breaking wall and tower," grace coming "somehow violent."

In his essay on "The Literarization of Theater," Brecht says, "Some exercise in complex seeing is needed—though it is perhaps more important to be able to think above the stream than to think in the stream." But the authority of the science which Brecht admired has already changed the picture: if it's all seeming—if we can't step into the same river not twice but even once (since we're already there)—there seems to be no alternative to thinking *in* the stream if we're to do any thinking at all, as if the stream carried every conceivable current of thought locked in its waters. In those new and wild tributaries of the mind that science describes, where mass is almost nothing (10^{-19} grams) or less than an instant's instant (a billionth of a millionth of a nanosecond), it's as if the cut brain of Lear or the ghostly tablet of Hamlet had released its shattered content to the world. In the reality of the outer and inner worlds, they tell us, spacetime may crumble and reform—as *foam!* Other-natured? Or the foam of old story? the many-headed foam of Salamis? the foam that Cuchulain fought? or—as the bedlam son says to the blinded father over the cliffs of Dover—"The murmuring surge/ That on th'unnumb'red idle pebble chafes"? For all we know of the mind-shattering brilliancy of the conception, we might as well have been dropped from the Milky Way on a field of diamond.

Back within the apparent measure of things, in the temporal behavior we think we know, we have all we can do to keep up with the surgings of inwardness. Suddenly, out of any concept of time the self confronts itself not knowing itself, as if it were fluency alone. Thus, in *Seeds of Atreus,* the royal carpet is the stream, a repetitive sequence of rehearsed blood, to which he who cannot believe in his symbolic status but can't refuse his role returns, a prophetess beside him, the chariot like a disenchanted juggernaut appearing out of ten years of catastrophic distance, not in a burst of martial speed, but *lente lente,* incomparably slow—no physical chariot, no stage property, except the prophetess joined to the king in the catatonic bodies of the actors—as if the wheels that are still turning are at the still point of turning thought. Before that, we saw the Messenger rise from a pedestal at the rim of the playing space to announce the coming. He steps into the space in an at-

Take Up the Bodie.

tenuation of time, as if swimming in a whirlpool back from the ruins of Troy. In Elsinore, remembered scenes sink through the face of the deep like the drowning Ophelia. Court Closet Garden and Graveyard transform each other and merge, chafing, upon the play within the play within . . . the stream thickens as the old plot thins. It is the heavy water of atomized energy. (Or another foam?) That is the story being told in Elsinore, a texture of self-dispersing fantasies, displacing the content of Hamlet with our own content and being displaced in turn by images of the play which return like the Ghost with the insurgent appeal of an originating cause.

The ghostliness begets ghosts. What happened in Hamlet—as Horatio knows in every painful breath drawn to tell the story—beggars the telling, and grows more untellable with the grievous burden of intervening years. Take, again, any quality of Hamlet, his seeming incapacity for action or the inability to love or the refusal to show it—any view we have of it is supportable or unsupportable. How accurate is Claudius when he says, "Love? his affections do not that way tend"? Is it a tending of the moment, and does Claudius mean it only now? or as a defect of character? a fault in nature? his nature? Hamlet is as opaque to self-scrutiny, for all his acuity, as he is to all observers. He is as complex as a human being can be (not being one) but lacks wholeness despite his protestation ("A whole one, I," that parcelling I), which no human being has (despite the illusion of entirety in the corporeal body). So, how to tell the story? One can imagine Horatio absented from felicity like another ghost, that graybeard loon, the Ancient Mariner, with glittering eye, rehearsing the words words words to no avail, as the images proliferate in the stream, including the image of the teller.

As we take up the burden in our ghostings, there is an essential duplicity in the form. It arises from the contraband of excessive tellings that undermines the irreducible thing we pretend to be after, what exhausts all speculation: the inarguable. It is related to the self-reflective dispersals of the missing persons. The superfluity which is at first a *means*—the instrument, attitude, and orchestration of inquiry—becomes itself an *ingredience* of the subject; more than that, its tonality and inflexion. It endows the subject with not only the character but substance, as if the catalyst had become an element of the reaction-formation, which is carried along on the overflowing stream. By then, it seems, the superflux of imagery is immured within a structure which we can no longer control. It is like a geyser in the whirlpool or, to change figures, the knottings at the dream's navel which, however exacting the interpretation, cannot be entangled and have to be left obscure because, touching on the unknown, nothing can be added, as

. . . at the edge of solipsism, the process is incestuous. . . , an echo of the figure of the

Freud says, to what we know of the dream-content. The duplicity of excess takes over the structure. It resembles the procedure of interpretation when—branching in all directions to every nerve end of thought—it narrows the network and takes over the dream. It also resembles (or is qualified by) that moment when the Ghost—who recalls us to origins and the imminence of meaning—takes over Hamlet's assault upon Gertrude in the Closet. There, it's as though the distortion were being displaced by the unconscious itself, which is never otherwise present, only reflected, except as a trace. As in the Closet, at the edge of solipsism, the process is incestuous. For all that, the struggle is to ground our theater work, like dream analysis, in something more theoretically powerful than our own self-encapsulating experience. That comes about by ghosting the Ghost, as we once pursued the Enemy—a vain project, endless, but raising the thought process of performance above self-perception, with all the attendant danger that we may be seeing nothing at all. But if so, we would see it accurately.

The recessions of the Ghost are infinite. No matter. We pursue them relentlessly in the ghosting, everywhere back to the overwhelming question: "Is there a divinity that shapes our ends?" It is once again the question of origins. (I have seen any number of productions of Hamlet in which that question, like "To be or not to be," is in the commonest sense meaningless, either lost in the stagings of our indifference or having been heard so much that it can hardly be heard at all.) The question is never answered but is dialectically ghosted—or rather ghosted into a dialectic, as if the whole pressure of performance cracked down upon the nutshell of that infinite space where, as Hamlet says, we might be king (the whole one, there) were it not for our bad dreams. In that space of thought, pushed to an answer, an echo of a figure of the Ghost: "Man proposes. . . . What makes you think the dead know more than you?" Before that, ghosts rising and falling—and after, ghosting in the grave: "I will question more in particular." A child is born a ghost, through Ophelia's ascension from her grave—in the maimèd rites the grass-green turf—becoming the Ghost: "I am thy father's spirit"; but it is a boyish woman's body, chest bare, mantic, like a breasted Tiresias. (In Seeds of Atreus, the Furies are "those gray and ancient children. . . .") The Ghost is in the Closet but in multiple forms. "I'd rather not believe in ghosts," says one of the actors in a long improvisation that ends up on the tape, but there's no rest, perturbèd spirit. The Ghost filters through our skepticism as it does through Horatio's—who remains a ghost among the living, dead. Fortinbras, who may not in fact believe in ghosts, nevertheless claims "rights of memory in this kingdom" and becomes, in the last words of Elsinore (he never appears), king of the kingdom of the dead. But where is "the beauteous majesty" of Denmark? I mean the majesty of buried Denmark. The Ghost's presence, like all seeming, subverts all systems of value. Even its own.

I shall return to that shortly. I am tracing these shadows of the Ghost to suggest more fully than before the working process involved in the theatricalization of such thought. Each actor, like Horatio, carries with him his version(s) of the story, or hers, each with its own compulsive life and course, intersecting and colliding (like the Donner Party in its versions of history), abrading each other, shaping, the murmuring surge, some of it lost, all of them rights of memory in this kingdom, forming the one structure of *Elsinore*. In the process, what's lost is lost. At the moment we start each night—in the research that leads to what we form—it's as if the source, history or text, all copies and versions, fair and foul, were lost. There is nothing to go on except what's remembered, and that shifts. What's there is all there is. The acting is a reconstruction, done collectively, in the perceiving and performing, one thought molding and correcting the other, anima(d)versions, enactment pressing back on thought raising the inevitable shaping question: "Who's there?" and the self-reflective response: "Nay, answer me. Stand and unfold yourself." The actors do just that, moving into the space.

I circle the area around the observers, asking sharply and repeatedly—at the intensity of the performer's emotion or pitched to an incipient criticism or out of an intuition of the observer's desire to know (perhaps my own)—what eventually (my voice and presence subsiding, another ghost) they ask themselves: *What do you see? what do you think? what does it mean?* (the words more conjectural, often metaphoric, less literal). *Speak!* Solo, duo, syncopated, a whole chorus—the murmur of inwardness outwardly projected, in an animated system of cross-reflection. In the act of acting, observing; in the most estranging watchfulness, performing. *Describe that. Analyze this. DO IT. Tell the story.* One response guides another, shocks it, deflects it, bevels the edge of an intuition, speaks your thought (even of the acting), makes it *responsible as performance,* observed of all observers. The reflection surrounding the specific enactment becomes, *as spoken,* a kind of conceptual music, throwing the anonymous body of the actor back, like the mysterious hebona, into the porches of the ear, where concept forms. As the actors contemplate the space of performance, "We say ourselves in syllables that rise," like the creation of sound in a Wallace Stevens poem, "From the floor, rising in speech we do not speak." Like the indeterminable story out of the rottenness of

Take Up the Bodies

Denmark, it is a speech which "is not dirty silence/ Clarified. It is silence made still dirtier./ It is more than an imitation for the ear."

Then, substitutions and displacements with no respite, like the compulsiveness of dream, one actor moving from the discursive level of thought right into the condition of the other actor, being where-the-other- *is*, out of the dirty silence, spontaneously, almost without transition from perceiver to perceived, seeing what is seen there in the actual body of thought. The specific qualities of each actor produce qualifications of what is *being-seen*, male and female codifications, through the substitutions proceeding at various levels of perception, intuitive and framed. Thought in this way becomes enactment, enactment thought—not abstract but active, active when abstract, blooded, taken up short, extended, *stage-struck*.

It's the fine suddenness of the substitutions which is critical, the unimpeded fluency of displacement, uncensored, like overlapping currents of the one stream. What we formally arrive at has been approximated in an almost infinite series of substitutions over a long period of time within the closure of a finite ensemble. While actors replace each other at the same level of emotion—the glyphs of reflection as identical as dissimilar bodies can make them—the stress is on the collectively *shaped* perception. It is not an ordinary kind of improvisation; that is, within the auspices of a character or a plot or a situation or a game. There is too much explicit mental activity, including narrative, and split-second jumps between apparently detached analysis (with no requirement that it be dispassionate) and totally "involved" acting, to almost purely dissociated kinetic states, as if hallucinating. The hardest thing for the actor to learn is—once the verbalizing of reflection begins—to keep speaking, not to stop, the temptation being at first to withdraw into internalizing thought. The actor will justify it with the conventional rationalization about not being "prepared" yet to speak. In this work, that preparation is not only a hindrance, but an irrelevance.

Two arbitrary rules in the method: one, told to go into the space or to leave the space, the actor does so instantly, carrying all doubt, or resentment, with him; two, told to speak, the actor speaks, keeps speaking—and under the pressure of cross-reflection is compelled to speak with greater accuracy of abundance. Asked to describe what he sees, for instance, the actor may want to associate away. But the insistence may be—by reflection or indirection—that he *detail*, point by point, with no interfering judgment or deflection, what is *out there* in the space. Or the suggestion may be more open and deliberately ambiguous, a cue for turning what is out there back upon the self, associatively, calibrating the inside against the outside in the other meaning of the word *seeing*. In the earliest training for the work—with all the accent upon the resources of the body—words are a seminal aspect of the method. As Hopkins writes of the forged verbal life of his poems, the instressed fastened flesh that bursts and darts, "it is the rehearsal/ of own, of abrúpt sélf there so thrusts on, so throngs the ear"—until the words are second nature, reflexive.

As the words begin to come more profusely, charging and parsing images, the liability is a scattering effect. The power of association that incites the method also subverts it. There may be random amplification of an image, spinning off (which we want) without a self-enforcing return to its core (which is also like a sculptural clarification). There is, however, a kind of spinoff which really stays with what's there, coming back to it, illumined, roundabout. What we've had to control is the tendency to diffusion—going off another deep end. As the work proceeds, it's almost as though we have to amortize the liberties of association until it becomes the case of last resort, the random leap only justifiable if it is a real quantum, undeniable, at the limit of an intuition. It is what Stevens and Hopkins and other poets understand, "that lovely riding thing, chaos" (Olson) or "the last kiss given to the void" (Yeats). Otherwise, as the images proliferate on the wing in a coruscation of words, the improvisational energy goes into the act of recovery. Gradually, the associations behave like the gathering repetitions of a refrain. In the ghosting, we look for the identifiable structures of reflection, recurrences, clusters of initiatory meaning, the volatility of emerging concepts. But *when* to do this is really hard to determine, a crucial perception of the work. It doesn't usually occur until after months of rehearsal; and there's no getting around the preliminary risks of diffusion, including the differential rhythms of the actors.

A group process depends on the sharing of available information. Each of the actors is, quite literally, a body of knowledge. (That may be self-evident, but if one thinks over conventional theater practice, it's easy to see the extent to which it is ignored within a "production scheme" or a "directorial concept.") Each project begins with a survey of the repertoire of information on the subject or issue being considered, which has already had something of a history within the group. The preliminary exercises gather up what is already known. As the materials come forth, first thoughts, first intuitions, they come with open, disguised, or unrecognized biases. The bodies of knowledge are out of phase. We see the structure of reality through the habits of our own minds. The mind settles easily into its habits. One of the purposes of the method is to cultivate the mind's restlessness. If there's any unity of thought, it's in the music of association. We're not really sure what we're after, but what enters the enveloping construct is what *belongs.*

Take Up the Bodies

Instead of a subject, a gravitational field. It moves outward through evidence which very soon appears endless, as well as images which seem incompatible—which is why the work's completion is almost always a surprise, a coming upon, the proposition of a cadence. There is an accrual of meaning in the music. The protracted time for the investigations is unavoidable and, for all the anxiety it causes, essential. After all that time, the cadence of the coming upon is like a series of remembrances. The repetitions and recyclings—the biofeedback in the process—gather up the residues of memory, causing them to sink in. The stored memory is the shifting ground of image and action.

Through all the association, we learn to develop a cold eye for the memorable fact. But as the images repeat and cluster, we also recognize that some of the material, older and almost forgotten, seems to insist on coming back of its own accord. We may cannibalize an image, cut away all but a minor part; or there are fusions and transplants of what appeared to be unmanageable or conflicting materials. We especially single out those images which, as we say, carry their structure with them—as opposed to enactments or occurrences which are essentially psychic states not easily recoverable, however useful they may be to the actor when they occur. Such states are subtextual, though not in the customary sense: they are rather the subliminal content of subsequent imagery, spilling over later into an ideogram that we can repeat. The run, for instance, at the beginning of *Elsinore* is a condensation of a whole series of atmospheres and prior images that came from the obsession of another actor with the lines in the First Player's speech on the death of Priam:

> Out, out, thou strumpet Fortune! All you gods,
> In general synod take away her power!
> Break all the spokes and [fellies] from her wheel,
> And bowl the round nave down the hill of heaven
> As low as to the fiends!

This led to weeks of powerful circular movements and monologues—an impulse toward personal confession combining with a sense of history as mere dispossessed and crushing momentum, a brutalizing force without purpose. The circular momentum was preserved, sparingly, in the run and with more or less intensity elsewhere in the structure, which sometimes has the character of that runaway wheel—as it does in *The Donner Party, Its Crossing*, where we were also reflecting on a runaway history, the hill of heaven reversed as the Pass.

Since what has to be told is indeterminate about the moment of its inception, we may choose an image as a provisional beginning, a way in, letting it work out its destiny through the inquiry: if this, what next? and if that, what then? image to image passing from rehearsal to discussion to rehearsal, the inaugural image shaken out as a concept, behaving as a growth, determining its own course. Sometimes an image will come in as a picked-up cadence and become a concept, though when it first appeared we hadn't the faintest idea what it was all about, nor the actor. Yet, unless it is absorbed conceptually into the structural rhythm, it will disappear or be eliminated. We are not interested in the mere serialization of material, as in some New Theater works, where the structure is mainly additive.

Sometimes the investigations, reaching toward meaning, remind me of the docking process of spacecraft when the interlocking mechanism fails. The images resist each other when the energy fields are not equivalent or, when equivalent, one comes from what seems like another galaxy, or another psychic or structural universe. Often images arise which are so completely ideographic—divorced from anything like the psychology of character—or so strangely idiosyncratic in design that no connection can be made at the moment. An actor will find himself trying to move in on what simply cannot be penetrated. I mean move in on with a regressive instinct toward a "relationship" that derives from the older psychology of acting. But the image, whose *existence* may be compelling, is as resistant as a stone. It is a *phenomenon* (the word we use) that may be *attached to*, but you certainly can't have a dialogue with it. Nor can it be logically enveloped in a narrative. It exists as an accretion or mutation of an imbedded concept, all construct, as when one of the actresses put the figure of her truncated body, spasmodic, jigging at the knees, into the *idea* of Jorick's skull. It (she) couldn't and wouldn't respond interactively when it occurred in an improvisational sequence, but it (she) could be played *with* in a structure, as Hamlet does with the skull that the Gravedigger throws up. Sometimes the actors will obtrude on each other's images before they have crystallized in their emergence—and while that may set off another ideogram or gestural train of thought, it may also abort a growth. Here, too, there are no strict guidelines, though they must be fast. We are dealing with the ubiquity of strange languages. In the instant of perceiving, there must be instinctual discretion. Or there is confusion, turmoil, scattering, and an irritable cacaphony of imagistic response that succeeds only in cancelling itself out. The ghosting question is the determining principle: what exactly is being *seen*? and how, in the instant, can it be seized? within the teleology of the impulse: to act, critically, in accordance with that.

The story, gradually, is no accident. There is a shadowy providence in the telling, the trial of error. The acted version is verbalized without interruption, sometimes with prefatory tags like "I saw . . ." or narrative connectives like ". . . and then . . ." (even when, especially when, there has been virtually no clear narrative in what was performed), the seeing reseen in words only, a ghost story, ghosted, and then replayed. The storyline, to the degree that it exists, is conceptualized by various modes of narrative: the straight physical sequence of motion and fact; sometimes analytically or philosophically (as if written by Borges or like the chapters on the whale); sometimes from a severely limited point of view (whether the actor's "own" or the fiction of a point of view). The rights of memory contend. Even what is screened tells the story. The material masses, at first inchoately, as the elements of the story are thought through, and their escaping. All information is recycled, all images. The texture eventually becomes anonymous. Something like a line of argument may appear as a tracery, indecipherable, assertion and rebuttal, incessant qualifying, additions and amendments, quarrels, annotations and marginal questions, echoes, loops, guesswork, and encodings. The faintest buckling sinew of a figure has its genetic code. The constant retelling is a grinding wheel, it sifts out. What is not told is oblivion.

Perseveringly, however, thought begins always afresh, in a series of ceremonial detours to what was first thought, a genesis. Usually the verbal tellings are done around a circle by the group—immediately after the enactments (which may have had verbal tellings within them). The individual versions usually overlap in a flush of desire to rehearse them, as if they *must* be told, with interventions and reflections (and, indeed, the actors *want* to recall, to justify, to hold in their minds what it is they did and saw), in one stream of consciousness. Sometimes the actors are asked (my intervention within the rhythm of the stream) to review, solo, what they think they saw, each in a synoptic chronicle like the gospels—and like the gospels an effort to achieve an affirming textuality that leaves the indeterminacy of origins behind. Occasionally, someone who is silent but seems to contain *the* story, like the veiled Word, is solicited for a sign. These differing versions are compared. Sometimes the tellings themselves become image-clusters which are incorporated into the enacted versions. Whatever the instance, they are a series of differentiations or laminations of the essential matter, building up remembered densities in the process. It's not unlike the consecutive pourings of a Morris Louis veil, the surface obsure with interior light; or eventually reticulated, hard, like a first century B.C. marble, showing the undergarments below the drapery, with a luminous delicacy of stone. The most difficult task is always to recover what has gone before: *to repeat the Story*, not in the sense of a stale retelling, but as if exactitude in the retelling were a matter of piety, as it is.

The methodology insists on images that become obsessions. They insist upon returning, as I said. The intensity of the insistence is a measure of validity, although mere obsession is not sufficient—and the obsession with a particular image introduced by one actor, perhaps months before, may (like the hyperventilating Ghost, performed by a woman but posited by a man) be taken up by another after the first actor has lost interest. The image, even if insisted upon, is subjected to the refractions, suspicions, and abrasions of further tellings, enactments, reflexions, and may still be returning even when it no longer resembles what it originally was. Our faith is that if we tell it over and over, we will eventually decipher what we *must* tell, in the most condensed form, like the morphology of a myth. The collective process checks out, eventually checkmating, the errant perception of the singular view, and the reliability of separate memories.

As that seems to occur, the written text begins to develop, as if it can be reliably founded. We collate the stored images. For a while, as the actors explore other aspects of the story, some of the thinking through may be done on paper. It gives still another perspective, and other laminations. We may feel at one point, for example, that what is being told is predominantly, and maybe falsifyingly, in sexual terms. Other aspects of image making subordinate themselves to that; maybe good, maybe bad. But the emphasis corresponds to the actors' particular concerns. What is seen depends after all on who, carnally, sees it. That may be a matter of sensitivity, values, determined passion, an absolute demand that something be represented which hasn't been shown or thought of—or which may have been dismissed, when it came up, by the others. Or swallowed up in association. Since there are no restrictions during the explorations on who does what, plays what, the claims can be openly made. At a given point, a single actor may be dominating the nature of the inquiry, as with the manic rolling versions of the heavenly wheel, the momentum of which was so fierce at times—both physically and verbally— that when the actor (Tom) careened around the space (his body large and powerful), everybody stayed out of his way. He was so intimidatingly compulsive—the monologues emerging like a speaking of tongues—that, for a while, unable to interrupt him, the others found it hard to be productive. It wasn't until we were deciphering a personal line for each of the actors through the long catalogues of their images that we remembered the many variants of an equal and opposite momentum, almost utterly passive, in another male actor (Jack) who, like Massacio's Eve driven from the Garden, moved with harrowed eyes and exquisite femininity, hands over genitals and breast, in a doleful round to the edge of the same doom. We composed a series of exercises for these opposing energies in which the two encountered each other more behaviorally

210   *Take Up the Bodies*

and dialectically—and the images that came of this (there is no such encounter in the piece) were *distributed* in the structure of *Elsinore,* the
initiating momentum never lost in the interchange of value. It is still
there, though rooted in a spot, in Tom's self-flaying at the start, while
it is Jack who circles around the space. The Massacio image remains,
but in another context, with Tom running around it, but in broken
angles, in a manic topological survey of the ramparts, beseeching the
Ghost to materialize and stand still. The momentum is there when, in
the appearance of the Ghost, he throws his hot heart against its im-
pregnability, and they fight.

In the course of the work, the actors have been acting better than
they know, not knowing really what they know. Often they've lost
sight of useful ideas which they introduced very early on, most of
which have been recorded, written down, from the start. As we go
through the record, and its amassing possibilities, we try to diagnose
what, behind all disparate behavior, action, imagery, is the overt or
unconscious motive of each actor in the project. Here are jottings from
my journal on two actors of contrasting sensibility (Tom again, to
detail the implications; and Peter this time, with a reference to Jack,
with whom he shares qualities but is more ironic). Traces of these
observations may be found in the Analytical Scenario which became
our guiding "text," the traces preserved as actual lines or other impulses:

PETER: laughing above the stream; Yorick side of the antic disposition; also Polonius, "purging amber and plum tree gum"; that
is, distancing/alienation. Being in the stream, acceptable; an
instrumentality, but not a conviction. While others (Denise,
Tom) might accept the commandment [of the Ghost] & rage
against it, P. derides it, not scornfully, puts on a grinning mask.
He believes in the Father but not in the commandment. *Is there a
divinity? Yes. That shapes our ends? Absurd. "What makes you
think the dead know more than you?"* Since it seems impossible
to function without a commandment, he accepts, now the *idea*
of aggression (the duel *scene*) but not aggression itself. [This
observation refers all the way back to the earliest discussion of
The Enemy, when Peter resisted the notion because conceiving
of it would encourage aggression. He was the one who said he'd
prefer to forget it.] Nothing Dostoyevskian about him.
Madness is always being *mused*—not quite reasoned; no
savagery of mind in Peter, though mindful, attentive to it, even
admiring; [yet] a disposition to *Let be* though going further, not
because he must know or is even convinced he will know by
following the Ghost; but because he *likes the experience* [em-
phasis added], the *feel* of it: "Is that the custom?"

Том: sin/guilt/remorse/madness/rage/grounds-for-being. Madness due to limit, contained by the body, unwilling to thaw, melt, resolve into a dew (cf. Jack, who càn & does, more neutral to will & matter); so can't take on the feminine principle, though he might mimic or allude to it. . . . The Faustian side of "I'll go no further": answer me! he tells the Ghost, and I'll follow alright. Refuse to answer, and I'll dig up the grave to find out. "I'll make a ghost of him that lets me." The side of him that is arbitrary, rigid, armored, moralistic. Like Denise, T. scruples. Concerned too, excessively, with honesty & betrayal. But mainly, rages vs. the ruled body. Refuses to be dominated by the act of fear. Instead of thawing, buckles; out of moral scruple, however, *forces* himself to his knees, *wants* to pray, then rending himself there out of resistance to intimations of impotency [if he does]. *Why am I not King?*

The notes already suggested, at the time they were written, what went into the scenario as motives to be pursued and, if necessary, surpassed. They were acted upon in subsequent rehearsals—and strategies were developed to explore the intuitions, or test the accuracy of what was being observed. Whatever we decipher for the individual actor—the major questions being played out by each one—we are inevitably dealing with intersecting paths. Through the particular questions, we look for the question that is absorbing them all, the meta-question. In *Elsinore*, that question was specifically the Ghost.

In time, things that were once random or deviate—what you might never have dreamed of joining together—are connected by a whole series of mediating images, the form emerging like the coordinates of a myth. As with myth, there is still a methodological problem. One tries to grasp the affinities before the splitting mechanism takes over again. This means for the actors an almost shocking imposition of a provisional order on the open-endedness of earlier improvisations and individual projections. It is in process like a reining in of the Id. The "finished" text puts a further dialectical constraint upon the actors. They are surprised to see things that they did, remembered images, displaced. The text seizes upon the centripetal energy of the investigations without surrendering the perceiving form back to mere process. The constraints are a disquieting energy in the performance, as if the findings were wrested from cross purposes in a terrific act of will, before going out of control. We always know there is something more, other, vast and, as in myth and dream, in-terminable. The felt experience of the work, I think, depends on that: the substance of a performance that is always, like the mirror's blank, open to what is not there and the dubious thing that is. There is a contrast between something intensely willed in form and that which reflects upon it or is reflected upon, which is always escaping.

We're not sure which is which. What pops in between the election and our hopes, even in performance, is afterthought and further association, the ghosting within the text, which cannot be stilled but which, theoretically, the performance excludes. We say it must be done *exactly*, as if there were a ritual order, knowing full well there's not. The exactitude is the impossible thing sought for. The sealed moment, however, is the final illusion, since there's no real stopping of the process of textualization except by the impatience of a closed mind. We are meanwhile exhausted by an excess which is unexhausted. Thus, there is always another reading, a spate of images, like Hamlet showing Polonius the clouds. The nature of the work is toward a bottoming out in still another interpretation. It is a kind of crash program whose major objective is a compulsion (ontological) to reach the ground by breaking it. But there is always something left over, the solid dark ground of wanting. That is where a ghost appears even when it is not the Ghost. Ophelia's are the watchwords: "T'have seen what I have seen, see what I see." *I saw*, say the actors on the tape in *Elsinore;* and even then, in performance, the ground shifts.

The trace of the Ghost liquidates thought, even in the releasing. To the question of whether "this thing appeared again tonight," the answer was "I have seen nothing." Nothing is behind what the Ghost speaks, which is a contradiction in thought. The Ghost is outside the categories which name a contradiction. We cannot say what the Ghost is, for it-is-not. The Ghost *should* frighten us out of our wits, for the fact is we have no wit for the Ghost. The Ghost is a meta-fact of an apprehension, an invisible event, at which we can only make mouths. By definition, it leaves us speechless, though the words come, defining, with every breath. As for what it represents, what else can we think but that the Ghost is what Hamlet says it is, a fiction, a dream of passion—which is to say, the vehicle of an absent meaning. (As Roland Barthes says in *The Pleasure of the Text*, "Ideological systems are fictions [Bacon would have said *stage ghosts*]. . . .") The Ghost is a metaphysical conceit, not a character. Whatever they did at the Globe to make him real, however Shakespeare played him, the Ghost has been corroded, abstracted, and dematerialized over time, the ghost of a ghost. He is unplayable, this absence, as a character. He is only good for an acting process, a way of thinking through the theater.

So we ask of the actors: where are you when you're with the Ghost? That depends upon the thing itself, whether it comes, and what you make of it—I mean the thing that makes the acting move. The methodology of subjectivity, the thinking that makes it so, is taken as far as we can imagine. Nothing is there but what you make of it. The subjective process becomes a means of understanding its own nature, consciousness turning on the massy wheel. This *thing:* not the Ghost alone, but what *inspires* the Ghost, drawn between word and breath? matter or spirit? Each actor is a ghost answering. The who which is there is the respiration of the Other. It is always a double unfolding, through the impedance of the act of fear. When Hamlet stops on the ramparts and says, "I'll go no further"—how far has he gone? When he says, "Go on, I'll follow thee"—where does he follow? and why does he stop when he does?

We think it has something to do—at the outermost limit of performance, where the spirit is most perturbed—with the desire to *stop acting.* The true subject of the acting process is the *resistance* to performance. The erasure of resistance is an illusion of the craft of acting. It is also an aspiration of the reflexive structure. Thus, with the actors: they must define, individually and collectively, the point beyond which they will go no further. *But they must not stop short.* Only when they've gone as far as they must will the Ghost speak. Which is to say, the performance *is* the Ghost, its own real subject, whatever it is in respect to which one lets be. Or, whatever it is, commanding us, that is there and not-there. "Stay, illusion." The one essential: it must somehow appear again tonight. If it doesn't, there is no performance.

When *Seeds of Atreus* begins, the actors are in their seats, in the audience, but distinguished there, like icons or Byzantine figures, hieratic, immobile, reflecting on the space. In *The Donner Party, Its Crossing,* the actors greet and assemble the audience, friendly but estranged. Even the greeting is reflective. There is no effort to break down the distance between performer and viewer. For one thing, the actors are in western costume, anachronistic. There is something odd about their behavior, jovial but removed—not entirely the same but somewhat like the people we met at the square dance clubs where, for months, we studied the dancing. In *Crooked Eclipses,* the actors are in the space, contemplating each other when the lights dimly rise. The audience is close, a breath away, at the same floor level, seated on a sumptuously-colored carpet shaped like a fleur-de-lys. They are reflecting on the actors and each other when the lights slowly fall. In each case, there is a calculated assertion of the reflective process. It already confers a meaning on the event. In *Elsinore,* the course of reflection is deliberately traced into performance, like the etiology of the acting process:

The actors start against the wall, watching and being watched, "neutral to will and matter," on the cliff's edge of the act of fear. The process of ghosting is to question more in particular, and most particularly about that fear. There is in the struggle for identity and certitude something restive and haunted. Is it the dream of that other time when we were whole, clean, unafraid? what the Ghost mourns in that one great short-lined breath of remembered being about the smooth body: annealed, uncorrupted, undisguised. "Are you honest?" Down deep, the problem in the cellarage for the actor, that mole. The presentation of the self in everyday life does make hypocrites and cowards of us all. But so does the presentation of the self in the theater, like the forms, moods, shapes of grief which Hamlet despises. The self anybody knows, for all we know, is utterly, unutterably, contrived: a structure. Stop acting? Another consummation to be wished.

The structure determines the *degree* of acting: The actor against the wall, who is he? withdrawn, by himself? when the director says ready? when the audience enters the room? when they are seated and ready? neutral to will and matter? still? when the tape starts? at the first approach to the space within the audience? at the acting circle? seated? When the player rises and goes to the "center" (where's that?), who is he then? having risen and being specifically observed by all observers, the others, who? and would he be the same if the tape weren't there describing, in advance, what he is doing? or when he speaks the first line: "My offense is rank"?—whose offense? Hamlet's? Claudius'? his? whose? etc., the lines between person identity self actor role character persona disappearing in the structure—which involves no more yet (except for the tape) than a progress from the wall into the room, the space previously there, but now the *subject* of an audience, the actor *giving* audience, in the precipitating audibility of appearance.

There is, however, in the audition of appearance, always the unappeased: the one we can't find, that life, the one we're holding back or (that hubris?) claiming to hold back ("that within which passeth show")—and the fear that it might not be there (that lie?). "Remember me." As it comes and goes, like the presentiment of a (dis)empowering ghost, we are caught up short, harrowed with wonder. And so for the actor—between the ghosting and the act of fear, in the breathing space itself—there is the ambiguous instance of *held breath:* a breach of self? the impulse to cease upon the instant? or the sign of release into another plane of being? Here again, our sense of technique crosses the desire for substance. What *is* the Ghost, this ghosting, the clamor in the nutshell for? One looks in the acting through appearances for the moment of pure existence, which is not the finished fact of being, but the premonitory silence (in the auditing of appearance) into which being rushes on the breath of meaning. We suspect that the sense of being haunted puts us nearer to an identity. The presence of the Ghost forces us toward action and definition. The specific hauntedness of the process insists upon a completion with all the power that seemed to have arisen from the grave. If the power is both insatiable and nonexistent, *we live on the desire for that which, even if it doesn't exist, we want.* I cannot call it faith. But the intensity of the performance depends on the strength of that desire. In *The Donner Party, Its Crossing,* it was felt as hunger: "that is the soul," says Géza Róheim in *The Eternal Ones of the Dream.* "There is only one story—that somebody was starved. But not really—only inside, in my stomach."

There, thinking, we give birth to these ghosts. The quality of hauntedness is what is also nourishing. Of course, we always assume that the Ghost is male, but what bourn and body is (conceptually) there under the character armor of that warlike form? "Perhaps truth is a woman," says Nietzsche, "who has reasons for not letting us see her reasons." He reminds us that the contemplative character "consists of male mothers" and suggests that what is being concealed is the female genitals. In *Seeds of Atreus* and *Elsinore,* there is this female incipience to the act of contemplation. Watching is a birthing. The eyes are virginal and invaginated. I have already mentioned the tenderly perverse sequence at the end of *The Donner Party, Its Crossing* in which—watching for the rescue party to appear "across the snow like a mirror thawed out"—one actor, regressing, (a surviving child) sucks sustenance from another's penis as if it were a breast.

Whatever the empowering thought in the ghosting, it corrodes the old theoretic forms of behavior which, by mimesis, we once abstracted into a repertoire of character. The residues persist and the remembrance. We measure ourselves against the memory but, in the evolution of our work, character is diffused into the act of perception. I am not speaking of "transformations" like those once practiced by the Open Theater. They were merely changeovers from one role to another. The technique was an adaptation of Stanislavski's later method of physical actions to Viola Spolin's improvisational games. The playfulness was still predicated on standard ideas of "characterization," whether sustained or not. In *Elsinore,* however, the remembered characters are dismembered: parsed quartered drawn refracted, suggested and alluded to through the qualifying presence of each actor. As opposed to the atomized figures in, say, the plays of Richard Foreman, the actor is still the dominant energy of performance, self-determining *in* the dispersal of character, ghosting and being ghosted.

What is left of the idea of character is a convention of feeling, a form of intuition, expression, nuance, concept, an *approximation.* Who's

Take Up the Bodies

there? Not entirely Bernardo or Francesco, but *something between them*, a proxy. Horatio is closer to the mark when he responds to the name by saying a piece of him. The other piece(s), as we see with Hamlet, has to do with the appearing and disappearing species of being in the actor. Whatever else it may be, a play is about the players who play it. The actor's presence is *at issue*. To the extent that characters exist in our work, they are coordinates, points of reference, fields of experience, persistent memories, moral and psychological imperatives— the enfigured names by which we may attempt to name ourselves in the structure of what there is to-be-played, one name glancing off another.

The idea of character, then, mediates between the actor and the lure of solipsism. Like the solipsistic self, it hovers at the extremity of performance, perceived by a kind of peripheral vision. In regard to roles, we say, Don't characterize Polonius, but *assume* Polonius, as in an animal exercise one does not imitate a cat but seeks the cat within, so that some *idea* of the feline appears. The assuming is, however, heuristic, a furthering, part of the ghosting. The actor might, in the playing out, assume in a sequence something of Gertrude or Claudius in order to further define what caused him to assume Polonius to begin with, or to extend the idea or assumptions about Hamlet. Or the actor might assume not an antic disposition but something feminine in *his* nature coming out of a reflexion on *her* image in an uninterrupted conferring of meaning in the assumings, like the "overing and aftering" of a Hopkins inscape.

Where there is no mediation of remembered character (no initiating text, no specific history), the actor still performs within a spectrum of expressive modes like a scale of perception on a keyboard: person role character self identity shadow double other, and diminished or augmented forms of each, down to the microtones, blending. Thus, the meaning of the actor in his or her own presence may also be at issue, the person to be ascertained. In *Crooked Eclipses*, where there was not even the names of characters to refer to, meanings accrued to self-determined projections, the range of otherness without the resonance of encroaching roles. In place of roles, there were other signs, among them male and female identifications and substitutions. There was, in the development of the "argument," a dialectic of genders. We were concerned with how the audience "read" each of the actors sexually, what associations were aroused by each presence, the degree to which the actors were "seen" as male or female, what roles were imposed upon them, what qualities of intimacy and eroticism were achieved and also projected, occasions of distance, anxiety, repulsion, attraction. To some extent, these are factors in any play, but in *Crooked Eclipses* empathy with the *person* perceived is significantly *played upon*—whether or not, say, a particular actor is *felt* as "desirable." The condensations and displacements—the sexual metamorphoses—in the structure were designed to alter and direct perception, though we obviously couldn't predict how and to what extent for whom. The palette is limited by the persons on stage. It is also limited by the dispositions of the audience. Each substitution was a changed measure of loving/hating, positive/negative, being/becoming. While the image or the action may appear, so far as we can make it, exactly the same, the difference in the person acting is a major signifying value, like suddenly dropping an octave or changing key. In *Crooked Eclipses*, who's there at any moment is specifically relative to who was there a moment before, male or female, and how that person is being perceived. Why the person is thus perceived is specifically relative to who is perceiving.

In *Elsinore*—where character is an interval on the scale of perception—we don't ask what Hamlet *is*, nor do we try to perform "him" in any conventional sense. If the Ghost is unplayable—buskined or flat-footed, in blue light or clear, stentorian or normal voice, miked or embodied, out of thin air or dry ice—Hamlet is impossible. *Who* is Hamlet? The role of Hamlet, which is obviously unplayable by a single actor or a series of actors, merges with other roles. It is not merely rotated or distributed from one actor to another, male and female, but rather dis-integrated in a kind of centrifuge of perception, a molecular dispersal of all behaviors through what we call a unifying *structural emotion*, to which all intuitions and manifestations of character adhere. Hamlet is nowhere and everywhere in performance, distributed in the field of vision. This took to its limit an impulse developed from the earliest work. In *Seeds of Atreus*, while there were mutating figures, each of the actors was assigned a role. In *The Donner Party, Its Crossing*, there was no fixed George Donner or Jim Reed, although there were certain actors who picked up the latency of the roles through the slippage, shifts, and allusions. With *Elsinore*, there were no roles assigned, there seemed to be no roles, only dissociated names, the ghosts of roles—the diffraction of character onto another dimension of understanding. Breaking up the concept of Hamlet perpetuated the essential mystery of the name, or revived it, very much as older forms of religious poetry were created out of a primal or cultic name which is anagrammatically disguised or distributed into the syntax or rhetoric of a poem. So the nature and name of Hamlet—the dismembered body of his thought—are scattered through the structure of *Elsinore*, like a *sparagmos*.

There is a kind of remorseless theatrical logic in the scattering. It has long been apparent that Hamlet is something other than his role or roles, at least since T. S. Eliot spoke of the absent objective correlative of his emotion. There is a politics in that absence, seen askance. There is no role because he doesn't seem to believe (as we can hardly believe) in the form of power that would accredit it, that once appeared within his reach and for which he was ambitious. History divests him of that function, not because it returns as farce, but because it persists as tragedy. We are stunned to inaction by dismay. There is a sense in which Hamlet had *too much* character, a series of roles broken off in the brain's momentum, like the spokes and fellies from the wheel. This whirling glut of character became, in our version, the splitting image of the characterlessness of our nonpolitics. We look for the authorizing image of power. Who? "Do you see nothing there?" "Nothing at all; yet all that is I see." The energy of the structural emotion comes from the collective intensity of the will to see, the ceaseless troubled thinking through the stream.

The displaced crosscurrents of a given sequence may be unmooring and strange without the anchoring character, but less in Brecht's sense than in Shakespeare's, which seems truer to the shifting mark: "Oh wondrous strange. . . . And therefore as a stranger give it welcome." The thing which appears out of the ghosting incorporates just about every conceivable level and style of acting in the superobjective of the thinking through. Still, one must think in respect to something. All theories of the world as illusion (strangeness?) subsist around a stratum (stream?) of assumed permanence. We may know most deeply that we don't live on solid rock but we behave rather as if we do—and even what we say about seeming depends on instinctive assent to provisional structures of understanding. *Elsinore* is such a structure, on the nave-edge of splitting apart.

When we talk about structure, we are not referring to the dry-as-dust manipulation of the formal elements of a piece—rather that limit of the irrational at which thought becomes intelligible because it can't any longer be thought about. While we may disintegrate the customary appearances of theater—behavior, purposive action, narrative, the last semblance of roles, etc—the structure is emotionally charged, so charged indeed that some have trouble determining where all that intensity of emotion comes from, an intensity usually attached to character-in-action. It is still humanistic emotion, though we're well aware of the structuralist theories that man is an almost useless interruption in the millenial space of knowing. We say: the emotion comes from the structure. It is the discharge of apprehension. The emotion is thought, full of desire. All desire is relational, but though we look for grounds more relative than this, there is nothing but the shifting, nothing in sight to attach to like the normal coordinates of dramatic action rooted in character. Nor is the structure purely or mainly graphic

What we have been trying to develop is a collective form in which, should anybody falter, it falls apart.

or formalistic. It is familiar emotion moving through the structure, emotion we associate with plays in the older tradition. But there is very little of that tradition legibly there. So it's as if the structure were haunted, ghostly. People ask, Where does all that emotion come from? It comes from the structure.

But the actors, what do they attach to?—what else but the consummation to be wished? They follow the Ghost. There is nothing else to follow. When it slips away, they are in a solipsistic bind. The structure is what relieves them of it, though they must break out again and again. There is a kind of rhythmic apprehension of a being-about-to-be. It happens over and over, a provisional shading off into the next work and the next . . . in a circle of beginnings that leave themselves behind. Every moment is another question, averting a dead end. So long as anything is taken for granted, there is no structure. Hardly a smooth body, merely an empty husk. At the psychological limit of the self's momentum, the self-scanning continuum is the structure. When I think of the process of ghosting, I am reminded of the topologist's version of a surface which is transforming itself in a continuous fashion, one point remaining where it was, like the whorl on the head from which the hair rises (when the Ghost appears?)—a fixed-point theorem in the mind. It averts the scattering of the continuum beyond thought. The hairline difference is that between a form of self-reflection which is solipsistic in a rut (the killing thought?) and self-reflexive action unable to rest.

What is really experimental is the risk, for the actors, in the open-field subjectivity of the inquiry. It is not mere reflective motion as nervous disease, but a superlatively aroused state of mind. It requires from each of the actors not the sentimental supportiveness of group process but the absolute attentiveness, no exemptions, of a highwire act, that dependency. So far as we can do it, the existential risk is made literal in the structure. The work is severely physical and even dangerous—most strenuous, however, in the swift tension of the teeming brain. That is what is characterized in the structure. There is no relief for the individual actor because the momentum of association is in the ensemble. What we have been trying to develop is a collective form in which, should anybody falter, it falls apart. In *The Donner Party, Its Crossing*, the crossing refers also to this dependency. Everybody, in the structural rhythm, has to be of the same mind. Each assertion (to use an image from the work describing the work) is like the rain stopped for an instant in midair, only that instant separating it from what follows and what went before, each line qualifying before and after, *every line everybody's line* in the common fantasy text, no waiting anything out because nobody is theatrically independent for more than that instant, no series of routines, no scene carrying the rest; nor any single performance.

The dependency can be seen in the movement of the language from text to subtext to fantasy text (many of the lines having come into the text from the improvisational studies), the performance of which is the ultimate *textuality*. Take this short sequence from *The Donner Party, Its Crossing*, when they are moving through the desert:

JULIE: Sand dust salt and my toes are cold.
PETER: Snow comes from below.
WES: One must have a mind of winter.

On the surface, the pattern of association is clear (including, for those who pick it up—but not essential—the stealing from a poem to compose a poem). Sometimes the leaps are murkier, less followable, and here they become more subliminal as they go on. The subtext, in the conventional sense, has to do with connections among the actors, what is overt and what is disguised (what "comes from below"). In this sequence, Wes' connection, on the behavioral level, is mostly to Linda. He is turning to Julie in the square dance when he says the line, but the line, while not specifically directed to Linda, is meant relative to her. What exactly Wes means by "winter" is his own association, but the resonance carries through to what we call the Snow Chorale (described before), in his particular nuance of the distributed refrain, "Snow is falling." The line is assimilated by Julie, however, at another level, as he touches her in the dance. She becomes later the (invisible) white-shrouded figure of an Indian who haunts the landscape, white on imagined white, when the Party is snowbound below the Pass. Wes, surveying the appalling prospect of the impassable mountain, says, "There is a trail of white between her teeth." The fantasy text—accumulating in the unrevealed personal associations—develops all the way through the journey, depending on that *mind* of winter, to the vision Wes has on the mountain when—after playing the ox upside down beneath the snow—he becomes the dying figure who sees "someone leaning down with a white string in her mouth." The three lines quoted above were preceded in the text, several lines back, by Michael's response to Julie's "Hot hot"—"Teach her to talk snow." She does just that in her Indian dance, though "Snow comes from below." It is Michael who feeds his semen to the child.

There is a nuclear packing of these associations so that they reverberate from text to subtext to fantasy text, the lines blurring between them. They are additionally ramified by the recurring figures of the square dance which, over time, acquire their own associations. Much of this is designed, but the design of the performance is always surprised by the accidents of sweat and motion. When the pulse is quick and binding, new associations arise, over and above the immaculate scoring. There is also a kind of auto-suggestion in the process, connecting words, gesture, dance, and remembered story. Take Peter's line about the snow coming from below. What that means to Bill at the moment Peter says it, only Bill knows. Behaviorally, it is not said *to* him, and yet structurally it is. Later, playing the teamster killed by Reed (the "role" associated with Peter), he will be rising and falling, saying "Snow is falling"—with his ear to the ground when he falls. Moreover, Bill's first words after Peter's line are, "We are all vanishin down a hole." What sticks in the hole, again only Bill knows. The vortex of the exhausting dance is slowing gradually through the ground. The hole—a cave beneath the snow, the cabin, the underworld of the journey—is an echo chamber for all the unspoken motives of these lines. This aspect of the performance is limitless, but within the tightest design, like music. Drop a beat, and the mystery turns into obscurity. No matter what, it takes some listening, by the actors, by the audience.

The impetus is to take everything as far as it will go, like the associations. The extensions are imagistic, the binding is rhythmic. The performances are meant to be emperiled by their intensity. The old chanciness of theater (scenery falling, forgetting lines, heart failure on stage) is raised deliberately to the nth degree within the structure we do control, so that it is always at the edge of error. The literal dangers—whether the mountain climbing in *The Donner Party, Its Crossing* or the long fight in *Elsinore* or the technical feat in *Seeds of Atreus* of splitting syllables in choruses at high speed across distances—are metaphors of articulation like the defiance of gravity in the lead-plate and rolling-iron sculptures of Richard Serra. In Serra's sculptures, the entropic force of gravity is made to do constructive work, on the edge of danger. The point of the dangers incorporated in our performances *is* that the actors very nearly get hurt. The fact that they could be hurt puts a different construction upon the work than if they were merely *acting at* danger. (I remember from years before the anxious labor that used to go into staging fights, for instance, so that in no conceivable way could the actor be injured, the degree to which he was protected being a measure of status and commodity value in the commercial theater, literally a matter of saving face.) The most perilous physical exertion is an inflection of an act of thought. The concern is always with the objectification of meaning, as elusive as meaning might be

In the period of minimalist sculpture—when our work was developing—it seemed possible to demonstrate the fragility of meanings by a reductive simplicity, as Serra did on a large scale. In the theater, there was during this time a "minimalist reduction" to the body. But it more often than not seemed to us the wrong kind of simplicity, without the scale. Our work also narrowed down to the body, but it was always tempted to excess because of a conviction that, even when the text is abandoned, the language of the body is always ghosted by words. (So, actually, is sculpture, as the minimalists had to confess.) Moreover, I insisted upon the words. If the language of sculpture is relatively down to earth, it is far less so with the language of theater, where the words are a structural force—for they are always defying gravity in their incurable separation from things. No matter what the motives, the words fly up, the bodies remain below. This levitating capacity of language can be considered either an escape mechanism or a saving grace. We took the *immateriality* of language for precisely what it is, another articulation of possibility. By inevitably failing itself, it generates a skein of meanings. In the striations of the body, words displacing, dividing, and repelling words. We almost couldn't keep up with the rapidity of association and reflection, but it seemed to us the most exciting task. For it is the problem at the heart of reflexivity: the shocks that flesh is heir to because of the disruptions in language itself—the radical discontinuity between its power to signify and its escaping subject.

The form tries to imitate the precariousness of the perceptual act without breaking up into the condition it approximates. The meaning of the act seems to be riding on the swiftest current of the stream, words flying in all directions even in silence. The specific hopelessness of the task is the ground of all the striving. So the teeth are on edge with the concentration—on preserving the image and performing the meaning—as the wagon train careens over the Great Divide and Donner shouts, "WILL MY GOLD BRIDGE HOLD?" Musically, it is the strenuous plainsong of structure. While the bodies of the actors are the wagons and later the beasts of burden that haul them high over the mountains becoming the snow which buries them, it is the mental burden which exhausts them. The stamina required, for the watcher and the watched, is like the 880 run, a savage race. You cannot do it in a single burst nor pace yourself as in the mile. The stitch comes you know not where, the catching of breath, and the question of whether it's worth it, a desperate need for second wind. That comes only from knowing, by some visceral instinct, *why* you're there. "What does it mean," we ask over and over, "to get over the Donner Pass?"

The meanings cross at various levels of consciousness from the ontological to the aesthetic. The Party came to the Pass with barely a

Take Up the Bodies

parcel of belongings but the disappearing self. They left their property in the desert and we left it in the dance. I mean the exchange value. Normally, we fail to see the value of things as a quotient of human activity—the more so as a flood of quite useless things, today, dominates our reality. So besieged are we by objects that we miss the significance of the stored labor in their making. We tend to forget that the things around us are the products of ethical activity. It's as if they are masked by familiarity like human motives. One of the powers of performance, and part of its value, comes from the degree to which it reminds us—in its consummation by disappearance—of the (illusory) relations of work and use. Performance is useless activity which often requires extraordinary amounts of work: so much expended on what exists in passing and in vain. (In this book I speak constantly and quite purposely of what we do as work.) The very gratuitousness of theatrical performance impresses us, paradoxically, with the complicated choices that have gone into the making. It serves to remind us that time and labor are constituents of everything we use, all the more because we can't use it.

To the extent that the structure of performance reflects the presence of time and labor in its passing, it acquires a dimension of history. As Marx and Engels pointed out in *The German Ideology*, our value-systems and the ideological reflexes *"have no history, no developments,"* except as terms of a real existence, defined by material production. "The phantoms formed in the human brain are also, necessarily, sublimates [*supplemente*] of their material life-process, which is empirically verifiable and bound to material premises." Depending on the quality of its consciousness, it's as if the theater reverses the process, and the phantoms released from the brain remind us of their material existence. They both sublimate and supplement reality, but if they're not to be owned like objects, at the expense of the life-process, they must think about the cost of production; that is, the cost in human terms. At its best, by willed labor and choice, the theater makes it harder to look at things without, as they say, factoring in the cost. The idea of performance as we understand it in the theater is a measure of the sometimes dehumanizing stress on performance as we encounter it in life. Because the seeming abundance of things obscures the ethical issue in the production ethos, we specifically intensify the labor in our work to stress the human cost. It is, ideally, the difference between a labor of love and an anonymous process of labor which leaves a sediment of suspicion on everything we use, and all the staged and masked activity of our estranged and ghosted lives. If we look out from the object to the social system which is required to produce it, we cannot help being mortified by our vulnerable complicity. It is that to which Brecht was trying to call attention with his technique of historicization. How many karats from hell is that mine where the gold is plundered to plate that watch on your wrist? or for that matter, Donner's gold bridge? *Who* is out there at some remote, disguised, forgotten distance, being exploited or exploiting in order to mine it and make it? Having asked the question which calls for change, we are left with the question of the power to change it.

Performance is double-edged: it makes us conscious of our actual frustration while renewing the illusion of power. The history of the theater is a chronicle of strategies for the renewal of that illusion even when the illusion is being denied. "There is a poetry/ of the movements of cost," wrote William Carlos Williams, "known or unknown." We are interested in that poetry in the theater. If there's any truth to the idea that the acting out of a possibility makes that possibility more possible, then theater contributes to the quantum of stored prospect even while using up in performance—the passing of an appearance, getting over the Pass—the actuality of stored labor.

"Continue," says Kierkegaard, "I'll know you where you sweat." Getting over the Pass is also an achievement of self-knowing. The physical exertion speaks for itself: there is a sense of history in the dancing bones. But the rapidfire intellectual activity is part of that exertion, the sweating out of thought. It is a metaphor of the senses in the act of understanding. In the high synesthetic altitude of the Pass, the taste of air becoming body in the mind's eye, a shadow of meaning passes among the actors, whose bodies can barely move. The transpositions of thought from one sense to another is like, in *Seeds of Atreus*, the visceral flaring in the voices of the beacon lights. We take in experience with the speed of light, as we take in metaphysics through the pores. Inner and outer energy reinforce each other in a mutual act of transmission and reception, turning the inside out. The endurance of the Pass breaks down the barriers. As we meet the world at the edge of the skin, we send out signals as rapidly as we take them in. Thought moves in our work with the swiftness of sensation, almost stunning experience into the volatility of the body. At the summit of thought, snowed over, is the unconscious—also sending signals to the surface.

The quick movement of mind is a structural rhythm ("as swift/ As meditation or the thought of love"), an inscription of what at every instant happens to us by virtue of our contact with the external world. It is, as played, the posing forth of an energy behind the customary appearances of communication and the seemingly sluggish peripheries of thought. What we take in or what we fail to take in, no matter, the information comes at us terrifically—and we take in even what we're not aware of, training ourselves to keep up with it. The actors in the com-

Take Up the Bodies

pany remark how hard it is for them to see a play conventionally performed because, aside from the usual linearity of development, so little
information passes (or is registered) from moment to moment. (There
are experiments which indicate that most of us are capable of absorbing more at a faster pace, and that slowing down for clarity often im-
pedes learning by dulling the senses.) I play with the calculator on my
desk. There passes through my mind Yeats' desire for a technique to
surpass the technicians. I can't outwit the circuitry, but if I discipline
myself I feel I almost can. I can almost see the number *before* it appears, the weirdness of the reflection intensifying the reflex. That's
what the style of *Elsinore* reflects, the circuitry of reflexion in the form
of its occurrence, including its speed—without which there is no approach to form given the experience we are concerned with. It's almost
a case, as with Hastings, of thinking ahead of yourself—the ear so close
to the mind it has the mind's speed; keeping up not merely with the
words as discrete entities (which they are not) but, as in the sonnets,
with the ecliptic fluency of phonic states, the soundings.

Thus, the dull substance of the flesh is enlivened by thought. The
thing which happens at the skin is—though we forget it in the bias of
body over mind—more *like* than different from what happens within.
The rhythms of perception cut across the skin, "enter, entered, transformed" (like the actors crossing the space in *Elsinore*), the world
presenting itself assaulting the inner world like those high-speed par-
ticles which shatter atoms. Keeping up with the prospect of that indis-
cernible world is exhausting, to be sure, but what takes the breath
away is the enigma of the space which can't be crossed. At the Pass, in a
glaze of dream, life fastens, and we know it is unknowable—as we
sense, for the moment, that thing on the other side of representation.
The unnegotiable demand of the Pass is that we think in the bones, as
we take up the bodies, of the unpassable.

It is virtually impossible to think about it. For we encounter at the
Pass, as in the thought of Elsinore, the insistent presentness of a non-
presence, one aspect perhaps of the power behind the Ghost, the idea
of death as the impervious structure of the living moment—what
causes us to shift back to the terms of representation and think of the
world as a form of theater. If all reality is seen as theater, a mere passing play-within-a-play, *Elsinore* sums up that experience and finds it
unbearable: the very power of theater, the most resourcefully self-
reflective symptom of the disorder we must inevitably bear. That self-
doubting consciousness in the thought of theater—if incarnated with
sufficient force—may finally deny itself, the theatrical *act* upholding a
reality which is *not*, however it *appears* to be theater, theater. *Elsinore*,
quite conspicuously, appears to *be* theater. The density of the perfor-

mance certifies that, the palpable strictness of the reflexive structure, as if determined to be an absolute object in time. Disintegrating *Hamlet*, it also reflects the *dis*appearance of theater, in the world and separate from it, stubbornly resisting the seeming by which it is seized.

The process, then, takes Brecht's theory of Alienation some way further because we are deliberately invoking the content of the unconscious as an agency of perception. The *gestus* includes that content. The tale is untellable, but it is told and told by every mode of discourse which can be imagined or remembered. Technically, the means of subjectivity and the means of Alienation are deployed against each other, shaping appearances in whatever form they come *as* they come, as if we're dreaming in the open and assessing the dream-content at the same time.

To review a series of images from *Elsinore*, as if the work were in progress: An actress crosses the space, her fingers crosshatched in front of her eye; an actor runs in a furious circle around the periphery, self-punishing and unstoppable, with the terrible momentum of history unhinged. As an actor moves diagonally from one corner to another, hand over genitals, very delicate, feminine, somewhat like the expulsion from the Garden, but with an oscillating motion like a clockwheel, a woman crawls with painstaking deliberateness across the floor, arm reaching to its full extension ahead of her, body like an arrow. I am already reading into them, but what else do these images convey? how are they related? It is like watching karma unfold, or reading the prophetic entrails. But we do not leave the mystery alone. We have seen shadows of these images before, or versions in other planes—as when the woman performed the crawling action vertically. Why has this thing appeared again tonight?

As the images spin out their combinatory puzzle, the observing actors move in a concert of speculation around them. They try to read the signs by every means at their disposal—mimetic narrative descriptive analytical—by mirroring and substituting, seeing and saying, criticizing, being and letting be. In his essay on Chinese acting, Brecht says that an acting process is liable to be murky in so far as it depends, as this does, on intuition and the subconscious: "The subconscious is not at all responsive to guidance; it has as it were a bad memory. . . ." Moreover, the trouble with actors, he adds, is that "subconscious memory is getting weaker and weaker, and it is almost impossible to extract the truth from the uncensored intuitions of any member of our class society even when the man is a genius." The method tries to make up for bad memory. And bad faith. The actors work in a space of collective memory. What appears to be an empty space is the circuiting ground of received truth, where individual memory is not permitted to slacken and withdraw. The space is surrounded, it is *being-watched.* It is the claustrophobic space (nutshell cellarage burrow cell) of an openly vanishing presence. Space of the actor, space of the Ghost, space *for* a ghost: the thing you want to come and fear will stay, or the reverse, space of illusion. Remember me. Are you honest? Is that the whole story? Investigations are sustained over long duration, so the actor can't back out of the flow of perception. The questioning is relentless. Even the most resolute absent-mindedness is registered. Defenses weaken. Enactment passes into analysis without a lapse, analysis into performance, another order of enactment with its own emotional content. But look again, is it honest? What is it asking? Go back to that illusion. Stay.

It is a space of crossing illusions, all faculties in motion at once. The actors are observed entering being entered transformed. The act which appears to be subverted is enabled, critically, by the disabling mind. An image presented by one actor is the further activated state or avatar of the one before or a reflection upon it, performed, the partial image gathered into the critical act, mind fastened on the disabling, reflexive, at the same pitch of perception as the thing seen in a veritable dialectic of seeming. The unstopping momentum is important, the psychic violence, and the insistence that what is being seen be said. The language comes at us in familiar and unfamiliar cadences, a lamination of voices remembering, mnemonic and referential, with a history in the words forgetting that words forget. Sometimes the words behave as if they are vocables without memory. They seem like autonomous agents, objects, facts of being, forces and tensions—as if in colliding with each other they might release the thought which has been dissipated in the dramaturgical syntax in which we usually find them, plotted, like the "To be or not to be" which can hardly be heard any longer sounding over the abyss. What we are enabling in the space is subconscious memory, which has to be recovered through the interpreted murmur of history.

In developing *Elsinore* from *Hamlet* each actor knows not the lines of assigned characters, but the lines of the whole play, so that they can virtually improvise, as we say, in *Hamlet*—what I meant earlier when I said it was the only language we had. There is no discussion of what Hamlet is or how a character behaves because the behavior *is* the discussion, the network of reflection, the discourse. An idea might be developed on a single structural image through allusions to two or three characters attached like valences to a remembered event—as if the whole play were always all there moving in and out of the associative pattern. Look: there in the distance is a smiling mask, a mock childish obeisance. "No shuffling," says one of the actors, observing. The actor smiling moves on a strict line of perspective toward another who is saying, "I'll observe his actions, I'll tent him to the quick." This actor is a woman. The other approaches, somewhat zanily, it seems—an antic disposition? It appears to be Hamlet now, but the gait is shuffling, and the extended arm goes limp, aging, something closer to but not Polonius, a piece of him.

The actors make use of this shifting ground for further discriminations. The problem of identity is at some hypothetical center, and the experience is one of ceaseless perceiving, the problem of identifications. A figure of the Ghost suggests the drowning Ophelia: a floating and circling motion descending, one actor going down upon another, two women, body to body, the images meeting in a watery grave, like thought floating in consciousness, all ground disappearing. "'Sblood," says the actress floating down, "there is something in this more than natural, if philosophy could find it out." And there we are, suddenly, at the center of *in*difference, in a fourfold version of the Closet Scene, the images reflecting upon each other, gravely, as a figure of the Mother, brutally raped, commingles with the figure of Ophelia, horribly abused, who rises from nothingness and, speaking portions of Hamlet's soliloquies through stages of the mirrored scene, reason going mad, becomes the Avenger. "Is this not something more than fantasy?" Whenever things proliferate to where the mind can hardly contain them anymore, there is something in the structure of the method, as of the performance, which asks of both actor and audience, "What think you on it?"

The action is mediated by immediacy. The actor who is performer becoming observer or in some no man's land between is perceiving actions he is enacting as if somebody else were enacting them. He speaks *about* those actions not in the third-person technique of Brecht, designed to detach and objectify (that, too), but in a partly hallucinated behavior like that of Macbeth's "Is this a dagger which I see before me?"—entranced at what is transpiring, describing what you are doing as you are doing it (more imperceptibly than this shift of pronouns) as if spoken about in the second person. The observer becomes performer without mediation and, sometimes, it appears as if the person watching and reflecting is the source of energy for the thing that is being watched, as if it were coming out of the mind. Thus, states of subjectivity become instrumental means of investigation. They are distanced and not distanced, valued and devalued, not as polar opposites but in a spectrum of sliding perception. Any subjective state, any emotion, is but a path to what needs to be told or an approach to understanding as much as can be told. There is a difference between clarifying a dream

Take Up the Bodies

and allowing oneself to be clarified by it. One of the purposes of the method is to let the fantasy do the thinking, without the discrediting of rational thought.

The same is true even when there is no text to match our fantasy, as *Hamlet* did. In the work we've done upon *The Cell*—which started without any text, not even specific documents like those from and about the Donner Party—politics, reflection, and subjectivity were structurally connected in a pattern of infiltration like one of those wire-beaded Chinese collapsing toys. Again, a whole spectrum of acting behaviors: personal encounters; dramatic scenes; group confrontations (what we called "struggle sessions," after Mao, or "political education"); ideographs; choral abstractions of purge trials (the actors up against the wall saying, as an abrupt tangent of a prior event, *"I accuse myself of . . ."* and drawing upon personal failings to fill it in, the confessions mythicized as in *The Enemy*); litanies; mono-obsessive sequences in a Beckettish mode, as if incarcerated; expostulations; "mass appeals"; verbal "trashings" (victims castigated and abused); "ripping off the media"—and through it all wide fluctuations of displayed and eruptive emotion, all of which becomes an instrument of exposure and analysis.

We adapted the paranoiac system from *The Burrow* and the questioning technique used in the Oracle. The structural ground is inquisition. We proceed by conspiracy theory. Everybody, everything is suspect. Without the buffering mediation of character, the actors increasingly adopt personae to collapse the distance between their own non-ideological capacities and the political deed. But here the assumption of another identity seems in the grain. They gear themselves through the process to do what at first they could barely fantasize or, in principle, would insist on denying; if not do (absurd to imagine it), to find images that would approximate the sensation of doing (and in that sensation more than imagining you could). The project came from the feeling of revolted powerlessness brought on by thinking of the contemptible "uses" of this world, the pure stink of Elsinore—what makes one feel deep down that the most radically destructive act would be a duty and a blessing. In mythicizing the politics, we were trying to bring within the compass of imagining the one deed that would undo it all.

Gradually, as we thought our way through the cell's mission, the actors did not even require any strict personae, the mediation. The imminence of possibility was a graduation of the self, a movement of personal will toward the prospect. One could begin to imagine being radicalized by the work—except that there is also an impulse in the work that is devastating in its counterrevolutionary tendency. A revolutionary would of course say we are parasitical, all the more as it is effective. Aside from retrospective questioning of every motive, it's like learning to lie (as we do) by observing how the truth is told. In thinking through *The Cell*, we tried to take the lie seriously. The political education sessions were remorseless in self-examination. Once more we realized, too, that no matter how often we return to each other for stimulus and sustenance, the projections are inexhaustible, replenished by the subject, and thus the exposures. The questioning may be endless and never use the Other up.

Studying the relationship between political motive and subjectivity opened up the prospect of unfamiliar transformations in the self, a sort of cellular reconstruction, like forms of evolution speeded up. One of the actors (Jack) described the mutations as different "atmospheres" or "oceanic levels." The construct of the Cell soon absorbed the following polarities in its structure: body/mind, active/passive, guilt/freedom, subject/object, victim/executioner, solipsism/purpose. We discovered that potentially deceitful terrain between revolutionary politics and radical consciousness, and the maybe more deceitful terrain between fantasies of radical consciousness and the real thing. Eventually we started to introduce each night's session with a tape, my voice reading dispassionately from a textbook on cellular physiology: the cell as structure and function, the basic unit from which we move to an understanding of the substance of experience. "The root grows downward in response to gravity while the stem grows upward"—so the text says, sounding like William Blake: "The sunflower follows the sun—as the minutest movement of plant growth can be demonstrated in time-lapse photography." Certain sequences in the work began to give that impression, as if the minutest impression of subjectivity were being stop-framed. During this introductory passage, the actors were being "revealed," a cell portrait, a "culture"—each actor being cell, multicellular organism, cells within cells: action/motive, growth/decay, creative instinct/destructive element, pleasure principle/death wish. The study of the cell, as the text says, is basic to the understanding of "the fundamental activities of human life." So politics: a function of the organic will-to-life, yet that part of us that wants to be secreted in the Cell forced to self-questioning by inward pressure to public exposure: change the world? change the self? change the genetic code? One realizes how strong the questions are at the most rudimentary levels of the organism.

Soon we found ourselves entangled in questions about the limits of intimacy. The form of questioning was such in the ideological crossfire of the struggle sessions that nothing previously known about the Other is reliably known, trustworthy; nor the most intimate self-knowledge. You think you've asked the deepest questions of yourself only to discover how much hedging there has been. An apparently aimless question in another voice tears away the masks down to the bone—confusing the self to the self, all over again, the other mask. So, too, with most of what we think we believe: that consists of more or less ordered, mostly unspecified, rarely criticized attitudes. Even the most thoughtful of us really don't know what we think until forced to say it. The inquisitional process, at which we grew relentless (playing at it improved the technique of cruelty), demands that nothing be left to random, that every attitude expressed be examined and lifted into a larger system of conviction. Nothing, absolutely nothing, was to be left unexpressed. In the Cell, every thought is held accountable, the more so as an orthodoxy defines itself. In that context, one begins to understand how one may indeed "sin" in word, deed, and thought.

Soon we were dealing again with an assault upon the theater frame. That's another peril in the work. How much of the actual can we safely let in? Too much "real life" can destroy the Cell—and carried far enough, the group. There was the night soon after the actors had begun to change their names within the Cell: Tom had chosen the strange word *Squamous.* He had complex (if not perverse) reasons for the name, but Julie (who had worked in hospitals as an X-ray technician) thought he meant squamous cancer, which metastisizes through the body. Seized by the idea—the cancer inexplicably raging in her—she seemed to lose control and began to assault Denise as if she would destroy the Cell if it didn't destroy her; that is, change her nature entirely. She had read the signals in Tom's new name, but something "real" was seizing upon Julie, something cancerous. Denise was stunned, mortified by the gratuitous intensity of the attack, which turned out to be very personal. She felt unprotected, exposed as never before. When we were home after rehearsal, she called me to say that if she had responded as she felt, it would have had to be outside the membrane of the Cell. I asked her what she wanted me to do—was she asking for some intervention? Denise has a background of fundamentalist religion. It was she who had asked, in *Elsinore*, "Is there a divinity that shapes our ends?"

The question was no mere formula; she wanted a definite response if not an answer. But the powers of the Cell were organic, systemic, political. I had nothing else to offer. Denise knew that if the work were to proceed we couldn't prescribe any limiting rules, except the rules of the Cell itself. Otherwise, no safeguards. Was the Cell cancerous, is that what Tom meant? Maybe. Each of the actors has gone, at different times, through something like this experience—an irruption of inordinate vulnerability, as if there were something virulent in the nature of the work.

There is also, however, a self-healing mechanism. I don't know how much more of that kind of violation Denise could have taken, but there is a toughening agency in the method. The Cell accentuated the liabilities of what was always there: *acting on the edge of violation*, losing singleness to extend the form through the impetus of an infliction. There was an unaccustomed savagery in the prospect of the Cell, but we counted on its structure to contain the assault, and we trusted the method to inoculate the actors against the vulnerability. At other levels, they had all been assaulted in the work we had done—as if some necessary wound were at the center—sometimes out of that reflex of love when love grows impatient with the limits of the Other, wanting it to be more, other than it is. On this occasion, Jack—normally mild-tempered, restrained—was driven beyond himself by the gratuitousness of Julie's ferocity. He attacked her physically and wanted, he said, to kill her, his rage aroused by hers, the *idea* meeting his emotion, and her original idea (for that's what it was) absorbing it formally. He saw what she wanted and wanted it. I am speaking about something quite murderous. The others sensed that this was happening, each out of some excess of irony responding now to the idea. It was one of those sequences when they didn't actually know any longer whether they were still acting, nor did I—and it was hard to decide, because of the outright physical risk, whether to stop it. At the same time, I wanted more of it, because I could see there the demonic substructure of the Cell. It is the mind which is virulent. The exercise—dangerous as it was—was swarming with mind, gray blood. It is this virility, almost out of art, and unquestionably, indefensibly cruel, which we would have to absorb back into the structure when the translation was made from investigation to form. It's also the hardest thing to recover, and recover from.

As for the personal cost, an unstable personality couldn't survive it, which is why we are very careful in our auditions for the group and the preparation before any work is done with new people. Is there therapy in it? Yes and no. There must be, though we never go at that consciously or directly as, say, the Performance Group has done as a result of its experiments with Daytop. For those who persist, it would seem that personality would be strengthened. I don't know. Sometimes it is, sometimes it isn't. Both therapy and personality are more problematical than we like to believe, even knowing the problems, one of which—in our case—is the liability of a transference on me, since even in silence there is the ongoing discourse of observing authority. It con-

Take Up the Bodies

stitutes a judgment whether I am consciously judging or not. In this particular investigation, there was a strengthening of the Cell, which came out of further definition of responsibility in the group, through the process. That same night, Tom—whose vulnerability exists at the level of pure will—was announcing: "I will not take orders from policy. I will not take orders from social law. . . . Fuck ideology! I want the truth!" He would, however, obey "the Central Committee" (which he invented right there), a metaphorical function of what Jack later described as "the emerging intelligence of the group" in respect to the Cell.

Therapeutically, the method permits Denise to return her assaulted feelings to a more rational and/or ideological context. While Tom manically supported Julie through her self-humiliating attack on Denise, he would another day—the questions differently raised—support Denise in an effort to focus what all of it meant; that is, why did it occur in the first place, that outbreak? out of what unspecifiable motives? from what personal sources behind the initiating ferocity of the idea? The whole thing, perversely, *was* in a theatrical framework. It can't be anything else inside the room in which we work. There is a line beyond which it is nothing but theater, which is worse, maybe, than its becoming real. I say, not quite knowing what I mean: "Even if you leave the Cell, you're in the Cell, even if you leave the room." I believe that's true, even now that we've stopped working on the Cell.

The theater is a place of emotion, but I have spoken of various kinds of emotion as instruments of perception. Given the confusions that still persist about the Alienation-effect—as well as Artaud's notion of Cruelty and the misleading folklore of body language—it is important to clarify the relation of emotion and meaning in the theater event. We must always remember, as we are cautioned by Brecht, that it's not that we see wrongly but that we see differently when emotion is not "cool." Even in life, people who are calm and detached do not necessarily see more or better than those who are aroused and involved. In the session described above, Julie's awareness of what she was doing was stupefyingly accurate. She remembered everything that happened down to the finest detail of behavior. There was a clairvoyance like that of Raskilnikov after the axe murder over Lizaveta's trunk. So there is the startled efficiency of our being more available to ourselves under stress. Blood marshals itself where needed in the body. Eyes dilate to meet the threat. The nervous system is alive with signals. We rise with almost spectacular spontaneity to emergency, as we could never dream of doing in ordinary circumstances.

Normally in the work we don't make any big thing about producing emotions. (Or their initial honesty for that matter, since the falsity may be heuristic.) *"C'est mon metiér,"* said Réjane, when asked how she could cry on cue. It's a knowing corrective to the primacy of individual feeling which often blunts feeling by reducing the area of experience in which it exists. For the actor, emotion is (and should be) cheap unless it is being seen for what it is—which, in the act of perceiving, becomes another emotion, more than what it is. "I know my madness," says Phaedra. "I recall it all." What is true of objective states is true of the objectifying principle. That too becomes a phase of the larger process. In some of what we do, the order of emotion is hard to describe or the order of reality from which it comes. It is hard to know sometimes the degree to which it is acting, not because—as in the Squamous incident—the emotion is extreme, but because it is very slight or demonstrative. Or, as in the following example, a mere evidential instant: there is the sequence in *Elsinore* when Karen takes off her jersey, exposing her breasts—before lying down on "the grass-green turf" (the bare floor) and becoming the Ghost. She speaks of guilt and innocence, pointing to marks on her body (which are not actually there). Marks of abuse? signs of struggle? She gives a contradictory view. The nudity is a constituent of the emotion. Suddenly, there she is, torso bare. There is nothing erotic or particularly sensuous about it, nor is there the faintest suggestion that it might develop that way. There is no tease. As I say, the pointing is evidential, a turn in an argument where terms are not yet (if ever) manifest. Karen's behavior is no more than it needs to be to state the ambiguous theme.

The "emotion" is over there with Julie. Yet there is something in Karen more than dispassionateness. It is not easy to make out. She is not a mere piece of evidence, a mere object in the structure. She is and is not what she appears to be. But what is that? The appearance is more than meets the eye, but it does thus, bluntly, meet the eye. Karen does what she does objectively (something about which she feels passionately), but there is no way to perceive it objectively, not as it occurs, following the strange eruptions in the state (or performance). Is she acting? The word wavers in what she is doing. As for the nudity, if we played someplace where it might have been a problem, they wouldn't quite know what to make of it, because I'm not even sure it feels nude. It would be superfluous, I think, to justify it on the grounds that it is a part of our experience too long denied by spurious taboos. The sequence is an almost purely conceptual piece within the intensely emotional structure, which will require from Karen in a moment a terrific surge of ideographic passion.

The critical intelligence on which Brecht insists is not, then, abandoned to the intensities of the process, but it is never certain that it won't be menaced and baffled, turning into a mist above the stream. In *Elsinore*, the device originally used in a rehearsal to cool a runaway emotion—the narrative "He said" borrowed from Brecht—was absorbed compulsively into the slipstream of subjectivity as it was used, thus becoming another dimension of content, the "He said" even more moving in its repetitions than the thing that moved us to use it so we could see what it was about. Brecht might have said that if our politics were surer we'd not be so unreliably shifting. Maybe he is right. But the only reliable politics we have is the politics of performance, which we tried to refine further in the inquisitions of *The Cell*.

"Canst thou remember/ A time," asks Prospero, thinking he remembers, "before we came into this cell?" Sometimes, it seemed, we couldn't. The politics inevitably came to the solipsistic dilemma which we didn't escape in *The Enemy* and which remains the recurrent liability of the work—even as it arouses perception. It is like Hamlet's madness being reasoned and reason going mad, an energizing power. If we can act at all, it may help us to see with a finer sense of distinction than we had before. There are no guarantees. What moves us, finally, to use anything is the thing behind the thing itself, *what* we are seeing, the substance of seeming, the ungrounded appearance of things, that paranoia, the look of the world leaking into the work, past the most supportable wishful thinking in the thinking through.

We must talk more about that—in the work, the world: that emotion—what anybody can see with his own eyes:

The one appearance that seems undeniable is that violence and evil rule the world. It's hard not to think that something wants to do us harm. There is no longer anything, it seems, by which we are not poisoned. Constantly, a bad taste in the mouth. Is that a mere figure of speech? Nietzsche thought so. If, as he thought, the world is made out of language, we are always swallowing a lie. So far as we can see, there is some deep hostility at the encrypted heart of things. Human frailty being what it is, human endeavor takes place over an irreparable breach. We are still licking the wounds. Even our structures of peace are based upon the rationalized lunacy of systemic brute power. I dislike the vermicular thinking, but could it be that Luther said it better than Nietzsche: the world is the Devil's wormbag? Whatever justifications there may be—no matter whose Terror, capitalist or guerrilla, institutional or personal—the atrocities continue. All over the world the screws are being put to human beings. In parts of the world things are so hideously oppressive people are putting the screws to themselves, or nails, or ground glass, or fishhooks in the stomach, or cutting a slice of thigh and eating it. Bizarre, it seems, to make a point of it, for what has that to do with the theater? As the theater keeps telling us, everything. We are familiar with the more repressed and therefore civilized modes of self-torment, the incidence of which is about as appalling as the environment it reflects, the landscape, the politics. No wonder we develop theories of man as an interruption of Being inserted allegorically or, in an infinite series of substitutions, parodically, into nature, a mere repetition, disposable. The best things we do—our art, our loves, our most redeeming labors—are designed, it seems, with forgetfulness at the rim, just out of focus. If art survives, it survives obsessively, with all the illusions of craft, just this side of selective inattention, refusing to be absorbed into the rest of life, we know sometimes to keep from going mad, but being absorbed like it or not, and in the process on the edge of madness. Is the actor in his role? beside his role? beyond his role? maybe beside himself, yet utterly *in* it—what can one say?—so carried away by the fear of it or the urge of it, we can only hope that despite the fear there would be the urge, the procreant urge, so that if the theater were abandoned he would insist on playing through, not oblivious to the danger but in spite of it, because it's *written*, written by history, as if the achievement of performance were—otherwise numb, mute, attending on the event—a last will and testament.

One would like a theater event so vividly inscribed on time it seems cut in stone, even the corrosions and deteriorations, the stream frozen, to keep the madness in check; like the Watchman at the beginning of *Seeds of Atreus* at the near inception of time, a breathing stone, the watchtime measured by years, or millennia, yet a "most strict and observant watch," eyes and reasons open, observation as a moral act, the watching as intense as what is being watched—the energy of the otherness infusing it becoming all that other as if it were the thing reflected—actual, here, now. The fantasy is that of an immense act of consciousness that would seize the madness and bring it to rest, consumed by that which it was nourished by; yet even then (even now) never losing sight, the stream cracking again, of the split space of difference between the dream-divining Terror from which the energy comes and that which "drips in sleep against the heart, grief of memory." To do it all formally without choking back on form, which *sees*, letting the fleshing idea find itself as it must if it is to be theater in the final finding of the air. Because it *is* fantasy, this madness, returning to the world and life-as-it-is.

For all the strictness of the watch, saying what we see, the abominations seem beyond our control. Perhaps there is no control, and we are only temporarily spared by some chancy arbitration of the cosmos. We surely can't count on the Eumenides. As always, one must earn an af-

It is time for the many destructions to cease." But we know it is wishful thinking.

firmation in art, or do without it; or, given our world, do without it even if earned. That may be the true cost of the movements of poetry. We just can't make it up. Which is the situation we were confronted with at the end of *Seeds of Atreus*, where it became a political issue within the group. At the end, the meanings of the beacon light are exhausted. The Furies invoke a Buddhist edict: "It is time for the many destructions to cease." But we know it is wishful thinking. We could barely say the words: "Keep the human seed alive." *Seeds of Atreus* was completed a few days after the truce was declared in Vietnam. It was no V-J Day, no dancing in the streets. Athena says, "If love be not in the house there is nothing." As I told the actors when we tried the line, there is more likely to be nothing. The line is not from Aeschylus but from Ezra Pound, chastened by his madness: "We cannot make it cohere." And then? And then? The great saga of the trilogy is another untellable tale. The grace summoned up in the final choruses of *The Eumenides* seemed, as I've said, like a foreign incursion. It could only be the perdurable longing for a fullness which is not there. When we said the line "Let us render grace for grace"—it inevitably sounded more like a convention than a conviction or it would have been a falsehood. But it was a convention that moved like a wish through the work in the opposite direction of remembered blood. Yet grace is no more the opposite of blood than entropy is the opposite of energy. So let us cut down the losses on illusion. If we can't count on the Eumenides, we can listen to Euripides: "Troy shall be no more." That Troy suggested this Athens. Maybe they didn't believe him; maybe it was unimaginable. They only gave him second prize. The Athenian Empire disappeared.

If there's any worse affliction than having to live with a lie, it is having to live with the truth. The truth never comes later. The truth denied now will never be available again, not *as* truth. Instead of the celebration, then, flowing from the stage back into the City (*what* City?), the final exit of *Seeds of Atreus* reflected quite another reality, not so much true as a refusal to be false. It also suggested another tradition: the Nōh actor enters, carrying his space with him; that gravity, if not grace. The actors filed out, drained by a dilemma they couldn't solve, taking their space with them. The vigil was a disappearance, stern and silenced, unappeased; that part of the Fury, its savage mind.

It was certainly nothing like the bullroaring rebirths of the many *Bacchae* of those apocalyptic years, with their exploitative, desublimated fantasies from the counterculture, which—when the theater did flow into life—brought us no closer to the Second Coming. In that euphoric period, releasing the Spirit of Play, one of the talismanic works was the *I Ching*, another manual of craft, undeluded about the powers of power, a mirror for magistrates. One wonders how the oracles were interpreted as they tossed the coins. As the character of Mêng or Youthful Folly implies, "He who plays with life never amounts to anything." How you read the coins, as Marx and Engels also suggest, determines not only the phantoms in the brain, but how you do theater— which is, like morality or metaphysics, an ideological offshoot of material life-process. The displacement of the Spirit of Play into life-style did not quite keep track of life-process in this Marxist sense, or it would not have been so quickly reappropriated into the bourgeois value-system which was financing it to begin with. Nevertheless, so far as the theater was concerned, there was something salutary in the desire to let more life in and more theater out. But the question is, how much?

It is a question which has been with us since the idea of theater emerged from whatever dark backward and abysm of time: where does play end and life begin? what is the relationship of in and out? To think that through is a necessary corrective to the Marxist emphasis upon material premises, empirically verifiable—with which the phantoms of the brain may be coterminous rather than in a relationship of cause and effect. In the same way, theater appears to be coterminous with life. Where, we may ask, does the play start? Which is another way of talking about how "real" it is or, I suppose, how "illusory." The irony has always been—both the irony at our expense, and the irony *in* it—that illusion may give us a coherent and credible image of reality while all that dispels illusion, that which mystifies, may strike us at first as incoherent. In the history of modern art, that is relatively easy to see: in the disjunctures of cubism, say, or in Brecht's technique of estrangement. Such innovations were troublesome and confusing, and were meant to be, until they became familiar. What they accomplished was a (provisional) dislocation of the reality which was in the perspective of illusion. The latter is suspended when we bring contradictions, which were "resolved" through illusion in separate planes of representation, onto the same plane—the original notorious flattening out. As I suggested earlier, meaning is then forced toward what is there on the surface rather than back through frames of reference which imply some ultimate plane of value behind it all, thus making everything contingent, symbolic, pointing to some other reality than itself.

These distinctions can be formally alluring, but what actually happens to meaning is that it is ideologically relocated. This is what Marx helped us to understand. And Freud. It isn't only that meaning is discovered but that prior meaning is unobscured by the undoing (theoretically) of the repressive mechanism which, in the disguise of perspective, gives meaning the appearance of a timeless value rather than an ideological moment in a system of historical transformations. We then see the class interest of meaning. At the same time, by letting in life, or history, we are *constructing* new meaning. The alternative to construction is a theoretical kind of *fusion,* letting history rush in, as it were, or releasing the form to embrace life. In the theater, the stretching of the membrane into life—that is, letting in more of the real—is an intensification of theater by the provisional denial of theater, more or less true of a play of Chekov as of theater in the streets. I want to say more about this in the last chapter, in relation to the other arts. But the problem with thinking of theater *as* life—a temptation more or less succumbed to but never lived out—is that it may, as in the sixties, disempower the form not by bringing more reality in but by giving too much of the theater away.

Nevertheless, the metaphor of the world as theater has had such a powerful hold on the imagination because there are real grounds for it. Good metaphors don't come out of thin air, no more than the Ghost really does. Just *how much* ground is the thing to be thought. Because of the element of theatricality in actual life, we must continually ask of whatever we see: real or illusory? true or false? a false truth or a true lie? acted or not acted? playing a role? the real thing? only a dream? thin air after all? These are the circular and ubiquitous questions that bleed through judgment in both theater and life, their abstracted common ground. I said before that in our work the desire to make it *all* theater—that is, to maximize the play of illusion—is to prevent it from being *mere* theater. Within that perception there may be—as there is likely to be where the play of thought is as volatile as the thought of play—an infinite series of substitutions (within the sets: real/illusory, life/theater, acting/being), as with the playing of the *I Ching.* But in a peculiar double vision, the *I Ching,* which may be stimulating illusion, knows very well where the world is. So does the metaphor which sees the world as theater. Seeing what is there includes, in the act of perceiving, being aware of the ideological moment within the transforming system of history. That doesn't make any the less mysterious the relationship, and order of priority, of consciousness and material existence, body and mind. The more we reflect upon it in theatrical terms the more we see, feelingly, that one is a reflex of the other—with history insisting for its own reasons upon redefining priorities. Over the last generation we saw, for instance, that there are not only phantoms of the brain.

Reflection, reflex. If a man has lost a leg and a stimulus is applied to the nerve path from the stump to the brain, the man will feel a phantom leg. In the theater of recent times, distrustful of mentalized value, we looked elsewhere for meaning. We had an extended and much publicized dalliance with body language, sphincter awareness, gut action.

Take Up the Bodies

There was political meaning in it and an assertion of personal identity. The Human Potential Movement is still living off of it, but even more profoundly the antioedipal schizoanalysis of poststructuralist theory. (One is reminded of the remark made by Marx's flamboyant follower, Ferdinand Lassalle, to the countess whose divorce suit he, a young Jew without influence, was upholding against all the secular powers: "You seem to overlook the fact that your body has been borrowed by an idea of permanent historical importance.") In our generation, we have had high liberating ambitions for the body, the desire for a new libidinal economy. There was good reason for it, but where, really, has it taken us? Have we not had to learn all over again that the wisdom of the body is a short-sighted wisdom? If the body is the book, it is surely clear now that it was never an open book nor indubitably sacred—and we did not, in embracing it, read the fiery handwriting on the impenetrable wall: "Mene, mene? Naked bodies?" says Hamm in *Endgame*, "*your* light." He didn't think much of it.

An imaginary arm is enormous after an amputation but it subsequently shrinks and is absorbed into the stump as the patient consents to its severance. There seems to be no alternative. Our bodies, we discover, are released so that life may hide with more dexterity. The body lies like the mind, and why not? for where exactly is the mind when it is lying? The unification of mind/body that we seek in emulating the holistic psychophysical disciplines of the East still fails to take into account the awful social injustice of the amputated arm. While some are "having their being," their *dharma*, there are multitudes being denied even the semblance of a life, if you're really keeping book. As for us, we should have known it: the resurrection of the flesh has its own limit. If mental hangups are body hangups, body hangups are mental hangups—and there is one unfortunate truth, specifically human, of hangups there is no end.

The rites, dances, and participatory revels of the New Theater are just about over, thank Dionysus. They had the virtue of freeing up conventions and releasing old inhibitions, but for all the talk of a liberated theater and super-post-technological unrepressive art, we were never really sensible about the backlashing repressive limits of springing all the taboos. I am not merely talking of the new conservatism, but that was inevitable. The revolutionary delusion was perhaps the most pathetic of the desublimated fantasies. "The date of the revolution," wrote Merleau-Ponty, "is written on no wall and in no metaphysical heaven." All action is open and menaced, and menaced the more when reflex *takes over* from reflection. I have been describing an idea of theater which, while very body-oriented, puts the emphasis on the thinking through. The emphasis comes, obviously, out of a sense of corrective necessity as well as conviction, within a system of historical transformations; with that consciousness. Also over the last generation, we have emancipated an array of conventions from the apparent impoverishment of behavior in theater—aside from the body and its lost dimensions, space duration rhythm light gesture mask incantation spectacle; theatricality for its own sake—only to end up with impoverished thought. In going from the fifties to the sixties through the psychopathology of everyday life to the theatricalization of everyday life—including the aborted hope of a transformed politics—we ended up in a muddle of seeming which led from Watergate to Ronald Reagan. It turns out that the Enemy is also a crafty manipulator of images. We forget, in the years of his disgrace, that Richard Nixon had developed in his apparently conservative presidency a model of advanced theatrical form and that we were saved from the manipulated illusions of a near-fascist state by grace of eighteen minutes of erased tape. If Satan was the first actor, then maybe the theater unavoidably serves the Devil's party, but it's a pretty poor shadow of itself when the seeing is not up to the seeming and its understanding of power is banal. Who is serving whom?

For all the justifiable devotion to love's body, we still need a deeper reverence of the mind's passion. ("Training! Training! Training!" cried Meyerhold. "But if it's the kind of training which exercises only the body and not the mind, then no thank you! I have no use for actors who know how to move but can't think.") If it becomes easier for actors, or "performers" or "shamans" (words used by recent theorists), to be possessed, it becomes harder for them to be intelligent—and, especially, intelligent *in* the act of performance. I am still surprised at how much more intelligent some actors are offstage than on, particularly if they're doing collective work fuzzing up ideas of ritual, and playing rather loosely with the relationship of acting and trance. When Mircea Eliade speaks of "family shamanism"—making a distinction between the real ecstasy and the new rudimentary means of approximating it— one thinks back to all that easy percussion in the New Theater, the ingenuous blood rhythms. One can range over the entire gamut of New Theater in this country and be hard pressed to find more than a few events (Joseph Dunn's austerely reductionist theater; parts of Lee Breuer's *Shaggy Dog*; aspects of Foreman, though antiseptic) that explicitly engage the mind in anything like the way in which the dramatists who opened up the new possibilities did: Genet, say, or Brecht or Beckett, who really *moved* us. The critical faculty, for all the dissidence, had been abused. All things waste from want of use. "Use your head, can't you, use your head," raged Hamm, "you're on earth, there's no cure for that."

I suppose Hamm knows that we deep down know it, which accounts for the rage, the compulsion to say it, over and over. There's a heart in that head, dripping, grief of memory. It's hard to tell what it will take to preserve us from ourselves. I often feel something out there, a whisper a rustle, in the polluted earth or the defoliated jungles, a sound out of hearing accumulating rage, crying out that we be desecrated that we might see—even then with no guarantee of seeing for they haven't seen elsewhere, and they *have* been ruined. The early warning systems, the actuarial deterrents, the maniac saving grace of equitable mega-death—we develop these vanities. Yet the world remains what it was, a scandal, and despite all the balancing of power the worst to be imag-ined is more likely to happen than not. Michelet, writing of the fif-teenth century, might just as well be questioning us: " . . . where is the life here? Who can say which are the living and which are the dead? In what party am I to take interest? Is there one among the various fig-ures who is not either dubious or false? Is there one on whom the eye may rest and find expressed in him clearly the ideas, principles, on which the heart of man lives? We have descended into indifference and moral death. And we must descend lower still."

And so we do, art reflecting what life there is, as if the reflections were the only life that gives life to what is otherwise so precarious and self-evident it can't be told. If we're not determined by the motions of history, we may be genetically programmed. We don't even have to wait for the unexpected horrors of recombinant DNA. We inhabit nature, nature inhabits us: stalemate. Worse than that, omniverously, the end of the program? "When we examine the great curves that pro-ject into the future the phenomena of our time, we see that practically all these curves lead to catastrophe." This is not the customary doom-saying of one of the prophets of despair, although such doomsaying is coming increasingly from quite resistant liberal minds. This comes from one of the technocratic leaders of one of the most bureaucratic powers on earth: Giscard d'Estaing. What are we to make of it? I have no illusions that if we cry out we won't disappear. The illusions only matter as they get into the work, but do they matter? "Reality, how-ever complete," said Brecht, who was rejecting illusion, "has to be al-tered by being turned into art, so that it can be seen to be alterable and treated as such." One wants desperately to believe this, but the idea still troubles. Social change? individual change? the eye altering alter-ing all? I suppose if it comes right down to it, I'd accept my own mini-mum: art changes nothing, but it at least changes that.

"Where is the beauteous majesty of Denmark?" That line is lifted from the context of Ophelia's madness and addressed, in *Elsinore*, to the world at large, even as it specifically deters the act of vengeance. When it occurs in the most radical disjuncture of that ungrounding work, it is another inflection of wishful thinking—which may, at the critical moment, be the very best thinking we can do. Elsinore names and suffers from the (suspected) crime of insistent judgment. The Hamletic figure that rises (like a ghost) and walks slowly into the center (?) of the initiatory circle is the presumptive image of Father-Uncle-Son, taking upon him "the primal eldest curse"—no sooner having said it, turning it around, critically testing it as "the eldest primal curse. . . ." Which? or neither? and if not, what then? why? If there is in all the questioning a lapse of grace, it's not from want of wanting. The recurring judgments are exhausted in the structure, literally run into the ground, by pure, unjudging desire.

The fractured final circle starts with its equal and opposite impulse: "With all my love I do commend me to you." In that warlike state where you may die in a lapse of judgment (over which, as in ours, you may have no control), some part of us also wants to remember the state of forgetfulness, without forgetting. As the circle splits and the actors disappear, there are the receding mutations of the fragmented emotions of the Closet: "Have you forgot me?" "Forgot." "Have you?" "Me?" "Who? In the closing zero of the self-consuming subtraction, only the void can say—the dead named, the bodies gone—, whatever moves us in the final absence. The playing space is empty. A last tape is heard, each of the (disembodied) voices remembering a loss:

> I saw Claudius, King of Denmark, dead.
> I saw Gertrude, Queen of Denmark, dead.
> Hamlet I saw, Prince of Denmark, dead.
> I saw Polonius, the old counsellor, dead.
> I saw Laertes, son of Polonius, dead.
> I saw the nymph Ophelia, dead.
> I saw Horatio among the living-dead.
> I saw Fortinbras, with rights of memory in this kingdom, king.

Moved by absence, power is still in place, invisibly. But the thing is we *are* moved, and the old paradox is that a particular life in art may exist with increased energy at the very selvedge of manic depression, as if nothing were worth redeeming, turning the helpless seeming into an enlivening assertion of form:

Journal note (June 1, 1975): " . . . no slack in the void; the outward pressure so core-driven as to present a surface bursting but still a contained surface, not an explosion but the unthinkable brink of it, as if concept were all mass expanding with no less density in the expansion as if mass were added to keep it constant—like Picasso's *Death's Head,*

Take Up the Bodies

solid and immitigable skull, the solid globe: a center that must hold as if there were nothing but center (center of nothing?), *even the Absence, all core.*"

The work was completed a year later and became *Elsinore.* It came up, as I have explained, out of the cellarage of *Hamlet* by way of the exercises on Kafka's *The Burrow.* Before that, we were twenty feet under the snow in *The Donner Party, Its Crossing.* The subject matter of these two works, like *Seeds of Atreus* before them: murder, vengeance, suicide, madness, cannibalism. Staples. There seemed to be two functions of methodology in the theater: the first was to open up a psychic space in the very center of indifference, where action occurs not as if foreordained, recorded, and available for reenactment, but as if it were dreamed into being on the margins of its impossibility in a cloud of unknowing. The tale is untellable because in truth there may never be a story again for the telling of which we all wait, to give us resolution and coherence in the common disaster of fracture we all live. So far as Horatio can draw a breath and tell it, it is summed up in Sallustius' description of the myths of Attis: "This never happened but it always is." The second function of methodology is to keep us intact, to keep if not death at least the deadening outside the circle of existence in the fantasy of longevity through which we all expire.

The core of a technique, repeating Kafka, corresponding to these two functions: "Two tasks on the threshold of life: To narrow your circle more and more, and constantly to make certain that you have not hidden yourself somewhere outside of it." In that circle, holding nothing back. Even so, even if it's deadening, the power comes from what stalks the outside of the circle, that fine line, which takes away our breath.

The Future of an Illusion

6

There was very good reason for St. Augustine, Tolstoy, and other penitent geniuses to have had their suspicions about the theater. If it's not obscene, and it is (in conclusion, we must come to that), it is a Platonic Cave, shadows upon shadows performing. The overlays of illusion can be demoralizing. If one dwells upon it, there is something alarming in the most normal theater event, the more normal the more alarming. I mean what we grant and what we take for granted. The habits of mind are so long ingrained they are essentially unexamined. They exist in and out of the theater. The consciousness we have inherited from the theater accumulates, determining behavior and expectancy in everyday life. We meet each day as if a curtain were rising, although it rarely occurs to us to ask why, in the theater, the curtain that wasn't there should have been there. Out of what queer longing did it come?

The language of theater—its grammar of motives and rhetoric of appearances—has filtered through history into perception. Outside the theater we see as if we were inside, the world gradually seeming what it is not. We come to see what we have seen like the photograph which tries to fix it, by negatives, coming up with only a surface. What is there is not there. What is there is an evanescence, an escapement, a slippery clockwork. The theater is the most time-serving of forms, literally, functionally, and metaphysically. It is by nature unreliable. The sum and substance is a moving fiction, a lie like truth, a mere cast of thought. All its strategies are deceptions. No matter how the theater denies it—for instance, becomes "strange," as in Brecht, to be objective—its power is the power of a thoroughly laminated illusion. The obfuscation is deliberate. It is surely illicit. Which is why, even against our will, we find ourselves conspiring with its most unreliable creatures, like Iago, who in speaking of reality as mere seeming make it better theater.

Once the mind is let loose on the inescapable content of illusion in the form, it can turn insidious—as if Iago and no mere phantom were in the brain. Or Genet. In the dead middle of *The Balcony*, there comes an impeccable emissary from the Power Structure, presumably to explain what's happening. A dramaturgical necessity, he seems extruded from the opacity of the play, forced up like a cipher from the Void. The mind, demanding explanations for the razzle-dazzle allegorical pornography of the previous scenes, awaits the Word. The Envoy is (or claims to be) an agent of the missing Queen. He seems quite at home in the Funeral Studio, ravaged by revolution. Instead of clarifying things, however, the Envoy impacts obfuscation with obfuscation, like pure illusion. Embroidering on the absence of the Queen, he says the Queen is at her embroidery. Does she exist? She is occupied with becoming entirely what she must be, either engaged in an infinite meditation heading rapidly toward immobility, or picking her nose. The explanation is mummy's cloth, the Envoy is a death-bringer, killing with words. When the ambiguities (seem to) cease, he is exposed as a thug, an ineffectual phony among the phonies in the Brothel who play out, in dread, their fantasies of power.

We are among them (hypocrite voyeurs) contributing to the illusions, unmoored and vulnerable. Genet plays with the power behind the scene, so to speak (and we do), which is (whether we admit it or deny it) the power of illusion, which is (even when the structure is exposed) the sustaining power of all performance.

Think of it: the systems of information within the systems of information, even at a more obvious level, that we take for granted in a theater event. We bring not-entirely examined fictions from life to support the probable impossibilities of the art. Think of all the tacit agreements around the play and in the rehearsal process—if the play is rehearsed or if it's improvised or if it's something other than a play, the latest mutation of a Happening perhaps, some hybrid that is not-quite-life but not wholly art—the whole conglomerate of supposition, arrangement, plotting, and pretense out of which an act of performance is made. Consider simply an object in front of your eyes: on stage it is no longer simple. A real chair used for a real chair in a "realistic" setting remains, though a real chair, a *sign* for a chair. It is what it is not though it appears to be what it is. The real chair may also be, by convention, something other than a chair. (With such ideas in mind, one may respect the intricacy of Desdemona's handkerchief or the profundity of Gogo's boot.) If we move from object to action, the thing is immediately complicated: a faked kiss may seem a real kiss and a real kiss may obviously seem faked or less obviously seem real, as between any two actors the faked kiss may develop in the heat of performance, as we say, into something more real.

In the construction of *Elsinore*, there is a combinatory system of escalated illusions. I have already mentioned the metamorphoses of the Closet Scene, which is really one of the metaphors for the whole piece. There is the sequence, however, in which we have three simultaneous, multi-focussed versions, as if one were mirroring the other in its worst fantasy of itself. In one of them, an actress—who may be Ophelia who may be Gertrude who is neither Ophelia nor Gertrude but an actress whose name (elsewhere) is Margaret—is raped by an actor (Tom) whose identity is similarly ambiguous though the action performed is very precise as, of course, a *signified* rape. The incident may be shocking, but since no sexual parts are exposed, what is really simulated is the violence, an actual physical force. The actress, as if caught up by the brute blood of the air, is dropped to the ground after the beast-with-two-backs, an image exhausted of being—neither Ophelia, Gertrude, nor even herself, not quite Margaret, to be exact. In what follows (referred to in the previous chapter), she passes around the rectilinear edge of the playing space. In the space, the center of attention is one, then another, back and forth, of the transforming versions of the Closet Scene. As "Margaret" registers these occurrences, there accumulates in her mind, step-by-demented-step around the space, through suggestions of Ophelia's madness and then Hamlet's but neither Hamlet nor Ophelia, the abstracted rage of the Avenger, a force which raises her hand *as if* it held a knife.

The audience stares at the threatening edge of air at the end of her clenched fist. (The knife might have been established by the stiffened edge of a straight hand, or it might have been an actual—I was about to say real—knife. Each of these knives is a different image, each of the images a different inflection of meaning.) Now she moves into the circle of performance to commit the long-suspended deed—the act which is *not done*, as with Claudius at prayer. Only the victim, prone and gentled, seems to be the dying Hamlet, the sweet Prince who could speak the lovely words, "Absent thee from felicity a while"—but who speaks instead (in a tone of self-reflection) the words of the mad Ophelia, "Where is the beauteous majesty of Denmark?" to the figure who was once maybe Ophelia and maybe Gertrude, whose hand trembles now, about to stab, but *un*able. It almost seems as if the memory of the deed-still-to-be-done is a resistance in the structure to its own necessity, as well as a reflection of the loss of (beautous/majestic) origins (still-to-be-redeemed) in the replicated images of the self-murdering self. The convolutions of ideas and identities are constructed, however, around a rather awe-inspiring series of assimilated conventions: I am referring to things we accept in passing through the impacted illusions of theater, as if that's what is really meant by the readiness is all.

Those who have followed the history of "non-matrixed" performance events outside of regular theaters have a repertoire of stories about real things that looked staged up to and including murder. There is a similar history in the conventional theater, somebody from an audience periodically jumping into the scene to assault or embrace an actor whose imitation seems only too much what it is. Once you imagine the possibilities that have been realized in actual performance, either accepted as a matter of course or developing unbeknownst, you see what a queerer system of unquestioned information is endorsed within a performance than is covered by the mere willing suspension of disbelief. It is also structured into the illusions by which we live. "Sancho," says Don Quixote to his skeptical consort, "if you want me to believe in what you saw in the sky, I wish you to accept my account of what I saw in the cave of Montesinos. I say no more."

The tradeoff, all things considered, may be the only means of psychic survival. It is (if you think about it) as shocking as it is amusing. "Pretend, pretend that you are just and true," says Alceste to Célimène in Molière's play, "And I will do my best to believe in you." We collaborate by laughing in perpetuating the deceit. We carry over the experience of our own relationships—and the necessary duplicities on which they are built—to establish the credibility of the thing being performed. If we don't laugh, we may miss the point of its appalling brilliance. The truth is that it takes just as much truth to play credibly false as it does to appear indubitably true; and sometimes to convince others (and even ourselves) that we are true we have to *play* at being true. The illusions by which we live are the illusions by which we sustain the fiction. Or is it the other way around? As Erving Goffman has extensively shown, in *Frame Analysis* and elsewhere, ordinary life imitates its formulations which are drawn, in time, from ordinary life. Theater is one of the formulations, perhaps the most summary of all. The exploitation of the circularity makes the theater seem suspect, but from its own perspective the more it does it the better it is. So, what's real?

If the theater were real, we wouldn't bother with it. When it's not real, we complain. The confusion depends, of course, on how we're using the word *real* and the degree of illusion which makes it so. We abandon that illusion at our peril. Some new modes of performance, in theater and the other arts, have put illusion up for grabs: either it's nothing but or not at all. Both attitudes, oddly, seem to intensify the

Renaissance conceit inherent in Shakespeare's Globe and expressed by John Donne, that "the whole frame of the world is theater." We have seen through the last generation a passage from concern with the psychopathology of everyday life to its conscious theatricalization, to deal with the psychopathology or to forget it. I have already indicated what was only too much apparent, that there was theater all over the place, in politics, in fashion, in therapy, and in the histrionic emphasis on life-style. There may be a conservative retrenchment, but once the stylization is there it's hard to get it out, and there's carefully barbered long hair among the Moral Majority, like marijuana among the squares. In the theatricalizing process, there was some fudging on the word frame or a desire to wrench it quite from its fixture. The period of radical activism was a period of revived illusions. Perhaps the wildest illusion of all is the one that really believes—as Don Quixote does not, as Shakespeare does not, though he wrote it—that all the world is a stage, failing to see through the seeming that not even theater is all theater.

What makes anything theater? To repeat: thinking makes it so. The same Fall which brought consciousness into the Garden also brought the first actor. I have tried to show how thinking, in my own work, re-cycles itself between the illusions of theater and the realities of the word, the illusions of the world and the realities of theater, arriving at a kind of theater whose express (and expressed) subject is the *disap-pearance* of theater; that is, the appearances from which theater is made and upon which it reflects are conceptually elaborated and in turn reflected upon until there is a denial, or refusal, by means of theater of the distressing and maybe crippling notion that in life there is nothing but theater. "I could be bounded in a nutshell and count myself king of infinite space," says Hamlet, "except that I have bad dreams." In developing *Elsinore,* we were particularly interested in those dreams. The performance consists of image upon image replicating, exhaustively, until it returns to that encircled nothing at the vanishing center which is the source of theater—but resists the vanishing into theater at the living end.

In life, it's almost harder to resist. The illusions seem irresistible, or salutary, or totalled into Total Theater. The attraction of theater as a type of reality has come about, in our time, by contrast to the type of reality which is divided, classified, static, and predictable. To review one strain: as we became disturbed over the mental fixations of the categoricalizing West, we looked for relief to the metamorphic experience of the Far East, where reality in its Oneness is held to be a performance in which identity has a thousand faces. In the accelerating dance of Shiva, the expanding illusory universe curves back, haunted, through

Take Up the Bodies

the electronic media. "In the mosaic world of implosion," wrote Mc-
Luhan, video invokes "archaic tribal ghosts of the most vigorous
brand." Once, not long in the galactic past, that almost seemed reason for rejoicing. Some of the ghosts acquired brand names: Steppen-
wolf, Frankenstein, etc. With oscillators, amplifiers, and light projection, or chanting pyramids of doctrinaire flesh, the senses were assaulted until illusion took over, disabling the boundaries between art
and life. But the release from duality was of short duration as our sense
of distinction wavered. Despite the hard rock, hard-core remnants, the
tribes of the counterculture have been dispersed and the decibel count
lowered. There may be less reason for celebration, but there are still reverberations. I don't mean only the discos or punk rock. Some of the
new "baby moguls" of the movie industry, weaned on McLuhan or
McLuhanism, have been conscripted from the drug culture and the radical Left. Embracing stimulus with stimuli, they are now conducting
transactions with the means of regimentation. For the generation of
Star Wars, the images are even more mindless, maybe more overpowering because regressively pacifying, and enormously profitable. For
some, there is a continuing dream of Eden in computer feedback.

Into this fantasy comes, too, a more commendable and ominous
source of illusion: the medical revolution with its promise of longevity.
The world of pseudoimage, afterimage, and doctored sound is further
complicated by the new bioethical dilemmas: transplants and transformations, genetic management, permutated sex, and programmed
dreams; and the agonizing question of when a prolonged life is officially death. Over the global village falls the veil of Maya. As we move into
the century of the close encounters, the ancient questions over the
tomb take on another inflection: "Are you alive? Where are you living? What is your life?"

The superflux of imagery—and, thus, the qualitative reality of life—
is additionally manipulated by the image-making propensities of our
politics. I suppose one never could count on political reality to be
transparent. There have been other societies predicated on the importance of appearance and show. History has had its masques of power
and comedies of manners and its self-cultivated dandyism. But then appearance was a matter of enunciated principle and conscious theatricality. Never before in history, however, have appearance and show
dominated so surreptitiously on so global a scale, and with such mind-
shattering means and consequences as in the atomic age. Yet the irony
is that our survival seems to depend on a disguised theatricality (the appearance of an appearance), as in realistic drama, where the illusion of
truth establishes credibility, and the actors—pretending to be sincere—
are really playing to an audience (at home or abroad), improvising

The Future of an Illusion

games of power and manipulating the image of truth as strategic policy. We could be more supercilious about it if the same now-instinctive practice didn't leave a shadow on all human activity. This is so even with the vanishing of the staged war in Vietnam and the theatricalized opposition, and would be so even if we hadn't elected an actor as President. The overall result is that our hold on reality, whatever it is, is further attenuated. In the play of images and afterimages, no appearance can be taken at face value. Or in desperation we create theories of value that are entirely based upon appearance. Which amplify our readiness to believe everything, and nothing. The conspiracy theories that arise with or without evidence around great public events, such as the assassinations, are virtually unavoidable in this context. After Watergate everybody seems to be working at the problem of credibility.

It is no wonder—despite Jacques Ellul's caution that they are *not* the same—that we tend to collapse the illusory political universe, where policy is a masque of pretense, with the elusive old perceptual problem of the philosophers, "who say we do not know the external world except through the intermediary of our senses and have no guarantee that our senses do not deceive us, or even that the external world exists and that, in any event, we can perceive the world only through images. . . . There is a world of difference," says Ellul in his book on *Political Illusion*, "between experimental knowledge of a fact and knowledge of it as filtered through the verbal screen. Diogenes already answered the question." But the fact is that many contemporary artists haven't believed him.

We are familiar in postmodernism with the many ingenious efforts to break down the barriers between art and life should there have been the illusory appearance that there was any real difference to begin with. (I spoke of certain of these ingenuities earlier.) John Cage's *4'33"* of silence, which has had a considerable influence on "experimental" theater, was designed to let music arise out of the illusory difference, passing indistinguishably from one to the other, cancelling the difference, as Robert Wilson's twelve-hour long presentation of *The Life and Times of Josef Stalin* also did. Wilson's highly graphic surrealist *Gesamkunstwerk* begins with a five-minute wordless speech-song by Queen Victoria (pure fiction) played by the "director's" ninety-year-old grandmother (pure truth?). People were expected to come and go during the performance, and even possibly to fall asleep. This was not preferred but it was acceptable. I suspect it was similarly acceptable when Cage did a reading of his *Writing through Finnegans Wake* at a recent symposium, which I attended. About that performance, an *aside* (as we say in the theater) that may become more relevant as we proceed:

Take Up the Bodies

It was apparent in that event how thoroughly, despite all theory, the reception of performance is still bound up with certain pernicious (Goffman's word, in conversation—I prefer to call them illusory) qualities that also establish the credentials if not credibility of performance: charisma, presence, reputation, or notoriety; in short, star quality. This is true even in the avant-garde, as Andy Worhol has dexterously demonstrated in making an uninterrupted performance of his life-in-art to his great and creditable prosperity. When Cage did his version of *Finnegans Wake*, we had a compounded irony: the archetype of obscurity in literature being presented by the tutelary deity of indeterminacy in music, and managing to find in the process (I think it was part of the process, counted upon now as it once couldn't be) a perfectly passive and acquiescent audience who, out of some combination of courtesy and intimidation, accepted the premises of performance even when they were bored.

In a prefatory explanation of his structural principles for *Writing through Finnegans Wake,* Cage had indicated that it was a work, given how much he had written, which might have gone on for twelve hours. After about a half hour or so, when it looked as if it might (admiring, nevertheless, the aplomb and achievement and unfailing *zazen* good humor of John Cage), I walked out. I didn't do so in protest or to set an example; there was nothing in the occasion to warrant that. My only justification has something to do with the time-serving aspect of performance, its temporal dependency, if I may get theoretical again in self-defense. Since I had stayed around (even through boredom) in the days when John Cage needed it, I felt I could satisfy my needs when he didn't. If it were to be as he suggested like a reading of the Koran, I thought I might return the next morning to look in on the worship as, on Christmas Eve, an unbeliever might attend a Mass.

I am analyzing the occasion as a performance because I also think it important to point out, as we discuss new forms, how much harder it is, within the ethos of postmodernism and the preëmptive capacity of bourgeois culture, to work powerfully at the acceptable center of performance than it is when you're a guerrilla at the margins. Cage had a remarkable situation—one which we have all desired or fantasized— and that is to have a large *a priori* receptive and reasonably sophisticated audience ready for anything. When we do, however—when the audience's ears are, as Cage says in the epigraph to *Silence,* "in excellent condition"—it seems more difficult to say anything of exceptional consequence. We almost require the resistance. True, this was also an occasion for celebration, a testimonial. But the one characteristic of Cage's performance that might have been more devastatingly ironic than we realized was the actual manner of the reading. Cage—who has certainly endured and is still enduring his quota of superciliousness from others, and outright rejection—assumed the parental role and reduced us all to children at last, as he read in a voice suited to bedtime stories his redaction of Joyce's locquacious phantasm of the rude awakening, which circles back riverrunningly on itself.

There are various shadings and motives in the art/life syndrome. There is the abandonment of old formal properties in order to facilitate the interchangeability of art and life. There are forms which suggest ecological feedback, life in art, art in life, restitution by recycling, as in Newton Harrison's lagoons or Joseph Beuys' self-exposing political pieces. There is the differential preservation of the *appearance* of art, as in the sociodeclensions of the new participatory Activities of Allan Kaprow. The following, from his *7 Kinds of Sympathy*, might have been performed in the home environment of the participants:

> A, writing
> occasionally blowing nose
> B, watching
> copying A blowing nose
> continuing
> (later)
> B, reading A's writing
> occasionally scratching groin, armpit
> A, watching
> copying B scratching
> continuing

Etc. This is like an experiment in quasi-guided behavior, Skinnerism absorbed or subverted into the widening context of the old Happening.

Kaprow is in fact studying here the primary and secondary messages, the artful increments and involuntary encodings of the participants, in which they mix up the socially acceptable and the elusively or obsessively private. The conception is influenced by recent studies of behavioral discourse and the presentation of the self in everyday life (which, in Goffman, drew its terminology from *conventional* theater and drama). There is a script and careful preparation in which the participants are briefed, and the artist doesn't want to relinquish his art entirely to the slipstream of experience as it simply happens. This Activity, however, is at the edge of a disappearance into something other than what was once art, even in the apparent open-endedness of the earlier Happenings. It is not unusual, even in more definite art contexts, to conceive of performance as a "personal inquiry," but for Kaprow, "It would reflect that everyday meaning of performing a job or service, and would relieve the artist of inspirational metaphors such as

Take Up the Bodies

'creativity' that are tacitly associated with making art, and therefore theater art." It is not difficult, he adds, "to see performance aspects of a telephone conversation, of digging a trench in the desert, of distributing religious tracts on a street corner, of gathering and arranging population statistics, and of treating one's body to alternating hot and cold immersions."

No, it is not difficult to see the performance aspects, nor has it become difficult to bring such performances back alive from life to art by restoring the idea of the frame, or by shifting it. Kaprow knows that: "The framework tells you what it is: a cow in a concert hall is a musician, a cow in a barn is a cow." He prefers to stay closer to the life-as-it-is, however, working judiciously, as always, in nonart modes and nonart contexts, ceasing even to call the work art, "retaining instead the private consciousness that sometimes it may be art, too." And sometimes not. It's chancy, to say the least—but not quite Cage's "indeterminacy" which, as practiced, was setting the stage for chance.

Art and performance have always, to be sure, referred themselves back to life when they were in danger of going stale, when the gestures become through long repetition mere pale relics of the thing itself. But what has recently been happening on the blurred margins between art and life is not quite the pressing of art back upon life that was the empirical insistence of the old realism and naturalism. Nor is there the determination to respond to the pressure of insistent fact, as in the charge given by Wallace Stevens to the performing imagination in poetry. Kaprow would probably dismiss the imagination (strategically) as another inspirational metaphor which has damaged art or been used up. But, as Stevens indicated in his statement on the poetry of war, we live in an age when the enormity of fact almost corrodes the reality and value of art. When reality is *that* real, we don't like to bother with it either.

I cannot help feeling that in the attempt to unify life and art by obscuring the difference, in whatever subtle ways, there is another order of illusion, which is to say another way of evading life. There is a world elsewhere, it should be out there, but we don't really know where, so it keeps coming back to where we are, a new solipsism, playful and plaintive, open-ended and recessive, still disinherited, apolitical, vain. The old modernists—Marx, Freud, Pirandello, Joyce—told us that history is the nightmare from which we are trying to awaken. The postmodernists would sometimes rather forget it. The tendency is either to bypass history or reverse it. In the paradoxical quest of the modern, that's normal. We are always reminded, or should be, that the avant-garde is not far out but way back, or laying back, reactionary. There is a desire for the elemental, to purify the words of the tribe, to dance us back the tribal morn, to find the little child who passes through the eye of the needle into the kingdom of heaven or some more intimate secular paradise. Clear the altar, sweep the stage! Grasp the root. *Per*-form: to carry through to completion, furnish forth, finish, perfect. But what there is to be perfected is also what has been forgotten. If the Plot stalled or disintegrated, there was something lost or abandoned that needs to be recovered so that the action can be resumed. Where's the action? they asked in the sixties. In the fifties we waited around for it in *Godot.* "Nothing to be done." *Pause. Do.* So far so good. The void is there to be filled. Make your scene. Live the moment. Do your thing. Put your body on the line. We are still more or less doing it, as we can see in the understated sophistication of Kaprow's Activities, but—to my mind —with a certain weakening of perception in the slipping phenomenology of performance.

The idea was to loosen us up, to keep things fluid, to lift the dead weight of history—including subjective consciousness and the scaly accretions of culture. "Habit," says Didi, "is the great deadener." So, as in *Waiting for Godot,* it may be just as well to forget. The failures of memory are the grounds of improvisation. If you don't know what it was, you have to make it up. The desolate landscape of the play, where everything starts over again, is a release of consciousness. (So too with play itself.) But habits form in thin air as they do in heavier climates. The culture scraped away is space for other accretions. We learn, for instance, that objects can be camouflaged on the surface as they were once obscured in the depths.

Take our chair again: Richard Foreman tells us that if we want to confront the chair we must allow it a life of its own, not as a "chair for sitting," supporting our habit, a mere object for human use. As such an object, it is varnished over with too much ego-determined and culturally made-up consciousness. If we're too close to the chair, according to Foreman, it becomes mere kitsch. Therefore, we must allow it "free play within the idea" of an "*articulating* process, the MAKING A THING BE THERE AS ITSELF (in its web of relations)." To declassify the chair as a chair for sitting, you may tie a string from the chair to an orange, so that it enters an estranging compositional scheme warding off utilitarian and anthropomorphized expectancy. Nor is the chair allowed to float off, "BEYOND, DEEPER, HIGHER . . . ," into the disguised or transcendental reality we have been trained to associate with art. (That would involve for both Kaprow and Foreman, I suppose, a sentimental and self-deluding emotion like Gaev's peroration to the bookcase in *The Cherry Orchard.*) The string anchors the chair in the here-and-now. It breaks up preconditioned notions about the chair. Whatever emotions come up through this process come from the

Take Up the Bodies

realization that the existence of the object is a kind of fallout, a "trace" from the energy of perception. But the mode of perception is reductive, minimalist, deliberately dehumanized—and thereby hangs a tail: an abrogation of the historical. Instead of an *experienced* trace (by the actor, by the audience) in a universe of traces, what we have (by *design*) is a didactic summary in theatrical form of deconstructionist thought.

As I remarked earlier, Foreman takes the idea of distancing further than Brecht, by whom he was influenced. The intention is to keep subjectivity from exuding the chair into atmosphere or absorbing it into self-consciousness as a mere extension of the self—as when we say everything that Duse touched became Duse. The caution is understandable when the actor is not Duse, and the chair becomes the extension of a not-so-interesting, self-indulgent, or imperceptive ego. Yet there is another possible relationship that confronts the chair *as* chair, no strings, penetrating its use, rerealizing it, as when someone's posture affirms *its* shape or when the *idea* of Cleopatra, not merely the subjectivity of the actor, converts the chair to a burnished throne. Or when Ekkehard Schall—as I remember from *The Resistible Ascension of Arturo Ui*—works himself up into an ecstasy of pneumatic self-pity resembling Hitler and Chaplin at once, and backflips over it. There is no romantic awe for the implicit otherness of the object in these encounters, but there is in each case a precise *aptitude* for the chair. One is moved *and* perceives, perceives the more deeply for being moved—indeed, what is perceived couldn't be perceived at all except in so far as the emotional state in which perception occurs is also realized.

Ideally, the environment of a staged event has both the reality and the surreality of an anechoic chamber or zero gravity, where things can be sensed and seen that could otherwise not be perceived at all. The emotional state within it does not necessarily imply "a perceivable, nameable *content*," as in conventional theater. It is true that Schall's performance or the web of relations named Cleopatra transforms the chair, but in the curious double vision of such perception, it also remains there as what-it-is. What is *just there*, however, strings attached or not, may be just that, better than nothing but not very much, the substance of the relations thinning out with the web. As for the body there on the line—whether committed by the sixties or neutralized by the seventies—it may tell its quota of lies.

They may appear to be very different, but Kaprow's Activities and Foreman's Ontological-Hysteric Theater are strung out on the same line. Foreman's theater arises from the artcontext established by the original Happenings, where the emotional flow (hysteric) of traditional performance is broken up into a series of arbitrary "found" moments, and the participant is caught up in a continuous present beginning. The Activities are behavioral (but nonmimetic), and the plays of Foreman are matrixed and mentalized—the one improvised in performance and the other improvised on the page but strictly conrolled on the stage. What they have in common, however, is the desire to deflect preconditioned responses and static judgments, either toward the activity at hand or the objects of attention, including the body, which may be the object of an activity or, like the chair, strung up. In both cases, the emphasis is on the momentary, an aptitude for what's happening *now*, rather than in a time-bound, causal remembering of experience, with a plotted afterlife.

There was surely good reason, during the sixties and after, for the released (matrixed or nonmatrixed) forms which disavowed the old behavioral illusion of reality and its structured disguises. But for all that, and total exposure too, the result has often been somewhere between a loose gestalt and a sterile formalism; at worst, parody, paranoia, and melodrama, illusion's revenge upon itself. There is something hollow at the center, and it is not the void. Occasionally, as in the Performance Group's *Rumstick Road*, there is genuine confessional substance, quite moving, the actor exposed, but breaking down into parody and not absorbed into a wider consciousness, therefore on the edge of exploiting its subject, the actual suicide of the actor's mother. In Lee Breuer's *Shaggy Dog Animation*, the inventive but loose-strung parody is absorbed, finally, into greater substance, the selfhood of the author increasingly defined by the emerging selfhood of the woman. The playing with time, however, is unsteady and desultory; and the work not only feels long, it is long, time escaping from concept.

The widening parameters of theater, meanwhile, include a lot of emptiness—even in quite interesting experiments. Some of it is disguised in a search for roots, by an aggressive neo-ritualism which is essentially regressive (the recent Grotowski) or by soundings in archaic languages (the Persepolis Brook), as if by losing touch with history we needn't bother with meanings. Whether or not exotic, the theatricalization of experience keeps us, at times, from seeing it. In recent years, we have had actors performing down the Mississippi on a raft or rolling out a carpet in an African village. Peter Brook's polyglottal troupe, which brought simple improvisations into the bush, might just as well have brought Shakespeare and the natives would have been similarly amazed or, if that was the objective of the long journey, communicated with across the barriers of language. As for accepting all history, all reality as histrionic, the liability is that, ultimately, you do miss the time-bound dependency of its deeper drama. That has happened in every period where spectacle subsumes reality, as in Brook's *Orghast*

Take Up the Bodies

financed by the Shah, and participation is up for grabs, as it was finally in the admirable but lamentable communitarian anarchy of the Living Theater.

"We wanted to make a play," said Julian Beck in the published version of *Paradise Now*, "which would no longer be an enactment but would be the act itself, . . . an event in which we (the actors) would always be experiencing it (the play) not anew at all but something else each time." That something else was a projection of the unaccommodated self, the increment of solipsism that thinks if you substitute the *is* for *as if* you have a revolution, which is what made the political urgencies of the group a misguided mess as performance careened into the streets, presumably annihilating the boundaries between art and life. The Brooklyn jail defined the boundaries. The Power Structure is more adept at game theory. Paradise now, reality tomorrow and tomorrow and tomorrow.

There has been little recent experiment as ambitious as that done by Grotowski, the Becks, and Peter Brook. The more valiant efforts to theatricalize experience ended rather abruptly with the Vietnam War. Where there are still repercussions, the scale has been reduced. And there has been no real critique, through the decline of radical politics, of the processes of representation, as there was in France (and later Germany) after the Days of May. Even there, it still comes—as in the widespreading apotheosis of performance in poststructuralism—with an antioedipal orthodoxy which continues to sponsor, with undeniable brilliance, the fallacy of an uninterrupted present. Which is more feasible in the sublimations of theory than in the actualities of theater, which remains undeniably in the service of time.

The political narcissism of recent times, the experiments with language, and the nostalgia for a ritual appropriation of the libido were aspects of the desire for wholeness, to be achieved through the aboriginal. We have, as I remarked earlier, been very foolish about this whole business of ritual in performance. If there has been anything but a mockery of it in our theater, I haven't seen it. We may envy, and even usefully remember, the ritual unity that appears to have been available to the aborigines in New Guinea or Gabon, but as the anthropologist Victor Turner reminds us, the *communitas* we desire in ritual is achievable only when there are sufficient occasions outside ritual in which *communitas* is experienced; and I might add not only experienced but admired. I suppose we have our rituals and our occasions, as we can see in the half-time ceremonies of any football game, but we may find them embarrassing or contemptible. Moreover, some of the new ethnological data makes us wonder whether the aboriginal unity was ever what it seemed. As Lévi-Strauss declared in a melancholy discourse on the painful separation of the ethnologist from his source, we shall probably never know. And Turner has recently written, after courteously deferring to Richard Schechner as a theorist, that his idea of " 'performance' is a fairly precise labelling of the items in the modern potpourri of liminoid genres—but it indicates by its very breadth and tolerance of discrepant forms that a level of public reflexivity has been reached totally congruent with the advanced stages of a given social form—Western capitalist liberal democracy." He then reminds us, too, that the "liminoid genres"—the historically developed forms that displaced ritual and other "liminal phenomena" of tribal and agrarian societies—are a considerable advance in human freedom, connected with the emergence of individual judgment and, I would suppose, the discriminating powers of language. "The concept of individuality has been hard-won, and to surrender it to a new totalizing process of re-liminalization is a dejecting thought."

I don't see how that can be denied, though the experiments with language and ritual, at their best, may present us with " 'subjunctive' possibilities" to be appraised. In the theater, they mostly just happened, and that was all. As for occasions outside ritual that support the idea of *communitas*, even more dejecting, they hardly exist. Nothing but fractures, factions, fragments, and splintering vested interests, all of which contribute to the general powerlessness. Against that we have to appropriate from the residuum of a common fantasy life whatever perspective we can—as Jean-François Lyotard puts it—on a necessary return of the will. That requires, I assume (lest the apocalypse really come), all the rational intelligence at our disposal, which has not been much encouraged in our new performance modes, where gratuitous and regressive play has had the upper hand. The kind of factitious and manipulative ecstasy that came up in *Paradise Now* and *Dionysus in 69* has gone out of fashion; yet the regressive impulse is still there, the desire to reproduce through performance some more fulfilling earlier state of being, some avatar of the old *homo ludens*, still polymorphous perverse. That is, for all practical purposes, the (somewhat weakened) orthodoxy, reflexive and unexamined, of the no-longer New Theater.

It is a desire we all share to some extent, to remain a child forever. "Me—to play," says Hamm in *Endgame*, himself his own object, but with a scabrously self-critical acerbity. The impulse is imitated, with more diffusion, in the newer drama, as in Sam Shepard's *Buried Child*. It is also reflected in the very sophisticated performance pieces by Vito Acconci, such as *Seedbed*, in which Acconci can be heard over an amplifier masturbating below a sloped ramp in an art gallery; or more specifically even in *Trappings*, where Acconci situated himself in a closet surrounded by foam, shawls, flowers, toys—and used his penis as a playmate and doll, dressing it, speaking to it, trying to dissociate it as a separate being. "An occasion for self-sufficiency—expanding myself," he said, "so I don't have to go outside of myself." The solo—and a rash of solo and "autoperformances" (Stuart Sherman, Linda Montano, Winston Tong)—follows the failure of the renewed communitarian dream.

Exposing the drama back in the closet may still be a refusal of the Freudian Reality Principle, though it may offer a perspective on the impaired condition of the will. I want to say more about Acconci in a moment; but what is it, first, that Freud asks of us that we seem to be rejecting? It is to confess, as he puts the case in *The Future of an Illusion*, man's (and woman's, for all the resurrection of the Great Mother), "utter helplessness and . . . insignificant part in the working of the universe." Freud adds, in his characteristically unilluded way: "But, after all, is it not the destiny of childishness to be overcome? Man cannot remain a child forever; he must venture into the hostile world." For this task, the only residual faith is "a certain measure of appropriateness" in our mental structure to attempt to understand the alien and hostile world which we are trying to know. Freud always knew that what we don't know *will* hurt us, but he also knew that there is a world of difference between the idea that the unexamined life is not worth living and the belief that we ought to know everything, more or less gratis, as if the universe were an open book.

What I am still talking about is the poetry of the movement of cost. In the world and on the stage, there has been an unexamined gullibility in the freeing up of the libido (which now has, as we might have expected, its conservative backlash). The assumptions behind "desublimated sexuality" (Marcuse), the newer "schizoanalysis" (Deleuze and Guattari), and the (necessary) defense of the obscene were to begin with more conventional than they appeared. What was considered radical was part of the fantasy life of bourgeois culture as well as the common stock of honorific sentiments attached since the Enlightenment to human sexuality. As Foucault has demonstrated in *The History of Sexuality*, rather than the suppression of sexual discourse, it has been sponsored through the Victorian period up to the present in every conceivable way. It is a text that has become part of the tolerance of discrepant forms reflexively mirroring the advanced stages of capitalist liberal democracy. What has been lost in the almost compulsive discourse of sexual liberation is an appraisal of the relationship of pleasure, power, and repression.

It is the measure of appropriateness in the mental structure that causes us to understand that impressing libido into the service of the

Reality Principle is not merely a denial of pleasure. Instead of being a wasted agency of undirected stimuli, energy is summoned to an "appropriate alteration of reality," very much as in Brecht's theory. The text is on the stage where the dreams are analyzed and interpreted. In this sense, repression is the ground of social and political action, as well as of new possible forms of gratification, the subjunctive possibilities. The metapsychology of Freud, so much more profound—because anthropologically more radical—than the revisionist therapies attempting to lift repression, sees experience as a mediating principle between Eros and Thanatos. In characterizing the nature of a dream, Freud compares it to the image of corpses on a battlefield. Take up the bodies, he says, like Fortinbras at the end of the play. Only he knows well that the play doesn't end, and there are likely to be more bodies. If he has to choose, he will choose civilization *with* its discontents, including more and not less theoretical understanding. It is that which takes us beyond the Pleasure Principle to the reparation of the will itself in the "will to repeat"—the play of thought which, as in Nietzsche, is an endless rehearsal of possibility in the act of interpretation, which never ends.

The dream—by projection into the stagings of thought—is absorbed into the ongoing procedure of distortions. The interpretative process cycles through the unconscious with no bottom to its depths, a palimpsest, a *verbal* dimension of time, like the actor reeling backwards through the text of *Elsinore*. (So the works of KRAKEN, bottoming *out*, have not been presented here as incontestable accomplishments but rather as ongoing forms of my own thought reaching for a terminus in theory, like a discourse on a dream:) The dream is incomplete by nature, and so its interpretation, a sequential abandonment of what it *was*, its assertions corrected, *taking itself back*, as another beginning. Whatever the nature of the unconscious, it retains the wish for paradise *in* civilization because, as Freud revealed, the unconscious is our oldest *mental* faculty. It is thus that the past reclaims the future. Experience alone is not at the center, but experience predicated on *memory*, which is an aspect of thought with truth-telling value. The appropriateness in the mental structure is related to the nature of language. The power of psychoanalysis is that it remains a "speaking cure." If it sometimes appears to become an incessant and inexplicable tale, overintellectualized and faltering in the mind, we must nevertheless remember that so far as civilization is concerned we have not, all told, been speaking very long—and in the theater of our time less and less well, even though the voices have improved. Moreover, Freud would have agreed with Nietzsche that "deep down" there may be "some granite of spiritual *fatum*," unreachable, obtuse, and unteachable, that will never know what its knowledge is for. Whatever the age of man, the intellect is still relatively young—though it has been much debunked for failing to do what instinct, which has been with us (I presume) from the primeval slime, has also failed to do.

The work of Acconci falls right into this abyss. *Seedbed* is as pure a solipsistic act as we are likely to find, as the idea of performance is appropriated by the art world and other disciplines. Recently, in a long and impressive video piece called *The Red Tapes*, Acconci has given us what amounts to a visual raga by an anal retentive. The images are lyrical and often elegant. The words, as usual with Acconci, are raw, iterative, mantric, improvised. He has a theory about the video image leaping out toward the audience to make contact as no other form does, but on tape the solipsistic system is conceptually looped, the narcissism unjudgeably doubled over. Acconci deliberately rearranges toys, plays with self-incriminating games, and at the recessive end of many of the visual structures is an aperture, a hole or egress, which is unreachable. If he can't discover, he says, *he* will be the discovery.

But what is he? The person on the tape? the person off the tape presenting it before the audience? the person remembered on and off? no one? though there is something remembered? We can't be sure. "Whatever the solipsist *means* is right," says Wittgenstein, not what the solipsist says or does. The solipsistic self is a tautology—all assertions curving back upon themselves in a kind of metaphysical redundancy. If the self is neither body nor soul but only self, not anything else in the world, it is only a metaphysical subject—it vanishes behind the mirror of thought. In gaining perspective on the return of the will, one has to take stock of that vanishing. The self's fiction empties itself out, as in the masturbation of *Seedbed*, in order to be itself, like the replenishing and replenished void of the Tao. The self-aggression is a negative capability. It would seem as if in this mirror there is only one future, and that is the future of an illusion. Solipsism, so seen, is an idealism arising from brute fact. There is only what is there is there is there, and that's *all* . . .

Whether the solipsist is right or wrong, the hinge of meaning is in the phenomenology of the unconscious. To reduce the privileged claims of the unconscious has been the mission of artists and philosophers alike. Politically, it seems, the unconscious is a bourgeois construct, an obscuring mechanism, confounding the will. We see this view of it in the stimulating thought of Lyotard, a French Marxist philosopher, who developed the concept of the libidinal economy. As Marcuse tried to do by deconstructing the Reality Principle with Orpheus and Narcissus, Lyotard tried to deflect the Freudian perspective on the will by examining "The Unconscious as *Mise-en-Scène*." In this analysis, he showed how Freud's structure of understanding was, so far as it can be said to be a staging, derived from nineteenth-century Viennese opera and theater. It is true that Freud makes practically no mention of newer currents in the theater, but while the Oedipus complex may have been better confirmed in the older theater forms, it came from diverse sources. Freud was enormously affected by Dostoyevsky, for instance, who took charge in the nineteenth century of what was most harrowingly Shakespearean in the history of Western theater. The closet drama was where the action was, the demonic having gone more powerfully into the novel. But no matter. Let us follow Lyotard, who concluded his lecture by shifting the staging place from theater to film:

The point was to show just how dependent Freud was on a premodernist aesthetic, in which the *mise-en-scène* of the unconscious overextends itself to the point of vanishing. In shifting to film, Lyotard left one crucial element behind—and that, intentionally, was *drama* (which is only in loose talk equated with theater). He cited an extraordinary film by Michael Snow, *La région centrale*, in which by a kind of phenomenological exposure we are even made aware of the apparatus by which the film was made. Snow had devised for this purpose a DaVincean instrument which scanned a landscape through all horizontal and vertical planes while a synchronized moving lens made it possible to show the base upon which the camera stood. There was a shadow on the landscape. I don't recall whether it was the shadow of the apparatus or the shadow of the cameraman. The shadow was, however, first of all a shadow, and the system appears to be (even the shadow) almost like the game of chess according to Duchamp, a perfect system or a system of perfect information. It seems to resist psychologizing. According to Lyotard, the changing focus and velocity of continuous sequences eliminates traditional framing, and by doing so dispenses with "the idea of a meaning hidden underneath appearances," and hence "the principle of distrust" inherent in the conventional *mise-en-scène*. What the film presents, through the swivelling materialist scrutiny of the lens' journey, is "all the tales born of all the images it shows," the *will* toward altering, and centripetal perspectives on reality. What is being staged is, thus, not the disguised content of the unconscious, but only what wants to make its potentiality manifest. I think that's true, but so does the shadow want to make its potentiality (or subjunctive possibility) manifest. The shadow is still troubling to me. It reminds me that there might be somebody there, more than a shadow, or surface—for the film presents a surface only, presumably undisguised by animistic or anthropomorphic projections.

I am not satisfied. I am not satisfied in the way Stevens suggests when he says that "the poetry of a work of imagination constantly illustrates the fundamental and endless struggle with fact." The illusions of performance constitute a field of truth. But it is only an apparency. An optical illusion *is* an optical illusion—it is only equal to its own facticity, that truth. Everything else about it is conditional.

The insistence on the world being what it is: why? There is no hidden meaning but the world—but if so, what is the meaning of our persistence in questioning beyond it or behind it? To call it delusion or false ideology is too facile. The persistence is as natural as breathing. Our very sense of something other than a here and now is not merely an addiction to what Barthes calls "the romantic heart of things," it is just as much a response to the specific, material promptings of a felt interior. What would be there to demystify if the mystifications were not themselves a mystery?—I mean not their accretions, as from an economic base, but what causes them to accrete whatever the base. There *is* an abstract world in our heads, there *is* illusion in our hearts (though I know the phrase is a metaphor), there *is* a concrete world out there, and they continue to inform and rehearse each other, despite the historically recurring (and necessary) exorcisms. Phenomenology is a corrective like any other philosophical perspective; that's the necessary and enlivening incongruity. The most stringent materialism contains the fatty tissue of surplus value.

That's the beauty of Snow's film. What seems true is true only to the extent that it has been lifted from the viscosity of experience into a more abstract realm of interpretation. What we normally take to be real is only more legible, but it's the illegible that substantiates the real texture of an event. So with the shadow. The fact is—as with the absent boy I keep remembering from Beckett's *Endgame*—there is a terrible desire to see someone there. And as Stevens says relevantly to that fact, too, "Nothing will ever appease this desire except a consciousness of fact as everyone is at least satisfied to have it be." So, put the case: I see a landscape, I want a man. Fact. That, too, is a time-serving desire; which is to say, I have been, like others, irritated by the excess of psychology and psychological projection in our theater, our art, our habits of mind. I have worked my own depredations on the convention of character in theater which is psychologically based and about which, in the acting process, we have to "excavate" the unconscious, to use Freud's archeological term, which we do in burrowing. But new realities, or views of them, conceptions, styles, perspectives on the return of the will are as much the result of (provisional) exhaustion as of discovery. When something comes to the end of the road, it doesn't mean it's going nowhere.

True, destinations inhabited too long may induce paralysis or blindness, especially if there's the shadow of some superhuman figure over the way—Milton with the epic, Shakespeare with the drama (as Eliot pointed out some time ago). In order to liberate ourselves from what has become troubling custom or overpowering or vapid form, we proclaim not only new freedoms and a change of heart, but new truths, structures, and even new existential data. Yet if, by whatever devious means, old forms return, it's because they were never absent to begin with, as Genet shows in *The Balcony*. The disturbing truth appears to be we are the same old performers of the hour. Things come round. Human needs being what they are, we find that new needs are a recycling of old denial. What was not absent was just strategically ignored, scrupulously overlooked, or refused validity on what could only be a trial basis. We look for breathing space, exemption, a new geography. The new perspective on the return of the will is a familiar coign of vantage, an open landscape which, we discover, has its margins, as every continent a land's end. Then, the turning back, the turning in: last year's freedom is another structure. It was already in the mind.

So, on Snow's landscape, there is a man. (I am tempted, having mentioned Stevens, to say a Snow Man, which is to say a man minimal, who hears nothing that is not there and the nothing that is—and knows that life itself is a poverty in the space of life.) It is a man projected out of thought, the shadow's shadow. Even when the technique attempts to reduce the human presence (as it can almost do in film) to a mere thing among things, the old Freudian questions are going to return like the repressed. In short, we are back through this perspective on the will's potential to memory and curiosity, projection and lamination, the desire to know more, to identify where the person came from, history and biography, and all the old incriminating and maybe crippling problems of the ego. The *mise-en-scène* passes out of the frame and back into the realm of the unconscious. We are not where we were. However much we would like to free ourselves of the obtrusive screen and selfish claims of the ego, it comes back to haunt us.

So it is in my own work that I have described in this book. No matter what is thought through in the play of thought, the play is about the players who play it. There is no *escape* into thought. Form is the ceaseless uroboric passage into the ego, preparing for the leap outwards, then only to be driven back like the creature in Kafka's *The Burrow* into the underground (that is, the unconscious as *mise-en-scène*) because reality feels realer that way ("Stay, illusion!") as it does in Kafka's story, and in the concepts of performance derived from it. The creature of the Burrow is, as I've said, a mode of consciousness, not a character, almost totally solipsistic. It is the hyperbolic version of the limiting condition of the actor, all mirror and painfully hidden. Yet it is desperate about what's out there, looking, tempted by it, in fact moves outside but is driven back in panic, helplessly inner, realizing finally that there may be no way to hide, there are countless others, many burrows converging, all the similarly frightened identities encroaching, accumulating like a great rough beast slouching but not, alas, to Bethlehem to be born. Rather, the Burrow is the Burrow is the burrowing. . . .

Thus, all the talk of going beyond Freud, so far as I can see—whether by structuralism, chance operations, objectism, projective verse, conceptual events, environmental theater, the phenomenology of film, or the false participatory democracy of open forms, you name it—hasn't gone anywhere in that respect, though they do provide perspectives. "In the fight between you and the world," says Kafka, "back the world." Such information doesn't outdate itself; and if you look at the world it seems to be that we are still juggling purpose and randomness, determinism and will, the diachronic and the synchronic, being and becoming (not as mere binaries), and all the successions of selfhood seeming between. Where the liminal is, the subliminal will be. Which is to say the wires are still crossed, the messages still scrambled, and the *mise-en-scène* inscrutable. Much as we'd like to say the world is what it is, neither significant nor absurd, *nothing is what it is, not singly.* The terms of what we're juggling are not merely polarities but soul mates, indivisible and insoluble. In this performance, we look for a third term to break the stalemate, but we look in vain, and that's the pathos of experience, another problem we can't solve. Chance has, maybe, "the last featuring blow at events," as it does in that great paradigm of human motives in the mat-weaving sequence of *Moby-Dick* or in the nonappearance of the pirate ship in *Hamlet.* But by no means does it have the last word. Chance—made strategically central in art or human affairs—is bound to be reductive, a far cry from the whole story. The same is true of self and surface. The task is still to read the indecipherable writing on the immutable wall.

Problems of destiny are still more entrancing than problems of chance (the dominant ethos of much postmodern performance), because it is within the compass of destiny that one requires perspectives on the desire for a return of the will: ". . . an unpleasant suspicion persists," says Freud in *The Future of an Illusion,* "that the perplexity and helplessness of the human race cannot be remedied. This is where the gods are most apt to fail us; if they themselves make fate, then their ways must be deemed inscrutable. The most gifted people of the ancient world dimly surmised that above the gods stands Destiny and that the gods themselves have their destinies." It is out of that perception, I think, that performance was born, dramatically. When, in the most burning desire for the performance—that is, the consummate, completed action—there is paralysis of the will, the best and most immaculate response may be the most moving poetry that Shakespeare ever wrote, the two simple words: "Let be." But we're not even satisfied with that.

The endless struggle with fact has by no means ended since Stevens wrote what he did during World War II. Letting be was never the finale of seem, only a nuance, the readiness which may not be all but as much as we've got if we're lucky to have that. The imagination of disaster, one of those literalized metaphors of the century, is still as much with us as ever, however much we'd like to say let's move on to something else. Since the sixties there has been a tendency to blur distinctions in a sort of monistic wish fulfillment. That was true of certain talismanic works of the period, like Norman O. Brown's *Love's Body*. Brown speaks there of the Reality Principle as "an unreal boundary between the real and the imaginary." But what makes it unreal? As a conception, it has a definite reality. As a phenomenal base reflected in a formulated principle it has another sort of reality. Then there is also the duplicitous thing itself to which the principle refers, prior to formulation, recurring in the psyche and mirrored in the world, beyond denial. Nobody draws the boundaries we deplore. Nobody can wish them away. In art, we try to cross the distance between the real and the imaginary (often losing direction in passage, not knowing from whence to where), making desire equal to the deed. We are always paying the cost.

In whatever ways art transforms reality, reality doesn't always oblige art. If the sixties and seventies were a period of sprung and unmodulated energy—with power threatened by the mirroring of its own paranoia—the eighties seem committed (probably the wrong word) to moderation of power in order to keep it from total impotency. The energy crisis—which had been adumbrated through the whole history of modernism—now seems to have its own momentum and objective reality. The dreadful thing which had already happened (Heidigger's phrase) as metaphysics is now a matter of fact. But the measure to be taken seem to be blocked by all the countervailing powers. To the degree that the crisis is political, it exists within a macrostructure of global cynicism. The criminality of nations has been diversified on a larger scale by the domination of pseudoinformation. There is nothing even resembling a moral accounting for the deeds performed, no less those behind the scene. The theater created at the UN for the moral drama runs a jaded repertory. The rival camps, in their conduct of worldly af-

Take Up the Bodies

fairs, think nothing of violating neutrality, borders, codes of justice, the rights of individuals, while continuing to pillage the earth with decolonialized abandon, and eyeing the stars. What used to be true of the colonial powers is true of the socialist states as well, including the relatively new-born revolutionary governments, like the Cubans in the Horn of Africa. In this context, congressional obstruction of an energy program seems like a minor booby trap in the cosmic farce. There is a further depletion of energy in the effort any sensible person must make in order to tell whether the whole thing is rampantly dishonest or utterly deranged.

What we require of society bears a relation to its ability to be real to us or to fulfill our sense of reality. There is no longer even the promise of anything like that. Nor can we grant the customary willing suspension of disbelief to our political fictions, since for a fiction to be credible it must bear some verifiable resemblance to presumed fact. Meanwhile, if the world came into being out of the boundless, there is still the fear that the opposite may take place. Things may be absorbed again into the infinite, as Anaximander said, as if we didn't deserve to be: "They render unto one another the penalty of their injustice according to the ordering of time." In the normal order of things, we keep our defenses up and weapons stockpiled, like the creature of the Burrow. Nuclear overkill, which dropped out of the headlines for a while, is revived in the energy tradeoffs, with a waiting grain of SALT. The military-industrial complex which Eisenhower blew the horn on is now complicated (and obfuscated) by linkages with the multinationals and the development of an arms industry with eager markets in the Third World that would make Shaw's Undershaft bloat with envy. It does make George Kennan—formulator of the Cold War policy of Containment—blanch at the prospect of the Bomb being available, willynilly, in the OPEC countries and, perhaps, to terrorists.

The new spectacle of terrorism is also part of the old endless struggle with fact. By the classical revolutionaries, the Terror was conceived of as in *Danton's Death*, as a rational instrument of virtuous policy. In our world, it is another function of the information system. The internationalization of politics brings the remotest atrocities closer in. The electronic media bring them sensationally into the living room. A modest bomb equivalent to twenty-five sticks of dynamite goes off, say, in a locker at LaGuardia. Eruption of metal and glass. Limbs all over. A woman sees a head on a shelf, as if it were guillotined. Or, as if "the evil humours" that Fanon described in *The Wretched of the Earth* —the absence of limits within "the permissive circle" of the native's dance—has had its sway. There is the "acute aggressivity" of an "impelling violence" from the same anthropological source as the theater.

The act of terrorism amends our political fictions with the harrowing lucidity ("maybe deciphered as in an open book") of long-thwarted purpose. Yet the terrible dilemma of a murderous idealism remains: Can it be justified? There's no quarreling with the Terror from a position outside the Terror—and within the Terror there can be no quarrel at all. Of course, violence can never be condoned by those who are not forced to it by victimization, but beware of the awful arrogance of those who are. In the taxonomies of atrocity, some appall us by being liberating. Who can deny it? In the constitution of history, some inexorable outrage does its unjudgeable work.

So the illusions of performance are still horrifically entwined with the performance of illusions. The terrorist act has always been designed theatrically. There is a plot, choreography, *coups du théâtre,* and all the attendant apparatus of a staged performance, especially advertising and PR. It's just that in our world the scale of it is immeasurably greater than ever imagined, and there is no way for this new diplomacy not to be absorbed into show business through the networks. As for the old show business—the profession of theater as it exists in this country—it is still qualitatively part of the Gross National Product. The activism of the sixties looked to the reorganization of human relations to achieve a redistribution of human resources so that power and coercion would not be necessary to enforce a common existence. Some of the newer performance modes still attempt to reflect this desire. They are admirable, though we have seen an abrupt diminishment of that renewed utopian illusion, as well as the forlorn grasping for power that sometimes went with it.

It was not the idealistic Left but a self-confessed pervert, Jean Genet, who gave us the great summary play of the period, *The Screens,* a political drama which incarnates an absolute refusal to be politically engaged. Genet later became naively enamored of radicalism in this country, aligning himself most particularly with the Black Panthers; but his antihero Said aligns himself with nothing. The drama rejects the politics. There is a convulsive and inviolable negativity in the poetic universe. The play is finally concerned not only with the decolonization of the psyche, but with its depoliticization. Said, like the archetypal whore Warda, is perfecting a role. His mission is nothingness: the absolute acceptance of himself as excrement by way of transition. In behavior, the process is one of progressive self-mortification: rigor mortis. It is a terrifying discipline that leaves us in principle bereft of politics, which is pretty much where we are. The play dramatizes the acute aggressivity of which Fanon wrote, but the power of the art is in its apocalyptic distance from convictions about mere social change. (As for Genet's rendezvous in Chicago with the Panthers, it was an in-

Take Up the Bodies

terlude of what might be called—for more than Genet, and by Genet at another time—a sucking ideology.) It is the difference between the most astringent radical vision and the promise of radical politics.

What we strove for in the radicalism of the last generation was—as Freud appraises it for all such striving—a golden age, "but it is questionable if such a state of affairs can ever be realized." If the understatement is not ironic, its ingenuousness is cancelled by the years of clinical experience and unstinting analysis that led to the irrefutable conclusion. It pains us to accept the verdict, but we have seen no evidence in human history to overturn it. Coercion and instinctual renunciation are almost synonymous with the idea of culture. They may be the ground for the very idea of performance. Why? As Angelo says in *Measure for Measure,* "We are all frail." One last message from Freud: "It does not even appear certain that without coercion the majority of human individuals would be ready to submit to the labour necessary for acquiring new means of supporting life." (Similar reasoning leads even liberals now to anticipate totalitarian measures in response to our massive social problems.) The sweat of the brow is as out of fashion as the rational intelligence.

We see that also in our understanding of the relationship between work and play, which comes up increasingly in social discourse as a redemptive principle. The one depends, however, upon the other. But they are as confused as the relation of the Reality Principle and the Pleasure Principle. Because work has become so undesirable for so many people, we have had to commercialize the alternatives, the domain of dissociated play, leisure, and ways of getting away from work. To the degree that people can't stand what they have to do to earn their daily bread, we must create an industrial superstructure to cause them to forget that the large part of their lives, the necessary part, is unlived and meaningless. To the degree also that our public institutions lose the element of ritualized play that Huizinga has described in *Homo Ludens,* it is no longer possible to have cultural forms in which we witness the reenactment of shared belief. There is no alternative then to the emptiness of distraction but distraction. In this overpowering vacuum, the ethic of modernism which led to the detachment of art from the social center—alienation in technique to oppose alienation in labor—reverses itself with an inexorable logic. The insistence that art remain critically at the margin, giving witness to absence, becomes the postmodernist demand that the *appearance* of art be abolished and resemble *reality* again, a process which makes it both accessible and marketable, and assimilable by fashion. That's of course the worst of it, but by no means uncommon and beguiling in principle. It's important to remember, however, that the great modernists—who insisted on critical distinctions with an unyielding intelligence—have never, even as we talk of going beyond them, been assimilated. To recognize that has nothing to do with refusing innovation in art (far from it), only with acknowledging reality.

We go at our own hazard. The yielding up of boundaries is always a risk, whether between playing space and spectator space, reality and illusion, theater and life. The yielding up has the apparent advantage of any holism. There is a unitary illusion, but it may be a further illusion, and less valuable than the one which insists, without being slavish to categories, that some distinctions are worth keeping, must even be ferociously kept. That, too, is part of the endless struggle with fact.

Take just one performance idea that still persists out of the abated turmoil of the activist years: the desire for participation, which is a function of the desire for an extended community, both positive values. "I don't see any middle ground," writes Schechner in his book *Environmental Theater.* "Either the audience is in it or they are out of it. Either there is potential for contact or there is not. I don't deny that the spectator in the orthodox theater feels something. Sure he does. *But he cannot easily, naturally, unconsciously, and without embarrassment express those feelings except within idiotically limited limits."* Aside from the fact that it sometimes encourages idiotically limited feelings, this is a nearsighted view of theater conventions. What is natural and unconscious varies with expectation and mores, and any theater design of consequence is a responsive evolution. The proscenium arrangement (which Schechner is taking to task here) is historically burdened and it has been abused; but it is an available perceptual field, not merely a foolish structure of class consciousness and invidious design. As the dull substance of the flesh is thought, so is a space. The limits are shadowed by the same burden of history, as with a text. A stage is a palimpsest of memory, value, and desire. The limits are what is useful, limned or illumined, depending on what you're looking for, and how.

Nevertheless, the participatory ideal remains one of the major experimental issues in the theater. Now that it's a lot clearer that it can't be taken for granted, how far can it be taken? The space is not the crucial problem. The basic impediment is that the gestures people make when they are participating are the gestures they have seen when they're not. What else would they be? The improvisational element is sought for in the participatory frame (and it *is* a frame), but even when it's practiced, improvisation almost invariably starts with cliché, as I've indicated before. The purging of cliché is a function of repetition and duration, the breaking down of defenses through either sustained challenge or boredom. But even unendurable time will not rectify makeshift reflexes and a haphazard state of mind. Since most of us are complexes of habits, attitudes, and instincts which are banal until refined by the stringencies of thought and method, what can we really expect of unprepared and instantaneous responses but the shallowness of which we know ourselves capable. Nor can we expect much more from the drawn-out responses. We don't after all *live* in an environment which encourages exactitude of thought and feeling. If anything, the opposite.

The participatory assumption of Environmental Theater is simply unsound psychologically. Poor theory, poor practice. There is inevitable bad faith. (Even by people striving to be honest.) Bad faith, bad acting. Reconstructing a space in a theater is no more reliable than rearranging the chairs in a classroom. The efficacy of the gestalt circle depends on who's there and what they really have to say. It's amazing how quickly the raised consciousness becomes new habit. I have often found behavior at the Performance Garage or other environmental theaters artificial, self-conscious, constrained, improbable, falsely focussed or unfocussed, and lacking the potency of concentrated reflection which one can experience in an orthodox theater, depending on who does what with the convention. For that's what it is, available, site and structure in potential, ready to be seized by an idea.

As for the idea of the performance occurring all over, in "the fullness of space" and its transformations, it's a good idea. Yet it's a rare performance in a new environment that gives one the sense of the infinite extensibility of space. The palpable fact is that too much of the space is likely to be dead space, as the audience straggles from one place to another, following scenes which are arbitrarily shifted. It is hardly a perceptual field, like the body itself, or an anechoic chamber. Of course one can stay where one is and not see at all, according to the principle of participatory freedom. But that's a pretty low order of choice in what one thought would be a very sophisticated conception of audience involvement. Renaissance illusion, by contrast, is in every sense far deeper. I don't deny the possible validity of a free-flowing space, but see no primacy in either convention.

The same is true of mediated and unmediated acting. Being oneself onstage may be more artificial than being a character. The important thing is to understand the powers of theatrical framing, the nuances of the convention, even when one convention bleeds into another. The actor's presence is a beguiling thought, with a multitude of possible articulations. I have tried to explain how we played the gamut of articulations in the work of KRAKEN, thinking of it as a virtual scale of value, or part of a valuing structure. Everything asked of an actor (not only in our work) is in some degree mediated, the shading of a convention—which is the idea of acting itself. To ask an actress, for instance, to be more or less feminine is to make a stipulation about presence that may be far more demanding than the motives and lineaments of a specific role. It's also important to understand the implications of abandoning or minimizing a convention. Take the idea of character: I'd like to review what has happened to it in relation to some issues already discussed: the problem of language and the problem of the self or person, and the dependency of work and play. These are in turn related to the deep structure and perspectival illusion of the proscenium theater, the old apparently fixed space of dualistic thought—and the *mise-en-scène* of the unconscious.

The issue of character in theater is like the issue of drawing in art. (I should say again that in the ordinary theater it is no issue at all, and we continue to see the same old character.) The attempt to render behavior on the plane of the unconscious came to seem, in due time, like the last ditch of the imitative faculty. The commitment to abstraction (character is an abstraction, but we'll come to that) minimizes those techniques which are in homage to the classical inheritance of mimesis. The effort to reach the unconscious goes to two extremes of method: improvisation and the mask. The one is presumably free in form, the other hieratic. Sometimes the two conjoin, as in the comedic mime. In the traditional use of the mask, the actor—after long study—draws up the fluid materials of the unconscious to fill the fixity of the facial gesture. In the relation between improvisation and the mask, there are permutations and combinations, qualified by the unhindered mobility of other parts of the body. Improvisation without the mask is something else. In what we called the Method in acting, improvisation was supposed to be truer to reality, closer to the actual sources of behavior, but it too grew increasingly abstract and iconographic, specious, passing through a phase (as with the imitators of Marlon Brando, and Brando imitating himself) where it parodied itself as if it were a mask.

In recent theater, the falling away from mimesis showed up first in role-playing and Transformations, then fractured roles, or none, then purer image, or the ideograph. The rejection of the mimetic also comes—even within the structure of the mimetic (Richard II, the Six Characters etc.)—from a sensed disjuncture in experience, a lapse of function or break in being, transpersonal or prehistoric, which indeed causes us to invent constructs such as the unconscious or a conception of the self. Whatever these are in reality, we know them only through language. (Even so-called body language, as I've tried to suggest, is the outward inscription of the anterior word.) The problem is how to *represent* the unconscious or find the "through line" again (Stanislavski's term) from self to nature to origins. How do we do it? Surely not by likeness to ordinary behavior in a recognizable social context. The likeness we want is the likeness of the missing person. That was to be achieved by pressing the historically determined figure back upon its ground. The fixed environment (in the older sense of time and place) became a shifting field, where action, object, and character were dematerialized by perception.

Here we encountered paradoxes where social value and aesthetic value could either support each other or clash, depending on where one stood in principle. If the actors could exchange roles, they could also exchange genders. In the transformative grammar of modern acting, the actor could increasingly say, like Lady Macbeth, unsex me here. In the same way, performance might become indifferent to color. The more abstract, the more miscegenated. While that is a distinct and meaningful change in vision, there is still the feeling that it somehow lacks the multi-faceted *humaneness* of the other tradition, which keeps us responsible to history, biography, psychology, and the systemic values of sex and race. (In the conventional theater, liberals were left hanging on this issue when, after they argued for mixed casting, Black Power came on the scene and, in theory at least, said you can keep those honky roles.) In a recent book, Roland Barthes used the homosexualization of experience as a programmatic (he would deny the word) metaphor for the erotic plurality of thought and fantasy, which he prefers to the double violence of mimesis and finite meaning. But if things are coming semiotically out of the closet, they quickly enter the realm of fashion. One might also say: the more abstract, the more homogenized. (At least, there is the latent danger, offset in somebody like Barthes by the obvious brilliance.) The denial of character, like the denial of drawing, persists in that antirepresentational ethic of postmodernism which fears more than anything else the premature falling into meaning. On the one hand, it is an extension of the modernist tradition of depersonalization; on the other, it comes from the unsatisfied incessancy of the mirroring self. In either case, it represents the validation of the formal and iconographic, and the diffracted, against the chronographic, the narrative, and the mimetic.

Explaining the change broadens into cultural history: vision seemed depleted by the long emphasis on behavior after the emergent individualism of the Renaissance. Photography in the visual arts took over the obligation of likeness, which spread over the social scene by mechanical reproduction. The whole repertoire of gesture codified by history—what we named behavior—seemed overproduced, staple, too much seen. It was also systematically studied by the social sciences and the form that grew up with them, the novel, and in a filial line through film, as well as other kinds of visual realism. What else could be said about it? Sometimes, it seemed, nothing. So we turned abstractly away—as from the self-destructiveness of the same coded behavior. Nonetheless, the idea of character haunts us in the theater like the absence of some pictorial metabolism in a color field painting (no referent, no analogy, no nature, no mimesis). In the most advanced forms of theater, the missing character is felt like the absence of some primary level of articulation. In art, the techniques of rendering persist in giving witness to the remembrance of nature. They are not easy to do without. A line or a drip in what appears to be a completely abstract painting will betray the dispassionate image or the action field and remind us that something is being drawn from somewhere else, *outside* the picture frame, not coextensive with it, even when the frames are stretched almost beyond the limits of peripheral vision. There is something in the field painting of a Pollock that still makes us think of a landscape, and in his case the particular virility of the tracings makes us know the artist is very much there. The image was not meant to be dispassionate. Depending on the immediacy of the image, we will feel through the serenest abstraction the presence of the activating person.

In the theater we can't miss it, unless—as in the marginal performances conceived for the American Contemporary Theater by Joseph Dunn and Irja Kolonen—the activating persons are immersed in the dark, devoutly, offering a kind of unexhibited sacrificial labor to unfolding perceptions of space and time. (Actually, in the traditional theater, there has always been such labor, *backstage,* though once taken away from the actors and given to the stagehands, it was transferred to the economy, unionized, and made part of the inequities of the profession.) Here the image in part depends on the expectancy that in a theater event people *will* be present. But in the performances of ACT, the actors either can't be seen or, in a minimal gesture of presence, are barely seen—in one event, pedalling on unicycles round and round a light-sealed space through a continuum of thick smoke. So long as the corporeal body is visible, however—even minimally—something in us will want it to act as humans act, in the bleakest finality of final form. That they don't act conspicuously so in the conceptual pieces of ACT is due to a scrupulous formal restraint and the integrity of the conception. As in Beckett—by whom the work is deeply influenced—the perceptual increments are the concentration of a living absence, tirelessly there.

You can feel it if you are similarly concentrated within the event. It's another sort of character that the actors show—the disciplined intensi-

Take Up the Bodies

ty of constituted will—in the realization of a rigorously programmed environment which is an extension of the missing self. The perspective is almost that, however, of the "characters" in Beckett's urns looking back to the most minimal source of light. In this darkling meditative space, the idea of Environmental Theater, loosely realized elsewhere, has genuine signifying value. The space is diversified and expanded by thought. And the actors—unlike those visibly there in other plays—are not mere functions of a conception, though the conception is strong, because one can feel in the thoroughly defined atmosphere the immanence of determined otherness, another conviction, the empowering will to repeat, *that* image. In political terms (ACT makes no claim whatever to being political theater) the meaning of the labor exchange value is interiorized, freely chosen, and arduously preferred. The acting is not mimetic, but it is the stuff from which new possibilities of behavior are drawn. It is a perspective on the return of the will which is something more than chance operations, a seriality of images, a random disjuncture of roles, or the simple-minded vagaries of participatory theater.

In its outer appearance, the work resembles performance structures or environments we have seen in art galleries (e.g., the light-sculpture of James Turrell or Robert Irwin), but it is not part of that system. It is profoundly different because of a humanistic bias rooted in theater and the memorability of the idea of acting, where the undeniable person is at the core, struggling to being through the form. One has the sense of a presence which is ascetic and hard-earned. If it has had to start over, it is with the powerful memory of loss. Nor is it easily accomplished. Unlike those who participate in an art world performance event, the actors have to be trained to do what they do, elementary as it seems. In this they differ, even when they are inside constructed figures which outwardly resemble those of the Bread and Puppet Theater, from members of that communal group. (I want to take nothing away from Peter Schumann's individual achievement in designing the puppets and their pageantry by calling attention to the fact that once the puppet is built almost anybody, like an interchangeable part, can "perform" under its skirt with a minimum of instruction.) In ACT, the play is difficult work. The puritanism of the work ethic comes with the force of thought-out conviction from the same humanistic legacy as the old convention of character. There are none of the appurtenances of an enacted play, but you see feelingly, if you see at all.

The concerns of ACT may not even seem real to some theater people. For one thing, most theater events—even Alternative Theater events—still take for granted that some kind of characterization or role playing is the major purpose of acting. And of course it is. We may

The Future of an Illusion

have had to come roundabout, however, to what may appear to be a self-evident perception. Those who are nostalgic for the glamour of the old theater, critics like the late Harold Clurman or Stanley Kauffmann, feel that our actors don't act enough or frequently enough, that they don't fashion careers *as* actors. That's certainly true of the theater most of us know, where opportunity is still scarce for the majority of actors, an egregious majority. The lucky ones often make reputations prematurely, sometimes with no more than a lucky role. Those who excel are with equal rapidity confiscated by television or the movies as superstars, where they become media phenomena or cultural signals rather than actors. Thus, there is some reason for Clurman's insistence that much of what remains is amateurism. Some of these actors don't know the difference or wouldn't care if they did, and some are accommodated by the ethos or approach of a particular group, where the qualities of the actor or the quirkiness is what counts, as in the Theater of the Ridiculous, which is still vamping with nostalgia through the campy eccentricities of the quasi-actors at the old Judson Church.

There are also actors who would never choose to be actors were there no alternatives to the conventional theater. They are nevertheless deeply serious about what they are acting for, the breadth of being demanded from them in what they do, and they are willing to train themselves systematically for doing what they must—which may or may not include the cultivation of the mimetic sensibility. Without that, there is no responding to Clurman's charge, for he is talking (knowledgeably) of performance as it is normally understood. To play the great roles in straight plays at a high level of achievement takes years of nurtured experience, there's no denying it—and many of the actors who have been involved with experimental groups never had the gift for it. Nor, with the emphasis on research, do some of them perform enough. Yet the work which will be of eventual importance to the theater is that which proceeds not as if it knows what theater is but as if the question has to be asked, as it does periodically, again and again. Nothing can be taken for granted, especially the nature of acting. The work of ACT—specialized and unseen as it is—returns to that elemental question. Rather than a character to-be-played, it aims to develop character *in* the actor without encouraging the egotism of the unmediated presence. By denying role-playing altogether, it is an extreme version of Stanislavski's dictum about learning to love the art in yourself rather than yourself in art—from which basis we may return, better grounded, to the renewal of character as it has been known.

The idea of character, which once seemed second nature to the actor, is in any case a complex phenomenon in the contemporary theater. Its sufficiency is deeply problematical. The characters in search of an

Take Up the Bodies

author are still on the scene, probably even more neurotic and fragmented, because we are now severely questioning the authorial principle (already undermined in Pirandello), the idea of a progenitor or parental figure as the beginning of our uncertain ends. That was one of the implications of the emphasis on group process and "collective creation," with its rejection of the authority of the playwright and the director. This movement has diminished and the call is out again for the authority of the playwright, if not the director, who has with overbearing presumption deranged too many classical plays. Yet the deeper issue is being ignored. To restore the playwright's eminence over the director is merely to replace one form of inadequate authority with another in the larger historical process. It's as if mere knuckle-rapping can reverse the disappearance of the idea of the single authority or forbid the diffusion of the text into history. Or as if the missing person can tell us of his whereabouts as on a ouija board.

What continues to pass for character doesn't, sad to say, have very much to tell us. One reason is the introjection of the realistic tradition of behavior even by those presumably doing experimental work. We are still prey to commonplace theories of verisimilitude in the appraisal of acting, and most of our actors still think and feel in the psychology that Brecht criticized and Artaud would have purged. The reality is that they *like* being themselves and not a critical attitude or a tectonic figure or an ideograph in whatever roles they play, and they mostly prefer to play the roles as they've seen them played, though naturally in their own "interpretations." That's surely understandable. The mimetic instinct may be only too natural (as Aristotle thought)— which is what both Brecht and Artaud didn't like. What I have been saying is that character isn't natural, though it depends on the mimetic instinct. Character is a formal construct, an abstraction, which is also (historically) an evolution. In the novel, that evolutionary form, Henry James called it "a compositional resource." It is important to remember that while Aristotle spoke of the drama as an imitation of an action in the form of action, he did not, in enumerating the parts of a play, list the actor. He listed character.

A play is fundamentally a formal idea. Lifelike persons are authenticated by the idea, though we always have the problem, and the value, in the theater that people are pretending to be what they are not, including other people, and even when they're pretending they're not pretending. We may say, as I have just said, that the actors are subserving a formal cause, but as a compositional resource they are also subversive. They won't hold still. That dynamic is a potential source of meaning-in-theatricality. I have explained how we tried to explore it in KRAKEN. There is a long tradition of trying to get the actor to hold still: the masks of ancient theaters, Gordon Craig, Meyerhold, even Eleanora Duse (who wanted to revitalize the theater by killing the actors off), and the director who behaves like a traffic cop. Artaud was also in this tradition when he exhorted us to replace the egocentric stasis of the psychologizing actor with the meticulous geometries of the Balinese theater. For the peculiarity of that stasis is its uncentered restlessness, self-indulgent, like a nervous tic in eternity, the ultimate playing space of Artaud's desire.

While character is a construct, its default is related to a weakening sense of personal identity, arising from the absence of a unifying bond in the culture. The incapacity of Artaud's culture-in-action is that he tried to achieve a cosmic identity by reducing the concept of the person to parity with space rhythm sonority shimmer and shadow—all those images which haunt the edge of trance—and therefore with the theater's Double or animating spirit. There is something aphasic in the ecstasy, which we see in Artaud's poetry and in the word-locked litanies of Robert Wilson's spectacles, where the actor is somewhere between a selfless image and a solipsistic incantation. In denying, however, the primacy of the person—or the character of the self-important actor—we are always uneasy that in gaining a compositional resource for the theater, or the icon/archetype of a cosmic identity, we may be losing its major figure. Given what I've said of language, I do mean a figure of speech—with all the hazards of an ego identified only by language, whose unpredictable *situation* is in the unconscious.

Shakespeare knew the situation in the sonnets: "Look what thy memory cannot contain, / Commit to these waste blanks. . . ." As the theater goes in and out of perspective, from the estranged to the familiar and the familiar to the strange, in the paradox of apparencies which draw a blank, the convolvulus of psychology is always there. We move back and forth from the depersonalizing of the inner life to its raw exposure. We distrust, like Brecht, the recessiveness of the unconscious. There is always the impulse to throw off the mask, to purge illusion, and get down to what is hidden. The problem is to discern what exactly is in hiding, and sometimes it appears to be the surface. In a psychological age, part of the surface is the currency of self-exposure. Now that we've been given permission, it's almost doing what comes naturally. If the landscape is polluted with noise, it is also littered with confession. Whether true confession or not depends, paradoxically, on the formal construct in which it occurs (with every therapy claiming the truth). But the missing person is recurrently there insisting that his story be told, both playing and giving up the ghost. In our work, we have tried to make this uncentering dilemma into the methodology at the heart of the story, what I have described as ghosting.

In the vacillations over depth and surface (that insoluble problem), I suppose the general bias today is that truth comes from the exposure. There is a half-conscious vanity to it (that we don't entirely escape in the self-conscious mania of our method). We make more of ourselves than we can really justify to ourselves by hinting that something else is there, really, underneath. But as Valéry suggests, what is hidden is likely to be the least interesting part of a person. All of us tend to hide the same things, more or less; it's in what we *show* that we differ—which is what makes the theater interesting. (The vanity of Hamlet, and the supreme theatricality of the conception, is in wanting to have it both ways: letting it all come out while insisting with equal vehemence on an impenetrable privacy of being.) We have all had the experience of awaiting a dark confidence from someone nervous about astonishing us. We brace ourselves for the exposure and see just about what we guessed was there. It's like the people in Chekov's plays who complain about where they are—oh, if I could only go to Moscow!—implying that if circumstances were different they'd show the suppressed and secret part of themselves. Only the tragedy is, and the comedy, that they are no more than what they appear to be.

Nevertheless, it is what is shown that brings along the damnable opacity of the not-shown. It arouses another vanity in the hermeneutical circle. There is the exacerbating act of penetrating appearance, reading what is there on the surface, interpreting the signs. "The hair that won't curl is the guilty one," said Denise in a preliminary improvisation on *The Cell*, where we were presuming to invent an ideology from scratch. There was an existential politics within the Cell that reflected these tensions between depth and surface, solipsism and objectifying purpose. The major issue was whether the ego could be surrendered to the Central Committee, the political figure which was a surrogate for the unifying authority of our own group. There was a certain glamour in the idea of renunciation, attractive to the actors as actors, resisted by the actors as persons—if I can make a separation that I have been strenuously avoiding because it may be untenable. In the Cell, the ego is in theoretical jeopardy. The process can be radicalizing. It is a fine and dangerous line between the surface commitment and the depth of individual resistance—a line that must be crossed in the acting. What emerged from the evolution of *The Cell*, so far as it went, is the ferocity with which the actors finally refused the extrusion of ego for an objective purpose making absolute claims upon it. That came out inarguably in the struggle sessions, where we saw again how stubbornly the ego is situated in the unconscious.

There, it seemed, was the real power. When it came to the crunch, the actors didn't like being named by History, conceived as a process outside the self; which is to say, they wouldn't be reduced to nothing but a sign, mere password of a function. The names they chose—like Tom's Squamous—were pseudonymous, not anonymous. The names were instinctively names for what they took themselves to be (with all the sophistication about vanishing selfhood), not what History may have wanted them to be. They were names for the complexities of a multiple self rather than for what, yielding up the ego, they might become within a new social order if that were to materialize. Of course they were *these* actors in *this* history, and it was all a fiction anyhow, the whole enacted thing. But how tenaciously they clung to themselves! though they were committed to a process which would presumably cancel, on ideological grounds, any affiliation with the unconscious. They would burn it out. The more they were interpreted, the more inturned they became. If they were going to curl, it would be in the shape of their own genetic codes. They couldn't surrender and they didn't want to be read.

Earlier, I tried to put speculation about depth and surface in the context of phenomenological thought. Michel Foucault points out how phenomenology, which started in a climate of opposition to "psychologism," has come full circle back to personality and actual experience of the experiencing self. (For instance: Diane Arbus shoots freaks, derealizes them onto the photographic surface, with no illusions, and gives us the empirical data of her own identity.) Phenomenology, says Foucault, "has never been able to free itself from this insidious parenthood, from its tempting and threatening proximity to the empirical study of man"—with its self-edifying hypostasis of the ego. It starts out intending merely to reflect what is there—by "bracketing" or "framing" or "mirroring"—but the reduction to the mirror absorbs what is there into the processes of thought. The thinking subject is inevitably and incessantly self-reflexive. Questions bounce off the surface back into the head. They cast a shadow on the landscape of thought. The surface dissolves in phenomenological description, becoming what is reflected. As we bypass the primacy of the thinking subject, we come to an ontology of what lies beyond thought: "What is your substance, whereof are you made/ That millions of strange shadows on you tend?" Once you describe the shadows, the surface is all over. It is the inscape of the crooked eclipse.

One of the problems with keeping the person in his place as a compositional presence is that there is something innate which refuses the idea that all objects in extended space are equal. The implication that they are was the vice of earlier forms, such as Imagism in poetry and cubism in painting, neither of which (nor the Bauhaus experiments

Take Up the Bodies

with abstraction of the body into its mechanics) flourished in the theater. It is the vice of any theory of surfaces—even when theory doesn't mean to equate things but rather wants them to be seen for what they are without the encrustation of psychology and metaphysics upon things. But things prostitute themselves. We are somehow solicited. And there are things and things. "What, has this thing appeared again tonight?" Coleridge was right about the mental dazzle of that omnibus word *thing* to describe the unspeakable presence of a ghost. But of course it is not a ghost; it is an actor playing a ghost, himself ghosted by his own unspeakable past. What thing in the endless reverberation of thingness are we really talking about in that appearance? Or any appearance? If only the ghosts would hold still. There is a sense in which the human figure sabotages any composition, most especially when the figure speaks. For the deep structure of language is the unconscious sounding, or whatever it is that constitutes the unspeakable reaches of the mind. So long as that thing called an actor is there, there is the possible echo of a reality that occurs in three dimensions and the fourth dimension of remembered, irrecoverable, and projected time. If there is a break in being, metaphysics comes in through the pause.

Something there is that can't be formed, or remain unmediated. Whatever we have our actors do nowadays, there is always the memory of the actor's playing a character. Then we remember that there is somebody playing the actor playing the character, and we are caught up in that cycle of performance, or the awareness of it, where the character is really the actor playing that character; and as you reflect further upon the process the concept of character is parsed into concepts of person actor role being and presence (only the words identifying the nuances) playing off each other in various degrees and inflections as in a tonal system, behavior returning to its source, the ubiquitous and slippery thing itself. In perceiving behavior on this sliding scale of appearance, we are caught, ghosting, between the thing itself and the thing among other things. Seeing is believing, but can we believe we saw? We find ourselves saying like the distraught Ophelia: "T'have seen what I have seen, see what I see!" The very looking at things becomes a model of what they are, and only the most rigorous discipline can dissolve the model back to where it came from—neither the looking nor the thing looked at having the autonomy of subject or object. At the most, glimpses flashes traces epiphanies, then dissolve, back to the falsifying opacity of things, which we think of as out-there, usually, before they in-here.

To the degree that the cycle of the thing's appearance has been projected in our work, I have tried to suggest that it is more than a tech-

The Future of an Illusion

nique of performance, it is an ontological strategy. As for the idea of character, it exists now as something of a memory trace, coming and going in the fictions of its appearance, now visible, now not. I suppose we get closer to its ontological source when we realize that the word has a double meaning related to the nature of language. There is not only the generic thing-to-be-played but the genesis of writing itself in the play of words, about which Shakespeare puns in *Cymbeline*, when Guederius speaks of (the boy actor playing the girl) Imogen disguised as the boy Fidele: "He cut our roots/ In characters,/ And sauced our broths. . . ." What we appear to be doing now, in the apparent shedding of the convention, is trying to reverse the process, stirring up the (progenitive) sauce, so that character may find its roots. A pun also puts things in perspective, but it offers no guarantees.

Nevertheless, through the shifting of its conventions, anything is possible in the theater. Anything. Years ago, when I was studying "Dramatic Art," they said that certain things couldn't be done on a stage. All of them are quite doable, like uprooting place and time, or suddenly changing scale. The issue of scale—foregrounded again by theories of participation and environment—is quite obviously not a function of perspectival geometry. Shakespeare's practice was, through all baroque controversy, always the case in point. The trial of Goneril and Regan by madman, Fool, and lunatic King not only abolishes perspective but virtually shatters, within the framework of the old drama, the concept of scale, in the new justicing of perception. "Bless thy five wits!" says the Bedlam, kinesthetically. The hovel contains the universe as the senses, according to Marx, contain the whole history of the world. "The murmuring surge," below the imagined cliffs of Dover, "on th'unnumb'red idle pebble chafes. . . ." The zone of performance may be phenomenologically reduced to pebble or button, or stretched to infinity by the manic play, in the world that's made of language.

Still, they were right for the wrong reasons, my teachers. The power of form depends not only on what we do but on what we disallow. The orthodox theater—and I am hardly recommending that we go back to old-fashioned scripts in a box set—accommodates accident in consequential ways, like the pirate ship circling in a zone of indifference and bringing Hamlet back. There is a pressure in the medium which demands tribute. It keeps you honest. There are those like Gertrude Stein who, on the contrary, object to a basic dishonesty in the form because of a factitious pressure in the old drama, whose assumptions still permeate the theater. The problem, Stein said, is that there has always been a discrepancy between what's happening onstage and what the audience is seeing; that is, the spectator is at a disadvantage, always a little behind or after his own time in watching. "Who's there?" The play knows more for that opening instant than you know, even when the play pretends not to be knowing. For Stein, however, the presented moment should be there for its own sake, not as a causal outgrowth of a previous moment or the prefatory cause of a moment to come.

This view has been influential on a whole series of performance events from John Cage to the Fluxus group through the Happenings to Richard Foreman. The solution is to replace any semblance of a narrative sequence with a moment-by-moment process. But the theater has always been aware of this problem, as Richard II indicates in prison, or Woyzeck, running through the world like an open razor, in the sweat and stink of the whirling dance or the black calling of the bloody water. It has always had the means to suspend the causal sequencing of time into the semblance of a perpetual present moment. Or the momentary and the causal may be played off against each other, as in Jacobean drama, Buechner or Beckett, or the wildest absurdities of King Ubu, where cause is both delivered and debrained.

True, the idea of a narrative in a play is also an abstraction. But the idea of a moment is another abstraction. This is especially true when it is being played. So what we have is really not the solution of the problem but a shift in stateable reality. There is validity in the desire to concentrate on what's happening without losing sight of the moment by anxiously looking forward or back. Historically, there is reason for the emphasis. But the discipline of the moment is what it appears to be, provisional. Actually, there is an unavoidable time lag in any mode of theater, those performing being ahead of those watching, which is one of the reasons for the participatory dream of everybody performing together. When the curtain rises or parts, or the lights go on, or the audience gathers and the play starts by whatever means—back in the lobby or in the shopping mall—there is only the baldest pretense that the actors don't know any more than we do, even if they are improvising. They still have the advantage of knowing that intention in advance, and being more practiced in improvisation. The time lag remains, like it or not. I happen not to mind it one way or another, except to recognize that distress over the time lag is what the theater is all about. If you ask who's there, sooner or later you're going to have to say who or account for the missing person, in the sobering adjustment of aroused expectancy, presence, identity, and perception. If, somehow, you don't ask who's there or don't care—denying the centrality of the theatrical person—the reduction pays a price for the provisional liberation from a certain kind of presence.

Whatever is absent in the theater will return. Which is why the old conflicts of form are never dispelled. That doesn't mean they are merely the same old conflicts. They are altered to the degree that we shift for the time being our way of thinking about them. No method is false, only partial, or conditional. One may be historically more expedient than another, facilitating discovery, for the time being. The problem with open forms in our time—the Happening, the multimedia event, things nonmatrixed or participatory, the miscellany of occurrences—is that they ordinarily lack the pressure *in* the medium that we feel in older forms. In approximating with ingenuity and strangeness the more random texture of life outside the theater, they want the sense of consequence that life seems to require, and provide, even when it's lost its savor or is, as in darkest Beckett, on the edge of nonexisting.

The play upon the moment is another manifestation of art's endeavor to cut the distance between itself and life, so that the creative act (even when, as in Kaprow's Activities, it denies the word *creative* and prefers rather to be doing a job) becomes a cognate of nature, not displacing nature but making more of it. Whether or not there's more or less nature (by the reversal of entropic leak or by the loss of a particle of cosmic dust) or always the same amount (by some Bucky Fuller synergy of the two), I can't say. The theater is equivocal about the question. The concept of theater seems to refuse the notion of an uninterrupted continuity between art and nature as an undeniable fiction. Yet the fiction is inherent in the life the theater dreams. If one must speak, however, in a practical way about making an act of theater, it must be conceded that it is not nor ever will be—though we may *imitate* it—the way in which life makes life. To the degree that it is, it wouldn't seem to be much of a theater.

When the pressure is not in the recognized conventions of the form, it must be resolutely supplied by the artist. There are performance works outside the theater that manage this; for instance, several years ago, Denis Oppenheim's multimedia installation at the D'Arc Gallery, where he reconstructed a vision of death as a dream of his seven-year-old daughter. A puppet (representing the artist?) lies face down dangling off the far edge of a large oriental rug, which floats above the floor of a darkling space. There is a knife stuck in its back. There is a TV monitor on the floor. The lit screen shows an identical knife, thrown and thrown again into an ambiguous slowly revolving surface. We hear a child's voice. It speaks disjointedly about the knife spinning in her dreams, a carpet travelling through space. She seems to be the lifeline of her father's art, whose limits in the reach toward life are suggested by the edge of the carpet. The child doesn't seem frightened; she

Take Up the Bodies

seems to find it beautiful. The piece is called *Search for Clues*. It is very intelligently conceived and executed. Our function in space is controlled. The boundaries are *observed*, so that we know what the word means. The space is organized for perception, though in a sense we participate.

What we usually find, however, in abandoning the performance space to whoever cares to enter, without such control, is that many who enter have nothing to say there, little to bring, or so little as not to be worth their own attention. Very often, insisting that they be expressive, the work doesn't give +them a chance. When everyone is onstage, moreover, there is likely to be no consciously seeing eye, no sense of contrast, a diminished capacity for judgment, time devalued as a structural potency, the tokenism of wholeness without the actuality, since wholeness depends on our classifying powers as well as our willingness to throw over classifications. We lose our sense, when everything is theater gratis, of the right thing in the right place. In fact, we lose our power of choice. For all our feeling that all is seeming, it may be a better solution to act on the equal and opposite feeling (always provisional) that it isn't so. Or we can juggle both illusions with perceptual discretion: choose the separateness of the stage or its apparent continuity with life, depending on what life depends on—which may be nothing or something or whatever we care to make of the life that gives life in the ambiguities between.

The act of theater is a splitting infinitive. The act is there and the actor is there, inseparable and divided, the intervening element being a kind of adverb of consciousness, linking the performer masked in the logic of theater to the person responsible to another life-system. The logic of that sytem, the one which gives life to the elusive person, is there in performance, inviolable, in the stream of consciousness. At the same time, the erotic capacity of theater is not a matter of secondary projection. It is right there, in the bodies (although some bodies in the theater do their inhibited best to deny it). If you're aroused or unsettled enough you can reach out and touch, as you can't do with an actor on film, which is not a seminal space but a strict apparency, factitious, whose presence wards you off. Whether you're touching the real thing or not is another question, having to do with human bodies as the means of representation, or reenactment, which is the essential ingredience of theater descended from archaic forms.

Going over the edge of the carpet or denying the separateness of the stage comes out of the desire to replace the idea of reenactment with the idea of the spontaneous act, to make things happen in performance not as if for the first time but *for* the first time. (If this desire seems to have abated in the theater it is very much alive in theory, as in Derrida's essay on Artaud, "The Theater of Cruelty and the Closure of Representation.") The idea is attractive but has the liability which the ethic of immediacy has always had in American life. It makes every moment either a crisis or a banality. It melodramatizes. It can become psychotic. In the end, by erecting attitudes of great moment around everything, whether of consequence or inconsequence, it tends to trivialize experience—the meaning of which has been one of the major concerns of this book. We idealize the exceptional experience, and at our most romantic idealize the exceptional nature of the individual experience. But somehow all our exceptions become samenesses. Mostly we live and act by resemblances and typicalities. If experience were as exceptional as we wished, we'd be demoralized by the a-normative volatility of things. That's why a trauma is a trauma. Life offers us, occasionally, the exceptional occasion. Theater occurs, however, at the edge of resemblance, when we do, and then we don't, recognize ourselves anymore.

It's not that the notion of immediacy or spontaneity is wrong, only that the structures of immediacy have become too recognizable. We have developed conventions of spontaneity like the Tradition of the New. We look for mediation again whenever the immediacies are overused. The logic of spontaneity is a function of time, like everything else in the theater. This also applies to the validity of content, what is credible, what not. Credibility is the measure of displacement or disfigurement. Just how much and what kind of content is plausible within a structure before reality becomes unrecognizable? The theatrical enigma is analogous to the structure of metaphor, where one thing is also being referred to another. Metaphor, we say, is a logical absurdity, but whether we "believe" it or not, it is really not the metaphor but the nature of belief which is at stake. Whether we compare great things to small or the familiar to the strange, there is the disfiguring limit where belief falters. The old conventions—which is to say, habits of belief—can contain only so much new, and hence devaluing, content. The disfigurement itself is an irruption of new content. It is also a breach of form trying to erase the difference between form and content. In performance, there is a contradiction at the groin: between the requirements of the form, conventionally remembered, and the insistent, irredeemably human violation—which is always disfiguring, because subject to time. Credibility defines the space in which the contradiction is not absent but no longer felt. That, too, is subject to time.

The contradictions may at any time be very complicated, especially with aspects of the theater which we take for granted. Consider an old irruption of content, specific and material, to which we have long

Take Up the Bodies

become accustomed and which we have appropriated (long ago) into the theatricalist vocabulary of everyday life: the curtain which I mentioned at the beginning of this chapter. The history books tell us that the Romans invented the curtain (the *auleum*). But aside from giving us some technical information about how it operated, the books let it go at that. But think of it: in the order of time, first it wasn't there, and then it was. Incredible! What alteration in the sense of reality (or the nature of belief) induced them to think of something like that?—the arbitrariness of the separation, the secretiveness, even if it arose out of a gradually rationalized sense of practical needs. Surely when that phenomenon inserted itself for the first time between the seers and the seen, there was a psychic break of some kind in human experience. It was not a simple invention, more likely an emergence, but an ontological and formal matter of great momentousness.

Then consider the evolving types of curtain: falling and rising, parting, in the center, side to side; the half-curtain (Brechtian: the carrying wire exposed; or Kathakali: feet below, headdress above); the curtain rolled and unrolled by attendants (Yeats approximating the Noh); or the curtain which, since the advent of collage or assemblage, is not only swagged or scrimmed, but stripped leached glued and scarred. When you reflect on not only the versatility but the phenomenology of the curtain, you realize that history has endowed it with considerable power as a convention, whether you take it for granted or not, and especially when you take it away. That too can be taken for granted, like the three knocks behind it which once sought the attention of a noisy audience, but which have since acquired other dimensions from history, becoming another signal which is conceptually available in a work—as it was in Eliot's *Sweeney Agonistes:* KNOCK KNOCK KNOCK.

As we continue to explore the possibilities of new forms, it's important to understand where the life-giving power came from in the old—especially in those which appeared in their time to be breaking down conventions and preparing the ground for us. Yesterday's innovation, in the accelerated pattern of postmodern breakthroughs, may not serve us in the same way. It has an unstable half-life in the most atomized sense. As for the instability of theater, it is always divided in mind. It wants to be what it is and it wants to be something else. No matter what it is, it is always pretending. Which is why theater cannot so easily give up its being theater (without being something else) when it most desperately or ingeniously tries to resemble life. Nothing that it does, except in a perceived spatial or temporal frame, can be designated as either real or untheatrical. At the very least, as theater approaches some kind of truth other than the theatrical, it becomes another state of mediation, to the same degree that we say truth is stranger than fiction.

That strangeness reminds us of the grounds for the shift in theatricality in any historical period, because the supposed abandonment of theatricality is mere strategy, another fiction, more disguise. At most the theater can deploy the instinct to abandon the theatrical against its stubborn immanence, as in Pirandello. The framed action of a Pirandello drama enables him to ask questions about the reality of behavior and action *outside* the frame even as they're leaking in; that is, real questions about real life, if you'll excuse that maybe illusory insistence. He deploys the stage's illusion of reality against the world's reality of illusion—the stage world is *both* real and unreal. It is real *as* theater. In contemporary theater, this corrective insight has often been surrendered misguidedly, and the result has been an impoverishment of resources, injuring the instrument of perception. The subtlety of the theater's resources may again be seen by analogy with another form: Leo Steinberg points out, in *Other Criteria*, how the more realistic the art of the Old Masters became, the more they raised warning signals about or against illusion, so the focus would remain on art. But why that? So they could safeguard the *meanings* as well as the *experience* (perhaps the major motive of open forms). The effect was one of alienation. The subject matter itself may be an Alienation-effect, as in a Dutch interior where a curtain is pulled aside to reveal a painting, the looker reminding us that we are looking, too, at a flat object. Steinberg recalls Velasquez's *Ladies in Waiting*, which juxtaposes a window pane with a framed painting and a mirror. There are three kinds of image, an inventory of three roles for the picture plane: a proscenium effect, a reflection, and the pigmented surface itself; three planes of reality on but one plane. The painting soliloquizes about the power of its surface to produce and correct illusion.

In the theatrical experiments of recent years, we have very little that approaches the richness of this internal awareness, the form thinking within the form about the limits of its competing powers—and thus the validity of its connection with life. The effort to break the illusory spell of theater by merging event and spectator succeeds, if at all, in substituting a vague and weak-minded theatricality for theater. The reality of both worlds is surrendered without a third world solution. I realize that we've passed out of the life-style enthusiasms of the participatory phase, but the motives for making art behave like life remain in the form, along with the recurring desire for a holistic art, unifying act and motive, the watcher and the watched, being and becoming, and the other dualisms from which, classically, the theater was made.

These motives give the theater strength, as the imagination is spurred by the pressure to replenishing fact. Yet while acting, for instance, may be derived from ordinary life and referred there for stimulus, sustenance, and credibility, it is given meaning in the context of theater by the attitude toward *division*. The *degrees* of impersonation, personification, or alienation are potential measures of understanding; and there are significant conceptual differences, in action, of a pretense of holism as opposed to binary or dialectical thought which, while both based upon division, are not the same.

These distinctions are important by whatever name they occur, and however instinctively, although they are not going to be very meaningful unless they are thought through in the act of performance. In contrast to the ideal of participatory (or Environmental) theater or the old psychological theater of empathy, there is still the problematic of aesthetic distance. It won't, as in orthodox theater, take the distance for granted; nor will it assume that not taking it for granted in any way diminishes the distance. If anything, it will increase. It almost needs to be increased in order to be revitalized. That was one of the better perceptions in Grotowski's early work, which orchestrated the placement of the audience in a tightly controlled, almost tyrannous, enviroinment in which the experience of intimacy was a function of tactilely felt division. The audience watches; it is clearly separate from what transpires. The sweat is on the faces of the actors. Yet the contemplative act is unnerving. The division is preserved and disturbed. There is a hard aesthetic at the surface, which wants to do itself in. There is little in the performance, however, that solicits the audience, up close as they are. It forbids itself what it can't depend on. It is almost a matter of spiritual pride. It is what made Grotowski's Poor Theater irredeemably elitist.

Years ago in San Francisco—divided from an aspiration toward *théâtre populaire* by an accelerating sense of the Absurd—we tried to turn the consciousness of the audience (suspicious of our elitism) upon this condition, when one of the tramps in *Waiting for Godot*—agitated by the emptiness of his affections, attracted and repelled by the surrounding otherness, knowing in the most immediate existential terms the inconsolable separateness of the actor's identity and the intimidating distance in the physical structure of that particular theater with its orchestra pit, *any* theater (a "charnel house")—smashed his fist against the proscenium to strike it down, crying out, "I'm hungry!" wanting to end all division by obliterating all binaries. That desperately ineffectual and contradictory outburst began as an improvisation, a feeling out of stymied possibility, playing through the unanswerable. The puniness of the Samson-like seizure was, it seemed then, a correlative of all desire for destroying barriers to intimacy, oneness, the holistic embrace. He broke the frame of the action, only to hurt his fist. The first time he did it, and then pretended to.

It was as if he knew right then, at the end of the fifties, that the abyss between the I and the Other would never be crossed, certainly not by the ubiquitous celebrations and callow solicitations of the sixties, when the actors came off the stage or out of the orchestra pit to whisper (or shout) into your ears, as if they possessed the alchemical secret to a redeeming unity or (if political) to the absolution of *your* guilt. In the course of our work, we have thought much about the impossibility of that crossing. As we reflected on the disastrous effort of the Donner Party to make it to California ("the long root,/ venereal soil"), a crucial figure of the crossing was the Great Divide. As one of the Party says, "We'll never get to California even if we get there." Something uncrossable in reality was also reflected in the long fight of *Elsinore*, when the ephebe son throws himself against the invisible wall of the Father, unable to bring him to light, having finally to struggle with the division, and only then, exhausted, being able to hear the impossible words which were presumably coming from beyond the grave. (The tale which doesn't quite unfold.) It was as though for the moment we had touched upon "the phenomenological voice," a difficult but relevant concept which Derrida describes as "this spiritual flesh that continues to speak and be present to itself—*to hear itself*—in the absence of the world." In the world—and as they usually occur in the theater—the words seem buried by the alluvium of history, including the repetitive sonorities of all prior performance, making an unhearable emptiness or shallowness of the Ghost—a floating armor, only a mouth. The division here was like an excruciating penance in the skin of words. There was no material proscenium arch to strike at, only the self-embodying desire in the outrageous image of an *a priori* Other upon which identity seems to depend. "By a strange paradox," writes Derrida, as if describing the sequence, "meaning would isolate the conventional purity of its *ex-pressiveness* just at the moment when the relation to a certain *outside* is suspended." As the two actors fought, the sequence was, in a narcissistic doubling of desire, a rehearsed assault upon every remembered primal image of the unimaginable Father in the prison-house of language. It was like fighting thin air, pure illusion, the nothing between them—baffling, forbidding, indisputably real.

So much of what passes for new kinds of performance gets in its own way. It leaves you speechless for the wrong reasons. That was true of the shock tactics of the desublimating sixties, and the experiments with obscenity. The theater is after all obscene, always was. The root is the Greek word *skene*, the background place where the actors dressed, or disguised the thing to be seen. *Ob* means against, down upon, out of, away from—so, against the scene (like "the stern apartness of I and Thou," as Buber says, "overarched by the wonder of speech"). There is in every performance an aggression against the scene of performance as a value, a breakdown of unity, a derealization (this doesn't and can't happen at the movies because of the absence of the disguised human presence), the parsing out of the seen into definiteness and categories, even when it appears to spread all over the place.

In the history of the physical theater itself, the architecture, the scene invariably tends toward fragmentation, closure, loss of outwardness, and a sense of the infinite behind. Perspective was fake infinity (which doesn't mean infinity is fake). With Racine, the scene becomes (with the finite narrowing of the Word to almost geometrical precision, the inverse wonder of speech closing upon itself) a hothouse, a suffocating system of released value, narrowed and specious, introverted and private, profound in self-consumption; like appetite, the universal wolf, the scene eats up itself. The terror is voyeurism, that the taboo thought *will* be seen. The scene is cannibalized by realism in time, or raped, and has to repossess itself in its fulness. (The secularized word weakens or disappears.) The pressure toward a surface makes you wonder what's behind. The scene remains obscene. The obscene submits what should be kept private to public scrutiny. By the time of Genet, we're almost "fucking in the open," as the hieratic whore Warda says in *The Screens*. As the value of the private is reduced, so is the possibility of unifying public value. The theater wants the unity it destroys. That is the perversity of theater. We can't afford to fool around.

Let me see if I can bring this long summary to some conclusion by perhaps raising some more problems. Those of us in the theater, as opposed to other scenes of performance, dream of an old, exemplary drama. But every time we look back at what it really was, we see the enactment of our humiliations. The divinity that shapes our ends, whether for tragedy or comedy, has a demonic face. There is no way to see it as benevolent. As the greatest dramas know, the worst returns to laughter, the imbecilic rupture of disbelief. Victimization is relative. The hero who seems in the old drama to be mastering his destiny is mastered. The slave acts the slave for his master, becoming the image of his own reality. (I am speaking here, too, of the evolution of the actor who was once a slave.) The pretense is the form by which he coexists with his oppression. The difference between the reality and the pretense is the measure of credibility; the more credible the pretense, the more endurable the reality. That is the deep politics in the deep structure of theater, right there in front of your eyes.

Illusion, in this sense, is survival. (The idea is sequestered in every play, but it emerges as the explicit subject matter of such plays as *The Wild Duck* and *The Iceman Cometh.*) At least that should be so. But as the pretense exposes the reality—which it does to the extent that it becomes real or credible or true (any of those words we use as standards)—it may become bearable. The illusion bursts with the truth that feeds it. The humiliation is structured by some derangement of meaning into reality. Like the victim on the scaffold from whom confessions were once extorted ("the least body of the condemned") so that he might then play the role (of "the living truth") that confirms the judgment, the actor in total exposure (the tortuous end of acting) condemns himself. That seems only appropriate since, once, he stood condemned by the very nature of his profession—and, for the most part, is still being humiliated by the economic and public inconsequence of his career. The actor, therefore, who *exceeds* his role creates a new illusion for the sake of bearing it—one which redefines for the moment the potentiality of the social order itself, though it may destroy (obscenely) the propriety of the theater form.

All this is remembered in the oedipal drama which we are trying to undo. The drama is by nature conservative, which is what disturbed Brecht and caused him to develop the theory of Alienation. His view, as I have indicated, was that the cadences and apparent inevitabilities of the tragic sustained, for all their imaginative glamour, the grip of the status quo. Brecht recognized that comedy, not content with the way things are, is more corrosive. Laughter requires a subversive distance. But when we fear the worst, we realize, as did Kafka and Beckett, that no distance is far enough. The form is trapped inside the form, as the actor seems trapped inside his career. It is this realization which hangs heavy today over the art of acting and over the very idea of performance, for which theater (as Cage explains) remains a paradigm.

As for what the actor represents, the same curiosities about human nature persist (despite Brecht's refusal of the concept), and people still like to see themselves enacted. But the mimetic is all in the family, only too familiar, and even when quite sophisticated, self-evident. When it stops being self-evident, it's hard to make it widely relevant. While there is still the continued primitive liking of a good story, new performance modes reject narrative, all theory telling us that the story is untellable. Who cares? A voice says (not all that naive), tell it anyhow. There are pleasures independent of theory, not to be denied. True. Yet time in the theater is dreary for some of us, not at all pleasur-

Take Up the Bodies

able—perhaps out of blind vanity, thinking we've seen it all before. But there is the evidence of our senses. Behavior is still the problem. For the purposes of art, it seems exhausted. Mostly, we *have* seen it, because since the Renaissance so much of life-as-we-know-it has gotten around, first in art, then in the redundancies of the media. When the stress in performance isn't on behavior now, it is usually so artless or formalistic, as in Wilson and Foreman, so engineered—even if improvised or ideographic, however exquisite—that it doesn't satisfy some residual dramatistic sense of the actor's potentiality. I have remarked that the actor doesn't really like settling (the more truly the actor) for being the manipulable function of a visual choreography or the cybernetic bit of an information system. But, then, with our suspicions about the drama, potentiality for what?

The secret is still in the creating of *that which was not there before being made present in the actor's body*. It has to do with the summoning up of powers, and this may still require the breaking of taboos—as Chris Burden does, almost immorally, in Body Art when he has himself shot, or crucified on a Volkswagen. Real nails, real hands. An urgency to extremes. Its testimony depends, however, even in these self-victimizing events, on a frank acceptance of the conventions being used—in the theater, the clear realization that a play is another and nether-reality. As Theseus says of the play put on by Bottom and the artisans in *Midsummer Night's Dream*: "The best in this kind are but shadows; and the worst are no worse, if the imagination amend them." The actor is (to use another term from Wallace Stevens) a figure of capable imagination. Everywhere, there is the unceasing slough of brutish fact, the stink of mortality. In performance, that's the undeniable center of gravity. It's the imagining that lifts the weight. The actor says: I refuse the banality I know I am.

One of the uses of the theatrical act is to perform the possibility of a belief, teaching oneself to believe it, if at all, so that whatever one believes it *feels* enactable. And believing it with a passion against all disenchantment, which in the poor grace of time comes easy enough. The actor is supposed to lead a charmed life in the magic circle of desire, endowed with the charisma of a profession haunted by ages past. But if it is privileged, it is only momentary; we know that well enough. At the sticking point of conviction, the actor is likely to be a convention, back with the rest of us, somewhere between emptiness and silence, of which we have heard too much, though it is real, not knowing what to believe. At the achieving edge of craft, the actor is unexpected, but known; exposed, but inadequate; there, but again, and always again, who cares? sincere, another mask. Here, too, we go back and forth along a scale of sliding desire. Nothing compares with our passions, desire outgrows us. We are always done in by what we can imagine, which seems to have a fulness always denied to life. It is only when life, imitating the elasticity of the imagined, takes on its capacities that it is really memorable. Which is why we still favor our dreams, the deeply remembered, which is always slipping out of memory. The purpose of reënactment is to keep them from slipping, because—whatever story they tell of repression—they seem to have some enduring relation to what we should believe. When we think about our dreams (as we do with all our craft) we may remember a great deal that doesn't seem to amount to much; but a technique of performance is not only to give perspective on the necessary return of the will but to fortify the will as it returns against its failures, which are inevitable, and its own evasions, which are legion—accounting for the slippage.

Thus, in doing the work, one looks for the whiplash against evasion which is not a fetish about truth in acting but an effort to refuse the heel of this world which betrays our dreams. If we could only believe that judgment is above and damnation below, we could maybe refuse to act or leave us to the mercy of time. But in acting we accord the name of action to the assault upon the ignominy which looks like this. There is nothing heroic (a word not to be refused at the last blush) that doesn't involve throwing the ladder up or hurling oneself down in a revulsion of unbelief. A mere peaceful coexistence on the level of the polluted earth is still a task for scoundrels, at the dubious end of ideology, at the possible end of history, when our lives are still dominated (incredibly) by the prospect of an actual disappearance. All theater comes against the inevitability of disappearance from *the struggle to appear*. The only theater worth seeing—that *can* be seen rather than stared through—is that which struggles to appear. The rest is all bad makeup.

"If reality is inconceivable," said Hegel, "then we must contrive inconceivable concepts." The greatest fear in our work is cowardice, that we are not up to it, that the utmost passion is an evasion, inadequacy to such concepts. But precisely because so much that surrounds us is at the center of indifference, ready to tell us so, *that* story, we must act upon that too, making ourselves credible to ourselves. The greatest outrage is wholly directed toward what we are most liable to, never mind *them*. I suppose the actors were actually right: what one hates most of all is not the Enemy but the corrupted *image* of oneself—more than that one's actual corruption, for which our nature and our methods have all sorts of ingenious disguises. We've lived through a period when the Doctrine of Credibility was at the apparent center of public experience. When President Nixon announced the bombing of "enemy sanctuaries" in Cambodia, saying we were not going to act

Take Up the Bodies

"like a pitiful, helpless giant," the hypocrisy (from Greek word for actor) defined by some clairvoyance, if not the scruple of a politics, a politics of theater, reminding us that not only our power but "our will and character . . . is being tested tonight"—a staging of credibility in the loomings of time.

At the level of personal experience, the actor may remain an image of the self's denial, or of the realities that are not-wanted, or the only realities we can have as reliable alternatives: *the strength of appearances*. The actor's body is still the vessel of the self's conception of itself, disinterred from exhaustion by every performance. *What is the theater but the body's long initiation in the mystery of its vanishings?* On the face of the evidence, inimical to appearances, the actor's most tangible asset is the void. He plays against his strength, consolidating it. Think. The appearance is his strength. We are told at every performance just how much life we are capable of living, individually and collectively. We may believe it or not believe it, take it or leave it, depending on the authenticity of the evidence, the appearance credibly there, a ventured possibility at the abyss of thought. It is—if the intelligence is scrupulous in the enactment—the model of limit, fallibility, and conceivable future. Once that thing appears again tonight, we may find outselves existing in a rupture of roles, holding on for dear life, or in the mad assertion of a powerful identity spinning off the self as the stuff of dreams—out of the carnage of historical longing. We cannot act what cannot be thought, and there's the promise. But even as the assertion is made, there is something in the theater which says: don't count on it.

Whatever the appearances, we act according to nature. The aim is to separate the liberation of what one is (the desire for) from the determination to be what one can never be, even with the purest returned will. We deal with the ingrained, which is no simple determinism. What is basic, we hear, is that we are genetically coded, with inimitable fingerprints. It is the record of ghosting. There are all kinds of performance but, like the faded score for the dance inscribed like a mandala on the floor of the Theater at Epidaurus, that's Destiny—illegible limit of the body's infinite closure, written; the illusion which is our future. My body, my time: that end.

The Future of an Illusion

Note on the Author

Herbert Blau, who was until recently artistic director of the theater group KRAKEN, was formerly co-founder and co-director (with Jules Irving) of the Actor's Workshop of San Francisco and subsequently co-director of the Repertory Theater of Lincoln Center in New York. He was one of those responsible for conceiving the new California Institute of the Arts, where in the late sixties the groundwork for KRAKEN was prepared—a radical departure from the already innovative theater with which he had been associated before, including some of the first productions in this country of various controversial, now exemplary playwrights of the contemporary period, such as Brecht, Beckett, Pinter, Ionesco, Whiting, Arden, and Genet. Blau has written about this early work in *The Impossible Theater: A Manifesto* and has published widely on theater, literature, and other subjects. After an undergraduate degree in chemical engineering from NYU, he took a master's in drama and a doctorate in literature at Stanford, and he has had during his thirty years in the theater a parallel career in teaching. He is currently Professor of English at the University of Wisconsin—Milwaukee, where he has also been a Senior Fellow at the Center for 20th Century Studies. He has had a Ford Foundation grant for his work in the theater and two Guggenheim Fellowships for the books he has written about it.

DATE DUE

AUG 0 8 2001		

WITHDRAWN

DEMCO 38-297